MW00364678

WHO REALLY WROTE THE BIBLE

Who Really Wrote the Bible

THE STORY OF THE SCRIBES

WILLIAM M. SCHNIEDEWIND

PRINCETON UNIVERSITY PRESS

PRINCETON AND OXFORD

Published by Princeton University Press
41 William Street, Princeton, New Jersey 08540
99 Banbury Road, Oxford OX2 6JX

press.princeton.edu

All Rights Reserved

ISBN 978-0-691-23317-8
ISBN (e-book) 978-0-691-23366-6

Library of Congress Control Number: 2024933652

British Library Cataloging-in-Publication Data is available

Editorial: Fred Appel and James Collier
Production Editorial: Karen Carter
Production: Erin Suydam
Publicity: Alyssa Sanford and Kathryn Stevens

Jacket/Cover Image: Courtesy of The Leon Levy Dead Sea Scrolls Digital Library, IAA. Photo by Shai Halevi

This book has been composed in Arno

Printed in the United States of America

10 9 8 7 6 5 4 3 2 1

CONTENTS

ILLUSTRATIONS

PREFACE

This book began from the simple observation that ancient Hebrew scribes learned by apprenticeship, not in schools. At that time there were no schools as we know them. From this observation, I began to wonder how this might impact the formation of biblical literature over the course of the centuries. I wanted to tell the story of the scribes, but I also wanted to make this story widely accessible beyond specialists. In this spirit, I've tried to follow the advice of Albert Einstein, which runs, "Everything should be as simple as possible, but not simpler."[1] I think it's best to begin with the simplest explanation as a place to stand and observe the complexity of biblical literature.

A catalyst for my thinking about apprenticeships was the recent publication of the Kuntillet ʿAjrud inscriptions. I published my interpretation of these inscriptions in an article as well as in my monograph, *The Finger of the Scribe*, which investigated the curriculum that scribes used for learning to read and write in ancient Israel. What was striking to me, although outside the topic of that book, was the firsthand evidence for scribal apprenticeship as a mode of learning in ancient Israel. This is something that had been widely assumed by scholars, but it plays out explicitly in the Kuntillet ʿAjrud inscriptions. The more I looked around, the more I found evidence for scribal apprenticeship. The other catalyst for me was anthropological research, mostly by archaeologists, that began reflecting on how apprenticeship learning created professional networks. The implications seemed profound but largely unexplored. In this respect, I believe this book takes us into new territory.

Scribal communities, and not individuals, collected, compiled, and preserved most of the biblical literature. Of course, there were individual scribes, and occasionally we glimpse these individuals among their communities. Scribes worked in different types of scribal communities associated with the state, the military, the merchant classes, the temple, and tribal elders, and each group created its own literature. Eventually, all these literary traditions made their way to Jerusalem, where they were collected and preserved by official institutions—first the palace and then the temple. This book tells the story of the various scribal communities that wrote and collected biblical literature and how these communities and their literature made their way to Jerusalem where this literature could be preserved, compiled, edited, and eventually canonized into our Bible.

I hope my scholarly colleagues forgive me for eschewing original scripts and using simplified transcriptions, except where I thought they were necessary for clarity. In principle, I have always tried to favor accessibility and readability. Unless otherwise noted, the translations in this book are my own, although I have tried not to deviate significantly from published translations except in the occasional places where I thought they were misleading or could be clarified to illustrate my argument.

This book certainly reflects my own indebtedness to several communities. In the words of the Babylonian Talmud, "I have learned much from my teachers, even more from my colleagues, and the most from my students" (bTa'anith 7a). I wish to first remember my old teachers who began teaching me at my undergraduate alma mater, George Fox College, especially Arthur Roberts and Cyril Carr. The latter pointed me toward Jerusalem, where I began to study Hebrew, archaeology, history, and geography at (now) Jerusalem University College with Gabi Barkay, Isaiah Gafni, Ami Mazar, Jim Monson, Chaim Rabin, and Anson Rainey. Anson and Jim taught me to appreciate the Land and to think with my feet on the ground about biblical history and literature, and Anson steered me to Brandeis University for my graduate studies where I sat at the feet of new masters, especially Michael Fishbane and Marc Brettler who set an example of scholarly imagination, rigor, and generosity. My colleagues at UCLA have been a delightful part of a small community, and I am indebted to Cate Bonesho, Aaron Burke,

Liz Carter, Kara Cooney, Gina Konstantopoulos, Rahim Shayegan, Willeke Wendrich, and Jonathan Winnerman. And the scholarly world is also a rather small world where I find myself indebted to many colleagues including Susan Ackerman, David Carr, Spencer Elliot, Dan Fleming, Yuval Gadot, Ron Hendel, Michael Langlois, Mahri Leonard-Fleckman, Mark Leuchter, Oded Lipschits, Drew Longacre, Sara Milstein, Lauren Monroe, John Monson, Matthieu Richelle, Seth Sanders, Omer Sergi, Mark Smith, and Abigail Zammit. Andrew Herbek did some wonderful illustrations for the book. Most of all, I have been blessed with extraordinary students who have contributed in numerous ways to my thinking in this book. I wish to acknowledge Andrew Bock, Bob Cargill, Lisa Cleath, Brian Donnelly-Lewis, Bryan Elliff, Tim Hogue, Moise Isaac, Alice Mandell, Roger Nam, Melissa Ramos, Matt Suriano, Elizabeth VanDyke, Stephen Ward, and Alex Youngstrom.

This book began to be written during a worldwide pandemic. If there was a silver lining to this time, it was that my wife and I got in the habit of taking long walks. I am most indebted to my lovely wife, Jeanne, who cheerfully entertained my musings on those many walks and asked many probing questions that have undoubtedly made this book both clearer and more accessible.

WHO REALLY WROTE THE BIBLE

A New Approach to the Bible

This book proposes a different way of understanding the formation of the Hebrew Bible based on apprenticeship learning and scribal communities.[1] Over the past forty years I have studied biblical literature, ancient inscriptions, and archaeology. From these studies grew the realization that communities, and not so much individuals, are central to the formation of the Bible. To be specific, I am speaking of scribal communities. These are the people who wrote, copied, collected, collated, edited, and preserved biblical literature. In order to understand the Bible, we need to understand the people who wrote it and the communities in which they worked.

In proposing an apprenticeship model for the formation of biblical literature, I am taking aim at the individualistic model of biblical authorship. The view of biblical *authors* is anachronistic. It transports modern views of writing and authorship back into the distant past.[2] It assumes the conveniences of modern technologies like printing presses and the industrial production of paper that make writing and books a much easier, more accessible, and more private enterprise. But producing and distributing literature in antiquity relied heavily on scribal communities and social infrastructure. A scribe could not just sit and write and then distribute their work. Writing and literature as well as their distribution and dissemination relied on communities.

In this book, I will emphasize the communities, not the individuals. I do not mean to completely dismiss individual authors, and we will find a few of them along the way. Rather, I believe we need to acknowledge that scribal communities were the primary setting for the creation, preservation, and transmission of literature. We have a tendency to interject our own worldview into the formation of the Bible, in other words, a worldview of authors and individuals. Scribal communities are a sharply different model of biblical authorship than assumed by the old question: Who wrote the Bible?[3] That question looked to individuals. Moses wrote the Pentateuch; Ezra edited it. David wrote Psalms. Solomon wrote Proverbs. The need to assign authors to ancient Israelite literature first began in the Hellenistic period. The Greeks had their authors—Homer, Herodotus, Plato, Aristotle—and as classical Jewish literature entered a Hellenistic world, Jews began to feel the need to assign authors to their literature. But authors were not part of the ancient near eastern context of the Bible. Rather, it was a Hellenistic idea that was injected into the history of the Bible in its reception rather than its production. A book like Genesis, for example, gives no hint of an author. And this is true for most other biblical books. Even the books of the prophets, like the Book of Isaiah, actually do not ascribe authorship to the prophet. The prophet is a character in the book, not the author. Thus, the book is introduced as "the vision that *Isaiah* saw" and not "the words that *I* wrote" (Isa 1:1). Likewise, books like Samuel are named after characters in the story rather than the authors of the texts. But we will get to this part of the story of the scribes later. For now, it is enough to point out that contrary to our expectations, the Bible itself is not a book that usually names authors. This is almost certainly because it was collected and produced by communities.

The emphasis on communities, as opposed to authors, fits well with the increasing dissatisfaction with the Documentary Hypothesis among biblical scholars.[4] For more than a century, the Documentary Hypothesis, which envisioned four documents (and by extension four authors) to the Pentateuch—J, E, D, and P for the Yahwistic, Elohistic, Deuteronomistic, and Priestly authors—reigned supreme. In 1977, a German professor, Rolf Rendtorff, wrote a critique of the hypothesis, suggesting that instead of *documents*, we should think about the *processes* and *traditions* that created the Pentateuch.[5] His work was largely responsible for introducing significant cracks into the old scholarly consensus, but a new consensus has not yet emerged.[6] Even as the influence of the Documentary Hypothesis has waned, the framework of authors and their documents still influences the field. It is not only a Hellenistic way of thinking about literature and authorship; it is the way that we operate in the modern world. But the world of ancient Israel was quite different— it was a world inhabited more by scribal communities and less by authors.

To be fair, the Documentary Hypothesis always recognized the problem with authors.[7] For example, in Julius Wellhausen's seminal work, *Die Composition des Hexateuch*, he suggested a long history of composition among the different sources—for example, J^1, J^2, J^3 and an E^1, E^2, and E^3—each of which reflected a stage in the composition of the sources that implied an ongoing scribal community as opposed to a series of different authors. Hermann Gunkel summarized it nicely in suggesting that "*J* and *E* are not individual writers but rather schools of narrators."[8] Unfortunately, biblical scholarship has tended to fall back into the convenient concept and terminology of individual authors.

This book also reflects my own personal journey with the biblical text. I was especially influenced by studying archaeology, geography, and languages in Jerusalem. I came to Israel fresh out of college, just twenty-one years old. I was particularly struck by one teacher who repeatedly admonished me, "Bill, you've got to think with your feet on the ground." It was his way of telling me to get out of my ivory tower. Part of this meant that I spent many days wandering around in an old Land Rover, hiking along wadis, and climbing up and down tells (artificial mounds of biblical cities). Today, in my air-conditioned university office in front of my laptop and surrounded by books, it is easy to lose perspective. But the ancient Israelites did not live in books, they lived along the dusty highways and byways of the land. Digging into the archaeology of places, walking the geography of the land, and reading the inscriptions of the ancients began to put my feet on the ground and helped me to think practically about how biblical literature came to be.

Thinking with your feet on the ground may upset some religious approaches to the Bible, which take it as the "word of God"—not of scribes. I didn't intend this book to be a broadside against a religious reading of the text—against divine inspiration, if one believes. Rather, I merely intend to take the human side of scripture quite seriously. Only the most conservative religious traditions adhere to a "dictation theory" of scripture and thereby eliminate any human agency. This book is interested in the human agency of those who created and preserved biblical literature.

Thinking with your feet on the ground will also upend some popular scholarly conceptions. For example, scholars often write about and refer to a "wisdom school."[9] But there was no such thing. It projects ourselves—us scholars and our experiences—onto ancient Israel. This vision of ancient scribes started by identifying a genre of literature, wisdom literature, and then conjured a school of sages that created the literature.[10] Sounds like a bunch of university professors wrote the Bible! In this instance, I do not think that I am misguided in suggesting that we often project ourselves onto the ancient world. Scribal communities must have social locations, but there was no social institution akin to a university for the "sages" of ancient Israel. A wisdom *school* of *sages* has no practical grounding in ancient Israelite society. Wisdom literature is merely a genre of curriculum studied by all scribes. There were no formal "schools." There were no classrooms. Fledgling scribes learned in apprenticeships. Scribes were attached to one another, and they were attached to institutions like the palace or the temple or to social groups like the military, merchants, or landowners.

Scribes were not venerable wise men hanging out with their books. Everyone needs to "pay the rent," and scribes were no exception. Learning to write was a skill associated with professions, not sages in ivory towers. Sometimes scholarly descriptions of these sages are almost comical. For example, Gunkel described the sages as men with long beards who sat together at the town gate exchanging the proverbial sayings from their youth surrounded by eager young people.[11] And yet we now know that wisdom and proverbial sayings were a fundamental genre of educational literature used in training all scribes.[12] Perhaps old men did sit at the town gate holding forth. But "the Sage" was not a title in ancient Israel in the way that "the Priest," "the Prophet," or "the Scribe" could be used as a title.[13] Priests and prophets were professions, but sage was not. All scribes, whether they were royal, military, temple, or mercantile, studied and learned proverbial sayings as part of the standard early scribal curricula; there were no "wisdom" scribes. There were no sages wandering around independent of social institutions like the court, the bureaucracy, the market, or the temple.

If we want to understand the formation of biblical literature, we need to think about the locations where scribes actually worked in ancient Jerusalem, Judah, and Israel. It is important to distinguish these three terms and locations—Jerusalem, Judah, and Israel. Jerusalem is where biblical literature was ultimately collected, edited, and preserved. But Hebrew literature made its way to Jerusalem from other locations in Israel and Judah. Although the term "Israel" became a general term to refer to both the northern and southern kingdoms—to a united people—it originally referred more specifically to the northern kingdom with its capital in Samaria (and earlier with capitals in Shechem and Tirzah). In this book, I use "Israel" to refer more narrowly to the northern kingdom, and "Judah" to refer to the southern kingdom. Literature comes to Jerusalem from Samaria and perhaps Bethel in the north as well as from the countryside of Judah, cities like Lachish as well as smaller villages. Literature also came back from exile and diaspora, from places in Babylonia and Egypt, to Jerusalem, where it gets collected and edited in the Jerusalem Temple. Finally, we should not forget that the Pentateuch also went out from Jerusalem to the north, where it became a foundation document for the Samaritan temple on Mount Gerizim when it was built in the fifth century BCE.

We also need to think practically about how scribes actually learned and worked. This began with relationships—master scribes and their apprentices. These master scribes were first employees of the government bureaucracy. They had official positions. They trained their apprentices—junior scribes. And while learning and working together, they created tight-knit communities. We can call them *guilds*, but that term can regrettably conjure up medieval associations (more on this in the next chapter). Although I do not mean to equate the medieval *guilds* with ancient scribal *communities*, the term *guild* is a useful synonym. In fact, I like scribal *guild* because it has more of a tangible sense than *community*. Scribes did form tangible associations while being apprenticed together and then sharing a vocation.

There were no schools in ancient Israel, at least not in the formal sense. Schools have buildings. Schools are public and institutional. In ancient Israel, however, learning was more like home schooling, to use a useful, if inexact, modern comparison. Scribes learned their trade through apprenticeships, and a master scribe could take on several apprentices. In the Book of Isaiah, the prophet refers to them as *limmûdim*, which can be translated as "students" or "disciples." These communities of scribal disciples grew out of the apprenticeship learning model employed in ancient scribal education. Thus, the Bible was formed and passed along on a collaborative model rather than on an individualistic model of learning and knowledge transfer. This has profound implications, as this model of learning created communities that created the literature of ancient Israel.

Scribal communities were related to professions, and writing was a skill learned for these professions. Learning to read and write was a trade, like being a potter learning to throw pots or a metalsmith crafting jewelry, tools, or weapons. There were many trades that used writing, including government bureaucrats, soldiers, priests, prophets, artisans, and merchants. These communities transmitted learning and knowledge, replicating themselves and transferring traditions and skills to the next generation. The scribal communities who wrote the Bible were no exception.

This book is the story of the ancient Hebrew scribal communities that gave us the Bible. It charts the emergence, development, multiplication, survival, and adaptation among the communities that produced the Hebrew Bible. Herein I unabashedly try to simplify the formation of the Bible by viewing it through the lens of scribal communities. Of course, everything is more complex and nuanced in real life, but it helps to have a working model. Scribal communities will be a way of simplifying the formation of biblical literature. The temptation will be to multiply and fragment the scribal communities themselves—in other words, to individualize them. However, the anthropological literature on "communities of practice," together with the archaeological and epigraphic evidence, should serve as a hedge against this temptation. I will insist that every scribal community has to have a tangible social context. Scholars are wont to endlessly multiply the "sources" and "redactions" of biblical literature, but the scribal community model requires tangible social contexts that will rein in this inclination. As a result, we will be able to weave together the story of the various communities of ancient scribes that should serve as a transformative template for the composition of biblical literature.

The apprenticeship model was certainly not unique to ancient Israel or Hebrew scribes. Scholars readily acknowledge that ancient near eastern scribes learned in apprenticeship-type learning contexts. For example, Dominique Charpin's *Reading and Writing in Babylon* outlines the extensive evidence for "apprenticeships in the art of the scribe."[14] Likewise, Niv Allon and Hana Navrátilová's book *Ancient Egyptian Scribes* details case studies of different types of Egyptian scribes that provide a window into how apprenticeship worked in the education of different types of Egyptian scribes.[15] Studies of ancient Israelite scribes like Christopher Rollston's *Writing and Literacy in the World of Ancient Israel* also acknowledge the role of apprenticeship in the education of scribes, but the observation is made in passing.[16] In James Crenshaw's study on *Education in Ancient Israel*, he actually misrepresents scribal education when he writes, "In Egypt and Mesopotamia, where complex writing systems existed, scribal training occurred in official schools."[17] The word "schools" is problematic even in Egypt and Mesopotamia. It tends to give us misleading mental images based on our own current educational experiences. To be fair, Crenshaw was using this statement to contrast the lack of evidence for "schools" in ancient Israel as well as to discuss two different periods for the development of Hebrew "schools"—the days of David and Solomon (tenth century BCE) or the times of Hezekiah and Isaiah (eighth century BCE). But there were no "schools" in our sense of the word in ancient Israel at any time. Nor is it a useful model elsewhere in the near east. Moreover, as I have shown in my book *The Finger of the Scribe*, the Hebrew scribal curriculum was already developing in the early Iron Age (that is, by the eleventh century

BCE). This curriculum for scribal communities served fledgling scribes who learned with masters as apprentices, not in schools as students.

This book will streamline the story of scribal communities into a simple narrative. First of all, I narrow the story by focusing on the emergence and history of Hebrew language scribal communities. In addition, my interest in the formation of biblical literature will keep my focus on Jerusalem and Judah because that is where biblical literature coalesced over the years. Although my interest is in the formation of biblical literature, I think it is useful to approach the question from the outside looking in—that is, from external evidence gleaned from Hebrew inscriptions, comparative evidence, and archaeology. The working model for this streamlined story comes from anthropological theory about education, especially the apprenticeship model of education. Although my use of this model will focus on the external archaeological, inscriptional, and comparative evidence, I will supplement and illustrate it through the Hebrew Bible.

The rise of new scribal communities is one of the most important developments for the formation of biblical literature discussed in this book. Up until the eighth century, the state was the main patron for scribes. But in the wake of the Assyrian empire, urbanization and globalization encouraged the spread of writing to different sectors of society. Writing became more than just an administrative tool; it also developed as a political, economic, and religious tool. Various sectors of society took advantage of this developing tool. New scribal communities developed and cultivated their own literatures, traditions, and forms of propaganda. Eventually, the Babylonian destruction of Jerusalem and Judah curtailed these other scribal communities. In the wake of destruction and rebuilding, the priests and the temple emerged as the leaders of a restored Judean scribal community in Jerusalem. They collected and preserved the written traditions from the Iron Age, but their own writings focused on the temple and on the reshaping of Jewish identity and community in their Persian and Hellenistic context, bringing us to the end of the narrative account of Hebrew scribal communities. By focusing on these scribal communities, I offer a simple and powerful framework for understanding the formation of biblical literature.

1

Scribes and Their Apprentices

COMMUNITIES AT WORK

Learning environments create communities. I made most of my best friends in school, particularly in college and graduate school. This is neither surprising nor unusual. I spent countless hours in class with fellow students studying for exams and learning ancient languages. I shared apartments in graduate school with my fellow academic voyagers. When one of my roommates from college died of multiple sclerosis a couple years after college, I felt like I had lost a member of my family. During my junior year of college, one of my professors—my advisor—died unexpectedly of a heart attack. I lost a mentor, a father figure, and I tried to help his widow in small ways, like mowing her lawn. Mentors become like family, and you never forget them.

One of the most striking reflections that I have now about my field is how our teachers and mentors shape the way we think throughout our lives. Students almost invariably follow the positions and opinions of the scholars they study with, even when we are encouraged to think independently and are praised for individuality. In fact, I chide my own students about it, reminding them that they do not need to follow me off every scholarly cliff. But it is not surprising that students tend to follow their teachers. We train, we study, we are taught to respect our teachers. We become part of a guild shaped by close learning and sharing. In this respect, we share a little part of the experience of ancient scribes, with one major exception: individuality was strictly discouraged among this cohort.

Ancient scribes were not encouraged to be independent. They were encouraged to be part of the group. They learned to follow and memorize their traditions and pass them on to the next generation. This ethos is striking in the classical Sumerian composition known as *Schooldays*: "My teacher said to me, You fellow, because you hated not my words, neglected them not, may you complete the scribal art from beginning to end. Because you gave me everything without stint, paid me a salary larger than my efforts deserve, and have honored me, may your pointed stylus write well for you; may your exercises contain no faults. Of your brothers, may you be their leader; of your friends, may you be their chief; may you rank the highest among the schoolboys."[1] There was a respected master and a group of friends. Not surprisingly, the scribal apprenticeship system encouraged students to form tight-knit social communities.

Scribes were a family—both fictively and in actuality. The nature of apprenticeship meant that a master took on apprentices that could be referred to as "sons." A master first trained his own sons, but the master could also take on apprentices who then became his "sons" in a fictive kinship relationship. Such a fictive kinship among students reminds me of my own schooldays. A doctoral mentor is referred to as a *Doktorvater* or *Doktormutter*, German loanwords referring to a doctoral advisor as a parent. Our fellow students become our family. (Indeed, the first diaper I ever changed was for the daughter of one of my fellow graduate students. To this day, she refers to me as Uncle Bill, though we are not in any formal sense family.) And now that I have supervised over thirty doctoral dissertations, I understand the sense of family among my students. I look out for them, support their careers, encourage their publications, and help them find positions. And they look out for and support each other in their careers. We are a fictive kinship group, and there is a strong sense of family. For ancient scribal communities, these bonds were surely even stronger.

A master scribe took on students who could be referred to as "sons." The Hebrew word *ben* (plural, *benê*), which is usually translated as "son," does not need to be understood as strictly familial and can also relate to a profession. For example, the "*sons* of the gatekeepers" (e.g., Ezr 2:42) are not biologically related but rather members of a temple profession. The use of the term *sons* for apprentices underscores the familial aspect to the scribal trade. We first see this relationship expressed in the administrative lists of King Solomon's officials, Elihoreph and Ahijah, in 1 Kings 4:3. They are referred to as "the sons of Shisha—scribes" (Hebrew, *benê shîsha' soferîm*). The expression "sons of" reflects the familial nature of the apprenticeship relationship within the scribal community. In this reference, the word *shîsha'* was an Egyptian loanword for a royal scribe that was translated by its Hebrew counterpart—*soferîm* "scribes." The original Egyptian term got garbled by later scribes, copyists, and translators so that a variety of different transcriptions are found in Hebrew manuscripts, parallel passages (i.e., 2 Sam 8:17; 2 Sam 20:25; 1 Chr 18:16), and translations (especially LXX). The confusion of this word in parallel accounts and translations tells us that the later scribes no longer knew the Egyptian loanword, but they did have a sense of its meaning so they added the interpretative gloss "scribes" (*soferîm*) as an explanation of the meaning of "sons of Shisha."

The familial nature of ancient learning is also reflected in the use of the Hebrew word *yeladîm*, or "children." This word, which in biblical literature normally refers generically to "children," can also be used to refer to scribal communities. For example, in the story of the division of Solomon's kingdom (1 Kgs 12), the "children" are an adult group of royal advisors. After the death of Solomon, a group of Israelites complain about high taxation and threaten to divide the kingdom if their burden is not lightened (vv. 3–4). Solomon's son, Rehoboam, considers the matter by taking counsel with "the elders" and the *yeladîm*. But these *yeladîm* are Rehoboam's contemporaries, and Rehoboam was supposedly forty years old when he came to the throne, so *yeladîm* are hardly "children." Maybe this is just a literary trope to contrast the wise elders with the foolish younger people, but "elders" can also be a technical administrative term in Hebrew relating to traditional tribal and social structures. One scholar has pointed out the similarity of the *yeladîm* to the Egyptian administrative group known as "the children of Pharoah's nursery" (*ḥrdw n kꜣp*).[2] This is an administrative term that was widely used during the New Kingdom period, and they were apparently people who were raised and groomed for service within the Pharaoh's administration. They were often foreigners, and one can assume that many worked in the sprawling Egyptian administrative centers in the Levant during the heyday of the Empire. Given this background, the *yeladîm* likely represented young people groomed for government service, including being trained to write. In this respect, they represented government bureaucracy over against the traditional tribal social structures represented by the "elders." The literary contrast, then, is not simply age; it is government bureaucracy versus the wise old *local* elders.

The Book of Isaiah also uses the term "children" (*yeladîm*) to describe a community of prophetic scribes. When addressing his "students" (*limmûdim*), the prophet Isaiah slips easily from the term "students" to "children" (*yeladîm*) as he enjoins his apprentices to collect his oracles. We read in Isaiah 8:16–18, "Bind up the testimony; seal the teaching among my *students* [*limmûdim*]. . . . See, I and the *children* [*yeladîm*] whom the LORD has given me are signs and portents in Israel from the LORD of hosts, who dwells on Mount Zion." Did Isaiah mean to refer to his biological children here? Probably not, since the text begins by speaking about his "students." But his students—apprentices of the prophet—*became* his children. The familial term expresses the relationship created by a close-knit community of students.

In the apprentice relationship, the master was also referred to in familial terms. Perhaps the most striking example of this in biblical literature is the relationship between Elijah and Elisha. As Elijah's time on earth is coming to an end, he appoints his apprentice—Elisha—as his successor. The traumatic departure is described in 2 Kings 2:9–12:

> When they had crossed, Elijah said to Elisha, "Tell me what I may do for you before I am taken from you." Elisha said, "Please let me inherit a double share of your spirit." He responded, "You have asked a hard thing, yet if you see me as I am being taken from you, it will be granted you; if not, it will not." As they continued walking and talking, a chariot of fire and horses of fire separated the two of them, and Elijah ascended in a whirlwind into heaven. Elisha kept watching and crying out, "Father, father! The chariots of Israel and its horsemen!" But when he could no longer see him, he grasped his own clothes and tore them in two pieces.

Elijah is the fictive father of Elisha. Appropriately then, upon the death of Elijah, Elisha became the head of his own fictive kinship group—namely, "the sons of the prophets."

One reason for confusion in the translation of the term for an apprentice—Hebrew, *na ʿar*—is that the apprentice relationship could last many years. So, for example, one could be apprenticed as a small boy, as Samuel was to Eli (1 Sam 1:24–26). Eli calls him "my son" (1 Sam 3:16), even though they are not biologically related. Samuel remains Eli's apprentice for many years even after being fully grown, and Samuel only succeeds his master and "father" when Eli dies.

The scribal profession was a family affair throughout the ancient near east. Fathers trained their sons in their profession, although outsiders could be integrated into a scribal family. Assyriologist Yoram Cohen, for example, reconstructs the history of a scribal family active in the ancient Syrian city of Emar at the end of the second millennium BCE. Using colophons appended to the texts with the names of the scribes, Cohen can trace a family tree of four generations of scribes through their lineages; for example, one colophon reads, "The hand of Ba'al-mālik, son of Ba'al-qarrād, scribe, the diviner of the gods of the city of Emar."[3] From such colophons it is evident that, in addition to training paying students, scribes passed on their trade to their biological sons as well. The scribal trade was considered an identifying element of one's lineage. The scribes had official titles in the Syro-Hittite administration of the city, and there was a clear hierarchy to the profession so that scribes could be working at the profession with the title "junior scribe" and then later advance and become teachers and masters themselves.

Anthropological "Communities of Practice"

My understanding of the relationships fostered by apprenticeship has been furthered by the seminal research by anthropologist Jean Lave and educational theorist Etienne Wenger.[4] In their book, *Situated Learning*, they explore how social networks are created by learning through apprenticeship, using case studies drawn from craft guilds like tailors, butchers, or midwives. I was first introduced to their work in a dissertation by

Nadia Ben-Marzouk, a UCLA archaeology student who was working on metalsmith guilds. My understanding was further enhanced by the research of another UCLA colleague, Professor Willeke Wendrich, who edited the book *Archaeology and Apprenticeship*.[5] The idea was first introduced to me in the wonderful book by Seth Sanders, *The Invention of Hebrew*; I first met him at a conference on ancient scribes that he organized at the University of Chicago.[6] This is the wonderful thing about being around such a talented and shared community—you get new insights, see new ways of looking at things. Over the course of several years, I began reflecting on the import of this observation that writing was a skill used in profession. A craftsperson learned their skills through apprenticeships, and this type of learning created long-lasting, close-knit social networks. Lave and Wenger emphasize that their model "is not itself an educational form, much less a pedagogical strategy or a teaching technique. It is an analytical viewpoint on learning, a way of understanding learning."[7] They point out that learning is a social practice, particularly learning within the context of apprenticeship. Although this model has been taken up and applied to modern learning contexts, Lave and Wenger emphasize that communities of practice have been around as long as people have learned together. To be sure, this type of learning can exist in both formal and informal contexts, and the social groups can likewise be quite formal or completely informal.

Communities of practice are defined by three characteristics: a shared domain, a community, and a practice. Lave and Wenger identified these characteristics based on a variety of different types of guilds like butchers or midwives. Guilds are simply professions—that is, shared domains—where you learn through apprenticeship. Learning in a shared domain creates networks, which can become formal. But they do not have to become formal; they can also remain informal. In antiquity, the most prominent guilds were for metalsmiths and potters, who formed informal networks. Scribal learning also created informal social networks, though these could be formalized through employment in societal structures—for example, the palace or the temple.

The term *guild* comes with some baggage. It is usually associated with medieval societies, which is where Lave and Wenger took their case studies. But Lave and Wenger also coined the term "communities of practice," which underscores some of the less formal aspects of education through apprenticeship. Scribal communities were loosely organized groups. They should not be equated with the formal medieval associations of craftsmen and merchants that wielded considerable political power. Could they wield political power? Of course. But the ancient scribal guilds were less formal associations within professions created by shared domains and practice. Scribes belonged to guilds in the ancient world like other craftspeople. For example, Charpin observes that in Mesopotamia, "the scribe was considered an artisan and was remunerated as such."[8] In this respect, professions that acquired scribal skills had parallels with metalsmiths, potters, and other artisans in the ancient near east. They learned in similar ways, namely, through apprenticeships. In fact, the early spread and standardization of the alphabet has been associated with the metalsmith artisan economic networks.

Writing was a practice within defined professions. In this respect, a scribal community fits the anthropological model especially well. The development of the scribal practice begins with the profession's shared domain that distinguishes its community from other people. The shared domain is a common aspect of "expertise"—in the case of scribes, literacy. The shared domain created a community that engages in joint activities. This begins with learning the practice but then extends to the application of these skills in a profession.

The "scribe" was a profession within a government context, but "author" was not an ancient profession. Examples of the title "scribe" in biblical literature refer specifically to people that are affiliated with the government. This includes the "sons of Shisha" as well as the famous scribe, Shaphan, who was working for King Josiah and involved with the finding and dissemination of a book in 2 Kgs 22–23. In contrast, "author" is an anachronistic idea for ancient Israel and the ancient near east. As Karel van der Toorn pointed out in his influential book *Scribal Culture and the Making of the Hebrew Bible*, "In the ancient Near East, it was uncommon for an author to sign his or her work." And he concludes, "authors, in antiquity, were scribes."[9] But this is a bit misleading. *Scribe* is not just another word for *author*. As van der Toorn himself observes, scribes in antiquity did not think of themselves as individuals but rather as part of a group. What van der Toorn does not sufficiently address is that there were different scribal groups or professions, such as military scribes and temple scribes, with different roles and functions.[10] They belonged to different communities, which were their professions. Authorship is an anachronistic idea because writing was a skill used in a profession—like a metalsmith, a midwife, a potter, or a bureaucrat. Writing was not the profession itself, at least not in ancient Israel.[11] By comparison, a metal-smith in the ancient world required the skills of smelting, casting, and forging, but none of these was considered his profession. Take the example of Ezra. He is indeed called a "scribe," but that is not his profession. He was a priest, who was literate—that is, a "scribe"—because of his profession. For an author, writing is the profession. But for an ancient scribe, writing is a skill used in a profession. I suspect this is why there are no ancient Hebrew seals that have the title "Scribe."[12]

It was not until much later, perhaps in the first century BCE, that scribe became a profession for Hebrew communities. For example, there are seventeen manuscripts among the nine hundred Dead Sea Scrolls that are written in a "calligraphic" style—that is, they were in-scribed by professional copyists whose job was likely only to make presentation copies of scrolls that could be used in synagogues, archived in libraries, or displayed as part of the collection of a wealthy elite.[13] The rise of such calligraphic copies were likely related to the emergence of synagogues by the second century BCE (e.g., in Modi'in) where ritual reading of texts became part of the activities (cp. Nehemiah 8).[14] Syna-gogues needed presentation texts, and this became part of the Jerusalem Temple economy, producing presentation texts for synagogues and other wealthy patrons. As a result, calligraphic scrolls were produced by professional scribes or copyists. But there were no such copyists in an-cient Israel. Writing was part of other professions. Scribes belonged to communities of practice, and texts were passed on from one generation to the next as tools and products of their professions.

The function of Hebrew writing and place of Hebrew writing in pro-fessions changed over time. Sometimes the patron for writing was the king and the palace. Other times writing found employment in the temple among the priests and cultic personnel. A scribal community could also find a voice outside of the state and the temple among "the sons of the prophets" or with "the people of the land." Writing could also be important to economic and mercantile activities. This is reflected in some of the titles for "scribes" in the ancient near east, and this included royal scribes, palace scribes, temple scribes, military scribes, overseer scribes, and administrative scribes. There are also hierarchies such as master scribes and junior scribes. Writing played different roles in different professions that increasingly utilized literacy, and the different professions that used writing created their own communities of practice. A scribal community in antiquity was a formal learning environment that was encouraged by its own curriculum and standards. The ability to become a scribe was decided by the masters of the craft.

Since writing was a skill, literacy need not be strictly limited to individuals holding the title "Scribe." This is perhaps best illustrated by the claims of literacy for kings. For example, literacy was attributed to the famous pharaoh, Tutankhamen; on a royal stela, we find the statement: "A copy of the decree, which his Majesty himself made with his hands." The account of an earlier pharaoh states, "His Majesty proceeded to the house of the scrolls, When his Majesty unrolled the texts with the officials, Then his Majesty found the texts of the mansion of Osiris."[15] Likewise, the Assyrian king Assurbanipal notably claimed to be literate: "Marduk, the sage of the gods, gave me wide understanding and broad perceptions as a gift. Nabû, the scribe of the universe, bestowed on me the acquisition of all his wisdom as a present. . . . I learned the lore of the wise sage Adapa, the hidden secret, the whole of the scribal craft."[16] Evidently, a near eastern king could train in the skill of writing without taking on the profession or title of scribe.

What about the kings of ancient Israel? One might assume that kings like David (to whom tradition ascribes psalms) or Solomon (to whom tradition ascribes wisdom texts like Proverbs and Ecclesiastes) were literate. The biblical text never quite claims this explicitly, but the "Law of the King" in Deuteronomy does imply literacy: "When the king has taken the throne of his kingdom, he shall write for himself a copy of this *torah* in the presence of the levitical priests" (17:18). The Hebrew text states quite clearly that the king himself makes a copy of the text, but scholars and translators have been so uncomfortable with this idea that most Bibles mistranslate the text. For example, the New Revised Standard Version, in translating it, suggests that the king "shall have a copy of this law *written for him* in the presence of the levitical priests"![17] Such mistranslations illustrate how uncomfortable even scholars are with the idea of literacy outside of the scribal elite. But writing was a skill that could be acquired by anyone. Usually it was tied to trades that used writing as part of the profession, but it was likely a reflection of the spread of literacy when the king was able to write his own copy of the law.

But surely some individual scribes wrote books, right? There were, of course, individual scribes in all sorts of professions. Sometimes we know their names because they appear on seals and seal impressions in Hebrew inscriptions or biblical narratives. In the near east, we find scribes' names in colophons sometimes attached to the end of literary texts or at the end of diplomatic correspondence. In such cases, the scribe is more of a copyist than an author. It is notable that classic near eastern works like the *Epic of Gilgamesh*, the Babylonian Creation Epic (*Enuma Elish*), and the Egyptian Book of the Dead have no authors. In that respect, the biblical book of Genesis fits in well. It is helpful to recall the verse in Proverbs 25:1 in thinking about authorship and communities: "These are the proverbs of Solomon that the men of Hezekiah copied." The text points to Solomon, but the compilers of the text were "men of Hezekiah" who lived more than two centuries later. The agency for the actual text is a community of scribes—the men of Hezekiah—not the famous king.

One individual scribe who claimed to be an author can be found in Egypt. The scribe, Tjanuni, joined the Egyptian army as a military scribe and rose in the ranks during the heyday of the New Kingdom period. Allon and Navrátilová tell his story in their book, *Ancient Egyptian Scribes*.[18] Tjanuni eventually garnered the titles "Overseer of Military Scribes" and "General." They point out that Tjanuni accompanied pharaoh on his military campaigns and claimed to "make firm" his victories by committing them to writing. They also note that "Tjanuni is the first to claim that he put a text, and a historiographical one, into writing" and that this "distinguishes Tjanuni from almost any other ancient Egyptian scribe."[19] Where does Tjanuni write down this claim? In his tomb. He boasts from the grave! It was not for anyone to see except those in the afterlife—and, of course, the modern excavators. The exceptional nature of the scribe Tjanuni's autobiographical claim in his tomb only highlights the general problem of authorship in the ancient world before the Greeks. Scribes do not normally claim to be authors.

The problem of authorship in the Bible has two high-profile examples—Moses and Isaiah. According to Jewish, Samaritan, and Christian traditions, Moses wrote the Pentateuch, or the *Torah*.[20] But the Pentateuch itself does not make that claim. In some places, Moses is depicted as writing a few laws or instructions (e.g., Exod 17:14), but not the books as a whole. Sometimes God writes (Exod 24:12), sometimes Moses writes (Exod 24:4), but their writing seems to be limited in scope. And these references to God and Moses as authors stand in an uneasy tension until later readers come along in the Hellenistic period to ascribe the whole Pentateuch to Moses. But the communal aspect of the literature is evident in the Pentateuch itself. For example, the Book of Deuteronomy begins, "These are the words that Moses *spoke* . . ." (Deut 1:1), and when Moses concludes his speech, he enjoins the community to write down the *Torah*: "Moses and all the elders of Israel commanded all the people. . . . You shall write all the words of this *Torah* on large stones covered with plaster" (Deut 27:1–3). In a literal and narrow reading, the community—all the people—become the actual scribes of the text of "this *torah*" (as Deuteronomy refers to itself). But then later in the narrative, Deuteronomy concludes by suggesting that "Moses wrote down *this torah* [presumably, the laws in Deuteronomy but not the whole Pentateuch] and gave it to the priests" (Deut 31:9, 24–25). And every seven years the priests "shall read out *this torah* before all Israel" (v. 11). Moses is also commanded by God to "write down this song [apparently, the Song of Moses recorded in chapter 32] and teach it to the Israelites" (vv. 19, 22, 30). So the Pentateuch suggests that Moses wrote a portion of the five books but makes no claim that he is the scribe who wrote down the whole Pentateuch.

The Book of Isaiah also provides a nice example of community transmission as opposed to authorship. The book is traditionally assigned to the eighth-century prophet Isaiah of Jerusalem, but scholars have long noticed that the book seems to have a complex literary history. Many believe that three "Isaiahs" are responsible for Isaiah 1–39, 40–55, and 56–66. Others have pointed out that the book is even more complex than that.[21] For example, chapters 36–39 are largely parallel with 2 Kings 18–20. Who wrote those chapters? Why are they part of two different books? It is also worth noting that the Book of Isaiah does not actually claim to be *written* by Isaiah but rather to be the *vision* of Isaiah: "The vision of Isaiah that he saw concerning Judah and Jerusalem" (Isa 1:1). In fact, Isaiah himself enjoins his students to collect his oracles: "Bind up the testimony, seal the teaching among my students" (Isa 8:16). This seems to make Isaiah's students—that is, his apprentices—responsible for the "teaching" in the book. This fits well into the community model of collecting, editing, and preserving biblical literature.

Master scribes took on students or apprentices, and they in turn would eventually pass on the tradition. In some cases, these apprentices could be family members, and so you get familial language like "brothers" and "sons." The familial language then becomes a reflection of the tight-knit social group. According to Lave and Wenger's research, such communities of practice were about the maintenance and reproduction of the group, which was "a historically constructed, conflicting, synergistic structuring of activity and relations among participants."[22] As we read in *Schooldays*, the ideal student did not hate the words of the master. The early education included a shared standard curriculum that included vocabulary lists and model texts like letters and contracts. This group learning created standards for spelling and script that are evident in Hebrew inscriptions.[23] Students also practiced and memorized "canonical" literature that included proverbial sayings (as we find in the Book of Proverbs), stories (like the ones in Genesis), or liturgies (as we find in Exodus 15 or Psalms). In this way, the shared learning environment over time created a tight-knit community.

Scribal communities were not a single community. Increasing urbanization and complexity in ancient societies created new communities of practice (see Part Two). For example, in small, isolated villages, everyone might have to make their own pottery, grow their own food, and build their own houses. But urbanization fostered craft specialization. A potter now made pottery. A vintner made wine. A metalsmith made tools, jewelry, and weapons. Craft specialization was part of the major urban centers of the ancient near east. Urbanization and complexity were part of near eastern cities like Babylon or Thebes as early as the third millennium BCE. Early Israel, in contrast, was largely a village culture, especially in the days of the "judges" (Iron I, 1150–960 BCE) or the early kings like David and Solomon (Iron IIA, 960–840 BCE), when there were no major urban centers. But the rise of the neo-Assyrian empire beginning in the ninth century brought massive changes to ancient Israel and Judah. By the end of the eighth century BCE (that is, during the Iron IIB period, 840–700 BCE), urbanization had spread throughout the near east. As a result, craft specialization and urbanization emerged in ancient Judah.

Writing was one of the skills that developed and spread as part of craft specialization. Writing would be employed in a variety of old professions that previously may have used writing only sparingly or not at all. So, for example, in the late eighth century BCE, we find an industrial complex for production of wine at the site of Gibeon, just five miles north of Jerusalem. Sixty-three wine cellars were excavated with a capacity for forty thousand gallons of wine![24] Vintners there used writing to label the jars of wines. More than fifty labels were found inscribed on the wine jar handles. They are not sophisticated inscriptions. For example, one of the longer labels, which was written across the two handles that span the top of the wine jar, reads, "Gibeon. The Walled Plot of Azariah" (see Figure 1.1).[25] This is basic literacy. They were not writing the Bible. But it illustrates the use of writing as a skill in different professions. A vintner or a tomb cutter did not require high levels of

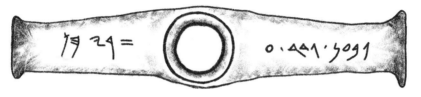

FIGURE 1.1. Label on jar handle from Gibeon. Drawing by the author.

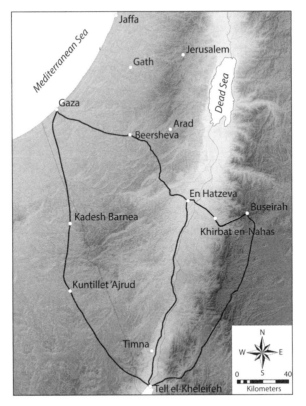

FIGURE 1.2. Kuntillet ʿAjrud along the road from Tell el-Kheleifeh (Eilat) to Gaza. Map created by Amy Carroll.

literacy. Writing was still a utilitarian tool. Palace or temple scribes, in contrast, would have required more sophisticated levels of literacy.

The inscriptions from Kuntillet ʿAjrud for the first time revealed the development of writing skills for the military-administrative profession.[26] Before these inscriptions were fully published, we knew very little about the actual curriculum for learning to read and write in ancient Israel. The location for these inscriptions is quite interesting (see Figure 1.2). Kuntillet ʿAjrud was a remote desert fortress sponsored by the kingdom of Samaria (northern Israel) in the ninth and eighth centuries BCE. It served as a trade station along a desert caravan route from Eilat on the Red Sea to Gaza on the Mediterranean coast.

A close examination of the Kuntillet ʿAjrud inscriptions shows master scribes and apprentices at work.[27] Why do we need to turn to such a remote location to illustrate learning within a scribal community? Normally, such scribal practice is not preserved in Israel because of the climate and the ravages of time. But the location of Kuntillet ʿAjrud in an arid region of the Sinai highlands was perfect for the preservation of inscriptions. And the function of the site itself as a military and trading fortress along the Eilat–Gaza road meant that military and mercantile activities that required writing might be expected there. In this respect, it is not surprising that another site along this trading route, Kadesh Barnea (about 50 miles north of Kuntillet ʿAjrud), also had several examples of scribal exercises.

At Kuntillet ʿAjrud, they used two large storage jars as a blackboard to practice writing. They would likely sit on the ground or on a bench, writing their exercises. When they filled up the top half of the jar with writing and illustrations, they flipped the jar so that they could use the bottom of the jar for more practice. Then they would wash it all off and start over. Excavators found illustrations, scribbles, and more formal exercises on these jars. In some places, the earlier exercises were not fully erased and can still be seen under the final inscription. As one can see in Figure 1.3, they doodled with letters (KA 3.15), scribbled their ABCs (KA 3.11–14), jotted vocabulary lists (KA 3.7, 8, 10), and even wrote model letters (KA 3.6, 9). On a second jar, we even have practice with accounting symbols. The jars illustrate the elegant hand of a master scribe alongside the rudimentary letter shapes of apprentices. One feature that we still use today is the use of red and black ink by a master and the students. This was actually an ancient tradition. In Egyptian educational rubrics, master scribes used red ink to write model texts and also to correct the writing of students. Hebrew education borrowed this use of red ink from the ancient Egyptians. Another common feature of teacher-student exercises was a vertical line separating the master on the left from a student on the right (note KA 3.6). All in all, the Kuntillet ʿAjrud inscriptions provide a remarkable glimpse into a community learning its trade with a very specific archaeological context. They were not training to be scribes as a profession but rather were learning scribal skills as part of their training in a military-administrative community stationed at a trading fortress. (We will examine this military-administrative scribal community further in chapters 2–4.)

FIGURE 1.3. Projection drawing of various exercises (KA 3.6–15) on a large storage jar from Kuntillet ʿAjrud. Adapted by the author from a drawing in Meshel, *Kuntillet ʿAjrud*.

The interaction continued when scribes engaged with one another in their professions. A community working within a domain developed a shared practice. This involved a repertoire of resources. For the scribes this might include writing technologies such as preparing ink or learning about different types of writing materials. But it would also include shared places (to learn and work), experiences, stories, tools, and other resources. Sustained interaction creates a community with shared knowledge and experience that becomes part of the community's repertoire for its practice—in the current case, for the scribal practice.

The education and organization of ancient scribes was comparable to the many craft guilds in near eastern societies. As Assyriologist Dominique Charpin points out in his book *Reading and Writing in Mesopotamia*, the archaeological evidence suggests that scribal masters "trained apprentices at home," and he goes on to observe, "All in all, scribal apprenticeship may hardly have been different in their sociological reality from other ways of transmitting knowledge."[28] This observation certainly fits with the learning model outlined in the research of Lave and Wenger. Literacy was probably only part of the training for many professions, for example, a temple priest or a military administrator. The Hebrew title "Scribe" (*sopēr*), as well as the other positions that required scribal training such as "Recorder" (*mazkîr*), "Royal Steward" (*'asher 'al ha-bayit*), or "Servant of the King" (*'eved ha-melek*), likely required complex social networks and hierarchies.[29] As Lave and Wenger have pointed out, a guild includes "apprenticeships, young masters with apprentices, and masters some of whose apprentices have themselves become masters."[30]

Traces of scribal communities can be teased out of the inscriptional records as well as biblical texts. I have already mentioned three biblical examples that allude to scribal communities. The first was the "sons of Shisha—scribes" that are listed among Solomon's officials (1 Kgs 4:3). The second was the "men of Hezekiah" that supposedly collected the proverbs of Solomon (Prov 25:1). And third was the "students" of the prophet Isaiah that were supposed to collect his oracles (Isa 8:16). This last example also points to the important role of apprenticeship in the development of scribal communities.

The Hebrew Title "Apprentice" (*na 'ar*)

The apprenticeship system in ancient Israel is indicated by the Hebrew title *na 'ar*, which is known both in biblical texts and inscriptions.[31] It is sometimes translated as "a youth" in the Bible, but in many instances the youth is serving as an apprentice in a profession. The translation of this term has been the subject of a great deal of discussion, partly because of its seemingly broad semantic range. The standard biblical Hebrew dictionary offers its first definition as "lad, adolescent" and its second definition as "young man";[32] however, this seems misleading, since many of the passages cited for such definitions could just as easily be translated as "servant" or "apprentice." For example, in the Joseph narrative we read about a *na 'ar* "who was the servant of the chief steward" (Gen 41:12). Joshua, the servant of Moses, is also given the title *na 'ar* (Exod 33:11). The prophet Balaam also has two servants who are called by the title *na 'ar* (Num 22:22). Gideon has a servant named Purah who is his *na 'ar* (Judg 7:10–11). Abimelech has a *na 'ar* who is responsible for carrying his weapons (Judg 9:54). One could be designated as a *na 'ar* from birth (e.g., Judg 13:7; Jer 1:5–6), but the *na 'ar* could be of various ages. Most famously, the young boy Samuel was made the *na ʿar* of Eli (1 Sam 3:1). He was his apprentice. How long did Samuel remain a *na ʿar*? Presumably until the death of Eli, at which time he took over the position of Eli and ceased to be a *na ʿar* (1 Sam 4:18). Being the *na ʿar* of Eli had nothing to do with Samuel's age but rather was related to Samuel's relationship to Eli. In short, he was apprenticed to Eli.

One of the most curious uses of a *na ʿar* is for King Solomon. Solomon actually calls himself a *na ʿar* when addressing God, even though he has just become king (1 Kgs 3:7). Obviously, Solomon uses *na ʿar* as a metaphor. It is a self-deprecation that has to do not with age but with *experience* and relative position. He is newly on the job as king. So he tells God that he is his apprentice. If we understand the metaphor of God as the ultimate king, then Solomon was indeed his *na ʿar*.[33] The metaphor further extends to the conception of the king as the "son of God" (e.g., Ps 2:7), since *son* is also a metaphor for apprentices.

One of the clearest examples of *na ʿar* as an apprentice is in a political coup by Jehu. Here, the *na ʿar* is clearly older and is part of a community of prophets:

> Then the prophet Elisha called *one of the sons of the prophets* and said to him, "Gird up your loins; take this flask of oil in your hand, and go to Ramoth-gilead. When you arrive, look there for Jehu son of Jehoshaphat, son of Nimshi; go in and get him to leave his companions, and take him into an inner chamber. Then take the flask of oil, pour it on his head, and say, 'Thus says the LORD: I anoint you king over Israel.' Then open the door and flee; do not linger."
>
> So the *na ʿar*, the *na ʿar of the prophet*, went to Ramoth-gilead. He arrived while the commanders of the army were in council, and he announced, "I have a message for you, commander." (2 Kgs 9:1–5)

Elisha delegates the role of anointing Jehu as king to his *na ʿar*, who is a member of a community of prophets. The age of the *na ʿar* is certainly not the issue. This could not have been a youth. Rather, the *na ʿar* is one from "the sons of the prophets." As Robert Wilson observes in *Prophecy and Society in Ancient Israel*, "the group labeled 'sons of the prophets' seems to have had a more rigid structure. . . . the group was capable of coordinated social action and had a hierarchical structure."[34] In this case, the term *na ʿar* gives us further evidence for an apprenticeship system in biblical literature.

Na ʿar is also a formal title in ancient inscriptions. It is worth beginning with examples derived from Ugaritic administrative lists, where the term is frequently used as a title.[35] So where is Ugarit and why is it relevant here?[36] Ugarit was a port city on the eastern Mediterranean (north of Beirut today) that was also under Egyptian control during the Amarna period and later was part of the Hittite empire. But it was culturally also part of the larger Canaanite world during the late second millennium BCE. Archaeologists excavated a large tell known as Ras Shamra—the ruins of ancient Ugarit—and found more than fifteen hundred tablets written in a language related to Hebrew. Most of the texts date to about 1200 BCE, which would be almost contemporaneous with the earliest Hebrew scribes. The texts are mostly administrative lists, but the literary texts have captured the most attention from scholars. The literary texts include the "Baʿal Epic" and other stories that find striking parallels in Hebrew poetry. For our purposes here, I am interested in the boring stuff—the lists. For example, there is a military list with the heading: *n ʿr mrynm*, or "Apprentices of the Chariot Warriors."[37] Another recently published administrative list from the "House of Urtenu" illustrates that *na ʿar* was a generic term for an apprentice in other professions as well (see Figure 1.4).

The title "Apprentices of the Field Master" (*na ʿarim ba ʿal šadim*) relates to the administration of agricultural holdings of the palace. The "Apprentices" (*na ʿarim*) were subordinates to the Master. This list illustrates that *na ʿar* has to do with hierarchy and social structures as opposed to simple age. Other Ugaritic texts (RS 92.2179; KTU 9.436) list *na ʿarim* among professions that include Priests, Cultic officials, Shepherds, Military officials, Guards, Sculptors, Smiths, and Merchants.[38] Thus, the use of *na ʿar* to refer to "apprentices" was apparently widely known in the Levant already in the late second millennium.[39]

Hebrew inscriptions nicely parallel the Ugaritic lists. At the fortress of Arad (about 50 miles south of Jerusalem), we have two lists of names that use *na ʿar* as a title (Arad 15:4; Arad 100:1, 2). The term also appears on several seal impressions, including four from the same individual, "Elyaqim, Apprentice of Yawkin" (*ʾlyqm n ʿr ywkn*), excavated at different

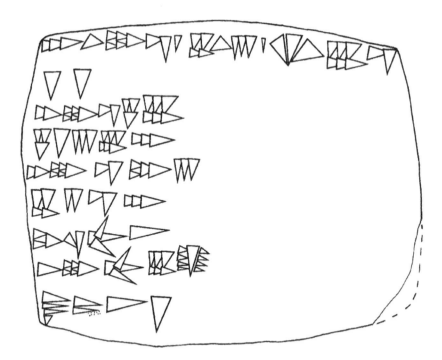

FIGURE 1.4. Ugaritic administrative list of apprentices (*na'ar*; RS 94.2439). Drawing courtesy of Dennis Pardee.

places.[40] Perhaps the most interesting example is the title of a fragmentary literary text at Kuntillet 'Ajrud that reads, "(For) the Apprentices of the Commander of the Fortress" (*n'ry . šr. 'r*; see Figure 1.5).[4] This plaster wall inscription—because of the general educational nature of the other inscriptions at the site—points to a scribal component of the apprentices' training.

Communities of Scribes in the Inscriptional Record

Archaeological excavations have uncovered two communities of scribes working in Jerusalem. One of these, the family of Shaphan, was already known in biblical literature.[42] Shaphan's family seem to be government bureaucrats, and Shaphan himself was the scribe who read the "book of the covenant" that was found during King Josiah's time and prompted

FIGURE 1.5. The title "Apprentices of the Commander of the Fortress" at Kuntillet ʿAjrud. Drawing by the author.

his religious reforms (see 2 Kings 22–23). There, Shaphan is introduced with an unusual three-generation lineage in the story of the scroll discovery—"Shaphan, son of Azaliah, son of Meshullam, the Scribe" (2 Kgs 22:3). The family seems to have been important and well connected. This is borne out by other references to family members. For example, Shaphan's sons, Gemariah and Elasah, were also bureau-

FIGURE 1.6. From a seal "Belonging to Gemariah, son of Shaphan." Drawing by the author.

crats mentioned in the Book of Jeremiah (Jer 29:3, 36:10). The former, Gemariah, son of Shaphan, is known from a seal impression excavated in Jerusalem (see Figure 1.6).[43] Another son of Shaphan, Ahikam, was also a government official (2 Kgs 22:12). Shaphan's grandson, Gedaliah, was appointed governor of Judah during the Babylonian occupation and was later assassinated (Jer 39:14, 41:2). The skill of writing was part of the family's education of these various figures, and they become employed in a variety of administrative functions. The excavation of a seal impression gives some some tangible evidence for this particular family of scribes.

Between the City of David and the Temple Mount in Jerusalem, a new and previously unknown group of scribes and administrators has come

to light in the Ophel area excavations. Eilat Mazar found thirty-four seal impressions in this area dating to about 700 BCE.[44] Seven seal impressions among a larger cache of impressions discovered in these excavations tell us about a scribal family related to a patriarch named Bes. Three of the seal impressions (published as B2, B3, B4) were struck by one seal that I have put together in a composite drawing (Figure 1.7b). This example nicely illustrates three generations of a scribal family. The other four seal impressions (B5, B6, B7, and B8) seem to come from four different individuals so that, as a group, they represent five different individuals of a scribal community of practice. The particulars of this practice are reflected by the use of a double line separating each register,

FIGURE 1.7. Bes seal impressions (top) and drawing of original seal impression from B2–4 (bottom). Photo courtesy of Ouria Tadmor/© Eilat Mazar; drawing by the author.

by short vertical strokes ("|") separating words (which is quite unusual), and by the naming of the patriarch, Bes, in the final register.

B2, B3, and B4
1) [l]yrḥm   "Belonging to Yeraḥmi-
2) [']l | bn | nḥm   -'el, son of Naḥum,
3) [bn |]bs   son of Bes"

B5
1) l 'ḥml   "Belonging to 'Aḥimel-
2) k | bn | pl[ ]   -ek, son of Pel[??,]
3) bn | bs   son of Bes"

B6
1) [...]   "[Belonging to ...]
2) l[...]   -ʾel, [son of ...]
3) h bn | bs   H, son of Bes"

B7
1) [...]   "[Belonging to ...]
2) [...]   [son of ...]
3) [b]n | bs   son of Bes"

B8
1) [...]   "[Belonging to ...]
2) [...]   [son of ...]
3) b[n] | bs   son of Bes"

The Bes cache is especially important because we know something of its broader archaeological context. First of all, the Ophel area of Jerusalem was a royal administrative district between the City of David and the Temple Mount. The excavator, Eilat Mazar, reconstructed a large building that she identified as a gate. It may have served as an internal passageway from the mostly residential areas of the City of David into the administrative, royal, and religious areas in Ophel and the Temple Mount. The cache was part of a larger group of thirty-four seal impressions. Most notable among these other seal impressions are one "Belonging to Hezekiah, son of Ahaz, King of Judah" and another "Belonging to Isaiah, Prophet" (see discussion in chapter 6). So this collection of seal impressions was part of a royal and administrative enclave in Jerusalem.

The excavated area also includes a building identified as "the Building of the Royal Bakers." The excavator, Benjamin Mazar (the grandfather of Eilat Mazar), found a jar with the inscription lśr h ʾw[pym], which he interpreted as "Belonging to the Official B[aker]."[45] However, other interpretations are possible, and I prefer lśr h ʾw[ṣr] "Belonging to the Official of the Tr[easury]." In either case, it provides further evidence for government administrative buildings in this area. It is also important to emphasize that two of the Bes family seal impressions were excavated in the same excavation square as the Hezekiah seal impression. Since

Hezekiah reigned at the end of the eighth century to the early seventh century BCE, this gives us a good date for this particular scribal community.

We should not imagine that there were many different and competing scribal communities. In early Judah, most scribes were likely related to the state, including bureaucrats and military officials (see chapter 3). Later, as Judean society became more complex, there were a few different scribal communities unrelated to the government in a variety of professions. But not many. Scribes were a part of closed communities of practice, and Judah was too small for there to be competing guilds vying for supremacy within the same profession. Rather, there were scribes in different professions. The evidence for this simplicity and singularity begins with the situation that we find in the Amarna letters from the Late Bronze Age (as discussed in chapter 2).

PART ONE

Hebrew Scribal Communities

The scribal art, receiving a handsome fee,
is a bright-eyed guardian, the need of the palace.

—MESOPOTAMIAN PROVERB

2

The Beginning under Egyptian Dominion

My daughter once helped me decipher a hybrid alphabetic-hieroglyphic inscription. I suppose that is more than adequate compensation for turning her back on the "family business"—that is, she turned her back on the idea of becoming a professor. She did an undergraduate degree in Egyptology at the University of California, Berkeley, and studied three years of hieroglyphs and hieratic writing. She became a good conversation partner as I was puzzling over an "undeciphered" early inscription. This inscription turned out to be a key piece of evidence in the transition for scribal communities that worked for the Egyptians in Canaan during the New Kingdom (at the end of the second millennium BCE) because these Pharaohs ruled over the southern Levant when the early alphabet was spreading and taking hold.

But I am getting ahead of the story. In this chapter, I explore the historical origins of the Hebrew scribal communities, which begin under the shadow of the Egyptian empire.

The Canaanite Amarna Scribal Community

I begin with some insights from the Egyptian city of Amarna. Amarna was the capital of Egypt during the reign of Pharaoh Akhenaten in the fourteenth century BCE. It is well known for the discovery of a cache of more than three hundred cuneiform letters written from the petty rulers in Canaan to Pharaoh. These letters are instructive in many ways, but the language is notable. They are written in an Akkadian dialect using the cuneiform writing system, not in Egyptian hieroglyphs. As such, they point us toward a variety of different scribal communities in various places throughout the eastern Mediterranean. They give us general insights into scribal communities a few centuries before the emergence of the Israelite and Judean kingdoms. Egyptian hegemony stretched as far north as the kingdom of Ugarit (on the eastern Mediterranean coast in modern Syria), and the Egyptians made use of cuneiform writing and the Akkadian language—a writing system and language from Mesopotamia— that served as the *lingua franca* for the ancient near east in the second millennium BCE.

On the surface, the Amarna letters seem to be written in the Akkadian language. This in itself would be interesting. The Egyptians did not require their subjects in Canaan to write in Middle Egyptian; rather, they accommodated and even encouraged the use of cuneiform. There are religious and nationalist explanations for this. The Egyptians reserved hieroglyphs for Egyptians. It was a national language. It was also a sacred language, given to the Egyptians by the god of the scribes, Thoth. It was not for outsiders. The Akkadian language written in cuneiform (or "wedge-writing"), in contrast, was a *lingua franca*, used throughout the ancient world by scribes to communicate with one another. So the Egyptians made practical, religious, and ideological language choices.

The language of the Amarna letters is not simple Akkadian. My former colleague at UCLA, Robert Englund, an internationally known cuneiform scholar, once dismissed the Amarna letters to me as "not real Akkadian." He had a point. The tablets look like Akkadian to the casual observer because they feature wedge writing (that is, cuneiform), but the language is actually a local Canaanite version of Akkadian. One scholar dubbed it "Canaano-Akkadian."[1] An analogy might be pidgin English—that is, a form of communication used by two groups without a common language.[2] It is often studied by scholars who do not specialize strictly in Akkadian. Indeed, my own teacher, Anson Rainey—who was a Hebrew and West Semitic scholar—wrote a four-volume grammar on the language. He knew Akkadian, of course, but it was not his specialty. And shortly before he passed away, he entrusted me to edit and publish his new critical edition of the Amarna letters.[3] But I am not an Assyriologist either. My expertise is in the Hebrew Bible and its language and inscriptions from Israel and its neighbors. Of course, I know Akkadian too, but it is not my specialty, and this tells us something about the Amarna letters. The Egyptians developed a standard, but pidgin, language based on Akkadian cuneiform for the local mayors who ruled the Canaanite cities that were under Egyptian oversight. This language—Canaano-Akkadian—was a hybrid, but it was not really anyone's language. The Egyptians encouraged a scribal community that used, perhaps even created, this language.

So, who were these Canaanite scribes who used Canaano-Akkadian? Sometimes the scribes rise to the forefront in their correspondence. For example, the scribe for the ruler of Jerusalem concluded a letter with a personal message to his Egyptian counterpart: "To the scribe of the king, my lord: Message of ʿAbdi-Ḥeba, your servant. Present eloquent words to the king, my lord. I am always, utterly yours!"[4] Such direct addresses from one scribe to another that are tacked on to the end of letters illustrate the scribal fraternity. The scribal fraternity in the Amarna letters was for military-administrative scribes. As even a cursory reading illustrates, military, logistical, and political issues dominate the correspondence for these scribes. ʿAbdi-Ḥeba, the ruler of Jerusalem, says, "Say to the scribe of the king [that] I am a solider of the king" (EA 287:64–69). In another letter he writes, "The king, my lord, stationed a garrison here, but Yenḫamu has taken it all away" (EA 286:26–29). There is a sense in the Amarna letters that the Egyptian control of Jerusalem (and Canaan more generally) was quite precarious. ʿAbdi-Ḥeba entreats the pharaoh, "If there are no troops this year, may the king send a commissioner to fetch me and my brothers" (EA 288:58–61). When ʿAbdi-Ḥeba refers literally to his "brothers," we understand this to mean his colleagues working for the Egyptian bureaucracy, including his scribes. Unfortunately, for such scribes and bureaucrats, the pharaohs would not bring them back to Egypt when their hegemony disintegrated in the twelfth century BCE. They were left behind.

Back in Egypt, scribes had an easier time. In contrast with Canaan, there were a number different professions for scribes. Writing was a skill that could be used in a variety of professions, and there were different scribal communities. As a rule of thumb, we may say that the more complex the society, the more professions incorporated scribal training into various jobs. The Egyptian title *seš* (or, *zḫ3.w*) "scribe" could be applied to a variety of different professions that required some scribal training.[5] For example, it was used in titles like *sš-ḳdw.t* "draughtsman," *sš-n-pr-ḥd* "Scribe of the Treasury," and *sš nswt* "Royal Scribe." The Egyptians also borrowed the word *mahir* from West Semitic (that is, proto-Hebrew) to refer to administrative scribes working in the eastern Mediterranean.[6] The proper Akkadian term for scribe, *tupšarru*, could also refer to a variety of occupations from mundane bureaucrats to royal scribes.[7] For example, the neo-Assyrian empire had several different kinds of scribes. This included chief scribes (*rab ṭupšarri*), palace scribes (*ṭupšar ēkalli*), and temple scribes (*ṭupšar bītūti*).[8] And the Assyrians and Babylonians also distinguished between cuneiform *tupšarru* scribes and alphabetic *sepīru* scribes. The *sepīru* scribes' work was purely administrative, using the Aramaic language to help the Assyrians (and later Babylonians) administer their global empire.[9]

Different Types of Scribes

I will begin with the most expansive view of scribal communities in ancient Egypt and then narrow it down to the community that gave rise to the early Hebrew scribes. Egyptologists Niv Allon and Hana Navrátilová take a snapshot of scribes during the period of Ramesses "the Great" (ca. 1279–1213 BCE). Their book, *Ancient Egyptian Scribes*, dedicates ten chapters to individual scribes and their various professions in New Kingdom Egypt. They recount the lives of a variety of people that had scribal training, including a mayor, a draftsman, a courtier, a royal scribe (tutor), an overseer, a general who became a Pharaoh, an artist (for tombs and temples), a copyist (for text preservation), a manager (in the worker's village of Deir el-Medina), and a military scribe. The military scribe is particularly interesting for our early history of scribal communities because these scribes worked in Canaan in the late second millennium BCE as the alphabet emerged. They will play a critical role in the emergence of a Hebrew (and alphabetic) scribal community.

Military-administrative scribes are celebrated in an Egyptian literary-school text from the Ramesside period known as *The Craft of the Scribe*.[10] There are more than eighty-five known copies of this text, which was composed during the reign of Ramesses the Great, and this suggests that it was a widely known school text. The best-preserved copy of the text is Papyrus Anastasi I (see Figure 2.1). The text is written as a satirical letter from Hori, a senior scribe, to a fellow scribe named Amenemope. Hori aims not just to teach, but also to entertain: "I will make you a document like a diversion, and it shall become entertainment for everyone!" But who is "everyone"? Actually, the text is not that entertaining unless you are a scribe, especially a scribe who works in the Egyptian administration of Canaan (which the Egyptians called "Retenu"). So this satirical text entertains while giving us a glimpse into the lives and training of military-administrative scribes that might work in Canaan. As Hori emphasizes to Amenemope, the *mahir* scribe (that is, the Canaanite military scribe) needed to know geography and logistics. Although the text is written in Egyptian, Hori uses fifty Canaanite words and mentions numerous Canaanite towns and places. Sometimes there are whole sentences written in Canaanite, from which we can glean that a scribe needed to know some Canaanite. And they needed to have the fortitude for the difficult life on the road during the military campaigns, negotiating with various local rulers, or dealing with the brigands that one met in this profession: "See, I have told you the manner of a *mahir*, gone around Retenu for you, and assembled the foreign land to you in one place, and the towns according to their systems. Would that you would see them for us calmly, that you might be able to relate them and become with us an esteemed official of the treasury."[11]

Hori calls Amenemope his "brother" and gives him several other titles, including "the royal command scribe." It is worth pointing out that Hori was not a "brother" of the addressee by blood but rather by the fraternity of scribes. In the conclusion Hori claims, "My father has taught me what he knew." Was this Hori's actual father? Probably not. No more than Amenemope was Hori's actual brother. The master scribe

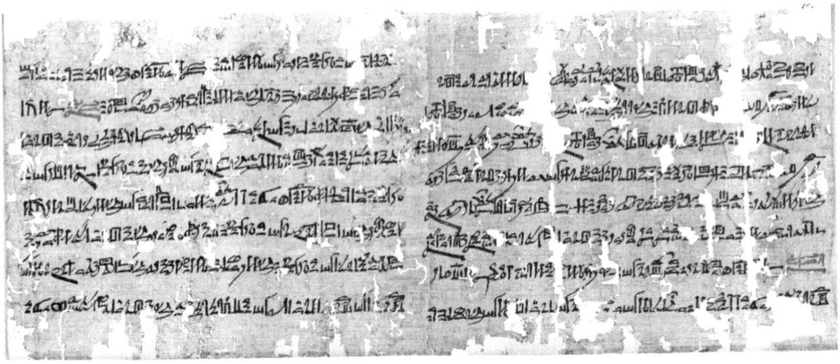

FIGURE 2.1. Papyrus Anastasi I, *The Craft of the Scribe* (EA10247,11).
© The Trustees of the British Museum.

often took nonfamilial apprentices that became his "sons." In turn, the master scribe was their "father." As already mentioned, it is like the German expression *Doktorvater* or *Doktormutter*, used for the dissertation advisor of a student. *The Craft of the Scribe* is a satirical text all about scribal relationships. Hori and Amenemope are "brothers"—namely, equals—but Hori accuses Amenemope of being "like an apprentice" when Amenemope claims superiority.

The *Mahir*, a Type of West Semitic Scribe and Administrator

One of the titles that makes *The Craft of the Scribe* especially relevant is one borrowed from proto-Hebrew (which scholars call West Semitic). This is the title *mahir*, which appears more than fifteen times in this text and is known from later biblical texts as a term related to scribes. Amenemope claimed, "I am a scribe [Egyptian, *seš*] and a *mahir*" (pAnastasi I 18:4), but Hori wants to set him straight about all that entails. Why did he equate the Egyptian term for scribe with a proto-Hebrew counterpart? Because these were scribes that worked in the Egyptian colonial administration of Canaan. It was appropriate for scribes belonging to the military-administrative guild in Canaan to be referred to with the local title *mahir*.

The *mahir* title becomes particularly significant for us because it gets retained in a few biblical Hebrew texts. But *mahir* was an archaic term when it was used in biblical texts; it belonged to a bygone era. After several centuries most Hebrew scribes didn't even understand it.[12] There are three examples of *mahir* in biblical literature. They reflect the difficulty of an archaism whose meaning was forgotten and lost. I would compare it to the use of Middle English in the writing of Shakespeare. Shakespeare's language is Elizabethan, but Shakespeare's audience could mostly understand when he used certain archaic terms. However, today, we mostly understand Shakespeare's archaic language but not Shakespeare's own archaisms.[13] This is instructive for the biblical use of *mahir* in Psalm 45:1 [Heb. verse 2], which is usually translated, "I address my works to the king, my tongue is the pen of a swift scribe [*sôfer mahîr*]." Most translations understand *mahir* as related to the Hebrew root *mhr*, which in later Hebrew means "to be quick, hasten." Other related languages like Ethiopic or Arabic have the meaning "to be skillful." But the easier way to understand *mahir* is simply as a gloss for the regular Hebrew title *sôfer*, "scribe." Thus, the text should be understood originally reading, "I address my works to the king, my tongue is the pen of a *mahir*—that is, a scribe." It was quite typical in the editing of the Hebrew for scribes to add a gloss to explain a word or term that was not well understood.

A second interesting example is Proverbs 22:29, which is usually translated, "Do you see a man skillful [*mahîr*] in his work? They serve kings, they do not serve the commoners!" Although modern translations usually opt for the meaning "skillful" for *mahir*, the activity or occupation is clearly related to kings. If we understand *mahir* as an old term for a scribe, then we have a simple observation: "Do you observe a scribe in his work? They will serve kings, they do not serve the commoners." This image recalls well-known ancient reliefs that use the motif of a scribe standing before a king (as, for example, in Figure 2.2). Indeed, there was no reason in early Israel for a scribe to work for the commoners. Only in later days did writing begin to be commissioned by the commoners, and then the proverb made less sense.

Looking a bit more deeply, the example gets even more interesting. This verse is part of a section in Proverbs that has a direct parallel with an Egyptian school text known as *The Instruction of Amenemope*. This was a collection of Egyptian proverbs dating to the end of the New

FIGURE 2.2. Aramean King Bar-Rakib with his scribe (at the Pergamon Museum). Photo by the author.

Kingdom that included thirty chapters of sayings written by the scribe Amenemope for his "son" instructing him in personal piety in the face of trials and tribulations. Scholars have long acknowledged that Proverbs 22:17–23:11 has close parallels with *The Instruction of Amenemope*; for example, Egyptologist Miriam Lichtheim writes, "It can hardly be doubted that the author of Proverbs was acquainted with the Egyptian work and borrowed from it, for in addition to the similarities in thought and expression—especially close and striking in Proverbs 22 and 23—the line in 22:20: 'Have I not written for you thirty sayings of admonition and knowledge' derives its meaning from the author's acquaintance with the thirty chapters of Amenemope."[14]

Another biblical scholar, Gary Rendsburg, has suggested that the introductory biblical verses (22:19–20) actually refer directly to *The Instruction of Amenemope,* even though the reference was obscured by generations of copyists. He reconstructs the original text as follows:

That your trust may be in YHWH,
  I make known to you Amen-em-opet,
Behold, I have written for you the Thirty,
  In counsel and knowledge.[15]

But one must ask how ancient Hebrew scribes would have gotten to know this text? When we look carefully at the parallels, it is not clear how well they actually did know the text. While some of the parallels are striking, many are quite general. Sometimes it takes some imagination to see the parallel. And the order of sayings differs in *Amenemope* and Proverbs 22:17–23:11. Perhaps this can be explained if we assume the text was known by memory, and we remember that the original was memorized in the Egyptian language. It was routine for scribes to memorize school texts, and the text could then have been adapted and reworked when it was translated into Hebrew by the *mahir* scribes that remained in Canaan. They did not have copies of the text, but they had studied and memorized it as young scribes in training for the Egyptian administration. These memories contributed to a new scribal curriculum using a new alphabetic writing system and the local language, Hebrew.

Not surprisingly, some things got a bit lost or garbled in transmission and translation. But it is remarkable that it was preserved at all when a new community of alphabetic scribes formed in Israel. The parallel between Proverbs 22:29 and *Amenemope* 30:15–17 is a good case in point. First of all, *Amenemope* 30 is the last chapter of the Egyptian text, whereas Proverbs 22:29 is in the middle of its biblical counterpart.[16] *Amenemope* 30:16–17 reads, "The scribe who is a *mahir* in his office, He is found worthy to be a courtier."[17] If we understand *mahir* in Proverbs 22:29 as related to "scribe," then we may translate it as, "Do you see the *mahir* in his work, he will stand before kings, not commoners."

The final example of *mahir* in the Bible comes from the post-exilic text in Ezra 7:6, where Ezra is called "a skillful scribe [*sôfer mahir*]." This borrows directly from Psalm 45 and applies it to Ezra. But this text was probably written in the Persian period nearly a millennium after the Egyptian text *The Craft of the Scribe*. Biblical scribes in the Persian period knew Psalm 45, but they were certainly unfamiliar with *The Craft of the Scribe*.

The history of the term *mahir* is quite enlightening. It was a common term in Egyptian school texts from the New Kingdom and refers to military administrative scribes working in Canaan. The technical term was retained in early Hebrew texts, including a portion of the Book of Proverbs that parallels an Egyptian wisdom text. But the term went out of use in Hebrew. Early biblical texts knew about this term for an old scribal community. But its meaning was eventually lost and transformed. Indeed, one might even suspect that the meaning was forgotten or transformed because the *mahir* scribal community had a sketchy past, namely because they were related to the old Egyptian overlords.

While the Egyptians had many different types of scribal communities and a significant number of scribes, Canaanite cities did not. Judging from the Amarna letters, Canaanite towns like Jerusalem, Jaffa, or Megiddo likely had only a handful of scribes—perhaps only one or two each. Their scribal community came from the other scribes working in Canaanite towns who shared their peculiar scribal language, idioms, and conventions. In contrast, Thebes at the height of the New Kingdom had a variety of professions that required scribal training. Different professions requiring scribal training were attached to the palace, the temple, the building programs, the military, and so on. These different contexts certainly reflect the quite different social, political, and economic circumstances of the small Canaanite polities and Egypt at the height of its expansion. In the same way, we should expect the role of writing to develop and change as the social, political, and economic circumstances of Judah and Israel evolved over the centuries.

Scribal communities were responsible for creating palace and temple archives. We have excellent comparative examples of this in Mesopotamia and Egypt. For example, the "House of the Book" (*pr mḏꜣ.t*) in Egypt stored ritual and historical texts. Pharaohs such as

Thutmose III and Ramesses II expressed interest in the history of previous dynasties and traditional rituals and ceremonies.[18] Another library-type institution in Egypt was the "House of Life" (*pr ʿnḫ*) that was attached to palaces and temples and was related to the training of scribes, which included a library of texts.[19] In Mesopotamia, Assurbanipal famously collected a library in Nineveh, and the king also portrayed himself as a scholar. This reminds us of the biblical recollection that "the men of Hezekiah collected the proverbs of Solomon" (Prov 25:1). Caches of bullae excavated in Jerusalem confirm that archives were collected in various places in Jerusalem dating back to at least to the ninth century BCE.[20] This all accords well with near eastern parallels, so we have good reason to believe that the palace complex in Jerusalem would have included annals, records, and other literary texts. In addition, it is likely that the Jerusalem Temple began investing itself with priestly literature and records as early as the eighth century BCE (see chapter 9).

Ancient Egypt is an instructive example for the difference between literacy and the scribal profession. For example, Allon and Navrátilová point out that "even though literacy and scribehood do at times converge, their sociology is markedly different."[21] There are several examples of Egyptian figures (including pharaohs) who are apparently literate but not scribes. In other words, attaining literacy did not mean that one participated in a scribal community. The account in *The Craft of the Scribe* also highlights a variety of skills that the *mahir*-scribe needed to acquire, including geography, logistics, math, and diplomacy. For example, Hori queries about math and logistics of building: "A ramp is to be made of 730 cubits. . . . The bricks needed have been asked of by the overseer of the workforce. The scribes are all assembled, without one who knows." Hori challenges the fledgling scribe, "Answer us the bricks needed" (14.2–17.2). Hori also asks about geography: "Come, put me on the road north to Akko," or "Where does the *mahir* march to Hazor?" (21.2–22.1). This profession was not just about learning to read and write. A *mahir*-scribe needed to acquire a variety of skills to work in the Egyptian colonial administration.

As the power of Egypt waned in the twelfth century BCE, so did the prestige and role of the *mahir*-scribes. The fate of Egyptian bureaucrats in Canaan is poignantly told in an Egyptian literary tale known as *The Report of Wenamun*.[22] Wenamun was an Egyptian official who worked in the colonial administration. His story is set in the fifth year of a pharaoh, probably Ramesses XI (r. 1107–1078 BCE). The work is historical fiction, but it nevertheless communicates a sense of the breakdown of Egyptian hegemony in Canaan at the end of the New Kingdom. The report tells of the misadventures of the envoy Wenamun as he is sailing along the coast of the eastern Mediterranean, where he is robbed and poorly treated. At one point Wenamun appeals to the harbormaster at the port of Byblos for help, but he replies, "I am not your servant, nor am I the servant of him whom sent you!" (2.10). Oh, how the mighty have fallen! In this account we see that Egypt no longer rules along the coast of Canaan. Wenamun commands almost no respect as an envoy of Egypt. One can only imagine what this meant for the many Egyptian bureaucrats—including the *mahir* scribes— who had been working in Canaan. As Egypt itself devolved into chaos at the beginning of its Third Intermediate Period (that is, the eleventh century BCE), the bureaucrats who were left behind found work among the fledgling Israelite, Judaean, and Phoenician kingdoms.[23] These bureaucrats had a role in the creation of new scribal communities for these kingdoms.

Deciphering the Egyptian Influence on the
Hebrew Scribal Community

There are a few telltale signs of the Egyptian bureaucratic influence on the emerging new alphabetic scribal communities in Canaan. Here I return to the story that opened this chapter—my daughter helping me decipher a mixed alphabetic-Egyptian inscription. As I was looking at an ostracon that dated to about 1200 BCE, I thought maybe this was some sort of hybrid text (see Figure 2.3).[24] The inscription was on a broken potsherd that was originally part of a large storage jar (holding about 25 liters). It was inscribed before the jar was fired. This means that

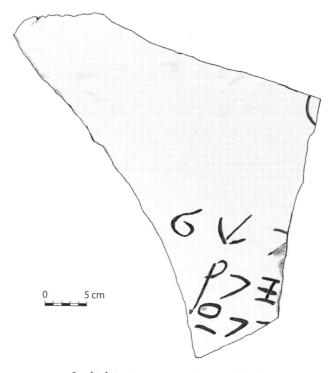

FIGURE 2.3. Lachish jar inscription. Drawing by the author.

the inscription was planned. It was not a piece of haphazard graffito, yet it was published as "undeciphered." Maybe I needed to look at the inscription through different eyes.

The first two lines, although broken, are easy to read:

1) [?]*pkl*   "[ ]Pikal,
2) [?]*spr*   [ ]scribe"

This was likely a personal name and then a title that could be translated "Pikal, [the] scribe." Alternatively, the second line could be read as a verb, "Pikal *recorded*." These two first lines are written in a clear early alphabetic script that we might call "proto-Hebrew" or "early Canaanite." The third line, however, was a problem. The oblong circle with the line underneath does not correspond with any letter in the old Canaanite or Hebrew alphabet, and consequently it was published as "undeciphered."

But I thought this has to be some sort of label. So I showed it to my daughter and asked if the third line might be written in hieroglyphic. She suggested that the last sign looked vaguely like the hieroglyph for *ḥḳꜣ.t* ( ), the Egyptian sign for a measurement of wheat. I sure invested well in that second major at Berkeley! I was off investigating, consulting colleagues and experts. The third line was written entirely with hieratic (that is, in a hieroglyphic cursive script) accounting signs, and I came up with a compelling decipherment: "[ ]5 *ḥeḳat* of wheat." The hieroglyphic sign was simplified to an oval in hieratic and sometimes written with a single line under it to mark it as a plural, and the symbol next to it could be read as the hieratic number 5. A *ḥeḳat* was an Egyptian measurement for wheat—5 liters of wheat, to be precise. So the third line turned out to be the actual size of the jar, 5 × 5 *ḥeḳat* = 25 liters of wheat. This was the standard size for the type of storage jar that the inscription was written on. More than this, we now had evidence of the use of Egyptian accounting symbols in an early alphabetic inscription. The two scribal cultures come together here in this twelfth-century inscription.

Egyptian accounting symbols became a regular part of Hebrew scribal communities beginning in the early Iron Age (that is, the twelfth century BCE). There are many Hebrew inscriptions that use the Egyptian hieratic accounting symbols, but these inscriptions mostly date to the eighth and seventh centuries BCE. The earliest good examples of these Egyptian accounting symbols appear in Hebrew inscriptions dating to 800 BCE, but there is one fragmentary example from Tel Arad that might date as far back as the tenth century BCE.[25] A remarkable example of this borrowing is a school exercise excavated at Kadesh Barnea in the southern Judean desert (Figure 2.4). A young scribe was doing homework, practicing the writing of hieratic numbers in a list. It is "Accounting 101" for scribes.

The symbols are borrowed from Egyptian by alphabetic scribes as early as the twelfth century BCE. By analogy, we borrowed "Arabic numerals," and all European languages use them. The early Hebrews borrowed "Egyptian numerals." We knew these numerals were borrowed from Egypt, but exactly when had been the subject of some debate.

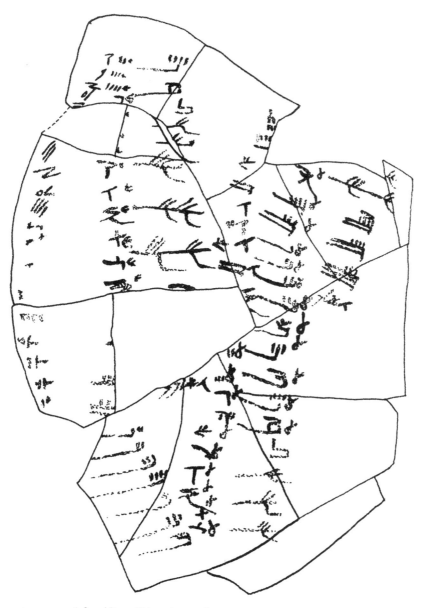

FIGURE 2.4. School list of hieratic numbers. Image courtesy of Stefan Wimmer, *Palästinisches Hieratisch*, 109.

Now we have the proverbial smoking gun in the Lachish jar inscription. They were a legacy of the Egyptian scribal community working in Canaan in the waning years of its hegemony in Canaan.

The borrowing from Egyptian scribal communities extended beyond the hieratic numbers and symbols. It begins with the very technology for writing—namely, the use of ink and papyrus (in contrast to the stylus and clay for cuneiform writing). These were Egyptian technologies. They were invented by the Egyptians and were borrowed by the early alphabetic scribes.[26] Not surprisingly, a whole host of Egyptian words related to the scribal enterprise made their way into Hebrew. These include basic words relating to the profession like "ink" (*dᵉyô*), "papyrus" (*gōme ᵓ*), "scribal palette" (*qeseṭ*), "seal" (*ḥôṭām*), and "signet ring" (*ṭabaʿaṭ*). In addition, accounting terms related to measurement also come from Egyptian: "ephah" (a measurement for grain), "hin" (a liquid measure), and "zeret" (a span of measurement). It is worth observing here that there are relatively few Egyptian loanwords in Hebrew, and most can be related to the scribal profession.

We might question why Hebrew scribes did not just use Egyptian hieroglyphs for their scribal communities. There are a handful of Egyptian hieratic inscriptions that have been excavated in various locales in ancient Canaan so it was at least a possibility. However, using hieroglyphs was not a viable option for early Hebrew scribes. There are no Egyptian school texts found outside of Egypt proper, even though some Egyptians working in Canaan were left behind at the end of the New Kingdom. But hieroglyphs and hieratic are purely Egyptian writing systems for the Egyptian language. They would have been awkward to adopt and difficult to learn for Judean scribes. And they were Egyptian. So it made sense to reject hieroglyphs in favor of the alphabet—a writing system that they could make their own.

Another writing system that early Hebrew scribes might have used was the cuneiform. For example, in the kingdom of Ugarit during the fourteenth century BCE, an alphabetic cuneiform writing system flourished.[27] And there are even a few examples of this writing system at sites in Israel and Judah like Hazor and Beth-Shemesh. Akkadian and the cuneiform writing system was the *lingua franca* of the ancient near east during the second millennium BCE, being used from Iran to Anatolia to Egypt. But it was still a foreign language and writing system. Ink was a more versatile technology than cuneiform, and the alphabet was more easily adaptable to the local languages. The alphabet, which seems to have been invented in Egypt in the early second millennium, was adapted by the Phoenicians in the twelfth century BCE and then used throughout the Levant in the emerging kingdoms along the Lebanese coast (e.g., Tyre, Sidon), Syria and Anatolia (Damascus, Sam'al), as well as Israel and Judah.[28] All the scribal communities of the Levant rejected cuneiform writing as a technology in favor of ink and the alphabet.

The *Mahir* Scribal Community

Was there any legacy from Egyptian rule beyond technology? Yes, the Egyptian bureaucrats who remained in Canaan were also a legacy of the previous era. As we saw in *The Craft of the Scribe*, the Egyptians borrowed the West Semitic term *mahir* as a title for a type of scribe working in the lands of Retenu (as they called Canaan), and the term *mahir* finds its way into the Hebrew Bible. This hints at some legacy of Egyptian scribal bureaucracy in early Israel. I would call this legacy the *mahir* scribal community. This scribal community had as its patron the new rulers in Canaan (which we will explore in the next chapter). They worked in royal bureaucracy, in diplomacy, and for the military. And they didn't just borrow technology from the Egyptians; their scribal training also borrowed and adapted educational curriculum and literature known from Amarna and more generally the New Kingdom period.

I have especially emphasized the Amarna letters, but school curricula to learn cuneiform have also been found in Amarna itself. In addition, there are cuneiform school texts excavated in Canaan that preserve the elementary curriculum of scribes learning to read and write cuneiform. For example, cuneiform vocabulary lists have been found in Amarna as well as Canaanite cities, attesting to the training of cuneiform scribes in Canaan. One vocabulary list from Amarna is bilingual—Egyptian and

Akkadian. Another vocabulary list, this one excavated at Aphek, an Egyptian governor's residence about 10 miles east of Jaffa, is trilingual—Sumerian, Akkadian, and West Semitic. This school text was a precursor of the Hebrew school inscription known as the "Gezer Calendar."[29] There were also advanced curricula. For example, there is a fragment of the famous cuneiform *Epic of Gilgamesh* excavated at Megiddo. This was likely a text memorized by scribes as part of an advanced curriculum. There is also a fragment of a legal text excavated in the Middle Bronze Canaanite city of Hazor, which we may call "the Hazor Law Code." This fragment seems to be a local Canaanite version related to the famous *Code of Hammurabi* as well as other Mesopotamian legal codes.[30] Biblical texts like the Covenant Code (that is, Exodus 21–23) also show some dependence on the Near Eastern legal tradition, but the lines are not direct. In other words, there are echoes of the *Code of Hammurabi* in biblical legal codes, but it is difficult to see places where biblical literature is borrowing directly.[31] Still, this cuneiform curricula influenced the Hebrew scribal education. But it was learned under the umbrella of the Egyptian empire in the late second millennium BCE.

Egyptian Literary Traces in Biblical Literature

Finally, there is the striking example of the Egyptian literary influence discussed above, namely, *The Instruction of Amenemope*, which was used and adapted in the Book of Proverbs. Proverbs and wisdom literature are typical parts of school curricula, and ancient Egypt is particularly known for this literature. The biblical Book of Proverbs is an unusual work inasmuch as it never alludes to the biblical stories in Genesis, Exodus, the Mosaic legal codes, or the Promise to David.[32] Why is this? Some have suggested that there was a group of "sages" that were disconnected from these other biblical traditions. But this hardly seems likely. The sages were not a defined social group in ancient Israel. Rather, a sage could be any wise person whether he or she was a king or a commoner, a prophet or a priest. We may use the Hellenistic wisdom book *The Wisdom of Sirach* as a guide here. *Sirach* frequently reflects on stories about the patriarchs, Exodus, and biblical legal prescriptions. No, it seems difficult to credit that there was some group of otherwise unknown sages that created Proverbs while ignoring other biblical literature and its literary themes. More likely, other biblical literature did not yet exist or was not relevant. They might not have existed if Proverbs was developed by the early Hebrew scribal community. And it might not have been relevant if Proverbs were part of early education, that is, preceded some of the more advanced topics in scribal curricula.

Proverbs seems early both in development and within the scribal curriculum itself. Clues for this can be found both internally and externally. For example, Proverbs 25:1 tells us, "These are proverbs of Solomon that the men of King Hezekiah of Judah copied." This hints at a few different things. First, a lot of this material seems to have been known orally for many generations. According to this text, it was only in the days of Hezekiah—that is, about 250 years after the famous royal sage—that these proverbs get collected and written down. This is not that surprising. A lot of education involved the memorization of traditional sayings, proverbs, and stories, and the creation of libraries of texts and literature was not necessarily a universal value. In fact, one of the famous early libraries in the ancient near east is associated with the Assyrian king Assurbanipal and was probably founded around the days of Hezekiah. Assurbanipal's library also collected the earlier cuneiform literary tradition. At about the same time in Egypt, Pharaoh Shabaka—a contemporary of Hezekiah—also collected earlier, classical literature, creating his own library.[33] So Proverbs could have been a classical text that was collected and edited by a later scribal community.

The Book of Proverbs itself is aimed at the education of the young. Indeed, the book begins with a stated purpose "for learning about wisdom and instruction, for understanding the words of insight . . . to teach the *apprentice* [Hebrew, *na 'ar*] knowledge and prudence" (1:2–4). I translate *na 'ar* here as "apprentice," but the young are also a frequent theme. For example, the master sage goes on, "Hear, my child, your father's instruction, and do not reject your mother's teaching" (1:8). Such statements universalize the Book of Proverbs as early education but certainly not strictly scribal education. There are likely elements of scribal curricula in the various collections of sayings in Proverbs, but the book is edited and framed to appeal generally to everyone to learn wisdom, instruction, and the fear of God (1:7).

The examples in this chapter establish that the emergent Hebrew scribal community did not invent its scribal tradition and literature from scratch. It also drew deeply from antecedent traditions. The most obvious example of this may be found in the borrowing of Egyptian words and symbols relating to the administrative profession. And there are also traces of an Egyptian school curriculum found in biblical literature. The Egyptians also used cuneiform writing and the Akkadian language, which was the *lingua franca* of the near east in the time of Egyptian colonial rule. As a result, the legacy of cuneiform scribal curricula is also found in the inscriptional record and in biblical literature. The Egyptians actually borrowed a local West Semitic word for a scribal administrator—*mahir*—and this word is preserved in a few biblical texts that gloss it by its Hebrew counterpart, "scribe" (*sôfer*). This old term became a convenient label for the early Hebrew scribes—the *mahir* scribal community.

3

In the Service of the State

We were in the middle of nowhere out in the agricultural fields along the southern coast of Israel, and the car wouldn't start. The battery was dead. Call for help, right? Unfortunately, the reception was not good. So Jimmy climbed back to the top of Tell el-Hesi to get a signal. He called the kibbutz where he was staying and tried to describe where we were. Professors Jimmy Hardin and Jeff Blakely had taken me out to see the sites of Tell Summeily and Tell el-Hesi, where they had excavated. The sites are nestled in the rolling agricultural fields of the coastal plain south of Tel Aviv. I was particularly interested to visit Hardin's excavations at Tell Summeily, where he had discovered a number of administrative seal impressions dating to the tenth century BCE. A bonus to our trip was a visit to the nearby site of Tell el-Hesi, which was first excavated by Sir Flinders Petrie (a pioneer in scientific archaeological method) in 1890. It was there that we broke down. Standing high on the imposing Iron Age mound at Tell el-Hesi, we could see the kibbutz pickup in the distance. A quick jump, and we were on our way again.

I especially wanted to visit Tell Summeily because I believe that Hardin's discoveries there are underappreciated. Among his discoveries are numerous seal impressions in archaeological strata dating back as far as the tenth century BCE (see Figure 3.1). The seals are all anepigraphic—that is, they have images but no writing. In this respect, they point to an early period in the development of administrative writing in Israel and Judah, a time when writing was not widely used in professions. At

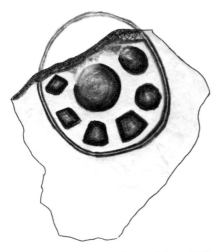

FIGURE 3.1. Anepigraphic seal from Tell Summeily. Drawing by the author.

the same time, they illustrate the development of early administrative systems among the fledgling kingdoms of the southern Levant. These administrative systems included the sealing of written documents. They point to the beginnings of scribal administrative systems and communities in the early Iron Age. Such administration systems were critical to the development of an early Hebrew alphabetic scribal system. They would be even more useful if they had used writing on the seals, but writing was not used on Hebrew seals until the eighth century BCE.

The discoveries at Tell Summeily support what I wrote in a book several years ago. In *How the Bible Became a Book* (2004), I described the spread of writing in ancient Israel and argued that the writing of biblical literature arose especially from the palace and early administration in ancient Israel. Of course, there were other contexts for scribal communities (as I shall describe in the chapters to come), but the first patrons were the king and the state.

I suppose one cannot expect scholars to completely agree, but it can be a bit disheartening when scholars disagree with you. A couple years after I published *How the Bible Became a Book*, another scholar published a critique that the primary context for scribal culture was the temple.[1] In order to assert this, the author located "the making of the Hebrew Bible" in the Persian and Hellenistic periods (i.e., the fourth century BCE) among temple scribes. This is not an uncommon position among scholars, but I find it a hard one to defend with extra-biblical evidence. To be sure, the scribal community in the Persian and Hellenistic periods was dominated by the Jerusalem Temple, but the making of the Hebrew Bible was a much longer process involving different scribal communities from earlier periods as well. This particular scholar's book illustrated the temple scribal community with remarkable parallels from neo-Assyrian literature, but such literature comes from a cuneiform royal library dating to the seventh century BCE, which did not exist in the fourth century BCE. To my mind, the external parallels undermined the argument! I thought it was wrong then, and I still think so.

As I argue in this book, we should not reduce biblical literature to one place, one time, or one scribal community. Nevertheless, the writing of the Bible began with a scribal community working for the king and the state. Early Hebrew scribes worked in the service of the Judean and Israelite states. As we saw in *The Craft of the Scribe* in the last chapter, the *mahir* scribal community learned Egyptian bureaucracy so that its members could work in Canaan. They were part of the legacy of Egyptian imperialism during the New Kingdom. Egypt sent their bureaucrats—people like Wenamun—to work throughout the eastern Mediterranean during the late second millennium. Egyptians set up forts and administrative centers at sites like Jaffa, Aphek, and Beth-Shean. Many of the people working in these towns and fortresses were left behind in Canaan. Some bureaucrats came from Canaan to be trained in Egypt and returned later. For example, we learn about such training from a letter sent from Canaan to the pharaoh: "When I was young, then he brought me into the land of Egypt and I served the king, my lord, and I was posted at the gate of the king, my lord" (Amarna Letter 296:25–29). This bureaucrat claimed loyalty to pharaoh in his service to the Egyptian fortress at Jaffa. He was likely a member of the *mahir* scribal community. But such bureaucrats could hardly have returned to Egypt as the local situation deteriorated in the twelfth century BCE. They got left behind, and such bureaucrats eventually found work in the service of the fledgling kingdoms of Israel and Judah.

What evidence do we have in inscriptions and biblical texts for these scribes? I like to begin with inscriptions because the biblical evidence is ambiguous. Biblical scholars have debated the historicity of the accounts of the first Israelite kings: Saul, David, and Solomon. A lot of this debate seems to depend on the temperament of the scholar. Are you naturally a skeptic? Or do you want to make the most of the (sometimes problematic) evidence that we have? I see myself taking a mediating position here. First, I think we have to acknowledge that most biblical texts that we are working with seem to have been composed or collected in the late eighth century BCE and later. That means most of our texts are at least a century or two removed from the events they describe. At the same time, there are indications of some early archival sources that biblical scribes used in composing and collecting biblical literature.

One example that I find particularly useful for thinking about the work of scribal communities is a passage that suggests that "the proverbs of Solomon were copied by the men of Hezekiah" (Prov 25:1). This seems like a good way to understand the process. There are three stages. First are the early oral and written traditions—"the proverbs of Solomon." In this case, whatever the proverbs of Solomon were, they were not formalized. At the same time, we know that proverbs are one of the most common types of school curricula for training scribes. We have a lot of examples in cuneiform where they are often written as individual small texts. Scribes wrote them; students memorized them. But we do not often find in the inscriptional record proverbs as a large collection or book. Proverbs tells us that they needed to be "copied," "collected," and "transmitted." What does this mean? There is a lot of debate about the precise meaning of the Hebrew word here (he ʿtîqû), but it has something to do with the transmission or passing along of tradition.[2] Since we know that proverbs were a typical type of scribal school curricula, perhaps they just needed to be collected and edited.

In the second stage of transmission, the "men of Hezekiah," namely, the royal scribes, preserve the collection. Here, the transmission moves from an allegedly old tradition to a community of scribes creating and preserving literature. Whereas individual proverbs or other texts may have figures (scribes or speakers) associated with them, the process of transmission highlights the role of the scribal community, not the individual. They collected, copied, and perhaps edited these proverbs into a compilation that stretches from Proverbs 25:1 to 29:27. Now, some scholars are skeptical of this claim about Hezekiah's men.[3] Personally, I cannot fathom why. There is no particular bias to this statement. I suppose one could suggest that the men of Hezekiah were just ascribing them to Solomon so that they had more legitimacy. Okay, maybe. Even if the Solomonic origins can be questioned, the proverbs were still an older collection. And there is no reason to question the collecting by Hezekiah's scribes. Why should we consider this matter-of-fact statement some devious attempt to deceive the audience? Note that the statement applies only to Proverbs 25–29, not to the whole Book of Proverbs. Moreover, by adding the statement, it actually distances this collection of proverbs from Solomon himself.

This leads us to a third part of the scribal process. This small "men of Hezekiah" collection is later edited into the Book of Proverbs as a whole. In fact, the reference to Solomon becomes redundant since the book begins, "The proverbs of Solomon, son of David, king of Israel, for learning wisdom and instruction . . ." (1:1–2). Such a general introduction to the book can be compared with other pseudepigraphic attempts to assign authorship to biblical literature, especially beginning in the Hellenistic period. This introduction actually stands in tension with Proverbs 25:1, which ascribes only part of the book to the editorial activities of Hezekiah's scribal community. Taken together, the book's introduction and the reference to Hezekiah's men attest to the *longue durée* of scribal communities collecting, editing, and preserving biblical traditions. Of course, we may also question whether the book's general introduction intended to refer to the whole book or just the first nine chapters. For example, chapter 10 has its own introduction, and there are several other minor collections of proverbs in the book.[4] The Greek translation rearranges some of these collections, which suggests that the book was conceived as different collections of proverbial sayings for a long time. The Book of Proverbs as a canonical work attributed to Solomon seems to be a later idea, no doubt influenced by the first verse of the collection. In sum, there are three identifiable stages among the scribal community: (1) an early source of proverbs attributed to Solomon; (2) a collection by a Hezekian scribal community; and (3) the placement within the Book of Proverbs as a whole.

Some of the best biblical evidence for an early scribal community are archival lists. We have many such lists in the Bible, and we also have them in ancient Hebrew inscriptions. But lists are a bit boring, so most

scholars do not study them. We are fortunate that the Israeli scholar
Anat Mendel-Geberovich collected all the Hebrew inscriptions with
lists in her Hebrew University dissertation.[5] I will draw upon her work
and add to it an examination of biblical lists, some of which include the
names of the scribes and their communities. For example, there are
three biblical lists of early administrative officials that include scribal
communities—two for King David and one for King Solomon. The lists
for David include 2 Samuel 8:15–17 (with a parallel in 1 Chr 18:14–17)
and 2 Samuel 20:20–23. The list for Solomon is in 1 Kings 4:1–6. Scholars
have usually understood these lists as deriving from archival records,
but sometimes scholars debate the date and origins of the archival records.[6] This debate can be put to rest with just one example.

The administrative lists in 1 Kings 4 will be our teacher. In the first
half of the chapter, it seems like we have two old archival lists:

[1]King Solomon was king over all Israel, [2] and these were his high officials: Azariah son of Zadok was the priest; [3] Elihoreph and Ahijah sons
of Shisha were scribes; Jehoshaphat son of Ahilud was recorder; [4] Benaiah son of Jehoiada was in command of the army; Zadok and Abiathar
were priests; [5]Azariah son of Nathan was over the officials; Zabud son
of Nathan was priest and king's friend; [6]Ahishar was in charge of the
palace; and Adoniram son of Abda was in charge of the forced labor.

[7] Solomon had twelve officials over all Israel who provided food for
the king and his household; each one had to make provision for one
month in the year. [8] These were their names: Ben-hur, in the hill country of Ephraim; [9] Ben-deker, in Makaz, Shaalbim, Beth-shemesh, and
Elon-beth-hanan; [10] Ben-hesed, in Arubboth (to him belonged Socoh
and all the land of Hepher); [11] Ben-abinadab, in all Naphath-dor (he
had Taphath, Solomon's daughter, as his wife); [12] Baana son of Ahilud,
in Taanach, Megiddo, and all Beth-shean, which is beside Zarethan
below Jezreel, and from Beth-shean to Abel-meholah, as far as the other
side of Jokmeam; [13] Ben-geber, in Ramoth-gilead (he had the villages
of Jair son of Manasseh, which are in Gilead, and he had the region of
Argob, which is in Bashan, sixty great cities with walls and bronze bars);
[14] Ahinadab son of Iddo, in Mahanaim; [15] Ahimaaz, in Naphtali (he had

taken Basemath, Solomon's daughter, as his wife); [16] Baana son of Hushai, in Asher and Bealoth; [17] Jehoshaphat son of Paruah, in Issachar; [18] Shimei son of Ela, in Benjamin; [19] Geber son of Uri, in the land of Gilead, the country of King Sihon of the Amorites and of King Og of Bashan. And there was one garrison in the land.

It is hard to imagine this being simply invented by a later scribal community. The chapter begins with a list of Solomon's officials in verses 1–6, then continues with a list of the administrative districts of Solomon. I already mentioned the first part in the last chapter when I discussed the "sons of Shisha." Verse 7 looks like the header to a second list: "Solomon had twelve officials over all Israel." Of course, the number twelve is significant in biblical literature; we may immediately recall the twelve tribes of Israel. We might expect the administration to be organized by the twelve tribes, but it is not. It does not correspond with the twelve tribes of Israel at all. As we shall see, this is one of the authenticating aspects of the old archival list.

Solomon's administrative district list has some unusual features. Besides being apparently unaware of the twelve tribes, the list also seems to be missing several first names. While many officials have a clear first name alongside a patronym (e.g., Baana son of Ahilud), several other figures are merely listed as Ben—literally, "son of" (e.g., Ben-hur, that is, "son of Hur"). The incongruity is curious and calls for an explanation. We might assume that the original list read something like "*blank*, son of so-and-so." One biblical scholar, Baruch Halpern, noticed this and suggested that the left edge of the original list may have been partially destroyed or effaced.[7] At first that seems plausible, if speculative. After all, it is supposed to be a very old list from a royal archive. He suggested that later scribes just preserved what was left. The damaged list read something like this, with the bracketed text reflecting names that were destroyed or effaced:

Solomon's Twelve Officials

[Name], son of Hur, in Mount Ephraim
[Name], son of Deker, in Makaz, Shaalbim, Beth-Shemesh . . .
[Name], son of Hesed, in Arubboth

[Name], son of Abinadab, in the coast of Dor
Baana, son of Ahilud, in Taanach and Megiddo . . .
[Name], son of Geber, in Ramoth-gilead
Ahinadab, son of Iddo, in Mahanaim
[Name, son of], Ahimaaz in Naphtali
Baana, son of Hushai, in Asher and Bealoth
Jehoshaphat, son of Paruah, in Issachar
Shimei, son of Ela, in Benjamin
Geber, son of Uri, in the land of Gilead
Ahinadab, son of Iddo, in Mahanaim
Ahimaaz, husband of Basemath, daughter of Solomon,
in Naphtali
Baana, son of Hushai, in Asher and Bealoth
Jehoshaphat, son of Paruah, in Issachar
Shimei, son of Ela, in Benjamin
Geber, son of Uri, in Gilead

In Halpern's reconstruction, the original first names in lines 1–4, 6, and 8 were effaced. Very clever, but not so fast. Administrative lists using "son of [personal name]" were quite common in Ugaritic economic tablets as well as Hebrew inscriptions, making Halpern's suggestion unnecessary.[8]

Just one example from Ugaritic can illustrate the use of "son of so-and-so" in ancient lists. A tablet[9] dealing with people, professions, and villages with a region reads as follows:

1. ʿEmalbu
2. Maharʿu
3. Urtenu
4. Son of ʿAmyenu
5. Son of Thanwana
6. Son of Nakalbu
7. Son of Barzanu
8. Son of Gargashu
9. Son of Ilyanu
10. Son of Barsanu
11. Son of Ilmanu, son of Yar[. . .]

12. 30 [...]
13. 30 citizens [...]
14. 1 citizen who [...]
15. 50 military [officials]
16. From [the town of] Margab
17. 10 apprentices [...]
18. [ ] servant [...]
_____

19. [place name] four [...]
20. Meʿqabu, three
21. Qartu, three
22. Zeranu, two
23. Thalḥanu, one
24. Thamrayu, two
25. Yakneʿmu, one

The list has three sections divided by two lines. The first section lists the organization of taxes and administration according to families—hence, "Son of..."—as opposed to individuals. The second section of the Ugarit tablet (slightly damaged, as reflected by [...]) lists the organization of officials within the region. The third section provides the towns within that region. It is worth pointing out that the word for "son" (*bn*) is actually the same in Ugaritic and Hebrew. But more importantly, the use of "Son of..." parallels our Solomonic list and points to its old archival origin organized around familial tribal structures. So the biblical list is not damaged or effaced; it just reflects old administrative lists and social structures.

There are also several Hebrew inscriptions that illustrate the use of "son of so-and-so" in archival lists. For example, the large cache of inscriptions excavated at Tell Arad, which was an old Judean military fortress, alternates between individuals and families ("son of"). Over a hundred ostraca were discovered, some dating all the way back to the tenth century, although most date to the last phase of the fortress in the early sixth century BCE.

The earliest example of an administrative list from Arad, ostracon 76, alternates between individuals and families. The ostracon is faded, broken, and difficult to read (see Figure 3.2), but it is the earliest one that

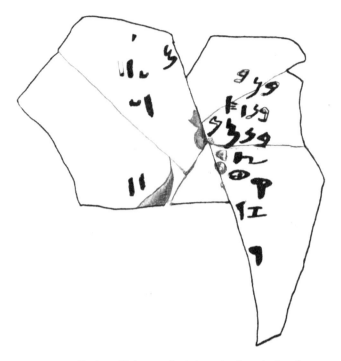

FIGURE 3.2. Earliest Hebrew administrative inscription from Arad (no. 76). Drawing by the author.

we have, so it is worth using it as an illustration. It was excavated in archaeological stratum XI, which Yohanan Aharoni dated to the tenth century BCE. Arad 76 has seven lines of fragmentary text[10] that I would reconstruct as follows:

Son of Ba[kbuk, whe]at	ḥeḳat	3
Son of Ḥa[m,]	ḥeḳat	2
Son of Men[achem,]	ḥeḳat	1
Zed[ek		]
Qaṭ[an?		]
Zer[aḥ,]	ḥeḳat	2
R[		]

The familial structures represented by "son of" in such lists parallel what we find in Solomon's administrative districts. So the unique features from Solomon's administrative district list reflect old archival rubrics. It is important to note that there are some traces of the later twelve tribes in this administrative list—Benjamin, Issachar, Naphtali, and Asher are mentioned—but it doesn't mention the rest of the twelve tribes. Why? Most likely because it was an early archival list that was made before later scribes created the neatly packaged portrait of the twelve tribes. 1 Kings 4 preserves an old list intact, even though the later biblical scribes used Solomon's twelve districts as a stylized pattern for the traditional twelve tribes. Such biblical lists tell us about the work of our early scribal community. They did accounting. They made lists as part of state administration.

There are other lists of the officials that worked for King David and King Solomon. First, there are two lists of King David's officials in 2 Samuel 8 and 20 that are somewhat similar to 1 Kings 4:1–6. And then there is another parallel version of David's officials in 1 Chronicles 23. The list in 2 Samuel 8 is given a scribal introduction in verse 15 as follows, "And David reigned over all Israel, and David administered justice and equity to all his people." Then the list follows in vv. 16–18:

Joab son of Zeruiah, over the army;
Jehoshaphat son of Ahilud, recorder;
Zadok son of Ahitub and Ahimelech son of Abiathar, priests;
Seraiah, scribe;
Benaiah son of Jehoiada, over the Cherethites and the Pelethites;
David's sons were priests.

It is worth pointing out that the Hebrew original for this list, in contrast to most English translations, has no verbs until the final line. The lack of verbs fits the structure of lists. In the Hebrew version, the only verb in the list appears in the surprising final statement that "David's sons *were* priests." This statement has caused commentators no end of consternation. After all, David's sons were neither Aaronites nor even Levites. So how did they become priests? Given that the statement has a verb, it seems safe to say that it was not part of any original list. It had to be added. The addition seems to marginalize the Aaronite priests while elevating the role of David and his sons in the temple. It is quite certain that later priestly scribes would not have added such a note! Who did it? I would point to those "men of Hezekiah" as the culprits here. They seem to be to elevating the royal dynasty—their patron—at the expense of the temple.

Curiously, King David has a second list of administrative officials in 2 Samuel 20:23–26. There are some similarities but also some striking differences. I have italicized the most notable differences:

> Joab, over all the army of Israel;
> Benaiah son of Jehoiada, in command of the Cherethites and the Pelethites;
> *Adoram, in charge of the forced labor;*
> Jehoshaphat son of Ahilud, the recorder;
> *Sheva, scribe;*
> Zadok and Abiathar, priests;
> *And in addition, Ira the Jairite was David's priest.*

Two additions contribute to the narrative context in the Book of Samuel. First of all, David has his own priest, who is added here. The Hebrew text actually uses a phrase, "And in addition" (*wegam*), that marks itself as a scribal editorial note. The mention of David's sons is gone, but the mention of David's priest was not a formal part of the list, so I have italicized it in my translation of the Hebrew text. Clearly, a later scribal community had a concern for who is a priest and connecting the priesthood closely with David and his house.

The second addition is the mention of a chief of the forced labor. This foreshadows the account of corvée labor that Solomon used to build Jerusalem and a variety of cities (see 1 Kgs 9:15). The Hebrew term for this corvée, *mas*, is an Akkadian loanword known from the Amarna letters. This loanword appears rarely in the Hebrew Bible and lends some credibility to the antiquity of the practice and its relationship to the practice under the Egyptian colonial rule. Indeed, such corvée labor is what the Egyptians used to build their pyramids and temples, and they also used it in their colonial rule of the Canaan. The person in charge of the forced labor in the list, however, presents some problems. In the Masoretic Text of 2 Samuel 20:24, he is called "Adoram." In the early Greek

translation, his name is "Adoniram." This recalls the reference that concludes the list of Solomon's officials in 1 Kings 4, "Adoniram son of
Abda, in charge of the forced labor" (v. 6). Are Adoram and Adoniram
the same person? It seems unlikely—though not impossible—that
someone could have held that position so long. The Greek translations
conflate the two people. This conflation highlights an issue of scribal
transmission. Later scribal communities had to make sense of the text
as they read and copied these lists for centuries. Names and identities
were a particular problem.

The confusion of names can also be seen in the two different scribes
in David's lists, Seraiah and Sheva. The Hebrew is similar enough to
suggest that these were one person in the original list. It is also worth
pointing out that a Greek translation has an alternative name (Σουσα,
2 Kings 20:25) that points to the original Egyptian title for a scribe, *sesh*
(mentioned in chapter 2). Biblical scribes, copyists, and translators had
a difficult time making sense of the Egyptian title *sesh*, and it created
confusion in the transmission of biblical texts. Later scribes tried to
make *sesh* into a simple Hebrew name. For example, in 2 Samuel 8:17, the
Masoretic Text has *Seriah*, which makes it good Hebrew name, but
this is probably the work of a late copyist because an early Greek translation reads *Sasa* (σασα), which corresponds with the Egyptian *sesh*. The
Masoretic Text of 2 Samuel 20:25 has the name *Sheva*, but that is not a
good Hebrew name. Consequently, the Masoretic reading tradition has
Shisha, and the Greek transliterates it as *Sousa* (σούσα), both pointing
to the Egyptian *sesh*. 1 Kings 4:3 has *Shisha*, but the parallel text in 1
Chronicles 18:16 has *Shavsha*. What a mess! And it all goes back to the
old Egyptian loanword *sesh*, which means "scribe." Sometimes things
get lost in transmission and translation, especially when the original list
included an old Egyptian loanword like *sesh*.

These lists incorporate the priests under the umbrella of the royal
administration. They were not separate. This recalls another famous
scribe known in Ugaritic literature—a certain Ilimilku.[11] At the end of
several different tablets, he signs his name. On the final tablet of the
Ba'al Epic, he seemingly boasts of his many titles: "The Scribe, Ilimilku,
the Shubbanite, student of Attenu (the Diviner, Chief of the Priests,

Chief of the Herdsmen), Vizier of Niqmaddu (King of Ugarit, Lord of Yargubu and Ruler of Tharrumanu)."[12] Ilimilku seems to claim to have studied under a master scribe named Attenu and to work for the King of Ugarit. The signature on another tablet of the *Ba'al Epic* shows a narrow focus of his patronage: "The Scribe Ilimilku, Vizier of Niqmaddu King of Ugarit."[13] Roles like "Chief of the Priests" also fall under the patronage of the king. Scribes were first and foremost employees of the crown, although writing was certainly a skill that could be employed in a variety of professions, including those related to the temple and the cult. For example, a variety of magical and ritual contexts use writing. Amulets use the power of writing. Curses employed writing. And, of course, the temple might need bookkeeping, especially when the temple and its operations grew in size and personnel, as the Jerusalem Temple did in the eighth century. But as long as the power of the king and the royal bureaucracy dominated, scribes remained under the shadow of the state.

The editions and sources for the royal historical work can be seen in the archival notices that frame the Books of Samuel and especially the Book of Kings. Each of the kings of Israel and Judah have accession notices and death-burial notices that follow a rigid pattern.[14] For example, the account of King Hezekiah begins, "In the third year of King Hosea son of Elah of Israel, Hezekiah son of Ahaz of Judah began to reign. He was twenty-five years old when he began to reign, and he reigned twenty-nine years in Jerusalem. His mother's name was Abi daughter of Zechariah" (2 Kgs 18:1–2). And his reign concludes with this notice: "The rest of the acts of Hezekiah, all his power, and how he made the pool and the conduit and brought water into the city, are they not written in the Book of the Annals of the Kings of Judah? Hezekiah slept with his ancestors, and his son Manasseh succeeded him" (2 Kgs 20:20–21). Such fixed notices begin with King Rehoboam, who ruled in the late tenth century, and continue to the last kings of Judah. They are clearly archival records, and the dates correspond with external records like those recorded in the neo-Assyrian annals. Who was in charge of compiling such records? It must have been the scribes of the royal court.

It is worth noting that we do not have accession notices like these for King David or King Solomon. King David does not have a death-burial notice either. Instead, there is a rather long story about his feeble old age, an attempted coup, and the installation of Solomon as his successor in 1 Kings 1–2. King Solomon does not have a typical accession formula, but the first death-burial notice begins with Solomon: "Now the rest of the acts of Solomon . . . , are they not written in the Book of the Annals of Solomon? The time that Solomon reigned in Jerusalem over all Israel was forty years. And Solomon slept with his ancestors and was buried in the city of his father David, and his son Rehoboam succeeded him" (1 Kgs 11:41–43). The length of Solomon's reign would normally be part of an accession formula, but as Solomon does not have one, it is inserted here. This points to a transition in scribal archives between the very earliest kings and King Rehoboam in the late tenth century. It is also noteworthy that Saul, David and Solomon all supposedly reigned for forty years—a suspiciously round number! Forty is the number for one generation. Moses' life, for example, is divided into three forty-year segments—forty years in Egypt, forty years exiled in the wilderness, and forty years leading Israel out of Egypt and wandering in the wilderness. The Mesha Stele, a Moabite inscription from the ninth century BCE, also uses forty years as the symbolic time period that the god Chemosh was angry with his land. So forty is a literary and typological number, not an archival number. We must assume that during the reigns of David and Solomon that the royal scribes began to develop various archival standards, but they were nascent. Yet royal scribes were already at work, and the archival accession formulae as well as the death-burial notices begin to develop among the royal scribes.

By the time of King Rehoboam (r. 931–913 BCE), the royal scribes were recording accurate dates and reigns archives. For example, we read in 1 Kings 14:25: "In the fifth year of King Rehoboam [ca. 925 BCE], King Shishak of Egypt came up against Jerusalem." This corresponds with an inscription on the Bubastite Portal relief on the Karnak Temple in Thebes. Scholars quibble about whether the biblical scribes have correctly dated and represented Sheshonk I's reign and his campaign against Israel.[15] The differences in the name—Shishak vs. Sheshonk—are easily accounted for by the different writing systems (Hebrew vs. hieroglyphs). Apart from minor issues in scribal transmission, the archival accounts of kings and length of their reigns from Rehoboam to the end of the Judean kingdom seem generally accurate. It is first of all the work of royal scribes. Of course, it is mediated by the interpreting and editing of much later scribal communities.

The lists from David and Solomon were written down by royal scribes and put into the archives in the tenth century. But it was not until at least the eighth century that scribes in the royal court in Jerusalem apparently compiled them into a longer annalistic narrative. This narrative itself would have a long life. First, they were compiled by the men of Hezekiah (see chapter 5). A century later that narrative was out of date. Josianic scribes compiled and updated the Hezekian narratives with royal archives into the so-called "Deuteronomistic History"—a historical work stretching from the Book of Deuteronomy through 2 Kings (see chapter 7). But history marches on. And the story becomes out of date after the Babylonians destroy the temple and exile the people. The earlier version of the Deuteronomistic History composed in the late seventh century BCE no longer told the end of the story. So an exiled royal scribal community updated the work in the sixth century BCE. They made another edition that included the destruction and the exile and concluded by explicitly explaining the fate of the monarchy (see chapter 10). Eventually, the priestly scribal community that survived the exile and returned to Jerusalem would rewrite the history of Israel in a "new" version known as the Book of Chronicles. Of course, they borrowed liberally from the earlier historical work, but they focused their new version on Jerusalem and the temple (see chapter 12).[16] This all reflects the *longue durée* of scribal communities that began with early royal scribes making archival records and lists.

What else were the early royal scribes writing? There are several royal liturgies connected with the enthronement and installation of the king. Scholars identify these texts by their language, which we call Archaic Biblical Hebrew.[17] We know from cuneiform school curricula that liturgy was a category of text that was copied and memorized by scribes in their training.[18] The biblical examples of this might include Genesis

49, Exodus 15, Numbers 23–24, Deuteronomy 32–33, Judges 5, 2 Samuel 22, and Psalms 18 and 68. Sometimes scribes would use these liturgical texts in stories and narratives. A good example is Psalm 18, which gets incorporated in 2 Samuel 22, so we have it both as an independent hymn and a section of a historical narrative. In some cases like Exodus 14 and Judges 4, we have a narrative retelling that introduces the related liturgy in Exodus 15 and Judges 5. Other liturgies like Deuteronomy 32 and Habakkuk 3 are essentially appendices to their respective books. They generally celebrate the divine enthronement and its corollary—namely, the king as God's human agent. So, for example, Psalm 18:50 concludes, "Great triumphs He gives to his king, and shows his lovingkindness to his anointed, to David and his descendants forever." Exodus 15 tells of God's triumph over the Egyptians and concludes with God's enthronement in the divine temple: "You brought them out and planted them on the mountain of your own possession; the place, O LORD, that you made your abode; the sanctuary, O LORD, that your hands established. The LORD will reign forever and ever" (v. 17). The divine procession and enthronement are described in Psalms 68:24 (Heb. v. 25): "Your solemn processions are seen, O God, the processions of my God, my King, into the sanctuary." Sometimes it is explicit, as we have here, and sometimes it must be imagined. But all these are psalms that can be connected to royal liturgy and processions.

The "Song of the Bow" in 2 Samuel 1:18–27 offers some clues about learning of liturgy within scribal communities. Although this poem is not considered as linguistically archaic as others, it has a telling preface in vv. 17–18: "David sang this lament over Saul and his son Jonathan, and he instructed them to teach 'The Bow' to the Israelites—indeed, it is written in the Book of Jashar."[19] This recalls the preface to another early song in Deuteronomy 32 in which God instructs Moses, "Now you must write down this *song* and teach it to the Israelites. Place it in their mouths so that this *song* will serve as a witness among the Israelites" (Deut 31:19). This preface makes aspects of the transmission even clearer. It is written down for pedagogical purposes. Placing it "in their mouths" is a metaphor for memorization. The expression might remind us of the Oral Torah, which is committed to memory and literally called in Hebrew, "the *Torah* that is in the mouth" (*tôrah she-be ʿal peh*). Like-wise, these songs were known first through memory. Just like the Oral Torah, *The Book of Jashar* eventually gets written down.

What is *The Book of Jashar*? The Hebrew term *yashar* (usually spelled as *jashar* in English translations) is related to the Hebrew words "to sing" or "song" (*shar* and *shîr*). *Yashar* comes from the Hebrew verbal form that prefaces songs like Exodus 15: "Thus *sang* [Hebrew, *yashir*] Moses." So, *The Book of Jashar* would be a compilation of hymns or lit-urgy. The lament that begins the Song of the Bow—"O how the mighty have fallen" (2 Sam 1:25, 27)—recalls the eclipse of the early Israelite chiefdom led by Saul and his son Jonathan. It also references the city of Gath (v. 20), a city destroyed by the Arameans around 840 BCE, never to rise again.[20] This points to a relatively early hymn that was written down in a liturgical collection. The Hebrew word *yashar* also means "upright," which actually gives the book a nice double meaning—the *songs* of the *upright*. Indeed, this is just the kind of pun that scribes love. The "upright" becomes a self-description of the owners of the scroll—namely, the scribes.

Liturgical collections were part of advanced scribal curricula. We have comparative evidence for such collections from cuneiform scribal curricula as well as some fragmentary alphabetic inscriptions.[21] The al-phabetic Hebrew evidence comes from a couple of sites excavated around ancient Israel—one at Kuntillet ʿAjrud (in the southern desert) and another at Deir ʿAlla (in Transjordan). At both sites there is evi-dence of the rubrics of student scribal practice.[22] Because such texts were for memorization, we don't find them in Hebrew school copies written down on parchment, papyrus, or ostraca but rather in large plas-ter wall displays. For example, a poetic inscription mentioning Balaam (the biblical prophet known from archaic poems in Numbers 22–23) was located in a large room suitable for a master scribe and his appren-tices (see Figure 3.3).

Several of my examples reflect the scribal communities from the north, from the Kingdom of Israel. This raises the question of whether separate royal scribal communities developed in the south and the north—in Jerusalem and Samaria. This would hardly be surprising. It

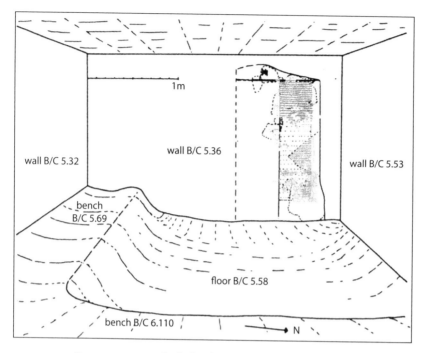

FIGURE 3.3. Reconstruction of a "schoolroom" at Deir ʿAlla with liturgical text written in ink on a plastered wall. Adapted from the drawing of Gerrit van der Kooij.

would make sense that Jerusalem and Samaria developed their own scribal communities since the two kingdoms were divided. This is borne out by a classic example of archaic northern liturgy in Judges 5 that begins, "Hear, O kings; give ear, O princes; to the LORD I will sing, I will make melody to the LORD, the God of Israel" (v. 3). It addresses an audience in the royal court.[23] Moreover, it points to female heroes like Deborah and Yael that helped free Israel and establish the northern kingdom, indicating its composition by northern court scribes. There is evidence for such court scribes during the early Iron Age in the excavations at Samaria, and the next chapter will investigate these court scribes in the northern kingdom.

In sum, writing during the early monarchy (tenth through eighth centuries BCE) was both robust and narrowly confined to the government and its agents. The military was a particularly important component of the early government scribal community. They compiled texts like royal annals, did accounting for the palace, and engaged in diplomatic service (e.g., writing letters). This scribal community would have also developed educational curricula that included literary texts, proverbial sayings, and temple liturgies. Such texts would have been a foundation for the later collection and shaping of biblical literature into a religious canon. But biblical literature did not start as a religious corpus. It started in the mundane life of an emerging monarchy and its military, administrative, and diplomatic operations.

4

Refugees from the Samarian Scribal Office

There is a certain disappointment when you find out someone has published an idea before you. On the other hand, there is a certain satisfaction that you had a good idea. On the (still) other hand, there's no prize for being second with an idea. I experienced this firsthand as I investigated a key site for the early Samarian scribal traditions—the ancient city of Bethel. Bethel figures prominently in biblical literature. But why? Why, how, and when did a small town just across the border from Judah and just a few miles north of Jerusalem—that is, in the northern kingdom of Israel—become so important in the biblical literature that it was preserved by the scribes in Jerusalem?

My own fascination with the ancient town of Bethel began in my early twenties, when I was getting a degree in historical geography at Jerusalem University College. I took a seminar called "Nineteenth Century Research in the Holy Land" that involved studying the accounts of the early explorers and roaming around the West Bank with my teacher and fellow students. Bethel was one of our test cases for identifying ancient towns using Arabic place names, geography, archaeology, and biblical literature—the four traditional disciplines of historical geography. In this case, the early American explorer Edward Robinson pointed out that an Arabic village called Beitin fit perfectly with the geography of the many biblical stories in Genesis as well as in the ancient accounts by Jerome

and Eusebius. The site was then the subject of early archaeological excavations by William Foxwell Albright and later James Kelso that gener-
ated even more debate about the early history of the town.[1]

Bethel is more than just a test case for historical geography; it was
also a prominent place in biblical stories. It has a role in the conquest
narratives (e.g., Joshua 7). It was the site of an Israelian royal cult center
that Jeroboam set up when the northern kingdom broke away from
Judah (about 930 BCE, see 1 Kings 12). It was the location of Amos' famous confrontation with the priests working at the northern royal
shrine that was located there (Amos 7). Bethel also gets explicitly mentioned in stories beginning with the promise to Abraham and throughout the book of Genesis (e.g., Gen 12:8, 13:3, 28:19, 31:13, 35:1). It was an
important place in the biblical tradition.

Why does Bethel gain such prominence in the biblical narrative? A
couple scholars suggested that these stories arose during the exile or even
the post-exilic period. They argued that Bethel must have become a
prominent place that grew in stature after the fall of Jerusalem, and this
explained why Bethel was featured so prominently in biblical tradition.[2]
I wasn't so sure. After studying their articles, I realized they had relied on
the old archaeological model of Albright, who thought that there were
two Babylonian destructions in the early sixth century—one in 597 and
a second in 586 BCE. They correlated Bethel's destruction with a first
Babylonian destruction in 597 BCE following Kelso, who thought the
city had been destroyed in the first Babylonian invasion. But Kelso got
the chronology wrong. Subsequent excavations at other archaeological
sites, particularly the city of Lachish, proved that there was no 597 BCE
destruction in the archaeological record. Lachish was a destruction similar to Bethel, but this destruction proved to be related to Assyrian campaigns in the late eighth century BCE.[3] This meant that the excavation
report published by Kelso needed to be updated. It seemed at the time
like this might make a good article, so I called an archaeologist friend,
Professor Ron Tappy, who was teaching at the Pittsburgh Theological
Seminary. Kelso had also taught at Pittsburgh, and all the excavation
materials from his excavations at Beitin were stored there. I thought I
would visit the museum, look at the artifacts with Ron, and write up an
article about Bethel. But when I called him, Ron thought that it was

curious that there was suddenly so much interest in the Beitin excavations. He told me that Israel Finkelstein, a well-regarded Israeli archaeologist, had just visited there to examine the excavation materials too. So I emailed Israel. Indeed, he told me he would soon be publishing an article, "Reevaluating Bethel," on just this topic.[4] I had been scooped!

Bethel does figure prominently in biblical narratives. Bethel, which is only about ten miles north of Jerusalem, is the place that Abraham stayed on his way to Egypt and also when he returned (Gen 12:8, 13:3). Later in the patriarchal narrative, Jacob wrestles with the Angel of the Lord there (Genesis 28). And Bethel is the among the first cities conquered by the Israelites (Joshua 7–8). The Ark of the Covenant was first located in the town of Shiloh, a town only another five miles to the north of Bethel (1 Sam 4:3). When Jeroboam rebels and sets up a new kingdom in the north, he builds a high place at Bethel (1 Kings 12–13), and it is there that the "prophet" Amos confronts the priests at the royal shrine. Bethel has a role in the Elijah-Elisha prophetic stories (e.g., 2 Kings 2), and it is mentioned in Josiah's Reforms that took place a century after the destruction of the town (2 Kgs 23:4, 17). So there is a concentration of important biblical stories located at Bethel, even though the city was destroyed by the Assyrians in the eighth century. The question is why? Scholars have reasoned that there must have been community of scribes there.

It is not just Bethel, but more generally there is a lot of Israelian literature in Judah's Bible. Of course, other scholars have noticed this.[5] For example, New York University professor Daniel Fleming points to *The Legacy of Israel in Judah's Bible*, as his book titles it. In an older book, *The Israelian Heritage of Judaism*, which suggests that the Book of Deuteronomy was "Israelian" literature, H. L. Ginsberg traced its impact on post-exilic Judaism. More recently, Israel Finkelstein tried to recover what he called *The Forgotten Kingdom*—that is, the northern kingdom of Israel—beginning from an archaeological and historical perspective. He points out that Israel was the larger, more populous, and wealthier kingdom, and that they had economic and political connections with the entire near east. And yet they were forgotten in favor of their poorer, smaller sibling—Judah. Why? It was the later Judean scribes who collected, copied, and edited our Bible. They did so over a long period of time beginning in the eighth century, and they made sure that Israel was not forgotten.[6]

So Israel was not really forgotten. The Bible is filled with its stories. The patriarchal narratives tell the origins of the northern tribes of Israel, and many take place in northern locales like Bethel and Shechem. The Joseph story, which gives an account of how the Israelites came to Egypt, prefaces the story of how Israel came out of Egypt. The Book of Judges mostly regales us with the early tales of the northern tribes in the land. Many psalms are set in northern locales like Mount Hermon and Carmel and clearly reflect a northern origin. Two of the prophetic books—Hosea and Amos—are set in the north. And Jonah is also a northern prophet, although his story focuses on Assyria. The prophet Samuel is a northerner, the son of Elkanah from Ephraim. The Book of Kings preserves many tales of the northern prophets Elijah and Elisha, and it also details the reigns and events of the northern rulers. The latter details about the length of the reigns of northern kings must have come from royal archives brought from Samaria down to Judah. In short, there were an awful lot of northern stories that got preserved by scribes in Jerusalem. It all becomes part of Judah and Jerusalem's sacred history. This needs some explaining.

Israel was not so much forgotten as it was appropriated. A story that nicely summarizes the appropriation of literary wealth from Israel to Judah is Melchizedek's blessing of Abraham in Genesis 14. The main character of the story is Melchizedek, whose name means "righteous king." He was the king and priest of Salem, a not-so-subtle allusion to Jerusalem. After the patriarch Abraham defeats some foreign kings in battle, he goes to Salem and meets Melchizedek and gives him a tithe. Melchizedek in turn blesses Abraham. It's an odd story, and Melchizedek is a cryptic figure who never appears again in the biblical narrative.[7] But it is not hard to see that Melchizedek, the ancient king and priest of (Jeru-)Salem, is honored above Abraham, the patriarch of the mostly northern tribes. Indeed, this literary relationship between the father of Israel and the predecessor of David foreshadows the transfer of wealth from Israel to Judah—not just material wealth but literary riches.

Jerusalemite scribes incorporated Israelian literature into their Bible and made it their own. Indeed, they were so effective in doing so that it is easy to forget that "Israel" originally referred to the northern tribes and kingdom. So how does Israel—or more specifically, the territory north of Jerusalem and Judah—come to play such a prominent role in

REFUGEES FROM THE SAMARIAN SCRIBAL OFFICE   79

biblical literature edited and published in Jerusalem? After all, David and his sons were the chosen dynasty. And it was in Jerusalem that God chose to build his temple and place his name. When the northern tribes of Israel went into exile in the eighth century, they were "lost" and "forgotten."[8] But not everyone was exiled. And some people—including scribes—made their way south as refugees to Jerusalem and Judah.

This chapter follows the scribal community that contributed to the Israelian heritage of biblical literature. Other studies have investigated the archaeological support for Israelian refugees or detailed biblical texts that may have originally come from the north, but this is circumstantial evidence. Here I want to search for the scribes themselves. I want to put faces on the general archaeological and literary theories about refugees and their literature. Can we find the fingerprints of these Israelian scribes that fled down to Jerusalem and Judah in the inscriptional record?

The Samaria Ostraca

I begin by examining the northern kingdom's scribal community. The largest group of northern inscriptions are known as the Samaria Ostraca—a cache of economic receipts excavated near the palace.[9] They give direct evidence for a Samarian scribal community working in the palace dating to the eighth century BCE. This collection of about one hundred inscriptions records the transfer of small quantities of luxury goods from the surrounding clans related to the tribe of Manasseh to the capital in Samaria.

The story of the discovery of the ostraca is worth telling. They were excavated in the so-called "Ostraca House," a building adjacent to the royal palace, but they were not excavated in an administrative archive. They were found in archaeological fills and secondary contexts dating to the later eighth century BCE. What happened? How did they get there? The ostraca—broken potsherds—were like scratch paper. There must have been a scribal office adjacent to the palace with a couple of scribes recording goods coming into the palace during the reign of Jeroboam II (r. 782–753 BCE). The receipts were probably recorded on ostraca, then later put down on a papyrus ledger, after which the ostraca would have been thrown on the trash heap. A major earthquake around 760 BCE severely damaged the scribal office and palace. The palace complex was then rebuilt, and these Samaria Ostraca—essentially old trash—became part of the construction materials used in rebuilding the palace complex. It is like finding an old diary in the wall of your house when you are doing remodeling.

The Samaria Ostraca are receipts of economic activity. Each receipt begins with a historical date such as "In the ninth year," "In the tenth year," or "In the fifteenth year." That we have different dates, essentially two collections, reminds us that these texts are not an archive but discarded receipts used in fills. These receipts point to a scribal community near the royal palace that developed its own scribal practice and was distinct from its later Judean counterparts. Although such economic texts have limited linguistic material, still we find distinctive spelling and vocabulary that reflect a northern royal scribal community. For example, they spell the common Hebrew words *št* "year" and *yn* "wine" instead of *šnh* and *yyn* as we find in Judean or Standard Biblical Hebrew. They also use a distinctive northern abbreviation of Yahweh's divine name prefixed or suffixed to personal names, e.g., Gaddi*yaw* (with *-yw*) instead of the Judean (and biblical) spelling Gaddi*yahu* (with *-yhw*). These distinctions extend to vocabulary. The words for the prestige commodities "old wine" (*yn yšn*) and "refined oil" (*šmn rḥṣ*) are northern dialectal variants that are different from their Judean counterparts found in the Bible (*šᵉmārîm* and *šemen kātît*).[10]

These spelling and vocabulary differences distinguish the Samarian scribal community from Jerusalem much the same way that words like *centre* (vs. *center*), *standardise* (vs. *standardize*), *flat* (vs. *apartment*), and *lift* (vs. *elevator*) distinguish British from American English. It was something learned and passed along as part of the Samarian scribal community of practice. However, when we move, our vocabulary and conventions usually adapt. For example, if I were looking for an apartment in London, I'd better ask about "flats." And if I were looking for an elevator, I'd ask where I could find the "lift." When I wrote an article for *Cambridge Ancient History*, my American spelling was conventionalized to British spelling. It helps to adapt linguistically to your context, and the same was certainly true for ancient scribes.

So what else can we learn from reading these receipts? Well, these are no ordinary receipts. The products are for the elite—for example, not

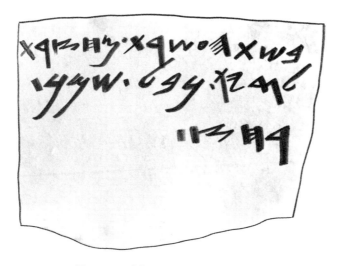

FIGURE 4.1. Drawing of Samaria ostracon no. 18. Drawing by the author.

just oil but *refined oil.* Not just wine but *old wine.* These are luxury goods, and taxes were usually paid on just such goods. Moreover, the quantities are quite small. Consider just two receipts (see Figure 4.1):

No. 3: In the tenth year, from Semida, a *jar* of old wine, for Baʿala.
No. 18: In the tenth year, from Hatzerot, for Gaddiyaw, a *jar* of refined oil.

The Hebrew word that is translated as "jar" is *nēbel.* It's not a large storage jar but more like a bottle of wine. Even if it's a large bottle, it's not significant enough for taxes. These were transfers of luxury items to individuals working in the palace from local clans or families. Emory professor Roger Nam, who specializes in ancient economies, explains that these quantities and types of products can be related to "elite political feasting" that was related to the royal acropolis at Samaria.[11] It is like bringing a big bottle of Dom Pérignon champagne to a party. Expensive but not a huge quantity.

Luxury goods actually fit quite well with what we know about Samaria both in the literary and archaeological record. Dame Kathleen Kenyon described the pottery from the acropolis as "the finest decorated ware of the Israelite period."[12] In addition to the fine "Samaria Ware," archaeologists uncovered finely carved ivory that adorned the furniture in the palace.[13] These archaeological discoveries accord with the biblical descriptions of the Samaria palace as a "House of Ivory" (1 Kgs 22:39; Amos 3:15). Indeed, critics like Amos—I hesitate to call him a "prophet" since he rejects that title (Amos 7:14)—railed against the luxury and excess associated with the Samaria palace: "Woe to those who lie on beds of ivory and who recline on their couches!" (Amos 6:4). All of this supports the idea that the Samarian scribal office was recording the receipt of fine wine and oil for elaborate celebrations in the palace.

The reach of the Samarian scribal community extended all the way to the Sinai desert. I pointed out in chapter 1 that the desert fortress at Kuntillet ʿAjrud included a fledgling scribal community of practice with a commander who trained young soldiers to read and write. This fortress was sponsored by Samaria and the royal palace. Many of the Kuntillet ʿAjrud inscriptions likely date to the period of Jeroboam II and might have been contemporaneous with the Samaria Ostraca. A couple of scribal writing exercises—a vocabulary list and a practice letter—even mention the city of Samaria. Most famously, a practice letter includes the blessing formula, "I bless you to Yahweh of Samaria and its/his Asherah." The personal names mentioned in the Kuntillet ʿAjrud inscriptions use *yaw* suffixes that are markers of the Israelian identity of the fort's occupants: Amar*yaw*, Shemaʿ*yaw*, Obad*yaw*, Ḥal*yaw*, Shekan*yaw*, Shemar*yaw*, Eli*yaw*, and Uzzi*yaw*. There are no Judean names mentioned in the inscriptions. The fortress also has a number of drawings on the pottery and fragmentary plaster walls that depict the image of the king on a throne (Figure 4.2), royal hunting scenes, and protective images.[14] These images further point to the royal sponsor for the fortress and its inhabitants.

Israelite Refugees in Jerusalem and Judah

So what makes the Samarian scribal community so significant for biblical literature? Some became war refugees, fled to Jerusalem, and worked for the state bureaucracy there. They brought their records, stories, and liturgy to Jerusalem. And we read their texts in the pages of our Bibles

FIGURE 4.2. "King on a Throne" at Kuntillet ʿAjrud. Drawing by Tallay Ornan; originally published in *Tel Aviv*, used with permission.

today. First let us look at the historical background to the stories of these refugees. In a series of military campaigns, the neo-Assyrian kings devastated the northern kingdom. First, Tiglath-Pileser III (r. 745–727 BCE), known as *Pul* in the Bible (2 Kgs 15:9), campaigned against Israel between 734 and 732 BCE, destroying Israelite towns in the Galilee area and along the northern coast. His son, Shalmaneser V (r. 727–722 BCE), and grandson, Sargon II (r. 722–705 BCE), besieged and then captured Samaria in 721 BCE. Many Israelites were exiled. Assyria created a brutal, though effective, policy of deportation for rebellious vassal states. People who had been dispossessed of their land were less likely to rebel. As a result, many fled from the Assyrians. Some went to Egypt; others most likely relocated to the southern coastal plain; and some from the Samarian scribal community fled to Jerusalem and Judah.

Striking archaeological examples illustrate a wave of Israelian refugees that came to Jerusalem in the wake of the Assyrian campaigns. First of all, there was a dramatic increase in population in Jerusalem in the late eighth century. Decades ago, Israeli archaeologist Magen Broshi recognized that the dramatic growth in Jerusalem's population during the late eighth century had to be related to Assyrian military campaigns and Israelian refugees.[15] This is hardly surprising. Even in our own times, we see how war and violence cause people to flee in search of peace and a better life. Notable recent examples include Ukrainian refugees fleeing war, Syrian refugees fleeing civil war, or Central American refugees fleeing violence. It was no different in ancient Judah. The population of Jerusalem may have doubled during the late eighth century.[16] The Western Hill of ancient Jerusalem (the modern "Jewish Quarter") was unwalled until the late eighth century BCE, but suddenly it was filled with refugees. Some of these refugees squatted outside of the walled city of Jerusalem. When the refugees needed protection because of the imminent threat of the Assyrian armies, Hezekiah "broke down the houses to fortify the wall" (Isa 22:10).

The biblical descriptions find support in archaeological excavations. After the Six-Day War in 1967, Israeli archaeologist Benjamin Mazar excavated the Western Hill. He uncovered a massive wall twenty-two feet wide that he dubbed "the Broad Wall," which was built to incorporate the Western Hill into the walled city of Jerusalem. And these excavations illustrate the words of Isaiah—old, poorly built houses were destroyed to make way for a major fortification wall. The foundations of the broad wall were built over the houses (Figure 4.3; note houses under the wall on the bottom left). These houses were originally part of an unwalled settlement outside of Jerusalem. Hezekiah destroyed the houses to enclose the refugee settlement within the city. Perhaps this should be considered one of the first examples of "eminent domain"!

Refugees left their imprint on the art, architecture, and bureaucracy of Jerusalem. Where exactly did these refugees come from? Some probably

FIGURE 4.3. Excavations of the "Broad Wall." Courtesy and
rights: Archaeological Excavations in the Jewish Quarter of
the Old City in Jerusalem.

came from just across the border from Judah, from the royal shrine at
Bethel mentioned in 1 Kings 12 and Amos 7. Others likely came from
the vicinity of the capital in Samaria. These would have included scribes
working in the capital.

One of the most noteworthy illustrations of Samarian influence on the
bureaucracy in Jerusalem was the emergence of royal storage jars and
the royal seal impressions used on these jars. These jars begin to appear
in Judah in the late eighth century—that is, in the aftermath of the

neo-Assyrian campaigns against Samaria. The shape of these Judean royal storage jars borrowed from the Israelian "hippo" storage jars. The storage jars reflect an advanced distribution system that was developed in the late eighth century. Indeed, some archaeologists have suggested—correctly, I think—that the Judean bureaucracy was informed by Israelian models.[17] This is supported not just by the shape of the jars but also by the insignia on the jar handles. The jars are impressed with a royal stamp (either a two-winged or four-winged scarab) and a two-line inscription reading "Belonging to the King" (Hebrew, *lmlk*) and the name of a Judahite administrative city—Hebron, Socoh, Ziph, and "*Mmšt*." The mysterious "*Mmšt*" probably refers to a place known today as Ramat Raḥel (its ancient name is still a mystery), which was a royal administrative site two miles south of Jerusalem built in the late eighth century.[18]

What is striking is that the four-winged scarab stamp was previously used in Samaria! In the 1930s, a British archaeologist, John Crowfoot, excavated nine seal impressions in the area around the palace at Samaria dating to the eighth century BCE. Another seal was later found and published by Canadian archaeologist A. D. Tushingham, bringing the total number of examples to ten. It seems more than coincidental that this motif then appears in Judah shortly after the fall of Samaria to the Assyrians in 721 BCE (see Figure 4.4 for a comparison of images).[19]

The parallel between the Samaria seals and the Judean royal seals has been noticed before. Many years ago, Tushingham noticed the similarity and suggested an Israelian origin to this Judahite royal insignia, but his suggestion was dismissed.[20] Several objections were made. First, there are only ten examples. This is fair. The four-winged scarab was not an iconic symbol for Israelian royalty in the same way that it became a symbol for Judah. But ten examples is still significant. It was obviously known and used at the palace in Samaria. In my view, that it was *not* an iconic Israelian symbol made it more palatable to borrow and use in Jerusalem. Second, this imagery is also known from Phoenician and north Syrian examples—in other words, it is not exclusively Samarian.[21] While the symbol was known elsewhere, Samaria was Judah's immediate neighbor, and refugees were coming into Judah from there. Why posit influence

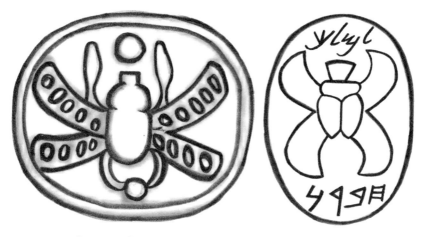

FIGURE 4.4. Samarian four-winged impression (left) and four-winged Judean LMLK impression (right). Drawings by the author.

from remote parts of the near east when there is a close and immediate vector of transmission from Samaria? Although the winged scarab was relatively insignificant in the Samaria palace chancellery, this imagery's appearance in the late eighth century must be more than just coincidence. Explaining this away as coincidental or circumstantial is unnecessarily skeptical. The borrowing fits well in the larger picture of Samarian scribal refugees fleeing to Jerusalem and Judah in the late eighth century. As we shall see, it is part of a pattern of data that fits together and shows the influence of a Samarian scribal community in Jerusalem.

Samarian Scribes in King Hezekiah's Court

A number inscriptions point to the wide diffusion of Israelian refugees. Some of the refugees can be identified by their personal names.[22] Features of Israelian personal names are well established from the Samaria Ostraca. Naming practices are cultural and distinctive. As I have pointed out, they spell names using a typical northern theophoric element (i.e., an abbreviation for the name of God). The Israelian prefix *yw-* and suffix *-yw* (often translated in English as *Yaw-/Yo-/Jo-* and *-yaw*) were used instead of the

FIGURE 4.5. Seal impression of "Eliakim, Apprentice of Yawkin" (*WSSS* no. 663). Drawing by the author.

longer spelling in Judahite names, *yhw-* and *-yhw* (usually translated in English as *Jeho-* and *-yahu/-iah*).[23] For example, a seventh-century papyrus from Wadi Murabba'at in the Judean Desert uses the Israelian personal name Yaw'ezer. But a name does not have to have an Israelian prefix or suffix to be identified as northern. For example, a personal name like Hosea seems distinctively northern. It was, for example, the name of a well-known biblical prophet. It also appears in the Wadi Murabba'at papyrus. It is an Israelian name, and it fits nicely with the name Yaw'ezer in the Wadi Murabba'at papyrus. Together they suggest that Wadi Murabba'at received refugees from the north. This is not surprising since the Judean Desert saw a dramatic increase in population—that is, refugees—after the neo-Assyrian campaigns. These personal names indicate that many of these new residents were Israelian refugees.[24]

There are also seal impressions excavated around Jerusalem and Judah that use the typical northern theophoric prefix and suffix. One seal impression of particular interest reads, "Belonging to Eliakim, Apprentice of Yawkin" (*l'lyqm n'r ywkn*, *WSSS* no. 663; see Figure 4.5). In addition to the example excavated in Jerusalem, nine other exemplars of the seal were excavated at Beth-Shemesh, Ramat Raḥel, and Tell Beit Mirsim. With regard to the title "Apprentice of," I mentioned these seal impressions in chapter 1 in discussing the social structure of scribal guilds. In this chapter we are interested in the individuals themselves. They use typical Israelian personal names. Yawkin and his steward Eliakim must have been particularly well-connected members of the Judahite bureaucracy given the number and distribution of the seal impressions at different places.

The Seal of Yawbanah, Son of Menaḥem:
A Case of Negotiating Refugee Identity

An even more striking example of Israelian identity in personal names comes from the seal impressions of a certain Menaḥem, son of Yawbanah. I counted at least seventeen separate seal impressions of this person that use three separate seals. Most of these come from excavations and include impressions excavated at Lachish, Beth-Shemesh, Adullam, Socoh, Ramat Raḥel, Gibeon, and Jerusalem.[25] This fellow got around! We also have examples of his seal impressed on storage jars that have the royal signia ("belonging to the king"). In fact, we know of no other example of a figure known from so many seal impressions in such a diverse set of locations. Most of these impressions come from one seal with the father's name spelled Yawbanah (*ywbnh*), meaning "Yahweh has built," using the Israelian *yw-* prefix for the divine name. The verb probably alludes to the building of a family through the birth of a son, as we see in the literary punning in God's well-known promise to David. David wanted to "build" a temple for God, but God turns that on its head and promises to build a dynasty for his family (see 2 Samuel 7).

In addition to the standard Israelian spelling, there are also a couple of impressions from a second seal with an abbreviated version of his father's name, *ybnh*, which might be understood as a simple contraction pronounced as "Yobanah." More importantly, the revised spelling in this contraction obscures the Israelian *yw-* prefix, and its meaning is now somewhat ambiguous. It could mean, "Y[ahweh] has built," or perhaps it should be read as *Yibanah*, "He shall build." I suspect both *ywbnh* and *ybnh* could have been pronounced as "Yobanah," which would still refer to Yahweh building a family. The different spellings in the prefixes were primarily a marker of identity and a reflection of scribal community practice. The difference was not about pronunciation; it was about identity.

Menaḥem's third seal illustrates just how closely spelling is connected with identity. There are two seal impressions from a third seal that corrected the spelling of Menaḥem's father's name. After the seal was engraved, it was modified by squeezing in two more letters, apparently to

FIGURE 4.6. Seal impression of Menaḥem, son of Yehobanah (*Y*ₕ*bnh*). Drawing by the author.

give his father a proper Judahite name (see Figure 4.6). It's important to see what was actually done on the seal. On the second line, the engraver squeezed in the letter *he* between the letters *yod* and *bet*. And before the *yod*, the letter *waw* was added to the seal. The letters had to be crammed in, and the *waw* erases some of the bottom of the double line separator. Very interesting. Why were they modifying a seal that originally read "Yobanah" (*ybnh*)? The additional letters—in the correct order—would give a standard Judahite name: Yehobanah (*yhwbnh*). But it was impossible to squeeze the letters in correct order. So they were squeezed in where they could fit. As it is written, the spelling *ʷyₕbnh* is nonsensical, but understandable. The added letters would create a standard Judean name, if they were in the correct order. The seal cutter did what they could to modify the name and give it a Judean spelling. We now have three different spellings for Menaḥem's father:

1) *ywbnh*   Yawbanah
2) *ybnh*   Yobanah
3) *ʷyₕbnh*   Yehobanah

By squeezing in these extra letters in the third rendition of the father's name, Menaḥem is redefining his identity.

The seal owner's own name, Menaḥem, has no identifying theophoric, but it is a typical Israelian name. In fact, Menaḥem was the name for one of the last kings in Samaria (r. 746–737 BCE; see 2 Kgs 15:13–22). Perhaps his father named him Menaḥem after one of the last kings—a patron of his Samarian scribal community? The king was long gone, but the memory is preserved in the naming of his son. This may even have been a family name, which might explain this refugee's prominent placement within the Judean administration. He had royal blood. In any case, the only explicit marker of identity for Menaḥem was his father's name. In the three seals, Menaḥem revises his father's name from *Yawbanah* to *Yobanah* to an apparent attempt at *Yehobanah*. Through the respelling of his father's name in his personal seals, he has redefined his identity! The interesting and perhaps unanswerable question, of course, is why did Menaḥem feel the need to revise his identity? Were Israelian refugees being discriminated against? This seems likely, but we can only guess.

The name Menaḥem is well known in the northern kingdom. To begin with, we find the name in the Samaria Ostraca (no. 112), which gives evidence external to the Bible affiliating him with the clan of Manasseh in the vicinity of Samaria.[26] We also find this name in biblical stories. For example, it comes up in the annals of the northern monarchy in 2 Kings 15. First, we read an account of the brief reign of Shallum:

> [13] Shallum son of Jabesh began to reign in the thirty-ninth year of King Uzziah of Judah; he reigned one month in Samaria. [14] Then Menahem son of Gadi came up from Tirzah and came to Samaria; he struck down Shallum son of Jabesh in Samaria and killed him; he reigned in place of him.

Next, we have an account of King Menaḥem:

> [17] In the thirty-ninth year of King Azariah of Judah, Menahem son of Gadi began to reign over Israel; he reigned ten years in Samaria. . . . [19] King Pul of Assyria came against the land; Menahem gave Pul a thousand talents of silver, so that he might help him strengthen the kingdom in his hand. [20] Menahem exacted the money from Israel, that is, from all the wealthy, fifty shekels of silver from each one, to give to the king of Assyria. Then the king of Assyria turned back. He did not remain there in the land. [21] Now the rest of the deeds of Menahem, and all that he did, are they not written in the Book of the Annals of the Kings of Israel? [22] Menahem slept with his ancestors, and his son Pekahiah succeeded him.

These accounts are highly formulaic. In such and such a year, so-and-so began his reign. But then there are details. He reigned for one month, or two years, or ten years. And there are the synchronisms with the Judean kings. And the accounts of the Assyrian campaign sync up with cuneiform records, although sometimes the editor muddles the details. For example, from Assyrian texts we know that Pul (v. 19) was an abbreviation of the name for King Tiglath-pileser III, who is mentioned later (v. 29). Later Judean royal scribes do not seem to realize this was the same Assyrian ruler, but they were just copying from archival records. It illustrates that they had records from the Samarian royal court. At the same time it does not mean they fully comprehended what they were reading. But we can still piece it together, and the details of the Assyrian campaigns accord well with what we know from Israelite royal annals preserved in the Book of Kings. This evidence also suggests that not all the northern literature came from oral tradition. Some scribes could have physically brought records from the palace in Samaria down to Jerusalem. From seal impressions, we actually know the names of some of these people—Yawkin, Yawbanah, and Menaḥem. Perhaps a person like Menaḥem was a second-generation immigrant? His father perhaps chose the name of the last king of Israel from a sense of pride in northern heritage or perhaps there was some royal family connection. The interesting and perhaps unanswerable question, of course, is why did Menaḥem feel the need to renegotiate his identity? Perhaps Menaḥem had been subject to discrimination as a Samarian. We know, for example, that there are decidedly anti-northern aspects to the Josianic religious reforms in the late seventh century (see 2 Kings 22–23).

Samaria's Imprint on Judah's Bible

The Books of Samuel and Kings reveal some profound differences between the kingdoms of Israel and Judah. As Daniel Fleming points out, "Judah's identity is bound up from the beginning with kingship," and in contrast, "Only in Israel was there a perceived need to explain this people's existence before and apart from kings."[27] Of course, this is the likely result of royal scribes working in the Jerusalem court. On the one hand, they naturally glorify the sons of David as the legitimate kings. For royal scribes in Jerusalem, the import of Israelian literature had to be outside of the royal court in Samaria. On the other hand, the stories in Genesis still tell the origin of the northern tribes of Israel, and Judah is secondary even though the stories were eventually copied and preserved in Jerusalem. The editorial process is nicely illustrated in the account of Judah and Tamar told in Genesis 38. Although the story is inserted into a Joseph novella (Genesis 37–50), which was a story relating to the northern tribes of Ephraim and Manasseh, it is clearly an intrusion. Indeed, the intrusion is marked in the scribal framing repetition that ends chapter 37, "The Midianites sold Joseph into Egypt, to Potiphar" (v. 36), and resumes at the beginning of chapter 39, "Joseph was brought down to Egypt, and Potiphar, an officer of Pharaoh, bought him from the Ishmaelites" (v. 1). The Jerusalemite scribes are letting us know that they're inserting Judah into a story related to the northern tribes through the editorial device of repetition.

The accounts of the two kingdoms in the Book of Kings are markedly different. Judah has one center for the king and the temple from its inception, whereas Israel has several capitals (Tirzah, Shechem, Samaria) and different sacral centers (e.g., Bethel, Dan, Mount Carmel). Judah had one dynasty—the sons of David—whereas Israel had a succession of different dynasties (e.g., Jeroboam, Omri, Jehu, etc.). Judah had no notable tribal divisions, where Israel was a collaboration of different tribes. But they did both worship Yahweh as their national deity, even if Israel's expression of this worship was markedly critiqued by later Jerusalemite scribes.

Jerusalemite scribal communities preserve Israelian literature even where Judah plays a marginal role. This begins in the patriarchal stories and Exodus from Egypt. The Book of Numbers includes Judah in its census as one among the many tribes, but Reuben is privileged as the firstborn and Levi is prominent for its role in the tabernacle. Likewise, Judah plays only a marginal role in the tribal stories in the Book of Judges. Most notably, Judah is not mentioned in the archaic poem known as the "Song of Deborah" (Judges 5). The Book of Judges as a whole was incorporated into the Jerusalem library by a process Sara Milstein has called "revision by introduction."[28] The book was given a new preface, beginning with an account of the conquest of Jerusalem and Judah (vv. 1–21). But then the next eighteen chapters ignore Judah and tell the tawdry tales of ten northern tribes. The book then ends (chapters 19–21) with a horrific political allegory fashioned by reusing the story of Sodom and Gomorrah to justify Judah and the hometown of David (Bethlehem) as against Benjamin and the hometown of Saul (Gibeah).[29] Such a political allegory suggests a scribal community in dialogue with a competing community as well as a live political debate. But how long could such a debate about legitimate kingship have survived after the destruction of Samaria? I doubt it would have long survived those events. After a generation or two, it just becomes irrelevant. The northern kingdom becomes old news.

So the question is, what literature did the Samarian scribes bring with them to Jerusalem? Certainly, some written documents, such as palace archival records of northern kings, must have been brought to Jerusalem. These documents included the names of kings, length of reigns, building projects, military campaigns, and the like. Such details were certainly not committed to memory by scribes. This is not oral literature.

Other physical texts are less certain. For example, were patriarchal stories brought down to Jerusalem orally, or did they exist in written parchments? Most of these stories were likely part of the scribal curriculum that was memorized, and in that respect not all of it needed to be transported as written documents. Some scholars think the legal core of Deuteronomy had its origins in the north (see chapter 7), but it is presented as a speech that was first written down when Israel arrived at Shechem beneath Mount Gerizim and Mount Ebal (see chapters 27–29, especially 27:2–4). The legal parts of Deuteronomy reflect textual study and editing;[30] this was certainly done later by scribes in Jerusalem. There are also the accounts of two northern prophets, Hosea and Amos, that are included among the prophetic books of the Judean prophets. These books were clearly edited in Judah (see Hos 3:1–5; Amos 9:11), but perhaps they existed as texts before they came to the Jerusalem court? There are also prophetic stories of Elijah and Elisha that were incorporated into the Book of Kings.

The story of the prophet Balaam in Numbers 22–24 is instructive for weighing the issue of oral literature vs. written texts. The account of Balaam certainly has some earmarks of oral literature. First of all, they are poems. Second, there are humorous tales like Balaam's talking donkey (Num 22:2–35), which works well as oral literature. But the dual nature of such literature—as both oral and written—was highlighted in the excavations at ancient Succoth (or, Tell Deir ʿAlla) mentioned in the last chapter. The wall inscriptions there featured the prophet Balaam and were placed in what seems to be a small schoolroom. While the plaster wall text was meant to memorized, it was also displayed as a written document. We might compare the well-known *Epic of Gilgamesh*, which also was likely meant to be memorized but existed in school copies as well. Just because something is oral literature does not mean there were not also physical copies. On the other hand, oral literature was memorized as part of scribal training.[31] In this way, physical copies of many Israelian texts did not need to have been brought to Jerusalem. One only needed the scribal refugees who had memorized such texts to be integrated into the Judean bureaucracy. They would then have the opportunity to integrate such literature into Judean scribal curricula and eventually into the canon of biblical literature.

What identifies a biblical text as northern? Some scholars have used content (e.g., patriarchal narratives, Judges). Others point to a northern dialect (e.g., Judges 5, Elijah-Elisha narratives). But even the texts that may have existed in Samaria and other northern scribal centers before they were brought to Jerusalem underwent editing and revision. Scribes revised both content and language as they copied, edited, and revised texts. The northern dialect was probably largely lost except when scribes wanted to preserve it. Language can be a stylistic feature—a classic example of this is the Book of Job, which is set in the foreign land of Uz and whose linguistic register is sprinkled with Aramaic and South Arabian features that fit its foreign characters.[32] By analogy, one thinks of the dialects of characters in *The Adventures of Huckleberry Finn*, which is a stylistic feature used by Mark Twain. So that brings us back to texts like the rewritten and updated history in the Book of Chronicles. Chronicles eliminates the history of the northern kingdom as much as possible. For Chronicles, the history of "Israel" is a history of Judah.[33]

And Chronicles uses "Israel" to refer to Judah. The northern kingdom was irrelevant. Or worse—it was anathema. So literature set in the north and dealing with northern historical figures in all likelihood originally came from the north. Sometimes there are features of the northern dialect that are preserved in the literature. It can be detected in narratives like the stories about Elijah and Elisha, but it is especially noticeable in poetry like Judges 5 and various psalms.[34] But in the end, all this literature is preserved in Jerusalem and Judah.

PART TWO

The Beginnings of the Bible

The beginning is the most important part of the work.

—PLATO, *THE REPUBLIC*

5

New Scribal Communities

After I finished my PhD at Brandeis University in 1992, I went to Jerusalem for two years as a postdoctoral fellow at the Albright Institute of Archaeological Research. My own arrival in Jerusalem coincided with a huge wave of Russian immigrants flooding into Israel. In 1991 150,000 came, followed by 65,000 in 1992, 66,000 in 1993, and 68,000 in 1994. Israeli society naturally struggled to cope with the influx of these refugees from the north. I vividly recall meeting a Russian immigrant who had been a concert violinist. He was working as a street sweeper. As he told his story, I realized how difficult it had to be to absorb the many immigrants that I was meeting on the streets of Jerusalem. Even though my violinist/street sweeper friend was thrilled to be living in Jerusalem, I saw how he and other refugees were forced into jobs where they were certainly over-qualified. Indeed, my personal encounter helped me understand that similar things must have been happening in Jerusalem during the late eighth century. Refugees do not usually come gradually. They come in waves precipitated by specific events. For Jerusalem and Judah, these events began with the Assyrian campaigns against Galilee (732 BCE) and the conquest of Samaria (721 BCE). Later Assyrian campaigns devastated the coastal plain of Philistia (711 BCE) and the foothills to the west of Jerusalem (701 BCE). These would change the nature of scribal communities in Judah.

The Flourishing of Hebrew Writing

The discussion must start with one incontrovertible observation. Putting aside the Bible, external evidence for Hebrew writing is concentrated in the late eighth through early sixth centuries BCE. To be sure, there are a handful of "Hebrew" inscriptions dating from the eleventh through mid-eighth centuries BCE. Most of them are quite short, and it is sometimes hard to tell the difference between a "Hebrew," "Phoenician," and "Canaanite" inscription.[1] The written language and scripts are quite uniform, although scholars can point to some distinctions. The point is, however, that there is not a lot of inscriptional evidence for early Hebrew writing. There is enough to demonstrate that a Hebrew scribal community existed, but writing was not widespread in all segments of society.[2]

The evidence gets even more meager after the Babylonian destruction of Jerusalem in 586 BCE until the Hellenistic period. You can count the number of Hebrew inscriptions dating to the Persian period (539–333 BCE) on the fingers of your two hands—and you do not have to use all of them! In stark contrast, there are literally thousands of Hebrew inscriptions of various types that date to the late Iron Age (about 725–586 BCE). I have already explained the limited writing in the early Iron Age by the restricted nature of the scribal community. Likewise, in later chapters I will account for the lack of Hebrew inscriptions in the post-exilic period (until we get to the Hasmonean Period) by the fact that Hebrew writing was largely restricted to the temple and was used primarily for religious purposes. In contrast, Hebrew inscriptions during the late Iron Age demonstrate that writing breaks free from small or restricted scribal communities. It is the flourishing of writing that I describe in this chapter, and I follow its implications—new scribal communities—in the subsequent chapters.

When we arrive in the late eighth century, Hebrew writing is everywhere. It is no longer confined to the palace or the elites. But what was the catalyst for the spread of writing and the emergence of new scribal communities? We must start with the Assyrian Empire. The specter of Assyria cast a long and growing shadow in the eighth century. By the mid- to late eighth century, the Assyrian Empire overwhelmed smaller kingdoms in the eastern Mediterranean. It devastated cities like Damascus (the Arameans), Sidon and Tyre (the Phoenicians), Samaria (the Israelites), Ashdod (the Philistines), and Jerusalem (the Judeans). In 732 BCE, Tiglath-Pileser III overran Galilee. In 721 BCE, Samaria fell. And by 716 BCE, Sargon II had reached Gaza on the borders of Egypt. From a wall relief showing Hananu of Gaza bowing before the Assyrian king, we can imagine the ultimate target of Assyria's relentless march—the riches of Egypt. But it is likely that the Assyrians began campaigning in the Judean foothills during the reign of Sargon;[3] in the days of King Sennacherib, the Assyrians would arrive at the doorstep of Jerusalem. But Jerusalem survived and with it, biblical literature.

So how does this impact biblical literature? The rise of the Assyrian Empire was accompanied by the three-headed monster of globalization, industrialization, and urbanization. These all encouraged the use and spread of writing. At the same time, the Assyrian military campaigns encouraged Israelite refugees to flood into Jerusalem and Judah. These refugees brought with them advanced knowledge of bureaucracy and engineering as well as the skill of writing. They were incorporated by Judean kings into the royal bureaucracy, but they also spread out more broadly across society.

The Curious Case of the Siloam Tunnel
Inscription—Refugee Labor

The Siloam Tunnel inscription is quite curious. I actually took up this case in an article that I co-authored a few years ago. I was sitting in the lobby of a hotel at a huge academic conference—ten thousand people. Four days, hundreds of papers. It was a zoo. I was taking a break when Gary Rendsburg, a scholar I knew, stopped for a chat. We had agreed on a few things over the years, and we had disagreed a bit as well—all quite collegially. For some reason, we started talking about the Siloam Tunnel inscription (Figure 5.1). We had both been working on a new approach to understanding the inscription. We discovered that we both thought it had been inscribed by northern refugees in Jerusalem. We had arrived at our conclusion in slightly different ways, and we decided to collaborate on an article that was

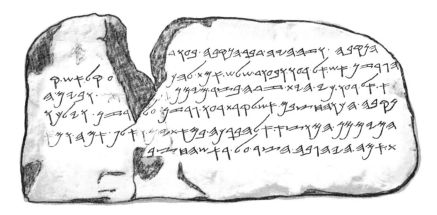

FIGURE 5.1. Siloam tunnel inscription drawing. Drawing by the author.

published in the *Israel Exploration Journal*.[4] I am always delighted to get independent confirmation for an idea, especially when I think it is a bit unconventional. The Siloam Tunnel inscription is a refugee text!

So what makes the Siloam Tunnel inscription so curious? And what led us to the conclusion that it must be a refugee text? The inscription dates to the late eighth century BCE, and it was discovered engraved on a wall near the exit of a tunnel. This tunnel is carved under and through the City of David, and it brought water from the Gihon Spring in the Kidron Valley to the Siloam Pool at the southeastern part of ancient Jerusalem's Western Hill. I have waded through its winding path a few times, knee-deep in water. My most memorable excursion was with my young family. My wife, Jeanne, carried our six-month-old daughter in front of her in a child sling. I transported my three-year-old daughter on my shoulders. She was wielding a flashlight to light our way through the tunnel's serpentine five-hundred-meter path. The water flows down from the Spring along a 0.06 percent gradient to the Pool. That's just twelve inches over its third-of-a-mile twisting path—quite an engineering feat. At one point, the height of the tunnel shrinks to only five feet, at which point my daughter slid down off my shoulders to ride piggyback. She still remembers the tunnel adventure.

We did not notice the place of the inscription—but no one could have seen it. The inscription itself had been removed more than a century ago and now resides in a museum in Istanbul, but we could not even see the place from where it was carved out. Although the tunnel was identified by the explorer Edward Robinson in 1838, the inscription itself was not noticed until 1880, when a teenager named Jacob Spafford was exploring the tunnel.[5] The inscription was located almost twenty feet inside the tunnel's exit, so no one knew it was there in antiquity, and no one could have read it! But Jacob, a typical curious teenager, was inching his way through the tunnel in the dark, and he felt with his hands that the wall was smooth and flat in a section with chisel marks that seemed like writing. That is how the secret inscription was discovered. The remote location of the inscription may explain one strange feature—the inscription does not mention its royal patron. Even though the tunnel must have been an engineering project financed by the crown, no mention is made of the king. This is very unusual. We have many dedicatory inscriptions from the ancient near east, and a prominent feature of such inscriptions is always the patron. You pay to build a building, a temple, or a modern concert hall, and you put your name on it. But here, the only people mentioned are the workers wielding pickaxes, and the dedicatory inscription is hidden. The workers themselves, seemingly aware of their extraordinary engineering feat, give their account in the dedicatory inscription:

> Now this was the account of the tunnel, while [the hewers were wielding] the pickax, each man toward his counterpart, and while there were still five feet to be he[wn], a voice was he[ard], a man cal[li]ng to his counterpart because a fissure was in the rock from right [to lef]t. Now on the day of the tunnel breach, the hewers struck, each man to meet his counterpart, pickax against [pi]ckax, and the water flowed from the spring to the pool through one thousan[d and eigh]t hundred feet. One [hun]dred and fifty feet was the height of the rock above the heads of the hewers.

Who were these workers who secretly monumentalized their work? They are anonymous, but one clue to their identity can be teased out of the execution of the inscription itself. Even to the untrained eye, the inscription is written in an elegant, flowing style (see Figure 5.1). It is beautiful. And the wall of the tunnel was carefully smoothed and evened out in preparation for the inscription. Given its location in the dark, the careful and well-prepared execution of this workmen's inscription is quite remarkable. We call it a graffito just because it is unofficial, but it is not a sloppy or hastily done scrawl that one might expect from workmen, even though we do have sloppy graffiti inscribed by workmen in places like the tombs at Khirbet Beit Lei and Khirbet el-Qom. This inscription is carefully prepared and expertly executed. These workmen made a statement with the quality and execution of their dedicatory inscription and hid it away in a dark recess of the Siloam Tunnel.

But I still have not answered the question of who these workmen were. Language experts can recognize some of peculiarities of the inscription, and these are detailed in the article that I co-authored with Professor Rendsburg. Although it is a well-executed inscription, it is not typical Jerusalemite Hebrew. This is a bit counterintuitive. The well-prepared wall as well as the elegant flowing handwriting suggest an expert, but the language itself is not the standard Jerusalemite Hebrew that we know from other Judean inscriptions. The dialectal peculiarities point instead to a northern Hebrew dialect. I can even see some similarities between the cursive script of the inscription and the (northern) Samaria Ostraca discussed in the previous chapter.[6] These workers had scribal skills that came from the north. But the workers were not bureaucrats working in the Judean royal court. There probably were not enough jobs for them in the Judean bureaucracy. They seem to have found work in a public works project and carved out their legacy in its inscription.

So what was the purpose of this tunnel? It is important here to understand that the Western Hill of Jerusalem was populated by many refugees from the north. The purpose of the Siloam Tunnel must have been to bring a fresh water source closer to the expanded refugee population of Jerusalem living on the Western Hill. More than this, the engineering project took advantage of this expanded workforce and their expertise. It is noteworthy that excavations in the northern kingdom uncovered elaborate water projects at Megiddo and Hazor that predate the Siloam Tunnel. It is possible that some of these workmen had worked on similar projects in the north.

Industrialization and the Spread of Writing

The fallout from the Assyrian campaigns was more than just refugees and immigrants. The Assyrian Empire forced Judah to pay tribute to support its militarization and imperial infrastructure. For example, King Sennacherib mentions a long list of tribute that Hezekiah gave to him—some of which was probably inaccessible to Jerusalem. Sennacherib's annals list "90 kg of gold, 2400 kg of silver, antimony, carnelian, ivory, elephant hides, ebony-wood, boxwood, multicolored garments, linen garments, red and blue wool, vessels of copper, iron, bronze and tin, chariots, shields, lances, armor, daggers, bows and arrows."[7] From where was Hezekiah supposed to get elephant hides or ebony-wood? Although there is undoubtedly a rhetorical aspect to Sennacherib's list, the Book of Kings also acknowledges that Hezekiah paid Sennacherib a hefty tribute. To help support the empire, the Assyrians encouraged their client states to develop industries. Judging from the archaeological record, what Judah actually could produce in abundance was olive oil and wine, which along with grain were helpful in sustaining the Assyrian armies. Supplying the Assyrians meant building an industrial infrastructure, and this prompted the use and spread of writing for commercial and administrative enterprises.

Nice examples of writing come from the wine and olive oil industries. For example, excavations at Gibeon (just a few miles north of Jerusalem) revealed the processing and industrial production of wine.[8] In total, archaeologists excavated facilities that would have been able to hold twenty-five thousand gallons of wine! Along with the facilities for crushing, pressing, and storing the wine, archaeologists found the remains of many ten-gallon wine jars with inscribed handles. One example (illustrated already in figure 1.1)[9] typifies the collection: *gb ʿn . gdr . ʾzryhw* "Gibeon, the vineyard of Azariah." This example illustrates two aspects of the Gibeon wine inscriptions. First, they were inscribed into pre-fired clay, which meant that the writing had to be carefully planned. Writing was part of the production process. In spite of this, the inscriptions are still pretty crudely written. The writing is not elegant like the Siloam Tunnel inscription. In other words, it is a mundane use of writing for economic purposes. Writing was now broadly part of commerce in the late Judean monarchy.

Excavations at several sites also point to an industrial production of olive oil, which was critical to the Assyrian economy. The most striking of these sites is ancient Ekron, where 115 olive oil presses were found that could have produced as much as one thousand tons of olive oil. Similar evidence for industrial production of olive oil was discovered in the excavations at the Judean towns of Timnah and Beth-Shemesh. So it is hardly surprising that inscriptions from Jerusalem mention quantities of "oil" (Hebrew, *shemen*).[10] Oil was an exchange commodity that could be traded, that is, it apparently served the same function as money. It also served a variety of mundane purposes including fuel for lamps and cooking.

The use of writing in everyday commerce is perhaps best illustrated by two common types of objects—weights and economic seals (see Figure 5.2). The object on the left of the figure is a seal inscribed as follows: "In the 13th year / first [crop] of / Lachish. For / the King."[11] The writing is pretty crude, and it just gives basic administrative notation. It is hard to interpret fully. It is a bit like finding an ancient receipt, and it points to the use of basic writing and reading in commerce. Likewise, dozens of weights used for measuring goods in the markets of Jerusalem and around the kingdom used writing. Nothing special, sometimes just a character or two to denote the weight. This is illustrated in the second example (Figure 5.2, right), where we find the Hebrew word *pîm*, written rather crudely. A *pîm* is two-thirds of a shekel (about 7.5 grams).[12] This use of writing on weights was something new to the late monarchy.

The mundane use of writing indicates that scribal training became part of the apprenticeship for merchants and people working in trades. Their curricula need not have become too advanced, but the very inclusion of literacy in the apprenticeship of merchants and craftsmen changed the role of writing in society. There were new types of scribal communities, and literacy became more commonplace. In order for biblical literature to flourish outside scribal elites, the use of writing had to spread throughout society. And in order for texts to have broad appeal and even authority, they had to become an integral part of the larger society.

FIGURE 5.2. Economic seal (left) and *pîm* weight inscription (right). Drawings by the author.

The Elevation of Literacy as a Social Value

One question that I am frequently asked is, What percentage of ancient Israelites were literate? I see numbers thrown around in scholarly literature—1%, 5%, 10%, 50%—but there is no way to answer this question definitively. To begin with, it depends on what we mean by literacy. Is a person literate if they can read a list or a label? Are they literate if they can sign their name, or do they need to be able to read a newspaper? Or perhaps they need to be able to appreciate a novel by Mark Twain? Certainly, very few could write like Twain or create the poetry of the Psalms. The point is that there can be quite different measures of literacy, and we do not have very precise ways of measuring this in antiquity.

Another way of tackling the issue of literacy is asking, What cultural value did people place on literacy and writing? Was literacy an expectation for many people? Was there a stigma to being illiterate? Was writing highly valued among wide segments of the society? We do have some hints to the answers to these questions beginning in our archaeological and inscriptional record. Perceptions of literacy were impacted by the spread of writing skills to new communities. Linguists have pointed out that in *nonliterate* societies, there is no stigma to being illiterate. Literacy is not a social expectation. In *literate* societies, it is an expectation. When literacy becomes a social expectation, then writing begins to play a very different role in society. We may have a clue to answering this question in "The Letter of a Literate Soldier."

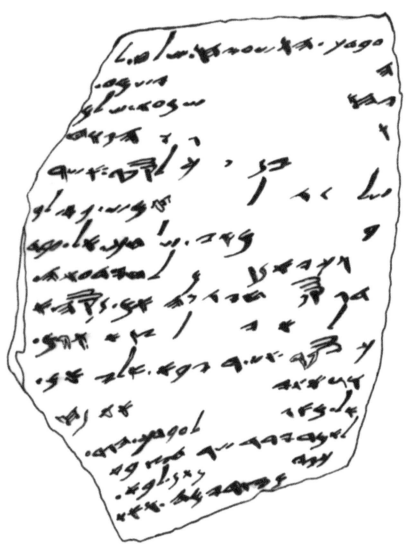

FIGURE 5.3. "A Letter of a Literate Soldier" (Lachish no. 3, obverse). Drawing by Abigail Zammit. Used with permission.

The first part of the letter (lines 1–13) gives a formal introduction, and then the body of the letter raises the issue of the junior officer's literacy:

> Your servant, Hoshayahu, sends to inform to my lord Yaush: "May Yahweh cause my lord to hear a report of peace and a good report.
>
> And now, please listen to your servant concerning the letter that my lord sent to your servant yesterday. For your servant has been despairing ever since you sent (it) to your servant. This is because my lord said, 'You do not know how to read—call a scribe!' I swear to God that no one has ever had to read a letter to me! And also, any letter that came to me, I could read it, and I can recount it in every detail!"

The junior officer here is despondent over the insinuation that he could not read a letter and that he would need a professional scribe. Although literacy was a skill associated with the military already in the Amarna letters or at Kuntillet ʿAjrud, here we have something different when a junior military officer is offended by the suggestion that he does not know how to read and write. It points to the growing role that literacy skills and scribal communities would have during the late Judean monarchy.

The First Word, Not the Last Word, in Biblical Literature

For the reasons that I have raised in this chapter, the late eighth century was a beginning for biblical literature. But let me be clear here. This does not mean that there was no Hebrew literature before eighth century. Of course there was. There were palace scribes, who learned curricula, kept records, and wrote correspondence. But the cultural conditions for writing, editing, and collecting biblical literature come together in a variety of diverse communities during the late eighth century. In this chapter, I have explained why writing spread. I have also illustrated the use of writing in everyday activities, but this type of writing did not give rise to biblical literature. This writing was mundane. It required only basic scribal training that became part of various trades—merchants, engineers, craftsmen, and stonemasons. Writing biblical literature required advanced literacy. Still, when a junior military officer gets hurt feelings because someone suggests he might need a professional scribe, then literacy has become a cultural value. This points to the spread of writing into different spheres of society that was the inflection point for texts to become authoritative for all people. Now we just need to look for the scribes that actually wrote biblical literature.

In the next several chapters I explore the implications for the spread of writing in the development of different scribes and scribal communities: prophets, the tribal elders, women, and priests. And we will explore the biblical literature produced in each of these scribal communities.

6

The Prophetic Scribal
Community

I just cannot take Amos seriously. Amos claims, "I am not a prophet,
nor am I the son of a prophet" (7:14). Oh really? That seems like a pretty
disingenuous claim given that his book is included in the biblical canon
of the "Prophets." What did he mean by such a disclaimer? One thing
we can learn from this is that there was something about Amos' understanding of the title Prophet that he did not want to be associated with.
And the Book of Amos respects Amos' objection inasmuch as it never
calls him a *nabî*, that is, the biblical Hebrew word for "prophet." Amos
also objects to the institutionalization of prophets in his rejection of the
title "Son of a Prophet." In rejecting the moniker and the description as
a son of a prophet, Amos both acknowledges and rejects prophetic apprenticeship. Amos does not conceive of the prophet as a solitary figure
called by God to speak for God; rather, he sees the prophet as an institutional position that can be learned through apprenticeship. Amos'
objections will make more sense in this chapter as we look at the title
Prophet in biblical literature and ancient Hebrew inscriptions.

Amos' rejection of prophetic titles is related to the context of his pro-
nouncements. The story is set at the royal shrine of Bethel, in the northern
kingdom, with Amos criticizing its leadership. The local priest, Amaziah,
tells Amos to leave and go to Judah but not to "prophesy at Bethel, for it
is a royal sanctuary and a royal house" (Amos 7:13). The town of Bethel

was one of the towns where the first king of the northern kingdom, Jeroboam I (r. 931–910 BCE), set up a rival temple to Jerusalem (see 1 Kgs 12:25–33). One story in the Book of Kings even mentions "the sons of the prophets that were in Bethel" (2 Kgs 2:3). Amos seems to be distancing himself from them and their royal patron. He equates them with state-sponsored religious and political power, and he sees himself as independent—something he does not equate with the title "Prophet." Amos treats the titles Prophet and Son of a Prophet as something associated with official political and religious power. He wants none of that.

As I discussed in chapter 1, the Hebrew term *ben* or "son" can be used in the familial relationships created by apprenticeship. The relationship does not have to be biological kinship, but it can be a fictive kinship created by apprenticeship. Amos seems to be thinking of just such a community in his rejection of the label Son of a Prophet. There is some evidence for this title in the inscriptional record, but it took some sleuthing for me to fully apprehend the evidence.

"Son of a Prophet" in Lachish Seal Impressions

My detective story begins in the 1960s with Yohanan Aharoni's excavations at Lachish, where he discovered two seal impressions that came from a single seal.[1] The seal impressions are poorly preserved. Using the advanced technology known as reflective technology imaging done by the Israel Museum, I was able to interpret and draw the combined original seal based on the two seal impressions (Figure 6.1). In his original publication of the seal impressions, Aharoni suggested reading the seal impressions as follows:

lyrmyhw	"Belonging to Jeremiah,
bn ṣpnyhw	son of Zephaniah,
bn nby[ʾ]	son of *a proph*[*et*]"

Aharoni's reconstruction is reasonable, but it is not the way these seal impressions have been read in recent publications.[2] Aharoni originally observed that reading the last line as simply *nby* "would be surprising as a personal name" and for this reason he offered his reconstruction, noting, "At the end of the line there is room for one more letter and . . . we may conjecture that נביא 'prophet' was intended, as a designation of the man's profession."[3] Even with the reflective technology imaging, the final letter is missing in line 3, but it is worth noting that the word "prophet" could also have been simply spelled *nby,* as it was in Aramaic.[4] In other words, Aharoni's interpretation can stand even if we do not supply the missing final letter.

FIGURE 6.1. "Son of the Prophet" seal impression from Lachish. Drawing by the author.

In assessing the title as a profession, Aharoni points to Nehemiah 3:31, where Malchijah is described as "the son of the goldsmith." He argues—correctly, I think—that in this example "son of" must refer to a guild of goldsmiths. Malchijah was apprenticed to a goldsmith. In both Nehemiah and the Lachish seal impressions, "son of" would then be a reference to apprenticeship. The title "Son of a Prophet" would also point to a community of practice related to the Judean state administration. The reading as a title gathers further support from its archaeological context. The two seal impressions were found in a jar with seventeen other bullae. Other items in the same archaeological locus included inscribed shekel weights and an ostracon with an administrative list (Lachish no. 22).[5] Another seal impression found in this group belonged to a royal official, "Shebaniah, [son/servant] of the king." This would fit well with biblical examples like Amos 7:14, where Amos rejects being an institutional prophet or the son of a prophet, as well as the Elijah-Elisha narratives where a prophetic community called "the sons of the prophets" (see below) is involved with politics and administration. Finally, the reading as a title is strengthened by the use of a third line in the seal. Typically, seals have two lines—the first for the owner and a second for the father's name. Occasionally, we have seals with three lines and often the third line is a title, just as we seem to have here. So far, so good.

Here's where the detective story gets interesting. Yohanan Aharoni published the Lachish seal impressions in 1968. Just two years after Aharoni's original publication, a new seal with the reading, *lš ʿp//bn nby* "Belonging to Shiʿap, *son of nby*," was purchased on the antiquities market.[6] Its immediate appearance on the antiquities market was all too convenient and well timed, rather typical of forged items. Forgers read publications too! It is also instructive that it is a seal and not a seal impression. Seals are easier to forge and more valuable to sell than seal impressions. But the fact that this seal came from the antiquities market did not stop scholars from using it to reinterpret the Lachish seal impressions. In an article published shortly after this object was purchased, Nahman Avigad rejected Aharoni's reading of "son of a prophet" based on the new seal from the antiquities market.[7] Even so, Avigad recognized that the personal name "Nobai" (Hebrew, *nby*) did not fit into our understanding of Hebrew personal names, so he proposed reading *nby* as a gentilic, that is, as relating to the hometown of the seal's owner "the Nobite." However, as Avigad himself would later recognize, place names are never used to identify people on personal seals. When another (probably forged) seal was purchased on the antiquities market with *nby*, Avigad recognized that the place name did not work and suggested reading it as a personal name, "belonging to Maḥseyahu//(son of) *Nobai*"—opting for the unusual personal name Nobai instead of returning to Aharoni's original interpretation.[8] But both Aharoni and Avigad had already considered this reading in their original publications and had quickly rejected it. Nobai would still be an unusual name with no obvious Hebrew meaning. Aharoni's original interpretation still remains the most compelling, and it is the interpretation that fits its archaeological context. The additional seals from the antiquities market had only muddled the interpretation. The "Son of a Prophet" title will also clarify some hitherto unclear biblical texts about prophets and a prophetic scribal community.

The two seal impressions from Lachish with the "Son of the Prophet" title are not the end of the prophets at Lachish. Another inscription from Lachish mentions a prophet. I already discussed the first half of this inscription, the so-called "Letter of the Literate Soldier," in the previous

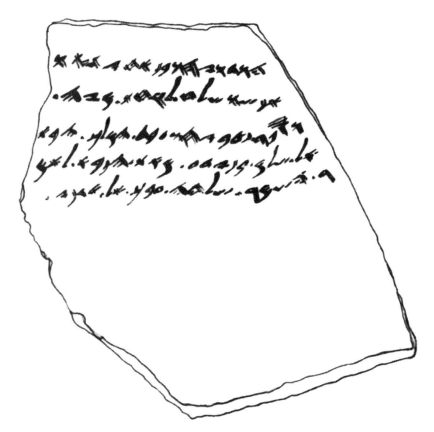

FIGURE 6.2. Lachish ostracon no. 3, reverse. Drawing by Abigail Zammit.
Used with permission.

chapter (Figure 5.3). Now I want to focus on the last few lines written
on the reverse side of the ostracon[9] that mentions an anonymous
prophet (see Figure 6.2):

> Hodawyahu, son of Ahiyahu, and his men, he has sent them from
> here. And the letter of Tobiyahu, the Servant of the King, which came
> to Shallum, son of Yada, *from the prophet* saying, "Beware," your ser-
> vant has sent it to my lord.

An anonymous prophet issues a cryptic warning at the conclusion to
this letter. Beware of what? We don't know. And who is this prophet?
We don't know. Indeed, the prophet's anonymity is one of the most

conspicuous aspects of this letter given that all the other figures mentioned in the letter have names—Hosha ʿyahu (sender), Yaʾush (recipient), Konyahu son of Elnatan (Commander of the Army), Hodawyahu son of Ahiyahu, Tobiyahu (Servant of the King), and Shallum son of Yada. Everyone else has a name. Many also have titles and/or patronyms. But the prophet remains anonymous. Sometimes scholars speculate as to his identity, but to no avail. Perhaps a better question is why he was left anonymous, especially since his anonymity stands in such stark contrast with everyone else in the letter.

We can tease out a few meaningful tidbits from the letter. To begin with, the nameless prophet can be put into a specific archaeological and literary context. This was an official letter found in a place of government business—the gate of the city. It mentions people that were in charge of official government business, including the "Commander of the Army" and a "Servant of the King." This prophet was included within the administration. Together with the two Lachish "Son of the Prophet" seal impressions, we can imagine a prophetic community at Lachish with scribal training.[10] Lachish was the second-largest city of Judah (after Jerusalem) and was a hub for official government administration and activity, and it provides some archaeological evidence for a prophetic scribal community.

Northern Origin for "Prophet" (nabî) and the Prophetic Community

The titles "Prophet" and "Son of a Prophet" in the Amos story suggest that the "prophet" was not an ad hoc calling but rather an official title. This will contrast with the concept of the prophet that develops in the postexilic period, when the prophet came to be understood as a solitary figure called by God (see, for example, Jer 1:1–5, discussed in chapter 10). As such, it can be compared to other titles (e.g., "Royal Steward," "Servant of the King," or "Fortress Commander") that we find in both inscriptions and the biblical literature. But "Prophet" was not a title native to Judean Hebrew, as we learn from 1 Samuel 9:9: "one who is now called a *prophet* was formerly called a *seer*." This comment contrasts "prophet" with the older Hebrew word "seer" (ro'eh), which it replaces. But where did the title "Prophet" come from? Judging from the repeated use in the Elijah-Elisha stories as well as the Book of Amos, it looks like the title originated in the northern kingdom.[11] The comment in Samuel then reflects the history of the prophets as a social institution as understood by a later scribal community.

The title "Prophet" was not used for the early prophets like Hosea, Amos, and Micah. Rather, it is a title used especially in the biblical books known as the Deuteronomistic History; for example, the title occurs fifty-five times in the Books of Samuel and Kings. That is a big clue. As we shall see in chapter 10, where the priest Jeremiah is retitled and remade as a prophet in the editing of the Masoretic edition of the Book of Jeremiah, the editorial note in 1 Samuel 9:9 was likely added in the late sixth century BCE in the final edition of the Book of Samuel when the title "Prophet" was being redefined and reapplied. But in the days of Amos, the title "Prophet" referred to someone who worked in and with the government.

The role of the "prophet" within the government is illustrated in another narrative situated in the court at Samaria about a certain prophet called Micaiah, son of Imlah (1 Kings 22). In this story, the Judean king Jehoshaphat wants to consult a "prophet of Yahweh," but his Israelite counterpart, King Ahab, complains that the prophet Micaiah does not support the king when he consults him (v. 8). The narrative thus sets up the tension between an expectation (namely, that prophets are patrons on the payroll of the king) and a rogue prophet Micaiah (namely, a prophet who answers to Yahweh rather than the king). Ahab, however, is also able to call upon his own group of "all of the prophets" (v. 10) who follow the protocol of royal patronage by giving support to King Ahab. The story relies on the tradition of the nabiʾ in the royal court as a means of critiquing and redefining a true prophet. One may surmise that one purpose in telling the story is to redefine the title and role of the nabiʾ. The need to revise it has to do with the origins of the figure of nabiʾ that was borrowed from northern social structures and later integrated into Judean government and society after the destruction of Samaria.

Likewise, the "sons of the prophets" specifically points to a northern social institution. The expression "sons of the prophets" (Hebrew, *benê ha-nabî'im*) is found exclusively in the Elijah-Elisha stories, appearing ten times in six separate stories among the narratives (1 Kgs 20:35; 2 Kgs 2:3, 5, 7, 15; 4:1, 38; 5:22; 6:1; 9:1). The expression is repeated so often in these narratives, is so consistent, and is so unique that it must point to a social institution, and I would suggest that the sons of the prophets are a "community of practice" that developed out of prophetic apprenticeships.[12] A related and unique term is found in a story about King Saul, who meets "a band of prophets" (1 Sam 10:5, 10; Hebrew, *ḥebel*). Again, this is a story set in the northern locale, and it again testifies to the concept of a prophetic community as opposed to the lone prophetic voice. Given these examples, it becomes easier to understand why Amos objects to the title "Son of a Prophet." He is aware of the close connection between the title "Prophet" and the social institution known as "the sons of the prophets" in the northern kingdom. Indeed, the relationship between Elijah and Elisha itself is an excellent example of a prophetic apprenticeship. Elijah is instructed to "anoint Elisha, son of Shaphat of Abel-meholah as prophet in your place" (1 Kgs 19:16). When Elijah's prophetic ministry comes to an end, Elisha replaces him. Elijah was the master, and Elisha was his apprentice. The purpose of the prophetic succession as described in the succession is political and militaristic, as the text continues, "whoever escapes the sword of Hazael, Jehu shall kill; and whoever escapes the sword of Jehu, Elisha shall kill" (v. 17).

A most telling example of prophetic apprenticeship is the anointing of Jehu as king by an apprentice of Elisha that I cited earlier. The full story in 2 Kings 9 begins with Elijah sending *one of the sons of prophets* to the Israelite general Jehu, son of Nimshi, in a military coup. Then the narrative refers to this figure as *the apprentice [na'ar] of the prophet* when he goes up to Ramoth-Gilead to anoint Jehu (v. 4). The terminology is revealing. Moreover, the story places the prophetic community closely within the political machinations of the northern royal dynasties, and this recalls our other examples. They apparently went in and out of favor with different kings and dynasties. From these stories, we can posit that a prophetic community of practice was closely associated with social structures in the northern kingdom.

The "Sons of the Prophets" and the House of Elisha

The role of Elisha in the political machinations of the Nimshi dynasty has been further elucidated from the archaeological finds at Tel Reḥov, a major Israelite city just east of Jezreel in the Jordan Valley.[13] On the acropolis of the site, archaeologists Amihai Mazar and Nava Panitz-Cohen found several inscriptions associated with an unusual large building and houses in its associated quarter (see Figure 6.3). They called the first large building located in the south of the quarter "the House of Elisha" because they excavated a rounded plaque with the name "Elisha" in the back room. The building is architecturally uncommon with a circular flow. A variety of cultic objects was found in all of its rooms, but the design indicates that it was not a temple. It was simply a unique large house or perhaps some sort of public building. The special artifacts included clay altars, a limestone figurine, a clay ritual chalice, and an incense stand decorated with petals. These objects, taken together with a plaque inscription, indicate a special meeting place. Mazar and Panitz-Cohen suggest that "Elisha sojourned in . . . a place where he received pilgrims, and rituals and feasts were held in his honor."[14] This building fits nicely with the biblical descriptions of Elisha, the prophet.

To the north of Elisha's house is a residential quarter that the archaeologists speculated might be related to the "sons of the prophets." The adjacent buildings contained cooking pots, storage vessels, and eating and serving dishes. In the house immediately to the north of Elisha's house, they also found the inscription on a storage jar with the name "Elzedek, [son of] Shachli." Such a residential quarter fits with the description of the sons of the prophets in the biblical stories. For example, the "sons of the prophets" complain because their living quarters are too small for them (2 Kgs 6:1). In another story, Elisha asks his apprentice to make a pot of stew for the group (2 Kgs 4:38). Was Elzedek one of the "sons of the prophets"? It's difficult to say for sure. Mazar and Panitz-Cohen note that a similar residential quarter was excavated at Deir ʿAlla, just across

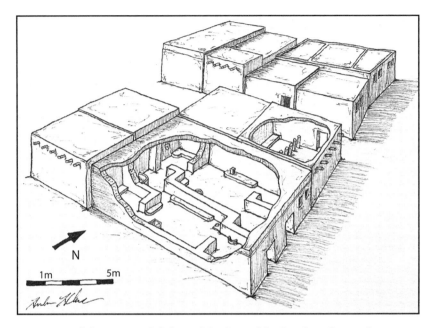

FIGURE 6.3. "The House of Elisha and the Sons of the Prophets Quarter."
Drawing by Andrew Herbek.

the Jordan River from Tel Reḥov, where archaeologists found plaster wall
inscriptions that mention the prophet Balaam, son of Beʿor. The inscriptions at Deir ʿAlla indicate that scribal education was taking place in this
residential area at Deir ʿAlla. Mazar and Panitz-Cohen suggest that "the
four small houses flanking the street between the two large, central buildings housed people who served different functions in the complex."[15]
Given the various lines of archaeological and inscriptional evidence, I
think we can call this the Sons of the Prophets quarter at Tel Reḥov.

The discovery that gave Elisha's house its name was an inscription
that had at least two lines that read, l[. . .] ʾlyšʿ "belonging to [. . .] Elisha" (see Figure 6.4). The second line is almost complete, and the restoration of Elisha's name is almost certain. But the first line is only a
small piece with the Hebrew letter *lamed* that is probably a preposition
that can be translated as "belonging to." I am tempted to reconstruct the
first line as reading something like "belonging to [the house] / of Elisha."
Or perhaps it referred to the "family of Elisha" or even "the apprentices

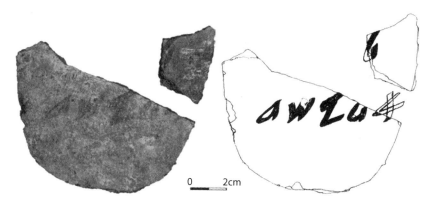

FIGURE 6.4. Plaque with the name "Elisha." Photos and drawing used courtesy of Amihai Mazar.

of Elisha." We can only speculate. What seems clear is that this is the prophet Elisha known from the Book of Kings. The archaeological stratigraphy as well as the radiocarbon dating places the inscription in the ninth century BCE. This lines up chronologically with the biblical Elisha. But why would Elisha be at Tel Reḥov? The hometown of Elisha in biblical literature was Abel-meholah (1 Kgs 19:16), which is usually identified with Abu-Sus, about five miles southeast of Tel Reḥov. This is indeed a hard question to answer, but the larger archaeological context of the inscription suggests an identification with the biblical figure.

A closer inspection of the Elisha inscription yields more insight. The pottery sherd itself is rather unusual. It is not a jagged, broken piece of pottery like other ostraca. Writing on broken potsherds is usually ephemeral; that is, they are meant to be discarded. This is different. The edges are rounded, suggesting that it was specially prepared as a display item. There isn't a single similar example in all the Hebrew inscriptions on potsherds that have been published. In this respect, it should not even be called an *ostracon*, which refers to an inscription on a broken pottery sherd. No, the rounded shaping indicates that it was prepared for display. It was not for ephemeral use. The special nature of the inscription goes further. The pottery sherd has a cream-colored slip that makes the red letters stand out. Red ink itself is exceedingly rare on inscriptions from ancient Israel.[16] The letters are unusually large, about twice the size as we see on other ostraca (e.g., Lachish 3; see above, Figure 6.2). It all points to preparation for display, and this is why I had the artist draw it on the back wall of the building near where it was excavated and perhaps where it might have originally been displayed.

But who was the Elisha in the inscription? Elisha was actually a common name in Israel. How can we be sure it referred to *the* biblical Elisha? The archaeological context and other nearby inscriptions point toward this conclusion. The house of Elisha was archaeologically unusual, and excavation in adjacent squares yielded other artifacts and inscriptions that point to Elisha. For example, the adjacent building (to the northwest) had been a commercial apiary for the cultivation of honey and beeswax.[17] The importance of honey and beeswax for consumption and trade are well attested in near eastern inscriptions. Honey and beeswax are mentioned in the Egyptian *Story of Sinuhe* in discussing his residence in Canaan. Beeswax was ascribed with magical powers in Egypt, and it was also used in medicine production. Perhaps most importantly, beeswax was used in the lost-wax technique of metal-casting and was thus vital to the ancient metal industry. Mazar estimates that the apiary at Tel Reḥov would have produced 500 kg of honey as well as between 50 and 70 kg of beeswax per year.[18]

The apiary itself yielded a strong connection to Elisha. In the apiary, they excavated an inscription with the reading *lnmš* "belonging to Nimshi."[19] This almost certainly can be associated with the Israelite general and later king Jehu, who was the grandson of Nimshi. The family's ownership of the apiary reflects enormous potential wealth. Another inscription referring to the Nimshide dynasty, *lšqy nmš* "belonging to Shaqai, (son of) Nimshi," was excavated in the northernmost building in that quarter (see Figure 6.3).[20] At Tel Amal, just a few miles away from Tel Reḥov, there is another contemporaneous ninth-century inscription referring to the Nimshide dynasty. The archaeological evidence suggests that the Nimshi family was both wealthy and well connected, and the location of two Nimshi inscriptions next to the "house of Elisha" point to a close relationship between Elisha and the Nimshide family.

The inscriptions from the Nimshi family call to mind the connection between Elisha and the Nimshide dynasty in the biblical narratives. There are several different accounts that place Elijah and Elisha as kingmakers for Jehu, son of Nimshi. At first, the prophet Elijah is instructed to anoint Jehu as king (1 Kgs 19:16). But Elijah dies, and Elisha is anointed as his successor. As we read in 2 Kings 9, the prophet Elisha eventually assigned his own prophetic apprentice, to find Jehu, grandson of Nimshi, at Ramoth-Gilead and anoint him king over Israel. Elisha and his prophetic cohort thus became the kingmakers for Jehu, son of Nimshi, but they also subverted the previous Omride dynasty. In this respect, they were squarely in the middle of dynastic politics. When the Omride dynasty rejected the role of Elijah-Elisha's community as royal advisors (e.g., 1 Kings 18), they turned to their neighbor—the general Jehu, grandson of Nimshi.

The organizational hierarchy, several inscriptions from the prophets quarter at Reḥov, and the connection of the sons of the prophets with the Nimshide dynasty suggest that scribal training became one of the skills of the prophetic community. Indeed, the plaque from the House of Elisha points to scribal training. Most important is the use of red ink, which was quite typically used as a teaching rubric with the master writing in red and the apprentices writing in black. Thus, when we later encounter the Elijah-Elisha narratives embedded in the Book of Kings, we may speculate that these stories were first collected and written down by the sons of the prophets. Judging from the Lachish seal impressions, the sons of the prophets survived as a social group within the Judean bureaucracy. And the prophetic scribal community preserved their stories—the tales of Elijah and Elisha—even though the neo-Assyrian campaigns destroyed Samaria and exiled many of its people. Refugees from this prophetic scribal community in the north must have fled south from the Assyrians, and they probably introduced the term "Prophet" as a title that started to be used in the administration in Judah.

Changing the Meaning of the Title "Prophet"

The meaning of "prophet" changed considerably after it was introduced in Judah. This can be illustrated by the distribution of the Hebrew term for "prophet" (*nabî*) in the Hebrew Bible. The Hebrew word for "prophet" occurs 287 times in the Hebrew Bible, but the books of the so-called "writing" prophets of the eighth century (that is, Isaiah, Hosea, Amos, and Micah) rarely use it as a title for a person. In fact, it is never applied to Hosea, Amos, or Micah. In the Book of Isaiah, the title is especially given to Isaiah in passages borrowed from the Deuteronomistic History—that is, from the Book of Kings (cp. Isa 37:2; 38:1; 39:3 with 2 Kgs 19:2; 20:1, 14). This biblical distribution of *nabiʾ* reminds us about an earlier comment in the Deutereonomistic History, namely that "the *prophet* was formerly called a seer" (1 Sam 9:9). This seems to be part of the later scribal reinterpretation of the prophetic office. The understanding of who and what a "prophet" is changed considerably from the days when the northern refugees first came to Jerusalem in the eighth century until the time when Judahites returned to Jerusalem after being exiled by the Babylonians in the sixth century (that is, when the final edition of the Deuteronomistic History was edited).

The Book of Jeremiah will illustrate the changing meaning of the term "prophet," as I will discuss in chapter 10. For the moment, it suffices to point out that Jeremiah is introduced as "one of the priests from Anathoth" (Jer 1:1), and his adversaries included the "prophets." Jeremiah is portrayed as an outsider, and the prophets were part of the government that Jeremiah criticizes. For example, in Jeremiah 26:7–8 we read that the priests and the prophets seized Jeremiah and had him imprisoned (see also Jer 18:18; 20:2). In another place, Jeremiah complains that "the prophets prophesied via Baʿal" (Jer 2:8)—these seem to be prophets working for the government bureaucracy that Jeremiah opposed. Jeremiah critiques these prophets who were working for the government (Jer 14:14–15; 23:15–40). Indeed, in several places in the book, lists of officials include kings, government officials, priests, and prophets together (e.g., Jer 2:26; 4:9; 5:31; 6:13; 8:1, 10; 13:13; 23:11; 26:11). In other words, the prophets were part of the state. In this respect, Jeremiah was not part of a prophetic community of practice. The confusion comes about because a later scribal community redefines the term "prophet" and changes Jeremiah's identity from a priest into a prophet (more on this in chapter 10). This changed title gets implemented by later scribal communities in framing biblical literature.

The Seal Impression of Isaiah, the Prophet

A main figure for the institution of prophet was the figure of Isaiah, who lived in Jerusalem during the late eighth and early seventh centuries BCE. The prophet Isaiah became a big deal. He became the quintessential "Prophet." He had his own disciples, and the book named after him became so important that it spawned significant study, editing, and additions over successive generations. Scholars generally speak of "three Isaiahs" (Isaiah 1–39, 40–55, and 56–66) to describe the Book of Isaiah, but it is much more complicated than that.[21] For example, Isaiah 36–39 largely parallels 2 Kings 18–20 and forms a separate section of the book. Isaiah 24–27 is a separate vignette within the book often called the "Isaianic Apocalypse." Indeed, the Book of Isaiah got updated and added to because Isaiah of Jerusalem, who lived in the late eighth century BCE, became the prophet in his own time, and his life and words spawned generations of reflection and supplementation.

A glimpse into the historical Isaiah of Jerusalem has come to light with a seal impression excavated by Eilat Mazar in the Ophel area of Jerusalem and dated by its archaeological context to the late eighth century BCE (see Figure 6.5).[22] Mazar read the seal impression as follows: "Belonging to Isaiah, [the] Proph[et]." But its interpretation has been debated, and the seal impression and its larger archaeological context warrants a detailed investigation here. To begin with, the seal impression is broken, so there has naturally been scholarly discussion about whether it belonged to the famous Isaiah of Jerusalem who was a contemporary of Hezekiah, the king of Judah.[23] If it did belong to the biblical Isaiah, some have questioned why Isaiah had his own seal—seals and sealing documents belonging mostly to the purview of government bureaucrats. Moreover, why was this seal impression found in the middle of an administrative area of Jerusalem? As we shall see, these are clues to the nature of the prophetic office in the Iron Age. The seal impression was likely impressed from the seal of the famous prophet of Jerusalem, and its location and interpretation have profound implications for understanding the development of a prophetic scribal community.

FIGURE 6.5. Seal impression of "Isaiah, (the) Prophet." Drawing by the author.

One might say that it was a stroke of fate (or coincidence) that the Isaiah impression was found about ten feet away from a seal impression of "Hezekiah, son of Ahaz, king of Judah." But this happy coincidence reflects the general archaeological context of the Ophel—the area between the Temple Mount and the City of David—that housed administrative buildings as well as the royal palace.[24] The Isaiah seal impression was one of thirty-four personal seal impressions discovered by Mazar in her excavations at the Ophel. The collection is quite interesting. In addition to the Isaiah and Hezekiah seal impressions, it includes the Bes impressions (discussed in chapter 1). There is also another fragmentary seal impression that has part of a two-winged scarab (that is, the royal insignia), so I would suggest that its owner was another member of the royal household.[25] There were also eight other royal seal impressions found in this area,[26] and a fragmentary storage jar inscription that I would read as, *lśr h ʾw[ṣrm]* "belonging to the royal treasurer," referring to a royal treasury that was located in this area of Jerusalem (see Jer 38:11).[27] None of these discoveries should be that surprising since the Ophel was an administrative area that housed a royal palace and other administrative buildings (see 1 Kgs 7:1–12). In sum, the archaeological and geographical context of the Isaiah seal impression reflects the royal administrative activities of ancient Jerusalem.

Unfortunately, the seal impression of Isaiah is broken and requires some reconstruction.[28] The seal impression has three lines that Mazar read as follows:

1) IMAGE   *Grazing doe*
2) *lyš ʿyh[w]*   "Belonging to Isaiah
3) *nby[ʾ]*   Proph[et]"

The first line is reconstructed as the image of a grazing doe—an image that actually appears on another seal impression from this cache (B17). We are not aware of any particular significance to this iconography.

The second line is missing its final letter (*waw*), but it is quite certain that it must be read as the name "Isaiah" (or, Yesha'ayahu in Hebrew). Mazar writes that Isaiah was a very common name based on inscriptions, but this is misleading.[29] In fact, Isaiah is only common on artifacts purchased on the antiquities market. That is hardly surprising. It is a great choice for a forger looking to make a little money. However, it is almost unknown in the *excavated* inscriptional record. For example, we can consider the register of all the seal impressions excavated in the City of David by Yigal Shiloh.[30] There are eighty-five names on forty-five published seal impressions. Several other names appear three or four times, but the name "Isaiah" never appears. This demonstrates that the name was in fact *not* common. To broaden the appeal, one scholar suggests we should include all the names that use the same root, *yš'* "to save," such as Hosea and Joshua, but this is also misleading.[31] There's no question that the root *yš'* is known and used broadly in Hebrew and Northwest Semitic languages. For example, the Moabite king Mesha's name uses this same root. But names are formed in particular ways, and each name is unique. For example, the related Hebrew names Hosea and Hoshiah create names using the *yš'* root in the Hiphil conjugation, which is a common refrain in biblical Hebrew meaning "Save, O LORD." But it is not the same name. Hosea, Joshua, Mesha, and Isaiah are different names in Hebrew and in English, even though they all use the same root. In sum, Isaiah was not a common name in ancient Israel. It had never appeared in a certain excavated context until Mazar's excavations.

The Son of the Prophet Isaiah

The fact that the name "Isaiah" was unknown in excavated inscriptions until Mazar's excavation makes it all the more remarkable that the name actually appears on another seal impression from the very same excavated assemblage. Another seal impression reads, *l'dyhw yš'yhw* "Belonging to 'Iddoyahu, [son of] Isaiah" (see Figure 6.6).[32] Who was this 'Iddoyahu? I would suggest that this is none other than the "son" of the

FIGURE 6.6. Seal impression of "ʿIddoyahu, son of Isaiah". Drawing by the author.

Isaiah mentioned on the other seal impression in this cache. There is actually another group of seals in this very group excavated by Mazar—the sons of Bes (discussed in chapter 1)—that demonstrate the familial scribal groups that must have been very common.

The name of the seal's owner—ʿIddoyahu (ʿdyhw)—is quite revealing. It is related to the name Iddo (BH, ʿdw or ʿdwʾ), which is well known in the Bible as the name of several biblical prophets (2 Chr 15:1–8; 2 Chr 12:15; 13:22; 28:9; Zech 1:1, 7).[33] The root for this name is ʿdd, and an Old Aramaic inscription uses a related word, recording that prophetic messengers (ʿddn) spoke to Zakkur about how the god had made him king and delivered him from his enemies (KAI 202A, 11–15).[34] The name ʿIddoyahu thus has deep connections to the prophetic profession. This would make the relationship between the Isaiah seal impression and the ʿIddoyahu seal impression even more interesting. Given the fact that the name Isaiah had not appeared elsewhere in an excavated inscription, the most plausible explanation is that the seal of ʿIddoyahu belonged to the son of the very same Isaiah known from the other seal impression. In this interpretation, the prophet Isaiah has a son or perhaps an apprentice with a name related to the prophetic profession.

The seal impression from Isaiah's "son" should remind us of the story in Isaiah 7, where Isaiah takes his son to meet the King Ahaz and give him counsel. Another story in Isaiah 8 has the prophet Isaiah enjoining his students (v. 16), whom he refers to as "the children that Yahweh has given me" (v. 18), to collect the prophet's teachings. These stories reflect the familial nature of the prophetic scribal community. And they remind us that it was through the community that texts were collected, preserved, and passed on.

The Title "Prophet"

The third line of the Isaiah seal impression is where things get more difficult. The impression is partially broken, but it has just enough space to squeeze in one more letter (note the drawing in Figure 6.5). The excavator, Eilat Mazar, offered an obvious reconstruction—the letter *aleph* which could fit into the spacing and gives us the biblical title *nby*[ʾ] "Proph[et]." But this reconstruction has met with some pushback.[35] Given the importance of this seal impression and its possible identification with Isaiah, the eighth-century prophet from Jerusalem, there are some technical issues that should be resolved.

First of all, the seal that made this impression was elegantly engraved. It was carved by a highly skilled professional. This means that the spacing and execution should be understood as carefully planned and intentional. Moreover, it suggests that its owner had means and standing. This observation is important for reconstructing the final line. Mazar argues that there is room for an additional letter and suggests adding the letter *aleph*, which gives the traditional biblical Hebrew spelling of the word prophet. But there is some debate about whether there is room at the end of the third register for an additional letter.[36] As my drawing illustrates, I think that this reading is possible, but I do not think it is necessary.[37] For example, the word "prophet" is also spelled *nby* (that is, without the *aleph*) in Hebrew manuscripts among the Dead Sea Scrolls, and the term is always spelled without the *aleph* in Aramaic. Since it is quite likely that the term was first borrowed into Hebrew perhaps through Aramaic, it is not necessary to reconstruct an *aleph* to interpret this line as the title "Prophet."

Some have suggested that the last line should be read as a personal name—"[the son of] Nobai." This is problematic for several reasons. First, this reading would require that the Hebrew word "son of" (*bn*) was omitted from the final line even though there was ample space for it when the seal was designed. The word "son" (Hebrew, *bn*) is almost never omitted when there is space for it on seals.[38] In fact, let me return to the control set of seal impressions from the City of David. There is not a single example where the word "son of" (Hebrew, *bn*) is omitted from a seal when the final name has only three or four letters. To be sure, sometimes the word "son of" can be omitted to save space in tightly executed seals, but there was plenty of space on this seal. It follows that "son of" was omitted because it did not belong there. It did not belong there because Isaiah was not the son of a prophet. He was not an apprentice; he was the prophet.

The problem of reading the final line reminds me of my own experience using objects from the antiquity market. In an earlier book, I cited a couple of ostraca that had come from the antiquities market to illustrate the spread of literacy. They were beautiful, well-preserved examples of Hebrew writing. Leading experts had published the ostraca in major journals.[39] The inscriptions were not critical to my argument, but they were pretty illustrations. Unfortunately, later research exposed them as expert forgeries. Lesson learned. Fool me once, shame on you. Fool me twice, shame on me. In my investigation of the "Isaiah, the Prophet" seal impression I encountered another sordid tale of forgery that illustrates how such artifacts can lead scholars astray. Forged seals bear directly on the reading of the third line of the Isaiah seal impression as the supposed personal name "Nobai" instead of the title "Prophet." I already discussed these readings above in the context of the Lachish seal impressions where I pointed out how the reading "Nobai" arose from the publication of forged artifacts and showing how "Prophet" is an obvious and commonsense translation.

The reading, "Belonging to Isaiah, *Prophet*," opens a new window into the history of the title "Prophet" and into the development of a prophetic community of practice. The title goes back to the northern kingdom, which had the community of the "sons of the prophets." This group had masters (like Elisha) and apprentices. They were connected with powerful families like the Nimshide dynasty. They seem to have had formal residences, and they were kingmakers. The title "Prophet"— and more specifically, a prophetic guild—made its way south to Jerusalem with the northern refugees. The title "Prophet" began to be used in the Judean royal administration in the late eighth century BCE, but it is a new term, as the Deuteronomistic scribal note, "a *prophet* was formerly called a *seer*," informs us. The Lachish seal impressions with "Son of the

Prophet" as a title as well as the mention of a community of disciples or apprentices under the prophet Isaiah provide both inscriptional and biblical evidence for the prophets as a *community* of practice. The ownership of official seals by the prophets as well as the use of scribal rubrics such as the messenger formula that are used in prophetic texts point to scribal training within this prophetic community.[40] Although the prophetic books seem to be collected by disciples or apprentices within the community, the very emergence and existence of such books seem to arise in the late eighth century, when the "sons of the prophets" emerged as a new scribal community of practice.

Perhaps it is best to begin with some evidence for scribal education among the prophets. The introduction to prophetic speech, "thus says the LORD," is in fact an adapted form from letter writing. We have several examples of practice or model letters used as scribal exercises from Kuntillet ʿAjrud.[41] One excellent example appears on a jar right next to scribal exercises for practicing correct penmanship of the ABCs—or, to be more precise, the *aleph-beth-gimels*. The letter exercise reads as follows:

> [Thus sa]ys Amaryaw, "Say to my lord: 'Is it well with y[ou]?' I bless you to YHWH of Teman and to its Asherah. May he bless [you] and keep you, and may he be with my lo[rd . . .]"

This is just the introduction or preface to the letter, which is what fledgling scribes practiced. The forms of prophetic speech are adapted from a letter from one person to another, often letters from or to a king. Using these rubrics of writing letters, the prophetic speech becomes a message from God. In antiquity, letters were sent and then performed by the messenger bearing the letter who would speak (i.e., read out the contents of the letter) on behalf of the sender. The performance is oral, but it begins with the learning and practice of a scribal skill, namely, letter writing. In other words, the very foundation of prophetic speech has its foundations in a scribal skill learned through apprenticeship among the sons of the prophets.

The prophets in the early biblical narratives were not associated with writing.[42] For example, in the Books of Samuel, the prophet Samuel is not an author. And the prophet Nathan is not described as a scribe. They do not write, even though Samuel gets a biblical book named after him. Their narratives do not describe them as writing anything. Then suddenly in the mid- to late eighth century, a series of prophetic figures appear whose life and oracles are collected in books under their names. The early "writing" prophets represent a new scribal community that first emerged during the spread of writing in the eighth century BCE. To be sure, there were prophets long before this time. In fact, anthropologists would argue that prophecy and prophets in various forms are part of a common human experience.[43] That is to say, there are always prophets and prophecy in some form in all human communities in all periods. So, what's new about the eighth century? The use of this title in the Isaiah seal impression suggests that the title "Prophet" was used already in the eighth century for court advisors like Isaiah of Jerusalem. But the meaning of this title changed over time, as we learn from 1 Samuel 9:9. Later scribal communities took the title and applied it to broadly to many different figures—e.g., Moses, Aaron, Abraham, Samuel. In the Elijah-Elisha narratives we see a community—"the sons of the prophets"—and prophetic apprentices. Later scribes reimagine the "prophet" as a lonely figure, called out by God (e.g., Jer 1:5). "Prophet" is no longer the title of a court advisor.

The introductions to the books of the writing prophets reflect a transitional phase for prophecy. We see this in the framing of their prophetic texts. For example, the Book of Isaiah begins with a classic expression of the writing prophets: "The *vision* of Isaiah, son of Amoz, which he *saw* concerning Judah and Jerusalem in the reigns of Uzziah, Jotham, Ahaz, and Hezekiah, kings of Judah" (Isa 1:1). This introduces a text, but it actually makes no explicit reference to writing, nor does it even suggest that the prophet himself is the author. The prophet is still a "visionary." But the visions are now recorded in writing, and this marks a seminal break with earlier prophetic figures known from biblical narratives.

The books of Hosea and Micah have slightly different introductions that give some hint about writing. Hosea begins, "The word of the LORD that came to Hosea, son of Beeri, in the days of Uzziah, Jotham,

Ahaz, and Hezekiah, kings of Judah, and in the days of Jeroboam, son of Joash, king of Israel" (Hos 1:1). This formula, "the word of the LORD that came to so-and-so," points to a genre learned in scribal education—namely, the writing of letters.[44] The Book of Micah begins in the same manner, "The word of the LORD that came to Micah, the Morashite, in the days of Jotham, Ahaz, and Hezekiah, kings of Judah," and it also hearkens back to the visionary introductions of Isaiah and Amos when it continues, "who saw concerning Samaria and Jerusalem" (Mic 1:1). In this respect, Micah's introduction fully embraces the transition from the visionary prophet to the writing prophet who adapts a literary form—the letter genre—to record his prophesy.

Scribal education, specifically as derived from letter writing, was the literary foundation for the writing prophets. Scholars have long recognized that prophetic books borrow the messenger formula as a way of depicting the prophet as the speaker for God's words. Hence, we find the frequent formula, "thus says/said the LORD," to introduce divine speech in the prophets. This formula was borrowed from letter writing and diplomatic correspondence. Essentially, a scribe would carry a letter from a sender to a recipient and then would read the letter aloud in the name of the sender to the recipient.

This becomes the paradigm for prophetic speech among the writing prophets, "Thus says the LORD," borrows from the scribal genre of letter writing and diplomatic correspondence. It looks like it is oral, but the scribes learned it from studying the formulas of writing and sending letters. We even have three nice examples of the scribal exercises in the Hebrew inscriptions found at Kuntillet ʿAjrud.[45] There are excellent parallels of this type of scribal exercise from Ugarit and elsewhere in the ancient near east.

The Book of Isaiah points to the existence of a prophetic community to account for the collection of some of his oracles. Isaiah enjoins his "students" (*limmûdîm*) to bind up his oracles: "Bind up the testimony, seal up the teaching among my students" (Isa 8:16). The technical terminology used here, "seal up" Isaiah's testimony, is a nice connection to the seal impression of Isaiah. The description uses technical vocabulary drawn from the scribal profession. The "students" are a community of prophetic apprentices. The students of the prophet would have formed their own community of practice, and this practice trained them with a knowledge of collecting and sealing up documents. If they could collect and preserve Isaiah's written oracles, we can assume that they were also trained to read and write. And if they were literate, their teacher—the prophet Isaiah—must also have been literate. This is not to suggest that a prophet was simply a scribe, but rather that scribal training was part of their community of practice. As I have emphasized, scribal training was part of many professions. The claim here is that it was part of the prophetic profession in the days of Isaiah and his prophetic apprentices. And this prophetic injunction to seal up a document now finds a striking archaeological reflex in the seal impression of "Isaiah, the prophet."

The prophetic scribal community as it was known in the days of Elisha or Isaiah did not survive. It was transformed. It was once a social institution embedded within the monarchy, but the Babylonians would destroy Jerusalem and put an end to the Judean monarchy. In the process, the figure of the prophet would be changed by later scribal communities. Just as figures like Elisha, Amos, and Isaiah illustrate the close early ties of the prophetic title with the state bureaucracy, later figures like Jeremiah (discussed in chapter 10) will illustrate the transformation of the prophetic title into a singular and lonely voice without a guild or community. The different figures of Isaiah and Jeremiah bookend the transformation of the title "prophet" and fate of the prophetic scribal community. Isaiah exemplifies the early prophet. As chance has fortuned us, we now have a seal impression that marks his institutional connections. And it is entirely appropriate that Isaiah's seal was found not far from the seal impression of Hezekiah, the king. And these seal impressions have their proper archaeological setting in the royal administrative district of Jerusalem. Nothing could be more appropriate! Jeremiah, in contrast, will exemplify the later transformation of the "prophet" into a solitary figure—someone exemplified as a lonely voice calling in the desert (see Isa 40:3)—and the complete disappearance of a community of the "sons of the prophet."

7

Scribes among the People of the Land

One of the more mysterious groups in the Hebrew Bible is the *Am Ha'aretz*, or "the People of the Land." I have been tracking them most of my career, and I think I have finally got them figured out. I wrote about them in a book two decades ago, but I had not fully solved the riddle then. The problem begins with the Hebrew term itself— *'am ha-'aretz*, which is composed of two common Hebrew words, *'am* "people," and *'eretz* "land." Therein lies some of the problem. You can use these words together without any special technical meaning as "people of the land." But sometimes it seems to refer to a specific group. Who are they? Scholars have offered a multitude of suggestions: farmers, the landed gentry, the common folk, etc.[1] Not surprisingly, different scribal communities used these common words at different times with different nuances. If you put all the biblical references together, then you have a mixed-up jumble that scholars have endlessly debated. But one scribal community used the term self-referentially in the Book of Kings, and I will oblige that community here and make this group into the *Am Ha'aretz*—namely, a technical term referring to rural elders.

Where did they come from? It will help to examine the Hebrew expression, *'am ha-'aretz*, in a little depth. The Hebrew word, *'am*, originally meant "clan" and can also be translated as "uncle." It hearkens back to the early kinship structures of ancient Israel. Early Israel was a tribal culture. It was configured around family groups and kinship relations. The translation of ʿam as "people" reflects a secondary development in the meaning of this Hebrew word—especially in the late monarchy when Judah and Jerusalem became more urbanized and the old rural kinship structures began to break down.[2] But rural towns and villages preserved this old meaning as well as old kinship structures. For them, ʿam ha-ʾaretz did not become the generic "people of the land." The second Hebrew term, ʾereṣ "land," also contributes to the rural and kinship background of the expression. It associates early Israel with the "land," that is, people who worked and lived on the land as opposed to in the city. The etymology of ʿam ha-ʾaretz suggests a need to look more carefully at the historical, social, and political world that created the *Am Ha'aretz*.

The World of the *Am Ha'aretz*

The *Am Ha'aretz* emerged in Jerusalem as a result of the continuing onslaught of the Assyrian empire that displaced many people. Up until now, I have focused on the refugees from Israel, but the *Am Ha'aretz* were related to a second and different group of refugees. The Israelian refugees were the result of Assyrian campaigns in the 730s and 720s in the north. But Assyrian campaigns in the 710s and 700s focused on the foothills and coastline directly to the west of Jerusalem, and these campaigns resulted in a completely different group of refugees that would associate themselves with the *Am Ha'aretz*. They were villagers who came from the foothills west of Jerusalem. They settled in the Western Hill of Jerusalem, but also in extra-mural suburbs just outside the city walls to the north and west of Jerusalem (see Figure 7.1).[3]

Judah had been a largely isolated and rural *chiefdom* in the early Iron Age. Scholars often speak about the rise of the Israelite Kingdom or the United Monarchy, but even if we allow for a brief unification of the early Israelite clans and tribes, the kingdom was still structured around tribes and clans. Scholars have debated the existence of a United Monarchy under David and Solomon from the archaeological record,[4] but I think archaeologists expect too much of the united clans and tribes of early

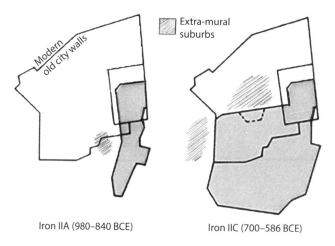

FIGURE 7.1. The growth and urbanization of Jerusalem.
Drawing by the author.

Israel. There are some unmistakable signs of the merging of the tribes—
for example, the uniquely shared allegiance to Yahweh as their major
deity. But the existing tribal structures did not disappear overnight. This
is obvious even in the biblical description of the division of the Solomonic kingdom: "When all Israel saw that the king would not listen to
them, the people answered the king, 'What share do we have in David?
We have no inheritance in the son of Jesse. *To your tents*, O Israel! Look
now to *your own house*, O David'" (1 Kgs 12:16). Early Israel was made
up of patrimonial kingdoms with power and influence still located in
tribal groups and clan elders, but the rise of the Assyrian empire reshaped the social structure of Judean society in the late monarchy.[5]

The changes can be understood from the demographics of Jerusalem.
The population of Jerusalem probably doubled in the late eighth century
BCE. This was due to two influxes of refugees. The second wave of refugees
came after the Assyrian campaigns by King Sargon and then especially
Sennacherib. Assyrian incursions into the region around the Judean
foothills began already in 712 BCE, when Sargon conquered the cities of
Ashdod and Gath.[6] Warfare encouraged the flight to the cities. But many
refugees probably did not choose to leave their villages and homes.
Eventually, Sennacherib focused his military campaigns on the Judean

foothills in 701 BCE. The destruction of Lachish—Judah's second largest city—is famously depicted on the walls of his palace, but the destruction in the Judean foothills was widespread. Sennacherib boasts, "As for Hezekiah, the Judean, I besieged forty-six of his fortified walled cities and surrounding smaller towns, which were without number. . . . I took out 200,150 people, young and old, male and female, horses, mules, donkeys, camels, cattle, and sheep, without number, and counted them as spoil."[7] Archaeological excavations and surveys confirm the essentials of Sennacherib's boast, namely, that the Judean foothills west of Jerusalem were devastated.[8] Many towns and villages were destroyed and never rebuilt. Large urban centers like Lachish were destroyed and then rebuilt. As a result, the demographics shifted from small settlements to larger urban centers. People left towns and villages in the Judean foothills and especially fled to Jerusalem and its surroundings.

In the early seventh century, the city of Jerusalem was bursting at its seams. Settlements spilled outside of its newly expanded walls to the north and west (see Figure 7.1). Further afield, new farmsteads grew in the close vicinity of Jerusalem, serving as suburbs for the burgeoning urban center.[9] This settlement was matched by increasing government bureaucracy. For example, recent salvage excavations in modern Jerusalem's Arnona neighborhood, just two miles south of the ancient city, discovered a major administrative center there dating back to the days of King Hezekiah and his son Manasseh, and nearby to the south of the Arnona complex was another administrative center at Ramat Raḥel.[10] Hundreds of royal and administrative seal impressions were excavated at these sites, suggesting their important role in servicing the urbanization of Jerusalem and Judah. The second wave of refugees coming into Jerusalem and its surrounding areas were from the towns and villages in Jerusalem's western foothills. Jerusalem and its suburbs were now overrun by two different refugee communities—the first from the north and the second from the west.

The second wave of refugees was related to the *Am Ha'aretz*. They also show up in the inscriptional record, particularly in seal impressions. There are two categories of seal impressions—those related to the activities of the state economy and those unrelated to the state economy. How can we separate these? Some inscriptions are obviously part of the government administration such as the royal *lmlk* ("belonging to the king") seal impressions. A related class of "private" inscriptions appears pre-stamped on jar handles—in other words, they are still part of the official economy. The personal names on these jar handles appear many times on jars excavated at different sites. And these "private" jar handle seal impressions are even found on the same jars as the royal *lmlk* seals. But there is also another class of the seal impressions that begin appearing at the end of the eighth century—"personal" seal impressions not affixed to jars. None of the "personal" seal impressions have the same names on them as the "private" jar handle seal impressions. In other words, they come from two different scribal communities. The scribes named on "private" jar handle seal impressions were part of the government apparatus—part of the administrative scribal community. But who are the people mentioned on the "personal" seal impressions? They participate in commerce, and they are probably paying taxes, but they are not part of the government administration. I identify them as belonging to the *Am Ha'aretz* scribal community. The *Am Ha'aretz* fled to Jerusalem and its environs as refugees that escaped the Assyrian invasions. Eventually, these refugees would become part of the urban and suburban sprawl of Jerusalem in the late monarchy.

The *Am Ha'aretz* Scribal Community and Its Literature

The *Am Ha'aretz* developed their own scribal community. The best example can be seen in the Josianic update of the Book of Kings, but they also have their fingers in other literature of the late monarchy such as the "Holiness Code" (Leviticus 17–26) and the updating of the Book of Deuteronomy.[11] These latter two texts focus on the fate of the countryside as opposed to the city of Jerusalem. The Holiness Code, for example, is concerned about the people in the "settlements" (Hebrew, *môshav*), that is, unwalled towns. It also repeatedly mentions displaced peoples using the Hebrew word *ger*, which is often translated "resident alien" although it is really a reference to refugees. At one point, the Holiness Code even talks about the *Am Ha'aretz* (Lev 20:2, 4), but they are not a regular topic.

Deuteronomy is also concerned about displaced people "in your gates" as well as showing mercy and kindness to "the widow, orphan, and the refugee [*ger*]." These are the casualties of war, of the Assyrian military campaigns. An interest in refugees as well as widows and orphans would reflect the results of Assyrian campaigns during the late Judean monarchy. Neither of these literary works is particularly interested in supporting the power of the king, the royal court, and administration or discussing the activities in the Jerusalem Temple. In addition to these books, the Book of Micah identifies its main character as someone who comes from the village of Moresheth in the Judean foothills. Although the reception history of the book includes him among the Prophets, he is never formally titled as a *nabî* in the biblical book and criticizes the prophets whom he includes as part of the urban and bureaucratic elite of Jerusalem (Mic 3:5–12). Jeremiah 26:18 remembers Micah as a prophet of doom, likely recalling the Assyrian invasions that ravaged the Judean foothills where Micah lived.[12] Micah levels a critique against Jerusalem and Judah's urban elites (1:5–9, 13), and he is particularly critical of the influence of "the survivors of Israel" in Judah (2:12; 3:1–10). This reflects the natural tension between two distinctly different groups of refugees—those from northern Israel and those from the Judean foothills. The Book of Micah reflects the interests of the countryside and the *Am Ha'aretz* scribal community.

A primary text of the *Am Ha'aretz* scribal community was a new edition of the Book of Kings. An early version of the Book of Kings had been compiled in the court of King Hezekiah (mentioned in chapter 3), but there is a long-standing scholarly consensus that there was a Josianic "edition" to the Book of Kings. I would argue that it was really just an update of earlier work done by court scribes, especially in the days of Hezekiah. As we shall see, the *Am Ha'aretz* had become part of the Josianic administration, and the general Hebrew expression was adopted as a self-description of this group such that it now became a technical term for the group.

How do we know that this scribal community that I am calling the *Am Ha'aretz* helped edit the Book of Kings? Because they appear in the book in a limited way, at two junctures in the story of the Judean kings—

moments that are critical to the editing of the Book of Kings. First, they play a central role in the overthrow of Queen Athaliah and the installation of Joash as the new king. Second, they figure prominently in installing Josiah on the throne. These two stories also have close literary connections, and these stories are pivotal to the narrative of the Book of Kings.

The story of King Joash in 2 Kings 11 begins with the ascension of Athaliah as queen. The queen's reign begins with her attempt to destroy the rest of the royal line, but the royal princess Jehosheba hides away her infant brother Joash (vv. 1–3). It seems likely that the little prince would have been taken out of Jerusalem and hidden in the countryside. After six years, the priest Jehoiada plots the coup. Jehoiada begins by enlisting a group of mercenaries, the Carites (vv. 4, 19), who are otherwise unknown in biblical literature. The scribes likely are thinking of the Carians, who were well-known as Aegean mercenaries in both Egypt and Babylon in antiquity. For example, the Egyptian pharaoh Psalmmetichos I (664–610 BCE) mentions using Carian mercenaries.[13] And Aegean material culture appears prominently in the archaeological excavations at the Judean coastal site of Meṣad Ḥashavyahu during the late monarchy, and scholars believe that Greek mercenaries might have been present there. So, this fits the context of a Josianic edition of the Book of Kings. Such mercenary groups would have been known to scribes working along the coastal plains like the *Am Ha'aretz* scribal community. In the biblical story, Jehoiada needed a group unaffiliated with the government and the official army for his coup, and the Carites filled that job description. It is unlikely that the Carites were present in the ninth century, in the days of Athaliah and Joash, but they were present in the late seventh century when the *Am Ha'aretz* scribes were updating the Book of Kings.

The story continues after Jehoiada has the proper support for the coup. They bring the seven-year-old child Joash into the temple and anoint him king in typical custom (vv. 9–12). When Athaliah hears the commotion, she goes to the temple to investigate. She sees the new king "standing by the pillar, according to custom"—a curious but important detail—and the rest of the cohort making acclamations. She cries, "Treason!" but they take her and put her to death (vv. 13–16). At that point, the priest Jehoiada makes a pact with the people reinstating the Davidic heir. The role of the *Am Ha'aretz* becomes prominent in the conclusion of the story, and it is worth citing the account here (vv. 17–20):

> Jehoiada made a covenant between the LORD and the king and people, that they should be the LORD's people; also between the king and the people. Then all the *Am Ha'aretz* went to the house of Baal, and tore it down; his altars and his images they broke in pieces, and they killed Mattan, the priest of Baal, before the altars. The priest posted guards over the house of the LORD. He took the captains, the Carites, the guards, and all the *Am Ha'aretz*; then they brought the king down from the house of the LORD, marching through the gate of the guards to the king's house. He took his seat on the throne of the kings. So all the *Am Ha'aretz* rejoiced, but the city was quiet. And they killed Athaliah with the sword at the king's house.

The *Am Ha'aretz* first protects traditional Yahwistic religion by destroying the Baal cult. Then they install a Davidic heir loyal to their worldview. It helps that the new king is only seven years old. The last verse provides a striking contrast: "the *Am Ha'aretz* rejoiced, but the city was quiet." This contrast seems intentional. It recalls typical societal tensions between urban and rural areas. The *Am Ha'aretz* represent the countryside, but they also wield political power in this story. They are not just the unorganized masses or a group of poor famers. The *Am Ha'aretz* are part of the power behind the throne here.

The story of Joash's coup points forward in the narrative to the second story of the *Am Ha'aretz* in the Book of Kings—the ascension of the young prince Josiah to the throne. The *Am Ha'aretz* reappear in the assassination story of King Amon (2 Kgs 21:23–24). Josiah's father, Amon, had ruled only two years when "Amon's servants conspired against him, and they killed the king in his own house. Then the *Am Ha'aretz* killed all those who had conspired against King Amon, and the *Am Ha'aretz* made his son Josiah king in place of him." History repeats itself. A young prince is again put on the throne by the *Am Ha'aretz*. The parallel is striking. In this story, Josiah is only eight years old when the *Am Ha'aretz* anoint him as king. We can assume that this is a proxy rule given the age of the boy-king. The *Am Ha'aretz* must again be the power behind the throne.

The matrilineal connections of Josiah are important to this story and to the biblical scribes more generally. For example, the Book of Kings makes a point of recording the name of almost every Queen Mother in history of Judah. So, the wives and mothers of the kings tell an important part of the story.[14] In this case, Josiah's mother comes from a rural Judean village called Bozkath (2 Kgs 22:1). The town is mentioned in the tribal lists in Joshua, where it is placed between the larger towns of Lachish and Eglon (15:39). Because it is not mentioned again in biblical literature, we can assume that Bozkath was a smaller town. Bozkath was such a small village in the Judean foothills that we are still not sure exactly where it was located.[15] Josiah himself takes a wife from another small town in the Judean foothills, a certain Hamutal from the city of Libnah (2 Kgs 23:31). And later in the story the *Am Ha'aretz* specifically choose her son, Jehoahaz, and install him on the throne when Josiah died suddenly in a battle at Megiddo. However, the Egyptians, not pleased with the choice of the *Am Ha'aretz*, depose him and install Jehoiakim, whose mother was from Rumah in Galilee (2 Kgs 23:36). The choice here again highlights the tension between two immigrant groups—one from the north and the other from the Judean foothills. These women are a window into the shifts in political leadership, in the latter case back toward the north and back toward the days of King Amon, whose mother was also from Galilee (2 Kgs 21:19). In these matrilineal connections, the tension between different social and political groups plays out, and the social background of the *Am Ha'aretz* comes into clearer focus. The Book of Kings makes a point of rural Josiah's origins. His family is also not affiliated with Galilee or the old northern kingdom and presumably more progressive and more prone to assimilating religious practices. Josiah is not a city boy, and his family is connected to the conservative rural politics of the *Am Ha'aretz*.

The installation of Josiah led eventually to religious reforms. As in the Joash story, a priest will play a pivotal role. In this case, it is the high priest Hilkiah who finds a book (22:8), which he passes along to the scribe Shaphan who reads it to Josiah. This precipitates a series of religious

reforms. Although the *Am Ha'aretz* are not explicitly mentioned in reforms (as they are in the Joash story), they were nevertheless the power
behind the throne, and there are literary hints about their involvement.
For example, the reforms begin by depicting Josiah standing by "the
pillar" (23:3)—a striking detail otherwise only found in the story of
Joash's coup. The stories of Joash and Josiah both employ women prominently. The princess Jehosheba hides away the young prince Joash, and
the prophetess Huldah is consulted by Josiah for his religious reforms.
This suggests that the *Am Ha'aretz* may have had a role in allowing
women a more prominent role in scribal professions. In sum, the accounts of Joash and Josiah are tied together in ways large and small. The
connection between the two stories was undoubtedly intended by the
scribal community.

The *Am Ha'aretz* scribal community made connections in Jerusalem
because many were forced to resettle there after the Assyrian destruction of their homes. But they retained their ties with rural leadership
even as they gained access to the royal court by helping establish the
young Josiah as king. Josiah was one of their own—a prince with family
ties to the Judean countryside, and the *Am Ha'aretz* remained connected to the traditional leadership among the clans and families in the
villages, especially in the Judean foothills. So it is not surprising that
when the *Am Ha'aretz* scribes describe Josiah's reforms, they include the
traditional tribal leadership: "The king sent and gathered *all the elders of
Judah* and Jerusalem to him" (23:1). The elders suddenly become an
important group in Josiah's story. This contrasts with the leadership
under King Hezekiah, which focuses on royal administration: "The king
sent Eliakim the royal steward, Shebna the scribe, and the senior priests
to the prophet Isaiah, son of Amoz" (2 Kgs 19:2). The *Am Ha'aretz*
scribes make their way into the royal court and write about themselves
and their community as they update the account of the Judean kings.

The *Am Ha'aretz* also appear at the conclusion to Josiah's reign. Josiah
makes a foolhardy attempt to block Pharoah Neco's march north to
meet the Babylonian king Nebuchadnezzar, and he is killed in battle.
After Josiah died, "The *Am Ha'aretz* took Jehoahaz, the son of Josiah,
and anointed him, and made him king in the place of his father" (2 Kgs

SCRIBES AMONG THE PEOPLE OF THE LAND   145

23:30). The political plans of the *Am Ha'aretz*, however, don't work out here. Pharaoh Neco returns from battle and replaces Jehoahaz with his own vassal king, Jehoiakim. And the *Am Ha'aretz* have to pay for their political machinations: "Jehoiakim gave the silver and the gold to Pharaoh, but he taxed the land in order to meet Pharaoh's demand for money. He exacted the silver and the gold from the *Am Ha'aretz*, from all according to their assessment, to give it to Pharaoh Neco" (v. 35). In sum, the *Am Ha'aretz* here are not just a group of rural peasants or farmers. They are obviously a landed elite with financial means as well as political interests and agendas, and their story was incorporated into the Josianic updating of the Book of Kings.

When the Book of Kings got revised and updated again by a still later scribal community (probably in the late sixth century), the *Am Ha'aretz* were no longer a defined social or political group. The *Am Ha'aretz* had been disbanded and disenfranchised by the Babylonian destruction of Judah and Jerusalem. So, for the later scribes, the *Am Ha'aretz* become quite literally just "people of the land" in its most generic sense. Indeed, the term became the opposite of an affluent, landed rural politic. It is understood as the poorest of the land. We see this in a chapter that was appended to the end of the Book of Kings. Chapter 25 says that there was no food for "the people of the land" (v. 3). Here the Hebrew expression ʿam ha-ʾaretz is used to refer to the poor masses. In exilic and postexilic times, the *Am Ha'aretz* and their scribal community no longer existed. They had been wiped out by the Babylonian invasions. All that remained was the legacy in their literary works.

A literary work often associated with the Josianic Reforms is the Book of Deuteronomy. However, an overly close association is misguided, as Lauren Monroe has pointed out in her book *Josiah's Reform and the Dynamics of Defilement*.[16] Monroe shows that the literary account of Josiah's Reform is not as closely connected with Deuteronomy as some scholars had suggested. Rather, the reforms are focused on issues of purity and defilement that are mostly connected to the literature of the "Holiness Code." This actually makes sense since the "scroll" was found by a priest, Hilkiah. In that respect, we should have expected Josiah's reforms to have a priestly influence (see chapter 9).

There has always been something unsettling to me about connecting Deuteronomy with the Josianic Reforms. First of all, the Book of Deuteronomy does not present itself as a "scroll" but rather is quite dramatically presented as an oral speech of Moses. The book begins, "These are the words that Moses *spoke*" (Deut 1:1). More than this, Deuteronomy focuses on the figure of Moses as the lawgiver. The book begins and ends with Moses. It starts with Moses giving a farewell speech as Israel is about to cross over the Jordan into the Promised Land. Moses' speech concludes in chapter 27, and then the book as a whole concludes with the story of Moses' death. The Book of Deuteronomy is all about the figure of Moses, but the scroll that is found by Hilkiah is not associated with Moses at all. This seems like a huge omission—that is, if the scribes telling the story intended us to think that this scroll was related to the Book of Deuteronomy in its final form. In fact, the later priestly scribes who compiled the Book of Chronicles (probably in the fourth century BCE) thought the omission of Moses from the story of Josiah's Reform had to be remedied. So in their account written during the Persian period, they make the connection quite clearly: "the priest Hilkiah found the scroll of the Torah of the LORD *given through Moses*" (2 Chr 34:14). But that note is not in the Book of Kings. Kings never attributes the scroll that was found to Moses. It is called "the scroll of the Torah" and "the scroll of the Covenant," but it is never suggested that Moses was in any way responsible for the scroll. The critical figure in the finding of the scroll is only the priest Hilkiah and then the scribe Shaphan, who gets the scroll from Hilkiah and reads it. This alone should suggest that we should look for priestly influences for the Josianic Reform, and this is just what Monroe found in her analysis. More specifically, the Josianic Reform addresses issues of defilement as articulated in the "Holiness Code," a section of the Book of Leviticus (chs. 17–26).

Another misconception about the Josianic Reforms is that they were concerned with centralization of worship in Jerusalem. This idea is perhaps part of the legacy of reading Josiah's Reforms through the lens of Deuteronomy, and in this case, Deuteronomy 12 (or "the Law of Centralization"). However, centralization is not really central to the Josianic Reforms. Rather, centralization was likely an aspect of the earlier reform under King Hezekiah, which was mentioned in just one biblical verse stating that Hezekiah "removed the high places" (2 Kgs 18:4). Archaeological excavations support this understanding of Hezekiah's Reform.[17] Several Judean temples and shrines outside of Jerusalem come to an abrupt end in the archaeological record in the late eighth century BCE. The late eighth century was about the centralization of Jerusalem— demographically, politically, and religiously. There likely continued to be a push toward centralization of Jerusalem in the seventh century, but that was not when it began.

Josiah's Reform was more concerned with a religious ideology about purity. For example, there is an interesting tension between the priests in the countryside whose shrines are defiled and the Jerusalem priestly hierarchy. But in the end the priests from various towns were allowed a place in religious worship: "The priests from the high places did not sacrifice at the altar of the LORD in Jerusalem, but still ate unleavened bread with their fellow priests" (2 Kgs 23:9). The *Am Ha'aretz* scribal community was allied with the rural priests and Levites. An alliance between the rural priestly community, the Levites, and the elders comes together to support the young king Josiah. The scribal community updates the Book of Kings as well as the Book of Deuteronomy, and they collect the priestly traditions known as the "Holiness Code."

An Inscription of the *Am Ha'aretz* Scribal Community

Is there evidence in the inscriptional record for the *Am Ha'aretz* scribal community? Perhaps. I have already pointed out that there are many personal seal impressions for people who seemed to work outside of the government administration. Some of these likely represent the *Am Ha'aretz* scribal community. A more solid example of the *Am Ha'aretz* scribal community may have been excavated at a small agricultural fortress known as Meṣad Ḥashavyahu, or "Fort Hashavyahu," where archaeologists excavated an unusual judicial ostracon. The fortress is far from any urban centers; it lies about 25 km south of Jaffa (modern Tel-Aviv) and about 1.7 km south of the small port of Yavneh-Yam near the Mediterranean coast (Figure 7.2). The ancient name of the fortress is

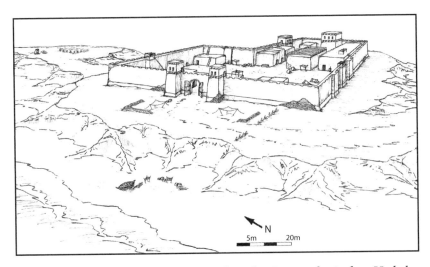

FIGURE 7.2. Artist's rendition of Fort Hashavyahu. Drawing by Andrew Herbek.

unknown, and the modern name comes from a fragmentary ostracon found at the site that reads, [ ]יא בן לחשביהו "belonging to Ḥashavyahu son of Yaʾa[ ]."[18] The epigrapher Joseph Naveh, who first published the inscriptions from the fort, already noted that this name was "common among the Levites."[19] There are at least nine separate priestly or levitical figures in biblical literature with this name (see Ezra 8:19, 24; Neh 3:17; 10:12; 11:15, 22; 12:21; 1 Chr 6:30; 9:14; 25:3; 26:30; 27:17; 2 Chr 35:9).[20] This name and the remote location both begin to suggest that the site and its famous ostracon may be related to the *Am Haʾaretz* scribal community.

The ostracon mentions another place, *Ḥatzar ʾAsam*, which literally translates as "an (unwalled) settlement of storing." The first word, *Ḥatzar*, known from many cognate languages and literatures such as Ugaritic and Akkadian, refers to a farmstead or an unwalled village. The word *ʾAsam* is known mostly as a noun referring to "storage" or "storehouses," although the verbal form might be associated with "gathering." It seems likely that Fort Hashavyahu protected a number of smaller farmsteads and settlements nearby. Such a configuration is described in Joshua 15:45–47 with fortified sites and related smaller villages and farmsteads (*ḥatzerîm*).

The main ostracon from the site seems like a judicial document. It is a reaper's complaint against his boss, Hoshaiah, son of Shobai. Hoshaiah seems to be a government agricultural administrator, and the worker addresses his complain to the "Commander," presumably, short for the well-known title "Commander of the Fortress."[21] This understanding makes sense given the location where the ostracon was found, namely, in the guardroom of the fortress, which is where official administrative business would have occurred. The complaint itself comes from an agricultural worker, but it is unclear whether the worker himself wrote the complaint. Probably not. More likely, he employed a local official at the fort as a scribe. The text may be translated as follows:

> May my lord, the Commander, hear the report of his servant. Your servant was harvesting. Your servant was in Ḥaṣer 'Asam, and your servant harvested and finished. Now he had stored the grain some days ago before the Sabbath. When your servant had finished [the] harvest and had stored the grain, some days ago, then Hoshaiah, the son of Shobai, came and took your servant's garment! When I had finished my harvest—this very day—he took your servant's garment! And all my companions will testify for me, those who were harvesting with me in the heat of the sun. My companions will testify for me. Truly, I am innocent of any gu[ilt. Come, let him return] my garment. Surely the power belongs to the official to retur[n the garment of your] serva[nt. May you hav]e mer[cy] on him [and return the garment of your se]rvant and not remain silent [. . .]

The inscription itself is a bit of a paradox. On the one hand, the script is elegant, obviously from a highly practiced hand (see Figure 7.3). On the other hand, the content of the complaint itself is awkwardly written and repetitious. This is not a great example of literature. So we have a poorly written text with very nice penmanship! Joseph Naveh, who published the ostracon, suggested that the text was written by an experienced scribe from the dictation of the worker. In this way, he was able to account for both the elegant hand as well as the rather awkward and repetitive style. But this does not explain some unusual features in the handwriting. For example, the Hebrew letter 'aleph is written normally sixteen times (𐤀)

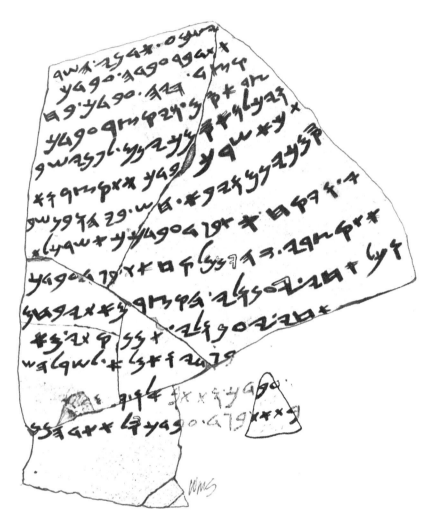

FIGURE 7.3. Meṣad Hashavyahu inscription. Drawing by the author.

but reversed five times (✗, lines 1, 2, 6, 8 [2x]). This has to be intentional, but it is hard to explain this given the elegant hand of the scribe unless it was a scribal practice from a different community. There are examples of this phenomenon on some seals, which are explained as mistakes.[22] If this happened once, we could explain it as a mistake, but five times indicates intentionality. It points to a different community of scribal practice. Another example is the open headed *dalet* (◁), which normally would have a closed triangle head and so does not fit with the general scribal practice or other administrative inscriptions like the Arad ostraca. If it were just one or two idiosyncrasies, we might dismiss it, but there are other idiosyncrasies in the handwriting that Naveh pointed out and some that I identified.[23] How do we explain them? We do know that different scribal communities developed their own unique styles. I think it is likely that this is a style related to a different scribal community—the *Am Ha'aretz*.

Scholars have based our typology of handwriting mostly on the basis of government administrative texts—because that is mostly what we have. But we have something quite different here in this ostracon, both in its content and the location where it was found. It suggests that each different scribal community had its own community of practice. Because reading and writing were learned through apprenticeships within different professions, each community of practice could develop its own particular practice. This would have included minor differences in vocabulary, spelling, and handwriting. On the one hand, the shared vernacular language and culture would have exerted a unifying influence; on the other hand, the different professions would have developed their own communities of practice shaped by the apprenticeship learning model.

Scholars have noted how the cry to return the worker's garment echoes issues of fairness to workers in biblical literature (see Exod 22:25–27; Lev 25:53; Deut 24:10–13; Amos 2:8; Prov 20:16; 27:13). One striking part of the plea is the apparent reference to the Sabbath: "he had stored (the grain) some days ago *before the Sabbath (lpny šbt)*." The Hebrew word *šbt*, which I have translated as "Sabbath," could also just be an infinitive verb, thus "before stopping." The objection to translating this as "Sabbath" seems to be mostly a debate about the history of the Sabbath as a religious institution, and I have no reason to think the Sabbath was invented in the post-exilic period. Rather, I think it is the earliest extra-biblical evidence for the Sabbath even though it's not clear that it carried all the later religious implications that developed. Indeed, references to the Sabbath in the Jewish archive from Elephantine in Egypt dating to the fifth century BCE presumes that the institution was known long before the exile.[24] The Sabbath appears prominently in the Decalogue as well as early priestly literature (e.g., Exod 20:8–11; 31:13–16), including the Holiness Code. Indeed, the Holiness Code emphasizes observing the Sabbath "in all your settlements" (Lev 23:3), an expression that points to the rural worldview that the Holiness Code reflects.[25] The interest in justice for a rural agricultural worker accords well with the concerns of the Holiness Code. This is another aspect of the inscription from Fort Ḥashavyahu that can be related to the *Am Ha'aretz* scribal community. In addition, a personal name on a fragmentary ostracon found at the site points to rural priestly and Levitical groups that align with the *Am Ha'aretz*.

As an originally rural social group, the *Am Ha'aretz* scribal community is hard to pin down in the inscriptional record. And their role in the political life of Judah was also transitory. They were forced to resettle in Jerusalem as refugees after the Assyrian invasions of the late eighth century BCE. Eventually, they managed to hold some political and social power in Jerusalem under King Josiah, but when he died the *Am Ha'aretz* lost their influence. They tried to reassert influence by installing Jehoahaz as king, but the Egyptians replaced him with their own vassal king, Jehoiakim, who had no ties with the *Am Ha'aretz* or the Judean countryside. The *Am Ha'aretz* and their scribal community then faded from history. Even their name, the *Am Ha'aretz*, was forgotten. They became just the masses, the poorest "people of the land," but some traces of their literary heritage survived in the Bible. The Babylonian exile forced a consolidation and a compiling of traditional biblical texts. The *Am Ha'aretz*'s literature was edited and reshaped when a library was later collected, compiled, and edited. The Holiness Code, for example, became part of a larger priestly book called Leviticus. Their edition of the Book of Kings was edited and further updated. A literary legacy of the *Am Ha'aretz* scribal community persisted.

8

Women in the Professions

My mother taught me to speak. But I didn't realize it until I was studying the anthropology of language change. Linguistic anthropologists point out that children learn language mostly from their mothers, not from their fathers. This certainly fits my own experience. My mother raised three boys, and my father worked two jobs to make ends meet, so he was not home much. So I first learned to talk and read from my mom. My own experience illustrates why women's speech patterns are so decisive for language change. The role of women in educational formation is underappreciated, but some biblical texts and inscriptions attest to a significant role. Women played prominent roles in society, even though the final editing of biblical literature took place in the hands of conservative, priestly scribes who downplayed women's positions in scribal communities.

The Book of Proverbs, in contrast, stands as a clear testament to the appreciation of women's involvement in education in at least one scribal community of practice. There's a certain tension concerning the role of women in the framing of the book. To begin with, the introduction gives it a distinctly patriarchal and elitist context. They are the proverbs of Solomon addressed to his son (Prov 1:1)—in other words, from the venerable wise king to the royal prince. Modern translations obscure this patriarchal context a bit by translating the Hebrew word for "son"—*ben*—as "child," but maybe they are onto something in attempting to be more inclusive. After all, Proverbs is also striking in the balanced way it includes female teaching, as we read in verse 8, "Hear, my son, your father's instruction, and do not reject your *mother's* teaching." Indeed, the parallel and balance for the teaching of both the father and the mother can be seen as one of the contributions of the Book of Proverbs, especially given its patriarchal cultural context and final framing. More than this, the main metaphor for instruction in Proverbs will be the personified Lady Wisdom. In this way, learning in Proverbs is gendered as feminine. Wisdom is introduced in the first chapter (v. 20) and then plays a prominent role as the tutor for the young in the first section of the book.

A role for female scribes is built into the very framework of the Book of Proverbs. Besides beginning with Lady Wisdom as a tutor, the book also concludes by extolling the *Eshet Chayil* or "Strong Wife" (31:10–31) in a scribal exercise.[1] Some have mistakenly suggested that this concluding poem is simply an ode to the characteristics of a good wife, but this misses the genre of this text as scribal education. The *Eshet Chayil* is an acrostic poem—that is, it is organized with each successive line beginning with the next letter of the Hebrew alphabet. This component is often lost in translation. I will give it a try:

> **A** strong woman who can find? She is more valuable than jewels.
> **B**ecause her husband trusts her, he has no lack of gain.
> **C**an she bring him good, not harm, all the days of her life? Yes! . . .

This is not the most literal translation, but it does capture the scribal curricular aspect of the text. The acrostic organization is a written device that does not translate to speech. This is not an oral component of the text. It is quintessentially a device of scribal learning predicated on a knowledge of the alphabet and its arrangement. Since the poem is a device for scribal learning, it has limited utility outside the context of scribal education, but there was likely also an oral component to this composition—namely, fledging scribes memorized and recited such texts. Memorization and recitation of written texts was an important part of scribal training.[2] But the poem's foundation is organized around a student learning her ABCs. Of course, many have also observed that the "Strong Woman" speaks of the activities entrusted to women, including the purchase of property and commerce in the town square—activities that require written contracts and for which literacy would be a useful skill.

In sum, Proverbs begins by introducing us to Lady Wisdom, the ultimate tutor, and concludes with a scribal ditty extolling a valorous woman. In this respect, it's not hard to see how the framing and content of Proverbs open a path for women learning scribal skills. It should be remembered, however, that a variety of professions and activities used scribal skills but were not defined by them. In other words, many women could have been literate but did not necessarily become "scribes" as a profession. Their professions included literacy as a skill, but were not necessarily defined by it.[3]

Female Scribes in the Ancient Near East

The figure of Lady Wisdom as a teacher in Proverbs nicely parallels the gendering of writing in Mesopotamia. The Assyriologist Eleanor Robson, in an article on gendered literacy in Mesopotamia, notes that cuneiform literature makes goddesses, particularly Nisaba, the primary actors in scribal education and literacy.[4] Robson points out that goddesses are twice as frequently depicted as literate in cuneiform literature as gods. And cuneiform literature depicts the goddess Nisaba—assuming a role parallel to Lady Wisdom in Proverbs—as responsible for a young prince's learning in the Royal Hymn of Shulgi: "When I was small, I was at the tablet house, where I learned the office of scribe from the tablets of Sumer and Akkad. . . . The fair Nisaba generously bestowed on me wisdom and understanding. I am an experienced scribe who does not let anything pass him by."[5] In a similar manner, the Book of Proverbs frames the tutoring of the royal princes—the sons of Solomon—as coming from a female tutor.[6] Although the Hebrew Bible does not have actual goddesses tutoring the royal princes, Lady Wisdom is a fair stand-in. According to Proverbs, she was created before the earth itself (8:22–31), which gives a primordial standing for her authority as a teacher.

Gendering of divine scribalism has implications for female scribes on earth. For example, Robson cites this gendered literacy of the divine actors to clear a path for seeing female scribes in Mesopotamia. She rejects scholars who just assume that scribes and their students were all male. Robson focuses specifically on cuneiform scholars, but the same bias can be found among those studying ancient Hebrew literacy. For example, one scholar asserts, "when discussing women's literacy, it must be recalled the profession of scribe was considered masculine—indeed, all ancient literature was masculine."[7] Another scholar asserts that "by the nature of things women would not serve as scribes."[8] What is this "nature of things," given that divine literacy actually has a prominent feminine bias? It is not surprising, therefore, that Robson can cite several examples of female scribes like Inana-amagu for whom scribal learning was a family affair that included her father and sisters.

Although writing in Mesopotamia was "predominantly a masculine space," an anthology of female authors shows that there was a broad array of female scribes responsible for scores of texts in all periods and places in Mesopotamia.[9] These include literary texts that reflect women copying and assisting in the transfer of texts within scribal communities—these are literary texts and school curricula. But there are also individual female compositions, especially texts like letters that were meant to serve a specific and temporary need. There are also texts that were dictated or commissioned by women that may have been written by a male scribe. Women often acquired writing skills because of their association with the palace or because of their professions. This would have been true throughout the near east. One neo-Assyrian cuneiform text mentions six female Aramaic scribes.[10] Since Aramaic was used as an administrative language in the empire, they must have acquired alphabetic literacy because of their work in the imperial bureaucracy.

There is also evidence for female scribes in Egypt. The most striking evidence comes from the Theban Tombs. Betsy Bryan identifies a number of tomb paintings that visually depict the deceased women with their scribal palettes below their seats (for example, Figure 8.1).[11] This demonstrates not only that women were receiving scribal education but also that they valued it so much that they wanted to represent it in the afterlife.

Interpreting the evidence for female literacy comes with its own biases. For example, in the ancient city of Ugarit—a major port city in the late second millennium on the eastern Mediterranean—there are a significant

FIGURE 8.1. Female seated with her scribal palette below her seat in the afterlife.
TT 162; courtesy of Betsy Bryan, "Evidence for Female Literacy from Theban
Tombs of the New Kingdom," plate 8.

number of letters written to or from the Queen or the Queen Mother.[12]
Other letters mention her position in palace affairs. One example suffices to illustrate:

> Thus says Iwaraḏanu to Iwarapazanu, "My son, my brother, say: 'May
> the gods guard you, may they keep you well.'
>   How about the tablet with the letter that I sent to Queen Tharri-
> yelli? What did she say? And now, may my brother, my son, ask

Tharriyelli, and may she mention my name to the king and to
'Iyatalamu. And now, may my brother, my son, ask Tharriyelli, and
return word to your brother, your lord."[13]

This certainly reflects the ability for elites to acquire literacy. But does
this suggest that Queen Tharriyelli may have been literate? Tharriyelli
was herself a well-known figure in the Ugaritic royal court. In the Ugaritic
letters, the Queen engages in diplomacy as well as in commerce. Even
when the king writes to the Queen Mother, he shows great deference:
"To the Queen, my mother, say: 'Message of the king, your son—at
my mother's feet, I fall. . . .'"[14] Several letters among the corpus were
apparently written by the Queen herself. The tendency is to dismiss
this as evidence of female literacy with the observation that these letters
were written by male scribes for the various royal women, and it is
possible that she dictated these letters. Even so, it suggests some basic
acquisition of literacy. Moreover, there is significant evidence in the
ancient near east for the education of young royals in the elementary
skills of reading and writing. Queen Tharriyelli is obviously well educated, and it would be normal for this education to include some instruction in reading and writing even if she had no obvious professional
goal to be a scribe. Her profession as Queen Mother made literacy an
important skill.

The Queen Mother was also a particularly important figure in ancient
Israel.[15] She is referred to regularly in the regnal formulas that introduce
each of the Kings of Judah. For example, we read in 2 Kings 24:18, "Zedekiah was twenty-one years old when he began to reign. And he
reigned eleven years in Jerusalem. And his mother's name was Hamutal"
(for other examples, see 1 Kgs 11:26; 14:21; 15:2, 13; 22:42; 2 Kgs 8:26;
10:13; 12:1; 14:2; 15:2, 33; 18:2; 21:1; 22:1, 36). There is nothing particularly
interesting about these formulas, except for the consistency in which
the Queen Mother is included. These must have been recorded in royal
annals that were used by later scribes. They reflect both prominence and
importance of the position. In certain biblical stories, these figures play
pivotal roles in events. Perhaps the most well-known Queen Mother is
Bathsheba, Solomon's mother. She played a critical role in his rise to the

throne (1 Kings 1), and then is presented as an advisor within Solomon's court (1 Kgs 2:13–25).

Female literacy and scribal education started at the top. The rich and powerful were the most likely to be educated and to acquire scribal skills, and this was no less true for women. So, it follows that scribal skills and training would begin with powerful women. Our examples can begin in the Bible itself. For example, the infamous Queen Jezebel fabricates charges against Naboth: Jezebel "wrote letters in Ahab's name and sealed them with his seal; she sent the letters to the elders and the nobles who lived with Naboth in his city" (1 Kgs 21:8). Shall we take this literally—namely, that Jezebel herself wrote the letters? That is what the text literally says, but some might suggest it is just an expression and she must have dictated the letter to a scribe. It would have been helpful for her to write the letters herself because this would have better concealed her plot. It is difficult to be sure, but we should not dismiss it so hastily. For example, there seems to be an ancient seal of Jezebel.[16] In a later period, the Queen Esther "wrote again with full authority to establish with a letter this Purim festival" (Esth 9:29). Such queens follow a well-trod path of women associated with the royal houses who were known for their education, literacy, and scribal training throughout the ancient near east.

Women in Hebrew Inscriptions

Although education for women started with the elites, some inscriptional evidence suggests that it trickled down to the lower classes. This can be observed in the examples of female Hebrew scribes known from inscriptions.[17] Presumably, such female scribes would have studied the standard curriculum. Their work seems often centered on overseeing large households—just as is described in the "Strong Wife" poem in Proverbs 31. Not surprisingly, as literacy in society expands, there often follows a larger role for female literacy.[18]

So just how common are inscriptions mentioning women in ancient Israel? That's not easy to answer. Gender is not always specified. So, unless there is a specific gender identifier like "daughter" (Hebrew, *bt*) or "wife" (Hebrew, ʾšh), gender may not be clear. On the other hand, it seems that when gender was important, it was likely mentioned. The other issue is that so many small inscriptions—especially seals and seal impressions—come from the antiquities market, which limits their value. Yet there are also some striking examples of women in the inscriptional record.

Let's take the excavations by Yigal Shiloh from the City of David in Jerusalem as a control to assess the extent of women's role in scribal activities. Two of the fifteen inscriptions that Shiloh published specifically mention women. The first is on a small storage jar that belonged to the "daughter of Yaʿamaʾ," and the second is an administrative ostracon listing several women by the title "wife of so-and-so." That two of fifteen inscriptions explicitly refer to women makes an important contribution suggesting that women could be active in commerce and administration that required writing and literacy. The context of these inscriptions is also significant. The City of David was the oldest part of ancient Jerusalem, an area presumably occupied by old elite families. While it was an elite quarter, it was not the royal quarter of the city during the late monarchy. These fifteen inscriptions all date to the late Iron II period, or more specifically from the late eighth through the early sixth centuries BCE.[19] None of the inscriptions are royal administrative texts, but they reflect the activities of elite families of old Jerusalem. They also date to a high point for writing in ancient Judah, and it follows that it was likely the period when women had the most significant role in scribal communities. Many of the inscriptions from this excavation are fragmentary, so it's sometimes difficult to know exactly what role female scribes might have played in their production or use.

Let's take a closer look at the first inscription, which came from a small storage jar (see Figure 8.2). We don't have the entire jar, just fragments, but it belongs to a well-known shape for small storage jars. It reads, *lbt . y ʿm ʾ ṭ* "Belonging to the daughter of Yaʿamaʾ, fine [wine]."[20] The final letter is probably an abbreviation, the Hebrew letter *ṭet*, from the word *ṭov* "good," which would likely refer to contents of the jar, namely, "fine wine." There is some debate over the interpretation of the final letter *ṭet* as an abbreviation for wine, but it seems best to read it in

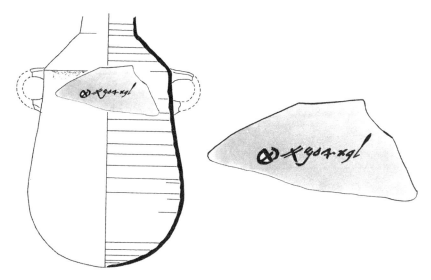

FIGURE 8.2. Small jar inscription of "Daughter of Yaʿamaʾ." Adapted from Donald Ariel, ed., *Excavations at the City of David 1978–1985*. Drawing by the author.

relation to the contents of the jar. The omission of the exact name for Yaʿamaʾ's daughter is not unusual, as many inscriptions—especially administrative lists (e.g., Arad 76 discussed earlier)—recorded people as "the son of so-and-so." And, of course, the designation of this jar as belonging to Yaʿamaʾ's daughter doesn't require that she herself was literate, although it is strongly suggestive. The designation "Daughter of Yaʿamaʾ" does likely mean that she was unmarried because if she were married, then we would expect her to be called "the wife of so-and-so," as we have in the second inscription. An inscription on a storage jar is also important because it points to women's professional participation in commerce. Many of the examples from the antiquities market are women's seals, which some have suggested are merely used on rings as decoration. But the inscription on a storage jar is not merely decorative, and it proves that we can reject such dismissive approaches to female literacy.

The second inscription from Shiloh's City of David excavations further supports women's role in the Jerusalemite economy. It is a fragmentary accounting record listing a series of women (Figure 8.3). Unlike the

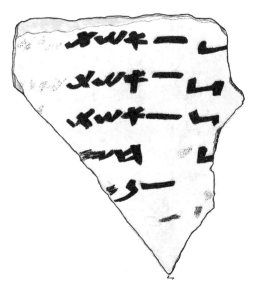

FIGURE 8.3. "Wife of" administrative list from
Jerusalem. Drawing by the author.

previous example, which was originally written on the side of a complete vessel, this is a pottery sherd, that is, an ephemeral accounting text
used to keep records. The inscription reads as follows:

1) [...] ↝ — ʾšt . xx[...] [...] ephah (of grain) — Wife of
   [so-and-so]
2) [...] ↝ — ʾšt . šx[...] [...] ephah (of grain) — Wife of
   [so-and-so]
3) [...] ↝ — ʾšt . xl[...] [...] ephah (of grain) — Wife of
   [so-and-so]
4) [...] ↝ ḥšb[n ...] [...] ephah (of grain), Balan[ce of ...]
5) [...]—nx[...] [...] — N[...]
6) [...]

Of course, the striking aspect of this list is the repeated mention of the
"Wife of [so-and-so]" in the first three lines. Unfortunately, it is broken.
Line 4 is missing the long dash—and I would reconstruct the Hebrew
word *ḥeshbon*, referring to the "balance."[21] Presumably, it would give the

final tally to conclude the administrative record. Line 5 might have begun a separate list. This particular list of wives reminds us of the economic aspects of the "Strong Wife" lauded in the scribal exercise in Proverbs 31. In this example, it seems that the text was essentially a scratch pad and that the record—if it was important enough—would have then transferred to a more permanent record—probably a sheet of papyrus. The irony, of course, is that such sheets of papyrus and parchment scrolls burned away, and the transitory pottery sherds withstood the burning of Jerusalem.

Both inscriptions belong to economic activities—the possession and transfer of goods. They remind us of the economic aspects lauded in the scribal exercise in Proverbs 31. Neither inscription requires that the women had scribal skills, but they are strongly suggestive. If one argued that scribal training was not implied by these inscriptions, I would suggest that this points to some inherent biases. It's reasonable to argue that only elite women had the opportunity to acquire scribal skills but not to argue that "by the nature of things women would not serve as scribes." This is just not true. As we have seen, there is some intrinsic female gendering to literacy and education. Women certainly acquired scribal skills in ancient Judah. Other inscriptions will further indicate that women were acquiring scribal skills.

A significant source for female literacy comes from seals and seal impressions. I did not want to lead with these examples because some have argued that women's seals might have been used only as jewelry. There is no reason to suggest this specifically for women, especially when we see women mentioned in other kinds of inscriptions. No, the seals and seal impressions are an important part of the evidence for women's literacy. There are at least a dozen seals and seal impressions that mention women as either "the daughter of so-and-so" or "the wife of so-and-so." Many of these, however, come from the antiquities market, but there are also some that have been excavated. For example, there was a seal impression "Belonging to Tamar" excavated in Jerusalem, although there is some debate about her exact name.[22] It was published as

ltmr b	"Belonging to Tamar, the daugh-
t ʿzryw	-ter of Azariyaw"

But other scholars have suggested reading it as "Belonging to Chana, daughter of Azariah."[23] Whether her name was Tamar or Chana is not really important. Her father's name, either Azariyaw or Azariah, reflects different interpretations of the family identity. The former would identify the family as refugees from the north, whereas the latter is just a typical Judean family name. The possible Israelian family name is a reminder of the significant deluge of refugees that came to Jerusalem in the late eighth century.

One particular Israelian scribal family that made their way into Jerusalem included a female scribe. Her name was preserved for eternity on a seal excavated in a tomb on the eastern slope of the Hinnom Valley in Jerusalem (see Figure 8.4). She belonged to an important scribal family, namely, the family of Menaḥem, son of Yawbana, discussed in chapter 4. There are nineteen individual seal impressions for the patriarch of the family (discussed in chapter 4), and he apparently taught his daughter to read and write. The seal reads,

lḥmyʾhl	"Belonging to Ḥamiʾohel,
bt mnḥm	daughter of Menaḥem"[24]

The seal belonged to the granddaughter of Yawbana, who probably came to Jerusalem as a refugee in the late eighth century BCE (see chapter 4). This would date the seal to the early to mid-seventh century, which fits with the paleography.

Seals belonging to women are relatively rare, and the name of Menaḥem's daughter—Ḥamiʾohel—is unusual. For example, the divider used between the first and second line on the seal is a fish, which is not known from any other seals. Most seals have a simple single or double dividing line. What could be the meaning of this fish? Some have suggested that this was a symbol of fertility. I doubt it. It seems like scholars like to make everything about sex and fertility when it comes to women in the ancient world. Here I think a more mundane interpretation is called for. Fish were an important part of the diet of Jerusalemites. In just one excavation in the City of David more than ten thousand fish bones reflecting a variety of species were collected dating to the eighth century BCE.[25]

The fish image on Ḥami'ohel's seal should not be surprising. The use of the fish image reflects a particular moment in the history of Jerusalem—namely, a time when Jerusalem had significant commercial access to the Mediterranean Sea. Jerusalemites are eating fish as a regular part of their diet, which may seem somewhat unexpected. Or maybe it should not be. The influx of refugees beginning in the late eighth century can explain this. First of all, the much larger

FIGURE 8.4. Seal of "Ḥami'ohel, daughter of Menaḥem." Drawing by the author.

population created the need for additional food in Jerusalem.[26] Second, many of the early refugees came from the northern kingdom, which had more access and experience with the Mediterranean ports like Akko and Dor. Finally, it also suggests the expansion of Judah's economic borders and a growing trade industry. The fish used as a divider makes for an ornate individual seal, but it also connects the fishing trade with this particular seal impression. This seal also indicates major vectors through which women would have gained scribal skills—namely, training within a family of professionals and participation in commerce. Perhaps the use of a fish in Ḥami'ohel's seal reflects her role as a merchant in the fish market in Jerusalem. Indeed, to account for all the fishbones in the Jerusalem excavations, we must imagine there was a "Jaffa Fish Market" in Jerusalem. Fish were brought in daily from the nearest coastal port at Jaffa and sold in Jerusalem. Maybe, Ḥami'ohel worked in this commerce. The truth is, we don't know for sure, but this would certainly make sense of the unusual fish image on Ḥami'ohel's seal.

Recently, archaeologists discovered a new seal impression excavated in the Givati Parking Lot, which was an ancient administrative area of Jerusalem just south of the Temple Mount. This finely executed seal read "Belonging to ʿElihana, the daughter of Gaʾel" (*l ʿlyhnh bt g ʾl*). Although ʿElihana or her father are not known in biblical literature, this seal was discovered in the Givati Parking Lot excavations, where a seal impression, "Belonging to Nathan-Melek, Servant of the King" (*lntnmlk ʿbd hmlk*), was also discovered. Unlike ʿElihana, Nathan-Melek is known from the story of Josiah's reforms where he seems to be an important bureaucrat (2 Kgs 23:11). More generally, this area of Jerusalem features prominent and large buildings that suggest it was an extension of the administrative area of the Ophel just to the north. We may surmise that ʿElihana also had some role in the Jerusalem bureaucracy.

The "Strong Wife" poem suggests that women did indeed work in commerce and that it involved scribal training. To be sure, a limited number of women probably received scribal training. At the same time, scribal skills were increasingly useful in a complex economy like we see in Judah and Jerusalem during the last several decades before the Babylonian destruction. To the extent that women participated in the activities of this economy, we would expect them also to be among those educated with scribal skills. It is certainly true that urbanization and an increasingly complex economy in eighth-century Judah led to the spread of writing throughout society. As the saying goes, a rising tide lifts all ships. In this case, complex economic activities led to the opportunity for more female scribes working in a variety of professions. We get just a glimpse of this in the inscriptional record.

A good parallel for understanding female literacy and scribal training can be found in the administrative texts from Elephantine in southern Egypt.[27] A large cache of papyri and ostraca dating especially to the Persian empire is known (ca. 539–333 BCE). The Jewish women in Elephantine are featured in a variety of legal and administrative texts. They had broad rights, held powerful positions, and played significant roles in everyday administrative affairs. These roles suggest that women acquired and used scribal skills in the daily activities related to corporate welfare and economics. They were able to own property and acquire wealth. To be sure, scribal skills seem to have been mostly pragmatic for women at Elephantine, but they provide an excellent comparison to think about female literacy in ancient Israel. They were primarily applied to activities of daily life, both economic and administrative. It certainly reminds us of the activities of the "Strong Wife."

Biblical Texts

Several biblical texts are attributed to women. Most prominently among these is the "Song of Deborah," which begins, "And Deborah (and Barak, son of Abinoam) sang on that day . . ." (Judg 5:1). One might object that this is not attributed to Deborah but rather to Deborah *and Barak*. Actually, this example is instructive. The Hebrew verb here is explicitly marked as a feminine singular. So Barak is an afterthought. More than this, the song is partially couched in the first-person voice of Deborah herself: "I will sing to the LORD," and even more tellingly, "I, Deborah, arose as a mother in Israel" (vv. 2, 7). Now some translations like to voice this latter verse in second person: "You, O Deborah, arose. . . ." This is possible. However, the Hebrew is grammatically in the first person and one must resort to preservation of ancient northern dialects to read it this way. Are we participating in the marginalization of Deborah when we translate the text by marginalizing her voice? It seems possible. Perhaps in a similar way the song points straightforwardly to Deborah as its ultimate author, but tradition somehow felt it necessary to include Barak. Was it necessary to include Barak's name to include the song in later canon of Scripture? This seems to reflect a marginalizing and patriarchizing tendency in the editorial and interpretive processes of the Hebrew Bible.

The case of Deborah and Barak reminds us of an even more famous example of woman's authorship that may have been supplanted by male scribes. Here, I am thinking of the so-called "Song of Moses." Exodus 15 introduces the triumphant song at the Red Sea (v. 1):

Then Moses (and the sons of Israel) sang this song to the LORD, "Sing to the LORD, for he has triumphed gloriously; the horse and the rider he has thrown into the Sea."

When Moses completes his song we find a short reprise of it (v. 21):

> And Miriam, the prophetess, Aaron's sister, took a tambourine in her hand, and all the women went out after her with tambourines and dancing. And Miriam sang to them, "Sing to the LORD, for he has triumphed gloriously; the horse and the rider he has thrown into the Sea."

It's the same song! Word for word. But Miriam only sings one verse. Moses and company get first billing, and they get the entire song in their name. I find it hard to believe that Miriam would have been mentioned at all unless it was first of all a song under her name. Later, the "Song of the Miriam" (or "The Song of the Sea") got sucked into a later scribal Mosaic vortex where everything gets ascribed to Moses. It gives the song Mosaic authority, but it also marginalizes the ancient female author. This was probably not an uncommon process in the copying, editing, and canonization of the Hebrew Bible.

The Book of Proverbs also has several indications of female authorship and influence. To begin with, there is the prominent place of Lady Wisdom as a tutor, which I have already mentioned. There are also multiple admonitions discussed above like "Hear, my son, your father's instruction, and do not reject *your mother's teaching*" (1:8; cp. 6:20; 10:1; 15:20; 23:22). Some might point out that the father comes first, but parallelism does not think that way. Rather, the final line is usually the climactic part of the parallel. The mother's voice should be understood as having at least equal importance here in education.

The most direct attribution of female authorship in Proverbs is the collection beginning chapter 31, "The words of Lemuel, King of Massa, that his mother taught him" (v. 1). This is a rather curious introduction to this short collection. Who is this Lemuel? Later Jewish tradition identifies him with Solomon, but there is no real explanation for why Solomon would be called Lemuel. Indeed, he is the King of Massa, not king of Israel. No, I would say this cannot be Solomon. Massa was an obscure Arabian kingdom (see Gen 25:4), and it makes sense to see these proverbs as part of the anthological impulse in biblical literature, in this case collecting various wisdom traditions in the Book of Proverbs.[28]

Proverbs are a bedrock of ancient scribal curricula throughout the near east, so it is significant that the collection here harkens back to a female sage. Another example of foreign wisdom sayings adapted and incorporated into Proverbs is the Egyptian text *The Instruction of Amenemope* used in 22:17–24:22.[29] So it is not unique to incorporate foreign wisdom literature into the Bible. What about the author—his anonymous mother? She is the fount of these proverbs, yet she goes unnamed and gets supplanted by her named son. It is also worth noting that these verses, the teaching of Lemuel's mom, serve as a preface to the final acrostic poem about the "Strong Wife." This juxtaposition seems intentional. Both texts can be attributed to the female scribal tradition.

Late biblical literature traces this female scribal tradition all the way back to the venerable King Solomon. Ezra has a list of "Solomon's Servants" that seems to include female scribes. In the NRSV translation, it reads, "The descendants of Solomon's servants: Sotai, *Hassophereth*, Peruda, . . ." (2:55). What looks like a Hebrew name here, *Hassophereth*, can be read as literally the Hebrew word for a female scribe (*soperet*) with the definite article (*ha-*). Confirmation for reading this as a term for female scribes can be found in the almost exact parallel text in the Book of Nehemiah, "The descendants of Solomon's servants: Sotai, *Sophereth*, Perida, . . ." (7:57). The variation in spelling is merely the lack of a definite article, but it also proves that this was originally simply the noun for a female scribe and not a personal name. But it is difficult to know what is going on in these lists. The variations suggest that an archaic list was being incorporated by later scribes into their historical works. The Persian scribal community that compiled the Books of Ezra and Nehemiah clearly thought this old list was important. But they did not seem to quite understand it. We might be critical and suggest that they were intentionally writing female scribes out of the record. I am not so sure, though. It must have been difficult to decipher old records from centuries before, and later Persian priestly scribes had little experience with female scribes. So it could be that they just could not comprehend a female scribe. But the result is the same—namely, a female scribe gets written out of the biblical record.

The tendency to write female scribes out of biblical literature in its transmission leaves us in a difficult position. We clearly see references to a female scribe or scribal community, but it's hard to do much with it other than point out that there seems to have been a tradition of female scribes dating back to the days of Solomon. The easy option is to dismiss examples like Sophereth as merely a personal name, but that just further obscures old traditions of female scribes, and that is the problem that we've been facing throughout this chapter—namely, the tendency to write female scribes and authors out of the biblical tradition.

Huldah, the Prophet

A particularly important figure during the late Judean monarchy is Huldah the prophet. She plays a key role in the Josianic Religious Reforms, as described in 2 Kings, and it all begins with the discovery of a book—a hidden scroll. And yet, Huldah is a relatively unstudied figure among biblical scholars.[30] The story is told in chapters 22–23, and it begins as follows: "The high priest Hilkiah said to Shaphan, the scribe, 'I have found a scroll of the *Torah* in the house of the LORD'" (2 Kgs 22:8). Shaphan then brings the scroll to Josiah, reads it aloud, and the king is stricken with remorse for their sins as well as concerned about their fate as a result. He sends a delegation to Huldah, a female prophet. It is quite a delegation—the high priest Hilkiah, the scribe Shaphan, and three others—the junior scribe Ahikam; a courtier, Achbor; and an official named Asaiah. Why a delegation of five people? Huldah must have been a person of some importance.

Huldah is given an unusually long description to identify her. She is "Huldah, the prophetess, wife of Shallum, son of Tikvah, son of Harhas, Keeper of the Wardrobe, who lived in the Mishneh Quarter of Jerusalem."[31] She has her own title, and she is connected by her husband to three generations of a family that had courtly connections as "the Keeper of the Wardrobe" (v. 14). I am not sure what this position is. It seems like some sort of royal valet, but I cannot help thinking of the wardrobe in *The Chronicles of Narnia*. In medieval Britain, the King's Wardrobe referred to his private household and closest advisors as well as a place where the king's clothing, armor, and treasures were kept. This seems like a good way of thinking about the position. In short, Huldah was an important and well-connected advisor to the king. This fits well with the title "Prophet," as already discussed in chapter 6. Huldah is a well-connected person within the Judean administration. It is striking that the biblical story turns to a female prophet, a woman government advisor, to give consul to the king. As Francesca Stavrakopoulou has emphasized, Huldah's story is clothed in the stuff of the state, even if she herself was not in the direct employ of the government.[32]

It follows that Huldah was likely well educated, including learning to read and write.[33] Her speech to King Josiah uses all the typical formulae of scribal learning. The contents are twofold. First, she outlines a program of religious reforms that Josiah follows. Second, she predicts that Josiah will go to his grave "in peace" because he has repented and followed the strictures of the found scroll. Ironically, scholars often suggest the antiquity and authenticity of her speech because the latter part of her speech was *not fulfilled*. In fact, Josiah died in a battle with Pharaoh Neco at Megiddo (2 Kgs 23:29).

Huldah's speech is often aligned with Deuteronomy because the Josianic Reforms have been loosely correlated with strictures in Deuteronomy. Judging from the central role that Huldah has in prompting the reforms, we can infer that she was well positioned with that scribal community. Some have even speculated that Huldah was the author of the first edition of the Deuteronomistic History,[34] but this has not garnered widespread support. She does seem to be affiliated with a scribal community, but which community? Judging by her spatial location— the Mishneh of Jerusalem—she was not directly affiliated with the government. The *Mishneh* (Hebrew, מִשְׁנֶה) or "Second District" of Jerusalem was located on the Western Hill, opposite the City of David and the Ophel where the old aristocracy and the royal bureaucracy were located. It is likely adjacent to an area known today as the Givati Parking Lot, which is currently being excavated by Tel Aviv University.[35] They have already found several prominent buildings and inscriptions in the excavations there, including the seal of ʿElihana and the seal impression of Nathan-melek. Presumably, the *Mishneh* was named for its secondary settlement and therefore importance. It was located on the northeastern side of the Western Hill, which is also where many of the Israelian refugees (post-721 BCE) as well as refugees from the Judean foothills (post-701 BCE) would have settled. Huldah seems well connected, but she did not have a seat in the halls of power or among the Jerusalem aristocracy. She does not live in the old town—that is, in the City of David. She lives in the Mishneh—an important, but secondary expansion of Jerusalem. These different neighborhoods probably tell us something about their inhabitants.

Huldah's real kindred spirit is Jeremiah, who was also an outsider in Jerusalem. For example, when Huldah's speech declares that Jerusalem "will become a desolation and a curse" (2 Kgs 22:19), she uses an expression that appears *repeatedly and exclusively in the Book of Jeremiah* (see chapter 10) but not in Deuteronomy (see Jer 25:18; 42:18; 44:12, 22; 49:13). In other words, Huldah's prophecy seems to have directly influenced the scribal community that compiled the Book of Jeremiah. Huldah is a critical and underappreciated figure in the early Persian scribal community that shaped the editing of the Book of Jeremiah. The point here is not that she *authored* the works but rather that she was an influential member of the scribal community, and this is the role she plays in the Book of Kings. A distinguished delegation appointed by the king comes to her, and she provides a vision for Jerusalem and a direction for the king and his people.

Summary

Ancient Israelite attitudes were undoubtedly complex with regard to gender roles, as all societies are. Just like today, societies can have orthodox or fundamentalist groups advocating for quite restricted roles for women outside of the household, but at the same time there are quite progressive groups advocating for inclusion and equality for women. There is no reason to think that ancient Israel was any different, and these different attitudes were likely felt on the ground through history in its ebbs and flows. In the end, we do see a tendency to minimize and marginalize the role and voice of women in the Hebrew Bible. At the same time, women's voices are not completely eliminated, and strong women like Miriam, Deborah, and Huldah remain. A significant and professional role for women began at the top with the pivotal role that the Queen Mother played in the royal court. Education and literacy undoubtedly began with the elite classes, but it spread to other professions in the late Judean monarchy. One might suppose that female scribes became more common during the later monarchy, but that is probably only because writing in general became more common. Early figures like Deborah and Miriam should warn us against dismissing female scribes in earlier periods. Indeed, female scribes are also attested in neighboring cultures in a variety of historical periods.

A grave error in seeking women in the writing of the Bible is to focus too narrowly on authors. For example, the idea the Huldah wrote Deuteronomy is as problematic as attributing to her the book of Jeremiah.[36] Women probably were not the sole authors of biblical books, but they were a part of the communities that produced biblical literature. For example, I would prefer to envision Huldah as an influential member of the scribal community that created the Josianic edition of the Book of Kings. Her respected position in the community is underscored by her role in the narrative of Josiah's reforms. There are other individual female voices in the Bible such as the "Song of Deborah," but the preservation of their voices depended upon their being a part of communities of scribes. As we have seen, there were female scribes, and they were part of communities and professions. We can hear their voices in certain scribal communities, and their voices were marginalized particularly by the priestly scribal community.

Women can be identified across many professions and positions in ancient Israel. Figures like Jezebel and Athaliah ascended to the throne and must have had support in some segments of society, even though they are portrayed negatively in the final editing of the Bible.[37] Deborah leads Israel into battle, and Yael plays a pivotal role in the defeat of the Canaanites in the Valley of Jezreel. Women are named as prophets who advised kings, and the role of the prophet(ess) particularly utilizes the literary forms of scribal education. There is every reason to think that part of their education included scribal training, even if "scribe" was not their profession. Biblical and inscriptional evidence also suggests that women were involved in economic and commercial transactions where reading and writing would have been an important part of their education. In most segments of society where writing and literacy may be found, we also may find evidence of women. To be sure, their numbers were probably limited, but they are not absent. The exception is in the temple and among the priests. There are no female priests in the Bible and little evidence for female priests in the archaeological record for Israel.[38] Priestly and temple scribes in the Persian, Hellenistic, and Roman periods were the final editors of the biblical canon. These were the gatekeepers that suppressed the role of female scribes in biblical literature, but they did not erase them. And when we look closely, we can glimpse the role that women professionals played in the ancient Judean scribal communities.

9

Priestly Scribal Communities

JERUSALEM AND THE PERIPHERY

I vividly remember the first paper I gave on priestly literature. It was at an international conference in Cambridge, and it was at the very beginning of my research into the anthropology of writing in the Hebrew Bible. I began with simple lexical studies. For example, where do you find the Hebrew verb "to write" (*ktb*) in the Bible? I was surprised to find that it was not really found much in the priestly literature. I dug a little deeper and discovered that there is no account of receiving a *written* law on Mount Sinai in the pentateuchal priestly literature. What about the Hebrew word *tôrah*, which comes to be associated with the Pentateuch in tradition? In pentateuchal priestly literature, *tôrah* is "teaching" and not a text. In contrast, in post-exilic priestly literature like the Books of Ezra-Nehemiah, Chronicles, and Jubilees, there is a keen sense of the *writtenness* of a *Torah*—that is, the Hebrew word *tôrah* becomes *Torah* with a capital "T." This seemed like a good observation to expound upon for my invited talk in Cambridge. But the lecture seemed to go down like the proverbial lead balloon. What did I do wrong? I had challenged a scholarly orthodoxy that believes that the so-called "Priestly Document" of the Pentateuch is an exilic or post-exilic creation. My observation still stands. But, of course, it is more complicated than that.

In this chapter, I will begin telling the story of priestly scribal communities. The priests have been a focus of biblical scholarship going back to the days of the famous work of Julius Wellhausen on the "Documentary Hypothesis" in the nineteenth century. Wellhausen identified a priestly source of the Pentateuch (usually referred to simply as P), along with three other sources. In brief, Wellhausen argued that the Pentateuch was composed of four documents—J, E, D, and P—the latest of these, the P source, was composed and edited in the exilic and post-exilic periods.[1] And it was a priestly author that ultimately edited the whole Pentateuch. Wellhausen's theory has dominated biblical scholarship during the twentieth century, but the consensus supporting it has evaporated.[2] Even as its influence has waned, the centrality of the P source for understanding the formation of the Pentateuch has not. There are some important insights that should form a foundation for biblical scholarship.

The beginnings of the Jerusalem Temple date all the way back to the tenth century BCE, and it makes sense to look for temple-affiliated scribal communities dating back to the earliest period of the monarchy. Priestly scribal communities certainly predated the late editorial and canonizing activities in the heyday of the rebuilt "Second" Temple in Jerusalem. To be sure, priestly scribes were central during the post-exilic or Second Temple period. In fact, as we shall see (chapter 12), they were largely the only game in town during the Second Temple period. This is because Hebrew writing would be essentially confined to the rebuilt temple, and Aramaic became the administrative *lingua franca* of Persian Yehud. Hebrew was something that priests used during the Persian period, but priestly communities acquired scribal skills and used writing long before the destruction and rebuilding of the temple. The main difference between the First and Second Temple periods is that during the Iron Age priestly communities were not the only ones writing in Hebrew.

Priestly scribal communities are both early and late. They date back to the Iron Age, and they come to the fore in the Persian and Hellenistic periods. In this chapter I will focus on the early priestly scribal communities during the First Temple period. When was the first priestly scribal community active? There might have been some priestly scribal activity dating back to the earliest establishment of the Jerusalem Temple, but that is hard to prove definitively. We can find some evidence of priestly writing and scribes among late Iron Age inscriptions. This includes priestly writing outside of Jerusalem among the peripheral temples and shrines. This will be especially evident in priestly inscriptions related to the Arad Temple. They represent some evidence for priestly scribes among the regional towns and villages. In the end, however, any literature associated with rural or peripheral priestly communities had to come to Jerusalem if it was to be collected, edited, and preserved.

Priestly Inscriptions

The priestly inscriptional evidence begins in the eighth century, when writing more generally began to flourish. Admittedly, the corpus of inscriptions from priestly scribal communities is small. It includes at least the following: inscribed bowls, the Arad Temple inscriptions, the Ketef Hinnom Amulets, and a few seals and seal impressions.[3] Taken together, these inscriptions point to unique scribal communities of practice that distinguished themselves from other scribal communities.

Where can we look for priestly inscriptions? You might think that we should start in Jerusalem. Unfortunately, the location of the ancient temple in Jerusalem (today known as the Temple Mount) has not been excavated. The Temple Mount became the location of Islamic sacred places, the Dome of the Rock and the Al-Aqsa Mosque, since the seventh century CE, so that means for practical reasons it cannot be properly excavated. So there will not be very much from the Jerusalem Temple scribal community. I used the words "properly excavated" because various types of digging have happened. For example, beginning in the nineteenth century various European explorers dug tunnels under the Temple Mount looking for the treasures of the Solomonic temple as well as the treasures of biblical history. Such activities certainly created a certain mutual distrust among the current caretakers of the Temple Mount, the Islamic Waqf authorities, which contributed to making any current archaeological activity near the Temple Mount particularly politically and religiously sensitive.

One recent construction activity on the Temple Mount—or as it is called by Muslims, the Haram esh-Sharif or "Noble Sanctuary"—has also provided us with some controversial archaeological material—

namely, the Temple Mount Sifting Project.[4] In November 1999, the Islamic Waqf authorities removed about nine thousand tons of dirt from the southeastern corner of the Temple Mount in order to construct the underground el-Marwani Mosque. Normally, such an operation might have been preceded by a lengthy and costly salvage operation, but not in this case. The southeastern corner of the Haram was excavated quickly using heavy machinery, and about 350 dump trucks of dirt from the construction activity were dumped into the Kidron Valley. Theoretically, this area of the Jerusalem might have included inscriptions relating to the temple and the priestly community. Afterward, a salvage project sifting the truckloads of dirt began in 2004 under the direction of one of my former teachers, Gabriel Barkay. Gabi, a recipient of the prestigious Jerusalem Prize, was horrified by the potential lost history, including the history of the First Temple. They have now sifted much of the recovered dirt and discovered many artifacts and inscriptions related to the history of the Temple Mount in Jerusalem.

The most interesting fragment of evidence attesting to the priestly administration of the temple is a fragmentary seal impression of the "son of Immer."[5] The seal impression is broken in half (see Figure 9.1), but it has been reconstructed as follows:

[lh]ṣlyhw   "[belonging to Hi]tziliah,
[bn] ʾmr   [son of] ʾImmer"

This is striking because Immer seems to be a member of a prominent priestly family known from the end of the Judean monarchy. The Book of Jeremiah identifies a certain Pashhur, son of Immer, who persecutes Jeremiah:

> The priest Pashhur son of Immer, who was the chief officer in the Temple, heard Jeremiah prophesying these things, and Pashhur struck him and put him in the stocks that were in the upper Benjamin Gate of the house of the LORD, and the next morning Pashhur released Jeremiah from the stocks. (20:1–3a)

Who is this Pashhur, son of Immer? Immer is a fairly uncommon name, and the date of the Immer seal impression would make Pashhur and Hitziliah contemporaries, perhaps even brothers. The archaeological location of the Hitziliah, son of Immer, seal impression—that is, from the Temple Mount—strengthens the identification of Pashhur and Hitziliah as brothers. The family was apparently strongly entrenched in the Temple administration judging by Pashhur's title "chief officer of the Temple."

The adversarial relationship between Pashhur and Jeremiah is an inner-priestly conflict that is emblematic of Judah in the Iron Age. There were two different locales for priests—Jerusalem and everywhere else. Pashhur (and his brother) were entrenched in the Jerusalem Temple hierarchy, whereas Jeremiah was an outsider. Jeremiah was born into a priestly family, but Jeremiah's family was from Anathoth, which is a village five miles north of Jerusalem. Jeremiah's family was not connected with the administration of the Jerusalem Temple like the family of Immer. This conflict introduces us to an inner-priestly conflict between the central priests (like the Immer family) and the peripheral priests (like Jeremiah).

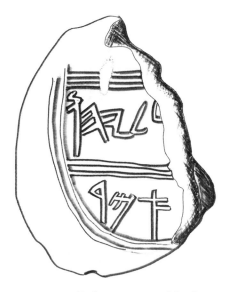

FIGURE 9.1. Seal impression of the "Son of Immer" from the Temple Mount. Drawing by the author.

The story of two different priestly scribal communities can also be told through the archaeology of temples and shrines in late Iron Age Judah. Looking outside of Jerusalem, there are not many Judean temples or shrines in the archaeological record, and they mostly seem to disappear after the eighth century BCE.[6] Yohanan Aharoni excavated one excellent archaeological exemplar at the Iron Age fortress at Arad (Figure 9.2). His excavations also discovered a cache of more than a hundred inscriptions. Most of the inscriptions relate to military activities, but he found eighteen inscriptions near the temple that can be related to the cultic activities as well.[7] Although most of the inscriptions are small and

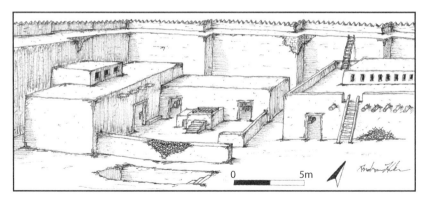

FIGURE 9.2. Temple within Arad Fortress. Drawing by Andrew Herbek.

fragmentary, the temple and its inscriptions give us the perfect place to start exploring a priestly scribal community.

Arad was a peripheral site for ancient Judean priests located about seventy miles south of Jerusalem in an arid region that receives about six inches of rain per year. The fortress was founded at Arad in the early Iron Age (about 1100 BCE), and seven different archaeological layers of the Judean fortress were uncovered stretching from the early Iron Age down to the end of the Judean monarchy (about 600 BCE). A temple was probably built within the fortress during the tenth century and then went out of use at the end of the eighth century BCE.[8]

The Arad Temple went out of use before the religious reforms of King Josiah. The eighth-century decommissioning of the temple accords with a brief notice in the Book of Kings about King Hezekiah: "He removed the high places, broke down the standing stones, and cut down the *Asherah*" (2 Kgs 18:4). In comparison with the account of Josiah's Reforms, which spans two chapters (2 Kgs 22–23), this is exceedingly brief. That it is preserved at all suggests that there was something to it. The decommissioning of peripheral shrines follows nicely with the centralization of political power in Jerusalem under Hezekiah, which also is quite clear in the archaeological record. The question remains: What would happen to peripheral priests working in local shrines if Hezekiah tried to centralize worship in Jerusalem? Any decommissioning of shrines would

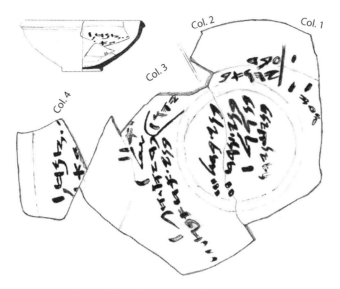

FIGURE 9.3. Priestly bowl inscription (Arad no. 49). Drawing by the author.

have been extremely disruptive to local economies in towns and villages. Of course, the Assyrian military campaigns were also quite disruptive and would have overshadowed and maybe even helped enable a religious disruption caused by decommissioning local shrines.

Who were the priests serving at the Arad Temple? One of the remarkable inscriptions discovered near the entrance to the sanctuary at Arad is a fragmentary bowl with names of the cultic personnel.[9] The text is written on the bottom of a complete bowl and seems a bit disorganized in its presentation (Figure 9.3). The inscription is not on an ostracon—that is, on a broken piece of pottery. It was originally written on a complete bowl that likely was still being used. Aharoni thought that there was also some writing on the inside of the bowl, but it was too faded to make any sense of it. So, the only text we can read is on the outside. We should assume that the inscription had to do with the purpose of the bowl. Some names are written on the base of the bowl, and there seem to have been four columns visible, separated by three lines—two visible and one reconstructed. I've added a line that I suspect separated column 2 (ll. 8–9) and column 3 (l. 10). Judging from column 4, the lists on the outside of the bowl would have had six or seven lines each. In total, there were four preserved lists with one on the base and three other lists of names written around the outside of the bowl. Beginning with the base, I would read the lists as follows:

Base

1) Apprentices of Beẓal,   3
2) Apprentices of Koraḥ,   2
3) Apprentice of Gilgal,   1
4) Apprentices of K[ona]iah,   1

*Col. 1 (around **from** right to left)*

5) [   ],   1
6) [   ],   1
7) [Yah]uʿaz,   1

Col. 2

8) Obad[iah,   X]
9) Jehoab,[X]

Col. 3

10) [ ]iah,   1

Col. 4

11) [Apprentic]es of Ṣemaḥ,   1
12) [ ]daʾ[ ]l[,   X]
13) [ ],   2
14) Shuʿal,   1
15) Pedaiah, W(heat),   11
16) Apprentices of Aḥab,   3

One interesting aspect of this inscription is the mention of "apprentices." Here I am translating the Hebrew word, *bn*, as "apprentice" based on my discussion in chapter 1, even though it is usually translated as "son." In this particular inscription, scholars have wondered why the inscription omits the fathers, but this is not a problem if we understand *bn* as relating to Levitical priestly guilds. The apprentice relationships are familial, but not necessarily family.

Several names on the bowl have direct priestly or Levitical affiliation.[10] For example, Beẓal (line 1) seems to be the shortened version of the name of the famous Temple craftsman, Bezalel, who supposedly knew how to do "any work in the construction of the sanctuary" (Exod 36:1; also see Exod 31:2; 38:22; 2 Chr 1:5). Although we should not directly connect the name Beẓal with the biblical figure, names do run in families or clans. The "Sons of Koraḥ" were a well-known guild of Levites who worked as temple singers (e.g., Num 26:58), and line 2 could refer to a similar Levitical guild. Many psalms are attributed to the Sons of Koraḥ; for example, "For the Director. A Maskil of the Sons of Koraḥ" (Psalm 42; see also Psalms 43–49, 84–88). Koraḥ was one of the principal clans involved in temple worship and leadership. According to biblical genealogies, Koraḥ was the grandson of Kothah, one of the three sons of Levi (e.g., Exod 6:18; 1 Chr 6:22–24).[11] The Levitical Kothahite clan, however, is associated with towns in the north—that is, in Israel and not Judah (see Josh 21:20–26). Were these Arad priestly workers originally from the north? Perhaps. But they would've lost their jobs when the Arad Temple was decommissioned in the late eighth century. Their names, however, still make it into the biblical psalter. This might suggest that the Jerusalem priesthood incorporated unemployed peripheral priests by giving them jobs as temple service personnel but not as temple priests proper. That would have been a very practical solution to the decommissioning of peripheral temples and shrines.

Several names in Arad 49 point to northern identities. For example, Gilgal (l. 3) is known as a northern town. We don't have Gilgal as a personal name, but maybe it refers to a clan that came from Gilgal. The name Aḥab (l. 16) is one of the more prominent names that have northern connections—Ahab was a ninth-century king in Samaria.[12] What are northern affiliated names doing here in the south at the Arad Temple? Actually, it fits with the pattern of archaeological evidence at places like Kuntillet ʿAjrud, an Israelian caravan fortress deep in the Negev. Although deep in the south, Kuntillet ʿAjrud was built and maintained by the northern kingdom. Although Judah was geographically closer to the Negev, trade in the southern Negev was dominated by Israel. This makes some sense since Israel had better access to the Mediterranean coast and an economic partnership with Phoenicia that could leverage maritime commerce. Judah may have participated in the trading partnership, but it would not have been the primary partner. Thus, these inscriptions from the eighth century and earlier could reflect aspects of early Israelian trading and economic activity in the Negev. Alternatively, northern refugees may have found employment in the fortress at Arad. The Levites also had connections with northern tribes, as we see in many biblical stories (e.g., Judges 18). Until the fall of Samaria, the stronger, wealthier, and more powerful northern kingdom overshadowed Judah, and these Arad inscriptions offer further tangible evidence of this relationship.

Arad 49 is part of a larger group of inscriptions found in and adjacent to the temple (nos. 50–57, 60–62, 65, 67–70, 87, 89, 94, 95, 100–103). Unfortunately, they are all quite fragmentary, but several have names with well-known temple affiliations in biblical literature (e.g., Meremot, Pashhur, Azariah, Shebaniah). The excavator thought some of the ostraca might have been used for casting priestly lots. Maybe. Some look like temple transactions; for example, ostracon no. 60 reads, "I weighed 27 ḥekats (of wheat)." All of these inscriptions were excavated in archaeological strata dated to the late eighth century BCE or earlier.[13] After the eighth century, no inscriptions were discovered in the area of the sanctuary. The dating makes sense in the history of the temple. Sometime after the destruction of Samaria in the late eighth century BCE, the Arad Temple was dismantled, and Arad became strictly a Judean fortress. Was the temple dismantled because the shrine had northern religious affiliations? That is a difficult question to answer.

Aharoni also excavated two "holy bowls" in front of the altar in the sanctuary at Arad. They are complete and have two letters, *qš*, scratched on the inside edge of the hard pottery after firing. The inscription on the inside is unusual since inscriptions usually are written on the outside of complete vessels. Writing on the inside probably relates the purpose of its contents. Most scholars think the inscription *qš* is an abbreviation for the Hebrew word *qdš*, meaning "sacred" or "holy."[14] There are several other holy bowls that have been excavated at other places that have the unabbreviated inscription *qdš* "holy." The writing itself consecrates a mundane vessel for its sacred purpose.

Another puzzling aspect of these holy bowls is that the handwriting uses Phoenician-style letters. Until the ninth century, there was a general form for alphabetic letters that was used widely from Phoenicia and Aram all the way down to Judah in the south. Scholars believe this standardized alphabetic writing originated in Phoenicia and spread throughout the Levant in the early Iron Age. However, by the ninth century, individual national scripts had supposedly developed, including a Hebrew national script.[15] But if this were the case, why are the Arad holy bowls still using Phoenician script? In this case, I think scholars have it wrong. There was no single national script, but rather certain letter shapes were learned in different scribal communities. They reflect the communities of practice in different professions. Different scribal communities could develop idiosyncratic scribal conventions of lexicon, orthography, and paleography. The differences in language between various Pentateuchal sources have long been recognized by scholars; this evidence would extend the observation to spelling and handwriting conventions. Many of these conventions were shared, but communities of practice would also develop their own unique features. What scholars have thought of as a single Hebrew national script is really the practice of the official governmental and military scribal community. Priestly scribal communities had their own conventions, which were conservative and retained some old Phoenician characteristics. The holy bowls are not written in Phoenician script; they are written in an old priestly script.

The holy bowls themselves continue a ritual tradition that stretches back into the second millennium BCE.[16] Examples of such votive bowls with inscriptions in Egyptian hieratic script are known in ancient Canaan from Lachish and Tel Sera during the Late Bronze Age. In some ways, this is not surprising. After all, this actually fits nicely with the general distribution of the sacred bowls found throughout Israel. In addition to examples from the Judean sites of Arad and Beersheba, we find examples of dedicatory bowls at the Philistine site of Ekron and the northern Israelite site of Hazor. The bowls are of different shapes and sizes, which suggests that they were used for different types of offerings. In other words, these sacred bowls are not merely a Judean ritual phenomenon. The various priestly and Levitical communities outside of Jerusalem shared ritual practices and also scribal practices.

There is one more unusual example of a dedicatory bowl that further illustrates ritual practices. Early in the twentieth century, Scottish archaeologist Duncan Mackenzie excavated at the Judean city of Beth-Shemesh, where he found a complete bowl with three letters chiseled on the inside: *ḥk* (see Figure 9.4).[17] But how could it be translated? The interpretation at first puzzled scholars. The letters were oddly shaped, and the meaning was unclear. More than fifty years after Mackenzie's excavations, Gabriel Barkay reexamined the bowl and suggested that the inscription should be related to the function of the bowl as an offertory for "your [poor] brother." It's very straightforward Hebrew, but unparalleled. Barkay related it to priestly texts like Leviticus 25:25–48 that use the expression "your brother who sinks into financial difficulty [*yāmûk ʾaḥîka*]" when discussing social justice and giving to "your brother." And "your brother" refers to general kinship with the people of Israel rather than a narrowly defined family. By this reading, the bowl was placed in a shrine or a temple for gifts to the poor.

The unexpected aspects of the "Your Brother" inscription extend to the shape of the letters themselves. All three letters are unusually shaped. For example, the *ʾalef* is written with a rounded c-shape and a vertical bar rather than the typical pointed c-shape that we see in other Hebrew inscriptions. And these letters are chiseled, which means that they were carefully written after the bowl was fired.[18] How do we explain the unusual handwriting? The eminent French epigrapher André Lemaire again identified them as a Phoenician-style script.[19] We have already seen that the two Arad holy bowls allegedly had "Phoenicianizing" script,

FIGURE 9.4. Beth-Shemesh "Your Brother" inscription. Adapted from Gabriel Barkay.

but this makes little sense. These are Judean cultic objects. The script must be Judean, but it reflects a priestly community of practice in peripheral settings. It is worth pointing out that we have not found any similar examples of holy bowls from Jerusalem. At this point, this absence of evidence seems significant. It may reflect a peripheral scribal community that was conservative and retained Phoenician influences. Phoenician script itself is quite conservative in its development, so in this respect it all comes together nicely. It is also important to reiterate that none of the bowl inscriptions are later than the eighth century BCE. That is, none can be securely dated later than the religious reforms of Hezekiah.[20]

Ketef Hinnom Amulets

One of the most striking priestly inscriptions are two amulets excavated in a tomb on the shoulder of the Hinnom Valley (in Hebrew, *Ketef Hinnom*), just outside the ancient city of Jerusalem. Ketef Hinnom was a family tomb complex, and archaeologists identified one tomb repository with the skeletal remains of at least forty-three people in the tomb dating to the late Iron Age. But the most sensational find was the silver amulets dating to the end of Judean monarchy (ca. 600 BCE).[21] The location of the tomb is also instructive—namely, it was a new tomb cut during the seventh century and far away from the Temple Mount. Normally, the dead are buried immediately outside the city. So, for example, the early tombs of Iron Age Jerusalem were located on the slopes of the Kidron

1
2
3
4
5
6
7
8
9
10
11
12
13
14
15
16
17
18

FIGURE 9.5. Ketef Hinnom amulet 1. Drawing by Marilyn J. Lundberg, West Semitic Research.

Valley and near the City of David—that is, where settlement began.[22] There are also tombs on Jerusalem's northern periphery, which would also have been close to the Temple.[23] The location of the Ketef Hinnom tomb reflects the expansion of the city to the west, mainly by refugees. The first tombs for the early refugees from the north were cut into the eastern slopes of the Hinnom Valley, like the tomb of the family of Menachem.[24] The well-known Ketef Hinnom tomb is even further away from the city, on the western slopes of the valley, reflecting the second wave of refugees from the Judean foothills in the seventh century.

The amulets are small. The first (KH1) is slightly larger, but still only 97 mm (3.8 inches) long (see Figure 9.5). The second one is smaller—only 39.2 mm (1.5 inches) long—but more complete. The script is small, which may explain some of its unusual features. But the authors also suggest another probable explanation—namely, that the paleographic and orthographic idiosyncrasies might reflect a "scribal school or locality."[25] Conservative spelling, for example, is something we have already seen in other priestly inscriptions.

These amulets lend evidence further for a specifically priestly scribal community, in this case in Jerusalem.

The two amulets may be translated as follows:

Ketef Hinnom 1: ¹May Yahweh ²[. . . ³the] grea[t, who keeps] ⁴the covenant and ⁵[the] loyalty toward those who lo[ve him ⁶and] toward those who keep [his ⁷ commandments . . . ⁸] the Eternal One [. . . ⁹the] blessing from any [. . .] ¹⁰snare and from the evil ¹¹because in him is redemption,¹²because Yahweh ¹³[shall] restore him. [¹⁴]May Yahweh bless ¹⁵ him. And ¹⁶may] he protect you, [may ¹⁷] Yahweh shine ¹⁸[his] face ¹⁹toward you.]

Ketef Hinnom 2: ¹[For PN, son of -ya]h, may he be blessed ²to Yahweh. ³the warrior and ⁴and the One who expels ⁵[E]vil: May bless you ⁶Yahweh, may he ⁷protect you, ⁸may Yahweh shine ⁹his face ¹⁰upon you, and ¹¹grant to you ¹²pe[ace].

The amulets made a sensation by their apparent quotation of the Priestly Blessing: "May Yahweh bless you and keep/protect you, may Yahweh make his face to shine upon you and be gracious to you, may Yahweh lift up his face upon you and grant you peace" (Num 6:24–26). This would make them the earliest known biblical quote in an inscription.[26] In truth, the picture is more complicated. First of all, it is not an exact quote. It is a paraphrase. At the same time, the similarities between the amulets and the Priestly Blessing are certainly striking, and there can be little doubt that the amulets and Num 6:24–26 come from a shared ritual tradition. In his book, *The Priestly Blessing in Inscription and Scripture,* Jeremy Smoak points out that the blessing in the amulets and the Book of Numbers fits with the so-called "Holiness Code" in the Bible.[27] The biblical Holiness Code is identified with ten chapters in the Book of Leviticus (chs. 17–26). These chapters form their own section with priestly literature, but holiness is not limited to a few chapters of Leviticus. It is a broader theme that can be associated with priests that had been working at rural sanctuaries and then came to Jerusalem.[28]

There are other ritual traditions used in the amulets. For example, Ketef Hinnom 1 lines 3–8 uses another significant shared tradition—the divine attribute formula known from a variety of biblical texts, for example, "the faithful God who keeps his covenant and loyalty for those who love him and for those who keep his commandments for a thousand generations" (Deut 7:9).[29] It clearly shares a knowledge of this formula, which is worked into the amulet. The divine attribute formula is a shared ritual tradition that was likely used in a variety of religious contexts judging by its repeated reuse in biblical literature.

The biblical texts used in the amulets have liturgical literary contexts. For example, the context of the Priestly Blessing in Numbers 6 underscores a ritual context: "The LORD spoke to Moses, saying: Speak to Aaron and his sons, saying, Thus you shall bless the Israelites: You shall say to them, 'The LORD bless you . . .'" (vv. 22–24). Likewise, Deuteronomy 7:9 shows clues of an oral and liturgical framework since it begins in v. 7 with a parallel to the liturgical text "Know that the LORD your God, he is God," using a well-known liturgy from Psalm 100:3.[30] And the divine attribute formula itself gets incorporated in a variety of ways into biblical literature (cp. Deut 7:9 with Exod 34:6–7, Num 14:18, and Mic 7:18–20). It is unlikely that texts using the divine attribute formula are quoting one another as textual citations; rather, they are recalling and reworking a well-known liturgical formula known from ritual contexts. The amulet engravers knew such texts from liturgy and from memory, not from consulting texts. They were not citing the Bible; they were recalling tradition and invoking memorized ritual texts.

The amulets were certainly made in a priestly scribal setting, but who bought the amulet? Was it a priest? A Levite? It is hard to know, and the tomb artifacts do not yield any further direct clues to the identities of those buried there. The location of the tomb itself is fairly remote from the Temple in Jerusalem, and it was a family tomb—as mentioned, archaeologists identified at least forty-three people in the tomb remains. It seems unlikely that it belonged to an old priestly family directly affiliated with the Temple because it was so remote from the Temple. The oldest burial ground in Jerusalem is Silwan, just across the Kidron Valley and close to the Temple Mount and the City of David. This is where the old families of Jerusalem would have been buried. Still, the Ketef Hinnom tomb is very nicely cut and elaborate, so the family had some financial means. Maybe the tomb belonged to a family of peripheral priests? Hard to be certain, but that is how I imagine the family. Priestly refugees from a small village in the Judean foothills who came to Jerusalem in the early seventh century. In any case, the content of the amulets certainly reflects priestly writing, even though the owners of the amulets and the tomb remain a mystery.

Priestly Seals and Seal Impressions

It is quite difficult to identify seals and seal impressions that might have belonged to members of a temple scribal community. The best way to identify a priestly seal would be the title "Priest" (Hebrew, *khn*). But no seal or seal impression has ever been *excavated* that includes this title. There are seals and impressions with titles, but none have priestly titles. Is this a problem with our evidence, or does it tell us something about the priestly scribal community? I would suggest the latter. For example, the huge Temple Mount sifting project has discovered several seals and seal impressions, but none with the title "Priest." This suggests that priests were not involved in everyday administrative tasks that involved owning seals and sealing documents. But there is the one seal impression from the Immer family, which shows that priests could own seals. However, they identified themselves by their family patronym rather than a title. Seals with titles tended to be owned first by government officials. The practice of using seals seems to have spread for economic purposes to a wider population. Even so, seals seem to have been owned by government officials, administrators, and even various types of merchants and craftspeople, not usually priests.

There is one famous example of a priestly seal, but it is probably a forgery. It is a seal set within a ring that reads, "Belonging to Ḥanan, son of Ḥilkiah, the Priest" (*lḥnn bn ḥlqyhw hkhn*).[31] Of course, we know someone with the name Hilkiah. He is mentioned in the story of King Josiah's Temple reforms (2 Kgs 22:4ff.). This could be his son's signet ring. Unfortunately, it came from the antiquities market, and that makes it quite suspect. And it is unique, which is also suspicious. We have excavated quite a bit in Jerusalem and around Israel, and we have no other examples like this "Priest" signet ring. In the hundreds of examples of excavated seals and seal impressions, we just do not find any from the temple or from priestly personnel with titles. In contrast, there is a wide variety

FIGURE 9.6. Seal impression of "Azariah, son of Ḥilkiah." Drawing by the author.

of administrative titles known from inscriptions, seals, and seal impressions (as discussed in previous chapters).

We can identify at least one member of the Jerusalem priestly scribal community from a seal impression. This is the seal impression that apparently belonged to a priest, "Azariah, son of Hilkiah" (Figure 9.6). To begin with, it was excavated in the City of David.[32] The owner is likely the same Azariah, son of Hilkiah, who is known from genealogical lists in Chronicles.[33] In 1 Chronicles 5:27–41, we find a list of high priests from the beginning down to the Babylonian exile. These include in verses 39–41 the last priests of the Jerusalem Temple before its destruction (also cp. 1 Chr 9:10–11 and Ezr 7:1):

Shallum begot Hilkiah,
Hilkiah begot Azariah,
Azariah begot Seraiah,
Seraiah begot Jehozadak,
and Jehozadak went into exile.

It apparently belonged to a high priest in Jerusalem, and it gives tangible evidence of the priestly scribal guild during the late Iron Age in Jerusalem. Hilkiah is, of course, the name of the priest who found the scroll that inspired King Josiah's religious reforms. This would be his son.

Azariah's seal impression was part of a well-preserved hoard of bullae found in a jar dating to the Babylonian destruction of Jerusalem in 586 BCE. Context is always important. In this case, the collection was excavated in a hoard of forty-nine seal impressions that included a seal impression from "Gemariah, son of Shaphan," a scribe who is known from the Book of Jeremiah.[34] Both fathers, Shaphan and Hilkiah, were involved in the Josianic religious reforms. According to 2 Kings 22, Josiah sends his scribe, Shaphan, to the high priest Hilkiah at the temple with orders to collect money and restore the temple. Then the high priest supposedly discovers a lost scroll and gives it to the king's scribe: "Hilkiah gave to the scroll to Shaphan, who read it" (v. 8). This unleashes a chain of events—Shaphan reports to the king, the king consults the prophetess Huldah, and the king orders religious reforms to be carried out in compliance with the words of "the scroll of the *Torah*." The biblical account as well as these seal impressions suggest that this priestly family was intimately involved with the political levers of power in Jerusalem during the Josianic reforms.

In sum, there is not nearly as much inscriptional evidence for priestly scribal communities as there is for royal, administrative, and military activity. But there is some evidence, and it suggests two different communities. Of course, there was one community in Jerusalem related to the Temple. But there is striking evidence, especially at the Arad Temple, of priestly scribes outside of Jerusalem. In addition, the phenomenon of the holy bowls found at a variety of different sites suggests that the peripheral priestly community was loosely affiliated and shared traditions. Ultimately, however, these traditions all come to Jerusalem, as we shall see.

Two Temple Reforms and the Priestly Scribal Communities

The history of priestly scribal communities has diachronic and spatial dimensions even before the destruction of the temple by the Babylonians in 586 BCE. During the First Temple period, there are two defining moments—the Reforms of Hezekiah and Josiah. These Reforms would also shape the spatial aspects of priestly scribes by marginalizing the non–Jerusalem Temple priests. The Reforms also provided the opportunity for peripheral priests and their literature to come to Jerusalem, even though they were marginalized. This seems to be the situation described in 2 Kings 23:9: "The priests of the high places did not make offerings on the altar of the LORD in Jerusalem, but they did eat unleavened bread with their fellow priests." This might suggest that the peripheral priests were employed in the service to the Jerusalem Temple rather than as priests offering sacrifices in the Temple. Eventually, the Babylonian conquest forced a consolidation of any diverse elements within the priestly community.

While two religious reforms (Hezekian and Josianic) in the late monarchy shaped the priestly scribal communities, the second one—the Josianic Reform—has received the most attention by scholars. This is a natural consequence of the amount of space it gets in the biblical narrative, fully two chapters in the Book of Kings (chs. 22–23). Historically speaking, the first reform—the Hezekian Reform—was probably at least as significant, if not more so. But Hezekiah's Reform is recounted in just one verse in the final editing of the Book of Kings: "He removed the high places, broke down the standing stones, cut down the sacred poles ['Asherah], and crushed into pieces the bronze serpent that Moses had made, for until those days the people of Israel had made offerings to it—and they called it *Nehushtan*" (2 Kgs 18:4). It is a striking statement, but there is not much there. Fortunately, archaeology can fill in additional background for the two reforms.

Archaeological evidence is no respecter of the editorial processes of the Bible. In this case, recent archaeological evidence points to a profound temple reorganization that took place in the late eighth century BCE—that is, in the days of Hezekiah (r. 715–689 BCE). For example, temples and shrines at Arad, Beersheva, Lachish, and Moẓa disappeared in the eighth century, long before Josiah's Reform (ca. 622 BCE).[35] This does not mean that some peripheral shrines did not continue after Hezekiah's reform, only that Hezekiah's reform began the centralizing process. It likely did not happen overnight. Still, according to the archaeological record we now have, Hezekiah's reform was a turning point for independent temples and shrines in Judah in the late eighth century. We should recognize here that religion and politics are intertwined. As we have seen, there was a growth and centralization of power in Jerusalem in the late eighth century. This was influenced by the rise of the Assyrian Empire—by globalization, by trade, and by profound demographic changes (urbanization as well as refugees). Both political and religious power were centralized in the capital in the late eighth century.

Hezekiah's centralization of worship in Jerusalem created two different stories for priests.[36] First there were the priests who had served in shrines and temples outside of Jerusalem, and then there were the priests in the Jerusalem Temple. With the destruction of rural shrines, both by religious centralization and by Assyrian invasions, many priests came into Jerusalem. They were essentially refugees. They brought their literature and traditions, but they were largely marginalized when they first came to Jerusalem in the late eighth and early seventh centuries. As refugees in Jerusalem, they became aligned with the *Am Ha'aretz*, another rural group that was displaced in wake of Assyrian military campaigns. The late eighth and early seventh centuries saw Jerusalem growing and economically flourishing. It was an ideal place to consolidate their traditions and create new alliances. They represented the conservative traditions of the countryside. They were marginalized, but their time would come.

The second group of priests were the old Temple priests in Jerusalem. The Hezekian reforms centralized political and religious power in Jerusalem. It placed the Jerusalem Temple and its priests in a position of prestige, privilege, and power. But there is an ebb and flow to political and religious power. Beginning in the time of Hezekiah, Israelian political and religious refugees (people like Menachem, son of Yawbana) were given positions of power and prestige in Jerusalem. Hezekiah consciously incorporated Israelian tradition into his court, including naming a newborn royal prince, Manasseh, after one of the prominent tribes in the north. The Jerusalem Temple even incorporated aspects of Israelian religious tradition during the days of King Manasseh (r. 689–642 BCE; see 2 Kgs 21:3).

The Josianic Reforms were a conservative reaction to these trends. The Josianic Reforms began with the rural political group, the *Am Ha'aretz*, who put Josiah in power (as discussed in chapter 7). The *Am Ha'aretz* were allied with the rural priests, who finally got a place at the table in Jerusalem during the Josianic Reforms (ca. 622 BCE; 2 Kgs 23:9). There seems to have been a merging of the interests and literature of the old Jerusalem priestly community with the rural priests during the Josianic period. Hilkah, who found the scroll in the Temple, is the critical figure here. The name Hilkah has a long Levitical tradition, but he also becomes associated with the line of the high priests in Jerusalem (e.g., 1 Chr 6:13–15). Hilkiah also happens to be the name of the father of the priest Jeremiah

(Jer 1:1; see chapter 10), who was from a group of priests from the village of Anathoth. So the name has deep priestly roots, including among the peripheral priests.

Biblical Priestly Literature

The inscriptional evidence has pointed us to two priestly scribal communities. One was associated with the Jerusalem Temple, which grew in power and prestige with the centralization of the temple and the cult beginning in the late eighth century BCE. The work of this group may be reflected in the Immer family seal impression. The seal impression of Azariah, son of Hilkiah, excavated in the City of David highlights the presence and scribal activity of this priestly community in the elite areas of Jerusalem. A second priestly scribal group, which I will now call the *Levitical priestly community,* was associated with peripheral shrines and eventually came to Jerusalem as a result of both religious centralization and Assyrian destruction of the countryside. Cultic and demographic centralization was important to the coalescing of these two priestly scribal communities.

Levitical Priestly Community

Who were the rural priests? I think they are best understood as related to the history of the Levites.[37] Who were the Levites? They were a landless group that became associated with the temple and Temple service. The landless status of the Levites suggests they were refugees, perhaps related to Assyrian military campaigns. Sometimes we see the expression "Levitical priests" in biblical literature, and this goes back to their origins. They were originally landless and tied with rural shrines, so they were not originally and primarily in Jerusalem. The Assyrian and Babylonian invasions change a lot of things, including the place and role of the old Levites (that is, Levitical priests). They come to Jerusalem, and eventually the Levites are formally affiliated with Temple service in the Persian period. The origins of this Temple service, however, may go back to the Iron Age.

I want to think pragmatically for a moment about the Levitical priests. They are a product of a clan-based and land-based society. The problem with this social structure is that inheritance and land can get subdivided among many sons and impoverish a family. So in order to avoid dividing property inheritance among too many sons, non-firstborn sons could be given over to temples as priests (or put into the military or even government). Children were apprenticed as priests in peripheral shrines and temples. They became landless and derived their livelihood as Levitical priests. A good biblical example of this is the boy Samuel, who was given by his parents to be an apprentice to the priest Eli at the temple in Shiloh (1 Sam 1:22–2:11). Samuel is one of the most famous Levites in the Bible (1 Chronicles 6), even though he originally seems to have been an Ephraimite (2 Sam 1:1). Judging from the example of Samuel, Levites apparently lost tribal affiliation and became landless when they were apprenticed at a shrine. The Hebrew word *Levite* literally means "joined to." So, becoming a Levitical priest describes this process of becoming joined to a shrine, that is, becoming a landless priest. As these peripheral sanctuaries increasingly included scribal training as part of the apprenticeship, the Levitical priests also became a scribal community.

The Levitical priestly scribal community aligned itself with other social groups that were disenfranchised by the centralization of power in Jerusalem. To be specific, the Levitical priests became aligned with the *Am Ha'aretz* (see chapter 7). They were both refugee groups in Jerusalem. It seems likely that as refugees the Levitical priests and the *Am Ha'aretz* were marginalized in the late eighth and early seventh centuries BCE. They both represented facets of the countryside that were marginalized by the growth of Jerusalem and the centralization of political and religious power. But there is an ebb and flow to power that would eventually bring them to the fore.

The Jerusalem Priestly Community

A natural focal point for a priestly scribal community was the Jerusalem Temple. And Jerusalem always seems to have been the focal temple in Judah. There is evidence of other shrines (e.g., Beersheva, Lachish) and smaller temples (e.g., Arad, Moẓa), but there are not a lot of temples and shrines in the archaeological record, relatively speaking.[38] For example, during the Late Bronze Age at least twenty temples have been identified from excavations, and this number is based on a much smaller excavated sample size than the Iron Age. There are many more excavated Iron Age sites. So, where were the Judean temples? They are hard to find in the archaeological record. Even the Jerusalem Temple, for example, is known mostly from literary records and archaeological parallels. The few other Iron Age temples that apparently existed—e.g., Arad, Beer-sheba, and Moẓa—apparently disappeared by the end of the eighth century BCE, that is, in the time of Hezekiah, not Josiah.[39] In this respect, the Jerusalem Temple had no serious rivals that could have served as alternative social locations for a priestly scribal community. This also seems different from the northern kingdom, which seems to have had multiple major shrines at Bethel, Samaria, and Dan. By contrast, Jerusalem seems to have been the central sanctuary in Judah. But Judah was quite a small kingdom compared to Samaria. One major shrine seems to have been enough.

The lack of other temples also raises a serious question about exactly what Hezekiah and Josiah's centralization reforms were. Indeed, by the time of Josiah's Reforms, there do not seem to have been many temples for Josiah to destroy. The reform seems to take credit for something that happened almost a century earlier. Even if there were some shrines that Josiah's reforms dismantled, Josiah still seems to have taken credit for his predecessor's actions. Josiah's Reforms also refer to foreign priests (kᵉmārîm) at high places around Judah, so this may refer to some shrines that arose in the wake of neo-Assyrian influence. Perhaps, but we do not find much evidence in the archaeological record. Maybe there were smaller shrines that did not leave a large archaeological footprint. Indeed, judging from the archaeological record, there never seem to have been large numbers of formal temples around Judah at any time. Most of the peripheral temples that might have existed were apparently dismantled in the days of King Hezekiah. Read in this light, we may notice that the Josianic account actually takes credit more for the cultic purification of the Jerusalem Temple and its environs rather than a destruction of other sanctuaries. While the Hezekian narrative mentions centralization, it is quite abbreviated. Hezekiah's religious reforms take just one verse (2 Kgs 18:4), but this verse focuses on the destruction of high places outside of Jerusalem. This contrasts sharply with the two chapters detailing Josiah's religious reform that are focused on Jerusalem itself (2 Kgs 22–23). The reforms were remarkably inclusive of the priests from the various shrines who "ate unleavened bread with their fellow priests" (2 Kgs 23:9). Josiah seems to have used the long disenfranchised peripheral priests to support his religious purification.

A focus of Josiah's reforms was on northern religious (and presumably political) influence in Jerusalem. It was a natural political and religious backlash to the influence northern refugees had in Jerusalem beginning in the early eighth century. Hezekiah seems to have invited it as a way of strengthening his power. With Josiah, the political and religious ebb and flow is in the reverse direction. The narrative of Josiah's reform mentions destroying shrines "in the towns of Samaria," and it lingers on the destruction of Jeroboam's high place at Bethel (2 Kgs 23:15–20). It suggests there was a continuing active cult in Samaria and the north in the late Iron Age (see chapter 11). This polemic against Jeroboam and Samaria wraps up a narrative trajectory that began in 1 Kings 12:25–13:32; in other words, it concludes a major narrative arc in Jerusalem.[40] In this respect, even the supposed destruction of Bethel is actually about Jerusalem. In sum, a careful reading of the Josianic reform suggests that Jerusalem priests had aligned themselves with the Levitical priests and were redefining normative cultic practice to exclude northern religious practice. They were trying to impose a new orthodoxy. This included an appeal to authoritative texts—alternatively called "the scroll of the covenant" or "the scroll of the *tôrah*." Texts were part of the new orthodoxy.

The priest Hilkiah finds a scroll in the Temple (2 Kgs 22:8). The scroll is first read to the king, and later the king himself apparently reads the scroll to all the people (2 Kgs 23:2). This also recalls Deuteronomy 17:18, where we are informed that "the king is to write out for himself on a scroll, a copy of this *tôrah* taken from the *Levitical priests.*" Apparently, the Levitical priests were caretakers of "this *tôrah*," which is a reference to the Book of Deuteronomy itself.[41] We should acknowledge, however, that it is unclear exactly what scroll Hilkiah finds in the Temple. Is it supposed to be Deuteronomy? Or perhaps it is the Holiness Code. We can see influences of both texts in some of the details of Josiah's Reform. It is also noteworthy that the references to the "Scroll of the Covenant" in 2 Kings 23:2 and 21 seem to point back to the covenant ceremony in Exodus 24:7 and yet another text, perhaps the Covenant Code. Or maybe the identity of the found scroll in 2 Kings 22–23 is intentionally ambiguous. The scroll's identity may have changed as the story was told and retold. In any case, the scroll is "found" by a priest, and that makes all the difference.

Writing and scribalism were not a focus of the temple community during the Iron Age. Temples are the place from which God *speaks* and where the priests *sacrifice*. This is borne out by the inscriptional record, in which priestly inscriptions are relatively rare. Most of our Hebrew inscriptions relate to the state and its administration, trade, and military activities—not temple administration and the cult. At the same time, writing was used in the temple and by priests. We have evidence of writing for the administration of temples, and writing served a numinous role in priestly rituals.

Priestly Writing in the Bible

What is characteristic of priestly writing in biblical literature? This is something that scholars have discussed for generations.[42] A lot of priestly literature was mundane and administrative—namely, lists of personnel, gifts, or sacrifices. It also incorporated temple rituals and liturgy. In fact, temple liturgies were part of general scribal curricula in Mesopotamia, and they likely were in Israel as well. Priestly writing also included laws and other legal matters. Finally, priestly writing reflected aspects of the divine and numinous.[43]

Several examples in biblical literature illustrate divine and numinous writing in priestly texts. My first example comes from the priestly account of the origins of the tabernacle, the temple, their paraphernalia, and the Sabbath law. These are framed by a biblical narrative that begins in Exodus 24:12. It begins, "The LORD said to Moses, 'Come up to me on the mountain, remain there, and I will give you the tablets of stone—the instruction and the commandment—that I have written for their instruction.'" Then God gives the instructions on how to build his temple in chapters 25–31. This section concludes in chapter 31 with the giving of the Sabbath commandment (31:12–17), and then the narrative wraps up as follows: "When God finished speaking with Moses on Mount Sinai, he gave him two tablets of a Pact, tablets of stone, written by the finger of God" (31:18). It has a classic priestly framing to a narrative that provides a divine origin to the desert Tabernacle, and by extension the later Temple, and also attaches the central priestly commandment—the Sabbath—as part of that divine writing and communication. It recalls examples of the divine plans for Mesopotamian temples that were written on the divine Tablets of Destiny,[44] and it has deep connections to neo-Assyrian technical literature that suggests that it dates back at least to the neo-Assyrian period (that is, eighth and seventh centuries BCE).[45] More than this, this example introduces us to a fundamental aspect of priestly writing—namely, its potentially sacred character.

The sacred character of priestly writing is well illustrated in its ritual use. A classic example of the ritual use of writing is the *Soṭah*, or "Ritual of Bitter Water," described in Numbers 5. This ritual uses writing as an ingredient for a ritual potion that divines whether a woman has committed adultery: "Then the priest shall put these curses in writing and wash them off into the water of bitterness. He shall make the woman drink the water of bitterness that brings the curse and bitter pain . . . if she has defiled herself and been unfaithful to her husband" (vv. 23–27). The written words themselves are put into the water as part of the potion! We see here that writing is a component of priestly ritual, and we can imagine how sacred bowls or amulets could function in priestly rituals.

There are excellent contemporary analogies to the ritual use of writing in magical texts elsewhere in the near east. For example, there are Egyptian Execration texts where curses with the names of enemies are written on clay figures or bowls and then ritually broken. The writing is part of the power of the ritual. Execration texts date back to the early second millennium BCE, so this kind of ritual use of writing in religion is quite old. The parallel with the Egyptian Execration texts brings us to a third biblical example of God's "Book of Life." At one point God threatens to wipe out Israel, saying, "Whoever has sinned against me, I will blot out from my book" (Exod 32:33). The divine book—which is also known as "the Book of Life" (see Dan 7:10, 12:1; Rev 20:15; 21:27)—is related to an old taboo in biblical literature about the taking of a census—that is, writing down names in a list. It apparently was thought to have a dangerous ritual component as we read in Exodus 30:12, "When you take a census, during their registration, you shall give a ransom for their lives to the LORD so that no plague may come upon them for being registered." Priestly law required that a sacrifice be given for each individual whose name was written down. Written words had power.

The ritual use of writing included priestly texts and even included priestly garments.[46] According to Exodus 28 and 39, the Aaronite priests were to make priestly vestments. Among these garments was the ephod, which was a vest adorned with gems, engraved with the names of the twelve tribes of Israel:

> You shall take two onyx stones, and *engrave on them the names of the sons of Israel*, six of their names on the one stone, and the names of the remaining six on the other stone, in the order of their birth. As a gem-cutter engraves signets, so you shall engrave the two stones with the names of the sons of Israel; you shall mount them in settings of gold filigree. You shall set the two stones on the shoulder-pieces of the ephod, as stones of remembrance for the sons of Israel; and Aaron shall bear their names before the LORD on his two shoulders for remembrance. (Exod 28:9–12)

The garments were topped off with a golden rosette, fastened to a turban, and engraved with the words "Holy to the LORD" (Exod 39:30). The writing here is important for making the priest himself an incarnation of divine presence and favor for the priests and all the tribes of Israel. Writing is here not an administrative tool but a ritual tool. The physical descriptions of writing in priestly literature underscore its powerful ritual use.

Priestly writing could also be mundane. The more mundane and typical type of priestly writing are lists. Priests needed to keep records and make lists, and lists were a staple of all elementary scribal curricula.[47] Indeed, lists and records are the foundation for the invention and development of writing itself. So, even if we do not quite understand the priestly list of names in Arad 49, it illustrates the more mundane utility for writing among priestly communities, and we see this in biblical literature as well. A classic example of this are stories of census taking and genealogical lists. In that respect, it is appropriate that the Book of Numbers begins with a priestly census of all the people. There are a variety of priestly lists including journeys, sacrifices, and temple utensils as well as other types of lists. Lists are not unique to priestly communities, but priests also took advantage of the pragmatic utility of writing.

These examples illustrate types of priestly writing that can be found throughout the ancient near east as well as biblical literature in all periods. In this respect, it is difficult to tie priestly literature to a scribal community in any particular time or place. When we look for ancient Hebrew inscriptions that might tell us about priestly scribal communities, we find three types of examples. The most sensational would be the two priestly amulets. The second kind of inscriptions are inscribed holy bowls that have been found in a variety of excavations around Israel. Finally, there are more mundane administrative texts—that is, lists, seals, and seal impressions—that inform us about the organization of priestly communities as well as their use of writing for everyday functions.

PART THREE

A Scribal
Community
Survives

Extinction is the rule. Survival is the exception.

—CARL SAGAN, *THE VARIETIES OF
SCIENTIFIC EXPERIENCE*

10

Exiled Scribal Communities

THE STORIES OF JEREMIAH AND EZEKIEL

Jeremiah and Ezekiel were both priests. In that respect, they continue the legacy of priestly scribes. But they came from different priestly communities and traveled very different paths. Their stories will help us understand the story of priestly scribal communities as these communities begin to unravel following the Babylonian invasions of Judah and Jerusalem. The Babylonians campaigned against Jerusalem and Judah at least three times—in 597, 586, and 581 BCE—and each campaign was followed by a wave of exiles. We tend to focus on the 586 BCE campaign that concluded with the ransacking and burning of Jerusalem, but the Jerusalem priest, Ezekiel, had already been exiled during the 597 BCE campaign. He illustrates the Babylonian "brain drain" of Jerusalem— that is, the taking of artisans, craftsmen, scribes, and other people that could be useful to the empire into captivity. The stories in the Book of Daniel also reflect the Babylonian brain drain that disrupted the various scribal communities in Judah. It reflects the realia of exile: "the king commanded his palace master Ashpenaz to bring some of the Israelites, who were schooled in every branch of wisdom and endowed with knowledge and insight, to serve in the king's palace and to be taught the literature and language of the Chaldeans" (Dan 1:3–4). Whether their stories are historical or literary, figures like Ezekiel or Daniel were useful to the Babylonians because they acquired scribal skills.

The brain drain from Judah also resulted from refugees fleeing to Egypt. The most prominent Egyptian refugee was Jeremiah. After the destruction of Jerusalem, Babylonians set up a puppet ruler, Gedaliah, in Mizpah. But he was assassinated, and this led to another Babylonian campaign against Judah in 581 BCE (see Jer 42:1–2). After Gedaliah's assassination, a remnant fled to Egypt as refugees, including Jeremiah, who seems to have been forcibly taken to Egypt. Jeremiah was a priest, part of a peripheral priestly community from the Benjaminite village of Anathoth (about 5 miles north of Jerusalem). According to the Book of Jeremiah, he was taken to Tahpanhes in the western Nile Delta (see Jer 43:4–8). Other large populations of Jewish refugees are known from southern (Upper) Egypt at Elephantine. Nile Delta cities like Leontopolis and Alexandria would later become home to groups of Jewish refugees. All of which is to say, not all Judahites were forcibly deported. Some fled and became refugees, mostly in Egypt. Thus, the depopulation of Judah and Jerusalem was a process that followed in the wake of several Babylonian military campaigns.

The Babylonians destroyed the larger cities and towns, but some small agricultural villages survived. According to archaeological surveys and excavations, over the course of a few decades, the population declined by as much 85 percent, and the continuity was mostly in smaller agricultural villages.[1] The entire economy and infrastructure of Judah collapsed. In other words, there was little context for the scribal communities that had flourished in Jerusalem and around Judah during the late monarchy. In order to follow the scribes, we must go with them to the places they were exiled or fled.

The Babylonians set up administrative centers that had their own scribal communities. These centers had their own related scribal infrastructure. For example, a settlement at Ramat Raḥel, just south of Jerusalem, seems to have continued as an administrative center even after Jerusalem was destroyed.[2] Archaeologists like Oded Lipschits have excavated and analyzed the lion stamp impressions that reflect Babylonian administration at sites like Ramat Raḥel. The Moẓa seal impressions are another vestige of Babylonian and early Persian administration. But we should be clear: such seal impressions from the sixth century are relatively few compared with earlier and later periods. More significantly, they testify to an emerging Aramaic administrative community that served the imperial administrative interests. This is not the place to look for a Hebrew scribal community.

Scholars have suggested that Hebrew scribes may have simply relocated. For example, there was a new center for Babylonian administration in the region around Mizpah a few miles north of Jerusalem. Was there a thriving scribal community there that collected and wrote a lot of biblical literature? Some scholars have suggested a robust scribal community at Mizpah writing biblical literature, but it is not likely. Why might such a theory arise? First of all, some scholars like to locate the composition of most biblical literature primarily in later periods—the Babylonian, Persian, and even the Hellenistic period. Mizpah gives them a convenient location to begin since it was an early location of Babylonian administration (2 Kgs 25:25; Jer 41:1–13). Scholars also noticed the prominent place that the Benjaminite town of Bethel plays in biblical literature, although I already discussed this town in chapter 4 because Bethel was destroyed in the eighth century BCE by the Assyrians.[3] Moreover, Mizpah isn't Bethel. One cannot simply interchange the two. Moreover, archaeological evidence still indicates that Bethel was destroyed in the eighth century and only very minor settlement continued. It was not the great Hebrew scribal center. Finally, if Babylonian administration continued in the Mizpah region, this administration would have used Aramaic and not Hebrew. The Hebrew language was still a marginalized vestige of the past in the scribal administration.

The sixth century, after the Babylonian conquest of Jerusalem, represented both a great crisis for scribal communities and the opportunity for unprecedented autonomy. It was a crisis that surely must have threatened the very survival of scribal communities. They had lost the social institutions that supported them; the disruption must have been profound. Writing takes money and patronage. Papyrus had to be imported from Egypt, and it wasn't cheap. Parchment requires an elaborate manufacturing process. Writing requires resources and patronage, especially in antiquity. At the same time, the crisis represented opportunity.

Scribes were no longer bound to strong institutions and well-developed communities of practice of the previous generations. They could forge a new path. That gave them a certain amount of autonomy even while it threatened their livelihood and indeed their very existence. But perhaps it is in such a crisis that the individual voice of the scribe, as opposed to the collective voice of the community, would be most easily heard. Indeed, the Book of Ezekiel gives us the first example of an extended literary autobiography. It gives us the voice of the individual, a priest detached from his community of practice.

Especially in the crisis of the sixth century, scribes still needed communities and patrons. So we continue in our search for Hebrew scribal communities during the Babylonian period. There are a few solid anchors in material culture to distinguish the (short) Babylonian period (586–539 BCE). To the south, the fortress at Ramat Raḥel continued as a Babylonian and Persian administrative center, but its occupants would have been imperial administrators. They would have worked in Aramaic; not surprisingly, only Aramaic inscriptions were found in the excavations there. To the north, there were only a few major conflagrations of cities in the Benjamin region that can be assigned to the Babylonians. Some sites like Gibeon were destroyed by the Babylonians, but others like Mizpah survived. Even though some towns in Benjamin survived, the population of the region still suffered a major decline during the Babylonian period. The number of towns and villages in Benjamin decreased from about 157 in the Iron Age to only 39 in the Persian Period.[4] There were no major cities. The attempt by the Babylonians to set up a local puppet government under Gedaliah at Mizpah failed.

Gedaliah, the Babylonian puppet, descended from the Jerusalem scribal family of Shaphan. In this respect, he might have served as a promising conduit for the relocation and continuation of a Jerusalem administrative scribal community at Mizpah. Shaphan, his grandfather, is mentioned prominently in the story of the discovery of the scroll that precipitated Josiah's Reforms. It is easy to imagine this scribal community bringing literature to Mizpah. But the Mizpah government was quite short-lived. Gedaliah was assassinated in 581 BCE—just five years

after the destruction of Jerusalem—and the Babylonian military returned. Judean remnants (e.g., people like Jeremiah) fled. Even if all the
towns in the region were not physically destroyed, there is substantial
evidence of a dramatic decline in population throughout the region. So
the territory of Benjamin was not a good center for a thriving Hebrew
scribal community. Was it a last, brief, shining moment? Maybe, but
there's not much evidence to suggest any thriving Hebrew scribal community continued there.

The Babylonian period also marks a major shift in the language of
scribal communities—Aramaic becomes the standard language. The
Aramaic administrative training is reflected in biblical literature after
the destruction. For example, six chapters of the Book of Daniel are
written in Aramaic. More importantly, the book depicts Judean youth
being trained in the Babylonian and Persian courts, that is, in Aramaic chancellery. Likewise, the Books of Ezra and Nehemiah tell
stories of Judeans working in the Persian administration; parts of
Ezra are written in Aramaic; and both books show knowledge of Aramaic scribal education. Aramaic education was a readily available
infrastructure for scribal communities. The Assyrians had already
incorporated Aramaic as the *lingua franca* in the West, and the Babylonians had made Aramaic the *lingua franca* of the entire empire. The
Persians further institutionalized and standardized Aramaic scribal
education.

From Iran to Turkey to Egypt, we find inscriptions written in Aramaic,
appropriately named by scholars "Imperial Aramaic." This imperial dialect shows a uniformity across the entire ancient near east. Unfortunately, there are almost no inscriptions found in the Judean Hills dating
to the Babylonian period. A major exception is the Moẓa seal impressions, which scholars usually date to the sixth century or early fifth
century BCE.[5] The seal impressions use Aramaic script and language
and thereby confirm the use of Aramaic as a local administrative language beginning in the Babylonian period. The infrastructure for Hebrew scribal communities had been destroyed by the Babylonians, and
Aramaic chancellery replaced it. We must look elsewhere to follow the
Hebrew scribes and their literature.

Exiled Communities

We must look to the Diaspora for surviving Hebrew scribal communities. Scribes were exiled to Babylon. We know about the Babylonian exiles from a variety of sources. For example, a cuneiform account of the exile is preserved in the *Babylonian Chronicle*: "In the seventh year, the month of Kislev, the king of Babylon [Nebuchadnezzar] mustered his army and marched to Ḫatti-land [i.e., the Levant]. He encamped against the city of Judah and on the second day of Adar he took the city and captured the king. He appointed a king of his own choice there, received its heavy tribute and sent [them] to Babylon." The Bible also gives its account of the campaigns of Nebuchadnezzar and the exile to Babylon. Along with the historical accounts in the Book of Kings and Jeremiah, there are also liturgical reflections in the Book of Lamentations as well as among the compositions in the Book of Psalms. So we know about the exile from a variety of sources.

What about the specific fate of Judean scribes and scribal communities? Traces of Diaspora Hebrew scribal communities have in recent years come to light. One of the most remarkable discoveries is collected in an archive of cuneiform tablets, *Documents of Judean Exiles and West Semites in Babylonia*, published by Laurie Pearce and Cornelia Wunsch.[6] The documents are a collection of receipts and records that include many Hebrew names that may be identified with Judean exiles. They record them living in a place called Judah-town (Akkadian, *al-Yaḫudu*). One cuneiform tablet even includes Hebrew writing scrawled on its side (see Figure 10.1). This document is a barley receipt, and it is worth reading in its entirety:

> [Cuneiform] 13 kor of barley are owed to Gummulu, son of Bi-ḫame, by Shalam-Yama, son of Nadab-Yama.
> **In Simanu**, he will deliver the barley in its principal amount in the town of Adabilu. Dala-Yama, son of Ili-shu, guarantees delivery of the barley.
> **Witnesses**: Shikin-Yama, son of Ili-shu; Balaṭu, son of Nabu-natzir; and the scribe, Nabu-natzir, son of Nabu-zer-iqisha.

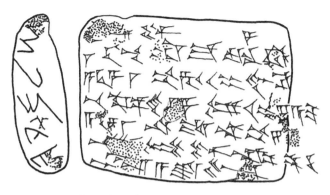

FIGURE 10.1. Cuneiform barley receipt with Hebrew name on the side. From Pearce and Wunsch, *Documents of Judean Exile*, no. 10. Drawing courtesy of Laurie Pearce.

Written in Judahtown, the 23rd day of Ṭebetu, the 6th year of the reign of Nabonidus, king of Babylon.
[Hebrew on side] *Shalamyah*[7]

The cuneiform receipt concludes with a time (ca. 550 BCE) and place (Judahtown) of the agreement. This place was a colony of Jewish exiles living in central Mesopotamia. This is only about thirty years after the last Babylonian exile from Judah, and this Jewish mercantile family retains the knowledge of Hebrew and the ability to write their name in Hebrew, although the writing of the cuneiform receipt required the services of a Babylonian scribe, Nabu-natzir. The name on the side of the tablet, Sha-lomyah (*šlmyh*), is written in distinctly paleo-Hebrew letters and parallels the name Shalam-Yama, written in cuneiform. It is ironic that the name for this Jewish exile means "the peace of Yahweh."

Given the date of this tablet (550 BCE), Shalomyah was probably born in the Babylonian Diaspora. His father, whose name in cuneiform *Nadab-Yama* may be translated into Hebrew as Nadabyah, was likely born in Judah and might have come as a young scribe with the exiles to Babylon. And so we get a glimpse here of the continuity of scribal communities in exile. Shalomyah probably learned Hebrew from his father while living in exile. At that time, Aramaic writing was also commonly used for administration in the Babylonian Empire, but

Shalomyah writes his name in a distinctly Old Hebrew script. But the cuneiform writing of their names does show distinct Aramaic and Assyrian influences. Thus, the cuneiform text writes using a typical Aramaic and Assyrian pronunciation, Shalam-Yama, and not Shalomyah as expected in Hebrew. There could not have been much economic reason for continuing to teach Hebrew scribal skills in the exile, but school learning and scribal skills are usually a traditional and conservative endeavor. A name like Shalomyah suggests an attempt to preserve culture and identity, and language is a critical part of the maintenance and preservation of identity. This family continued teaching the Hebrew script, and we may assume that other scribal families continued to teach Hebrew to the next generation. Exiles like the priest Ezekiel apparently continued to write and teach Hebrew. This meant that they also had to preserve texts as teaching curricula for their students and apprentices.

Another important collection of cuneiform tablets mentions the king of Judah, the royal family, and some of his administrative entourage who were living in Babylon. An archive of 290 cuneiform tablets was excavated in the Ishtar Gate leading into the city of Babylon during the 1930s. The documents are administrative lists that include dates spanning from 595 to 570 BCE, that is, beginning shortly after the first Babylonian exile. Several of the tablets mention the king of Judah, his sons, and his officials. Here is one example listing Judean figures receiving royal rations:

> 6 liters (of oil) for Jehoiachin, King of Judah
> 2½ liters for the 5 Princes of Judah
> 4 liters for the 8 Men of Judah[8]

The princes and men of Judah were likely still first-generation exiles. This reference to "Men of Judah" reminds me of the note in the biblical account of the Book of Proverbs: "These are the proverbs of Solomon that *the Men of Hezekiah* copied" (Prov 25:1). The phrase "Men of Hezekiah" in the Book of Proverbs refers to scribes working for the royal bureaucracy. Here, it's likely that the "Men of Judah" in the Ishtar Gate cuneiform text were also a remnant of the royal administration who likely had scribal training. They were in a good position to collect and preserve royal records and traditional literature from the old Judean kingdom. Let me foreshadow where I am going with this critical bit of information. I believe this is a huge clue that will lead us to a royal history of Israel (the Book of Kings) and the editing of books like Isaiah and Jeremiah later in the sixth century.

Before we get to the exilic collecting and editing of biblical literature, we should mention one other critical group of texts from Egypt. Thousands of papyri and ostraca were discovered from the island of Elephantine, which was a border town and fortress on the southern Egyptian border.[9] The documents include texts in Aramaic, Egyptian, Greek, Latin, and Coptic. The Jewish documents are written in Aramaic, date to the fifth century, and include letters and legal contracts. Some of the more notable documents include "the Passover Letter," which provides instructions for celebrating the Passover, and "the Request to Build a Temple" (ca. 411 BCE), written to the governors of both Jerusalem and Samaria requesting permission to rebuild their temple that had been destroyed in civil unrest in the town. They give us first-hand evidence for a mixed community of Jewish refugees living in Egypt following the Babylonian campaigns against Judah in the late fifth century. The first refugees may even have come from Samaria following the Assyrian campaigns and destruction of the northern kingdom in the late eighth century. Unfortunately, there is no evidence of Hebrew being written among these particular exiles. In that respect, they seem to have assimilated into the local and imperial linguistic culture.

One of the most fascinating texts from exiles in Egypt is known as Papyrus Amherst 63 (PapAm 63)—named after Lord William Tyssen-Amherst who purchased it—and it includes a biblical psalm! But it is not a strictly Jewish text. The papyrus is a diverse compilation of about thirty-five literary texts written in the Aramaic language using Egyptian Demotic script. It includes many different texts, including liturgical texts that relate to the Babylonian New Year festival as well as a court novella about the Assyrian king Assurbanipal (r. 669–631 BCE). Scholars think it may have originated in Elephantine, and the whole papyrus looks like it could have been compiled from various parts of scribal curricula.[10] This complicated text was already known at the end of the nineteenth century, but the texts remained mostly undeciphered for almost a century. The unusual combination of an Aramaic text written with Demotic characters baffled scholars. It was not until the 1940s that scholars realized that the unusual text was Aramaic written in Demotic script, and it was not until the 1980s that scholars realized that the text contained an Aramaic translation of Psalm 20![11] That begs the question: How does a biblical psalm get translated into Aramaic and end up in a fourth-century BCE literary papyrus from Elephantine? That is a good question. But it is an exercise in following scribes and scribal communities—that is, figures like Ezekiel and Jeremiah.

The translation of Psalm 20 into Aramaic distances it from the biblical psalm, but one can still recognize the general correspondence. It is best to put the two texts in parallel[12] to appreciate the similarities and differences:

Psalm 20	Papyrus Amherst 63, column XII, lines 11–19
[1] The LORD answer you in the day of trouble! The name of the God of Jacob protect you! [2] May he send you help from the sanctuary, and give you support from Zion.	May Yaho answer us in our troubles. May Adonay answer us in our troubles. Adorn a bow in heaven, O Moon! and sends your messengers from all of Rash! and from Zaphon, may Yaho help us.
[3] May he remember all your offerings, and regard with favor your burnt sacrifices. [4] May he grant you your heart's desire, and fulfill all your plans.	May Yaho give to us our heart's desire. May the Lord give to us our heart's desire.
[5] May we shout for joy over your victory, and in the name of our God set up our banners.	

<table>
<tr><td>

May the LORD fulfill all your
   petitions.

⁶ Now I know that the LORD will help
   his anointed; he will answer him
   from his holy heaven with mighty
   victories by his right hand.
⁷ Some take pride in chariots, and
   some in horses, but our pride is in
   the name of the LORD our God.

⁸ They will collapse and fall, but we
   shall rise and stand upright.
⁹ Give victory to the king, O LORD;
   answer us when we call.

</td><td>

Every wish, may Yaho fulfill.
May Yaho fulfill, may Adonay not
   diminish
Any request of our heart.

Some by bow, some by spear—
Behold, as for us, my Lord, our God
   is Yaho!
May our Bull be with us.
May Bethel answer us tomorrow.
Baal-Shamayin shall bless the Lord:
"By your loyal ones I bless you!"

"By your loyal ones I bless you!"

</td></tr>
</table>

It is not a simple translation of Psalm 20. It is more like a liturgical translation and adaptation of an earlier version of the psalm. When we look at the two together, we can see how Psalm 20 itself might have originally derived from a northern liturgical tradition before being bought south to Jerusalem by refugees in the late eighth century. It was then adapted and updated in Jerusalem, but it left echoes of its northern origin in expressions like "the God of Jacob." There were also Jerusalemite adaptations, like verse 6, which mentions the Lord helping "his anointed," an action that is quite typical of David royal ideology. In verse 2, the psalm refers to "Zion"—an allusion to Jerusalem—but Papyrus Amherst has "Zaphon," which in biblical poetry often refers to Mt. Hermon in the Golan region of northern Israel but could have originally referred to the mountain home of Baʿal (Mt. Zaphon/Jabal al-ʾAqraʿ) that was in northern Lebanon.

To be candid, the story behind Psalm 20 in PapAm 63 is still a mystery. I have only a working hypothesis. Namely, an early version of this psalm—an Israelian liturgical text—came to Jerusalem in the late eighth century with the Israelian refugees. But it also ended up in Egypt where

Israelian refugees also fled. The refugees in Jerusalem and Egypt would have known the psalm orally. Maybe it was a scribal community associated with shrine at Bethel, given its injunction, "May Bethel answer us tomorrow!" The deity names in PapAm 63—the Bull, Bethel, Baal-Shamayin—all would fit nicely into Israelian religious culture before the destruction of Samaria in 722 BCE. That means there were three centuries of independent development of this liturgy in Jerusalem and among the Israelian exiles in Egypt.[13] The Israelian exiles in Egypt eventually ended up in southern Egypt, and they translated it into Aramaic and adapted it for the local population. It was later transcribed using Demotic letters and incorporated into PapAm 63. Given such a long and winding history, it not surprising that Psalm 20 and PapAm 63 have only general correspondences. But it's still a remarkable story of an ancient Israelite liturgy over the centuries. PapAm 63 remains a puzzle. Its story is still being written by scholars, but a key to unraveling this mystery will be tracking the scribes and their communities.

The Book(s) of Jeremiah and Their Scribal Communities

The textual history of the Book(s) of Jeremiah is one of the most complicated in the Bible.[14] There are two dramatically different versions—we might even call them different books—known from the traditional Masoretic Hebrew text, the Dead Sea Scrolls, and the Greek Septuagint. These "books" of Jeremiah reveal an interesting part of the story of scribal communities. Scholars have long recognized two books of Jeremiah—a "long" Hebrew version and a "short" Greek version. The short version of Jeremiah is about 15 percent shorter, but it also significantly reorganizes the order of the later chapters.[15] The discovery of the Dead Sea Scrolls, however, changed our understanding of these two books when they found a "short" *Hebrew* version of the Book of Jeremiah along with the "long" version among the Dead Sea Scrolls. But a "long" and a "short" Hebrew Jeremiah still does not tell the whole story, because the first twenty-five chapters are largely the same in both the long and short versions.

Let's try to understand the relationship between the different versions of Jeremiah by comparing them in various ways. The "long" Jeremiah is the version we encounter in most English Bibles, which is based on the Hebrew Masoretic Text. It will help to lay the organization of short and long versions out in a chart:

"Short" Jeremiah	"Long" Jeremiah
1:1–25:13a	1:1–25:13a
25:13b–19	49:34–39
26:1–18	46:1–18
27:1–28:64	50:1–51:64
29:1–23	47:1–22
30:1–5	49:1–5
30:6–16	49:28–27
31:1–44	48:1–44
32:1ff.	25:15ff.

Both versions begin the same, and in the middle of chapter 25 the organization of the book diverges dramatically. The short version seems to follow a more chronological organization, while the long version seems to have a more thematic arrangement. The differences also highlight that the first half of the Book of Jeremiah follows the same order, which suggests that an early version of the Book of Jeremiah existed up through the middle of chapter 25. And that is the way Jeremiah 25 presents itself, concluding in verse 13a as follows: "I will bring upon the land all the words written in this scroll." This seems to be the ending to an early scroll of the priest Jeremiah, but it is not the end of the story of the Book of Jeremiah.

The missing parts in the shorter Jeremiah are concentrated in the second half of the book, but there are a few expansions and additions in the first half as well. Some of the major omissions include

10:6–8, 10 (poem about God's greatness)
11:7–8 (divine warnings for obedience)
17:1–4 (the sin of Judah)
39:4–13 (fate of King Zedekiah and the exiles)
48:45–46 (condemnation of Moab)
51:44–49 (condemnation of Babylon)

The differences are significant and reflect two different paths for the traditions about Jeremiah. These two paths likely followed the exiles and refugees themselves, one to Egypt and a second to Babylon.

One of the most striking differences between the short and the long version of Jeremiah is the consistent description of Jeremiah as a "prophet" in the longer version. The long Jeremiah adds the title "the prophet" twenty-seven times where it is missing in the short version.[16] In other words, the long version transforms Jeremiah into "the prophet" through its editing. Here are just a few examples:

Short Jeremiah (LXX–NETS)	Long Jeremiah (MT–NRSV)
26:13 What the Lord spoke by the hand of *Jeremiah* . . .	46:13 The word that the Lord spoke to *the prophet Jeremiah* about . . .
35:5–6 And *Jeremiah* said to Hananiah in the sight of all the people and in the sight of the priests who stood in the house of the Lord, and *Jeremiah* said, "Truly, thus may the Lord do . . .	28:5 Then *the prophet Jeremiah* spoke to the prophet Hananiah in the presence of the priests and all the people who were standing in the house of the LORD; [6] and *the prophet Jeremiah* said, "Amen! May the LORD do so . . .
36:1 And these are the words of the book, which *Jeremiah* sent from Jerusalem to the elders of the exile and to the *pseudo-prophets*, an epistle to Babylon for the exile to all the people . . .	29:1 These are the words of the scroll that *the prophet Jeremiah* sent from Jerusalem to the remaining elders among the exiles, and to the priests, the prophets, and all the people . . .
39:2 . . . and *Jeremiah* was being confined in the court of the guard that was in the house of the king.	32:2 . . . and *the prophet Jeremiah* was confined in the court of the guard that was in the house of the king.
41:6 And *Jeremiah* spoke all these words to King Zedekiah in Jerusalem . . .	34:6 And *the prophet Jeremiah* spoke all these words to King Zedekiah in Jerusalem . . .
43:8 And Baruch did according to all that *Jeremiah* commanded him . . .	36:8 And Baruch did according to all that *the prophet Jeremiah* commanded him . . .

Short Jeremiah (LXX–NETS)	Long Jeremiah (MT–NRSV)
43:26 And the king commanded to arrest Baruch and *Jeremiah* . . .	26:26 And the king commanded to arrest Baruch and *the prophet Jeremiah* . . .
44:2, 3 . . . the words of the Lord that he spoke through *Jeremiah*. And King Zedekiah sent . . . to *Jeremiah*.	37:2, 3 . . . the words of the Lord that he spoke through *the prophet Jeremiah*. And King Zedekiah sent . . . to *the prophet Jeremiah*.
44:6 The word of the Lord came to *Jeremiah* . . .	37:6 The word of the Lord came to *the prophet Jeremiah* . . .
44:13 . . . Sarouiah, son of Shelemiah, son of Hananiah arrested *Jeremiah*.	37:13 . . . Irijah, son of Shelemiah, son of Hananiah, arrested *the prophet Jeremiah*
45:9–10 You acted wickedly in what you did to kill *this person* . . . bring *him* up out of the cistern so that he will not die!	38:9–10 My lord king, these men acted wickedly in what you did to *the prophet Jeremiah* . . . pull *the prophet Jeremiah* up from the cistern before he dies!
45:14 And the king sent word and called for *him* . . .	38:14 And King Zedekiah sent for *the prophet Jeremiah* . . .
49:4 And *Jeremiah* said to them . . .	42:4 And *the prophet Jeremiah* said to them . . .

From this consistent titling of Jeremiah, it becomes clear that *the priest* Jeremiah has been systematically changed into *the prophet* Jeremiah in the longer version. This refashioning of Jeremiah from a priest into a prophet was likely done by a priestly scribal community in Jerusalem during the early Persian period. They did not want Jeremiah to be identified by his priestly heritage but rather as a prophet.

Why would a priestly scribal community in the early Persian period want to reinvent Jeremiah? Jeremiah the priest was apparently a problematic identity. Perhaps this is because Jeremiah was not among the priests serving in Jerusalem. He wasn't part of the Jerusalem Temple community. The key to understanding the two new editions of Jeremiah is understanding that one retains the identity of Jeremiah as a peripheral

priest and the other retitles Jeremiah as "the prophet." Jeremiah himself
does not have the "right" priestly heritage—namely, he is not an Aaronite priest. His family comes from the village of Anathoth, and they
have no connections with Jerusalem and the temple. This Jeremiah gets
taken into exile into Egypt. We must assume that the "short" Jeremiah,
which retains his identity as a priest from Anathoth (and not a prophet),
is an edition that gets updated among the Egyptian exilic community.
The Egyptian "short" Jeremiah originally and appropriately settled with
those in Egypt (see LXX, "short" Jer 51 ["long" Jer 44]).

I must admit that I was surprised that the retitling of Jeremiah as a
"prophet"—indeed, in this respect, the invention of Jeremiah the
Prophet—is not a major part of scholarly discourse. For example, in an
exhaustive edited volume on *Jeremiah's Scriptures*, four scholars reflect
on the question, "Why Jeremiah? The Invention of a Prophetic Figure."[17] None of the scholars ever reflects on the very titling of Jeremiah
as a "prophet." This title is fundamentally a reflection of the Masoretic
Text as opposed to the earlier, shorter version of the Book of Jeremiah.
And here we are fortunate to have objective and concrete evidence of
the transformation of the figure of Jeremiah in the process of the editing
of the book, as evidenced by the Septuagint, the Dead Sea Scrolls, and
the Masoretic Text. The conclusion must be that Jeremiah was not originally known as a prophet at all. This was not one of his titles. He was
simply from a priestly family that came from outside of the Jerusalem
Temple priestly community. This observation must be the beginning
for a reflection on "The Invention of the *Prophet* Jeremiah." What do we
learn here? Namely, that the portrayal of Jeremiah as one of the major
prophets by the Persian scribal community that produced the proto-
Masoretic text completely succeeded!

The Book of Jeremiah claims that oracles were sent to the Babylonian
exilic community. For example, Jeremiah 29:1 (LXX, 36:1) refers to "the
words of a scroll that Jeremiah sent to the elders among the exiles." Thus,
there is a tradition of a scroll of Jeremiah that would have existed among
a Babylonian scribal community in exile. We know about such a scribal
community from cuneiform records, especially the community in Babylon that associated with the royal family. Moreover, one critical addition

in the "long" Jeremiah is the story of the last kings of Judah told in 2 Kings 24:18–25:21 and appended in the "long" Jeremiah as chapter 52. I think this is a case of *self-plagiarism*. In other words, the scribal community that wrote the final "deuteronomistic" edition of 2 Kings that ended with the fate of the royal family was the same scribal community that thought this chapter would make a fitting end to the story of *the prophet* Jeremiah. Both the "long" Babylonian and the "short" Egyptian books of Jeremiah return to Jerusalem in the early Persian period (i.e., late sixth century BCE). There, the two versions of Jeremiah—the "long" Babylonian and the "short" Egyptian—were partially harmonized by later copyists in Jerusalem, but not systematically. For example, the two versions would get the same introductions and conclusions to make the "short" and "long" versions seem similar, but they also retained the unique characteristics of their different scribal communities.

The most important of these characteristics is the title "prophet." Here it is worth noting that the refashioning of "the prophet" itself is something characteristic of the Deuteronomistic History (i.e., Deuteronomy–2 Kings). The concept of the prophet is introduced in the book of Deuteronomy and then used especially in the historical books (Samuel–Kings). This creates a nice illustrative contrast. The title "the prophet" occurs very rarely in the early Former Prophets (e.g., Hosea, Amos, Isaiah, Micah), but it is used regularly throughout the Deuteronomistic History. And, as we should remember, the Book of Samuel itself alerted its readers that it was redefining the meaning of the title "the prophet" when it noted that "formerly in Israel the one called a prophet [*nabiʾ*] was called a seer" (1 Sam 9:9; see chapter 6). The scribal community that added this editorial note in 1 Samuel 9:9 is likely the same community that systematically added the title "the prophet" to Jeremiah in the long version.

The editorial conclusion to Jeremiah that is borrowed from 2 Kings reminds me of the editing of the Book of Isaiah. The first section of the book, called by scholars "First Isaiah" (chapters 1–39) ends with an extensive parallel from the Book of 2 Kings (cp. 2 Kings 18–20 with Isaiah 36–39). The borrowed ending details the reign of Hezekiah, who was the main figure for whom Isaiah served as "prophet" in the royal administration. The same royal and administrative scribes that edited the Book of

Jeremiah would also have edited the Book of Isaiah and used a similar technique—a borrowed passage from the Book of Kings—to wrap up the first section of the Book of Isaiah. King Hezekiah was an apparent hero to the exilic and early Persian scribal community because he was inclusive of the northern scribes and peripheral figures like Jeremiah. So the books of Jeremiah and Isaiah get the same treatment—the inclusion of some of the royal narratives from the Book of Kings in the final editing of the book.

So, how do we know these were royal administrative scribes? The telltale clue is in the conclusion to the Book of Kings itself. It tells the story of the last days of Jerusalem and especially the fate of the last Davidic king:

> In the thirty-seventh year of the exile of King Jehoiachin of Judah, in the twelfth month, on the twenty-seventh day of the month, King Evil-merodach of Babylon, in the year that he began to reign, released King Jehoiachin of Judah from prison; he spoke kindly to him, and gave him a seat above the other seats of the kings who were with him in Babylon. So Jehoiachin put aside his prison clothes. Every day of his life he dined regularly in the king's presence. For his allowance, a regular allowance was given him by the king, a portion every day, as long as he lived. (2 Kgs 25:27–30 // Jer 52:28–34)

This conclusion tells us about the scribal community that put the finishing touches on the Book of Kings. They were affiliated with the royal family and were concerned with its fate. We know that the royal family and its scribal apparatus survived during the Babylonian exile from the cuneiform administrative documents from Babylon (mentioned above). The rebuilding of the Jerusalem Temple involved one of the later sons of Jehoiachin, Sheshbazzar, "a prince of Judah" who returned to Jerusalem to help rebuild the Temple during the days of the early Persian province of Yehud (see Ezr 1:8–11; 5:14). Zerubbabel is another Davidic prince from the early Persian period who is named as helping rebuild the Temple and restore the Jewish community in Yehud (e.g., Hag 1:1), but the Davidic leadership of the early Persian period did not last. The scribal community associated with the royal administration did not survive past the sixth century, but they did preserve and update some of the royal archives that came into the Jerusalem Temple library.

In sum, Jeremiah himself was a peripheral priest. He survived the first (597 BCE) and second (586 BCE) exiles, but he ended up in Egypt with various refugees at the time of the third Babylonian campaign against Judah (581 BCE). At that time there was already a first scroll of Jeremiah that included an early version of Jeremiah reflected in 1:1–25:13a. This first edition of Jeremiah then had two different fates—one ended up in Egypt (with the priest Jeremiah) and another in Babylon with the royal family and its scribal community. The Book of Jeremiah itself gives hints about a Babylonian version: "These are the words of the scroll that the prophet Jeremiah sent from Jerusalem to the remaining elders among the exiles . . . whom Nebuchadnezzar had taken into exile from Jerusalem to Babylon" (Jer 29:1 MT; 36:1 LXX). This would become the basis for the "long" Jeremiah that would transform him into "the prophet."

The two scrolls of Jeremiah tell the story of two different scribal communities—the peripheral priests that reflect the original figure of Jeremiah, a priest from Anathoth, and the royal administration that was exiled to Babylon and survived in a palace in the Babylonian capital supplied by rations from the royal table. The scrolls will eventually make their way back to Jerusalem to the library of the rebuilt Temple. They are updated, even partially harmonized, but the two Jeremiah editions continue to have their own lives. These two editions were preserved by the scribal community that would survive the Babylonian exile—namely, the Jerusalem Temple priestly scribal community.

Jeremiah, as a priest, showed an intimate concern for the priesthood and the temple, but mostly as a critique of the Jerusalem priesthood. That is hardly surprising given his family's status as an outsider among the Jerusalem priests, but his priestly concerns are still etched throughout the pages of the Book of Jeremiah. Perhaps the best evidence of this is merely the prevalence of the Hebrew word "priest" (*kohen*) in the Masoretic text of Jeremiah—it occurs forty times! The priests are everywhere, as are their concerns—the temple, ritual, purity, and so on. Jeremiah repeatedly condemns the *Jerusalem* priests because he is a priest but is not one of their group.[18] The Jerusalem priests are among those Jeremiah will blame for the exile. That critique worked well for the later royal/administrative scribes who could appeal to Jeremiah to direct the focus away from the Davidic family as the explanation for the fall of Jerusalem, but they could not appeal to Jeremiah's priestly lineage for his legitimation. They found legitimation elsewhere, namely, by labeling Jeremiah as "the prophet." The story of Jeremiah being called by God to speak for God as a prophet becomes the new harmonized introduction to the Book of Jeremiah (see Jer 1:5).[19] This introduction reframes Jeremiah as "a prophet to the nations." In this refashioning of Jeremiah, not only Jeremiah himself but also the traditional office of the prophet itself is transformed (compare chapter 6).[20]

The Story of Ezekiel

Who was Ezekiel? Unlike Jeremiah, he was a Jerusalem priest. He was exiled to Babylon after the first campaign of Nebuchadnezzar in 597 BCE. He was undoubtedly chosen because he offered special skills for the empire—namely, as a Jerusalem priest, he had received scribal training. A most useful part of his training would have been knowledge of Aramaic, which was the empire's administrative *lingua franca*. Aramaic seems to have been part of scribal training in Judah already during the monarchy,[21] so there was a utility in exiling people like Ezekiel to Babylon. The Book of Daniel gives a nice vignette about training foreigners to work in the Babylonian court: "Nebuchadnezzar commanded his palace master Ashpenaz to bring some of the Israelites of the royal family and of the nobility . . . to be taught the literature and language of the Chaldeans" (Dan 1:3–4). These positions involved learning Aramaic, and the Babylonians literally referred to the position in cuneiform writing as ^{LÚ}A.BA—a person of the "ABCs"—using the Sumerian logograms that represented A and B. The Akkadian pronunciation of this logogram was *sepīru*, which referred only to Aramaic or alphabetic scribes. The *sepīru*, which is cognate to the Hebrew word for scribe, *soper*, worked alongside the cuneiform scribes who were known by a different Akkadian title, *ṭupšarru*.

So, young Ezekiel gets taken and settled "by the river Chebar" (Ezek 1:1) in central Mesopotamia not far from the capital of the empire. The Chebar river was a canal known in Babylonian as the *Nār Kabari* mentioned in cuneiform commercial documents from the sixth century BCE.[22] It was part of the canal system used both for commercial transport and for agricultural irrigation. Ezekiel lived near the capital of Babylonia on a commercial hub. His work there undoubtedly involved working in the Babylonian administration as a scribe, but we hear little of this in the Book of Ezekiel. From Babylonian cuneiform records—both the "Judah-town" documents and the Murashu archive—we read about Jewish diaspora communities working in commerce along the canal systems of central Mesopotamia.[23]

The Book of Ezekiel encourages and reflects integration into daily life in Babylonia. As someone living in Babylonia, it is not surprising that Ezekiel would begin using local words and phrases—that is, Akkadian loanwords. There are as many as eighty "Akkadianisms" in the book, which reflects its Babylonian context. More than this, Ezekiel also exhibits a knowledge of the classic cuneiform literature like the *Epic of Gilgamesh*, Maqlu, and the Poem of Erra.[24] The use of Akkadian loanwords and awareness of Akkadian literary classics suggest that Ezekiel lived his adult life in contact with communities of cuneiform scribes. However, when we look carefully at Ezekiel's knowledge of cuneiform literature or his use of loanwords, they reflect contact with cuneiform scribal communities but not necessarily cuneiform scribal training. For example, Ezekiel's loanwords specifically reflect commerce and daily life. Ezekiel's borrowed words come from local mercantile experiences, and he knows legal terms from marriage contracts that draw on his exilic experience.

Some scholars have suggested that Ezekiel himself learned Akkadian cuneiform and became intimately involved in the Babylonian intellectual culture, but there is no concrete evidence for this.[25] He was a first-generation exile. He was a former Jerusalem priest. He probably came to Babylon as a young adult. It seems unlikely that he started learning Akkadian with the local schoolboys. But Ezekiel did apparently have scribal skills. Advanced scribal learning in Judah probably even included some introduction to Aramaic, and as an alphabetic scribe Ezekiel would have had access to Babylonian scribal culture without necessarily becoming a cuneiform scribe. Indeed, Ezekiel even seems to admit that he does not know Akkadian when he writes about being sent to speak to his own people rather than "to peoples of obscure speech and difficult language, whose words you do not understand" (Ezek 3:6). Ezekiel could have gotten acquainted with Babylonian literary culture and acquired technical language and knowledge as an alphabetic scribe, even though he still would have remained a foreigner and an outsider.

There is considerable debate among scholars about the composition of the Book of Ezekiel.[26] Scholars question whether Ezekiel actually wrote his own book. I do not subscribe to this skepticism. One characteristic of the Book of Ezekiel is its unrelenting first-person voice. In this respect it is unlike any other book in the Hebrew Bible. Ezekiel is consistently and entirely autobiographical. Indeed, Ezekiel's voice is uniquely autobiographical. We do have other examples of first-person voices in the Bible. For example, Isaiah 6 begins, "In the year that King Uzziah died, *I saw the Lord.*" This is followed by a couple of chapters in the Book of Isaiah where we seem to have the autobiographical voice of the prophet Isaiah speaking out of the past, but this contrasts with the rest of the book, where the prophet Isaiah is presented in the third person. Isaiah is generally a character in his book; he is not depicted as its scribe. Likewise, we see the figure of Moses as a character in the Pentateuch, almost invariably presented in the third person. For example, the Book of Deuteronomy begins, "These are the words that Moses spoke . . ." and not "I, Moses, spoke these words." In other words, biblical literature is presented as being transmitted by a community of scribes rather than by individual authors. Ezekiel is different. The book begins, "In the thirtieth year, in the fourth month, on the fifth day of the month, *as I was among the exiles* by the river Chebar, the heavens were opened, *and I saw visions of God.*" The book begins autobiographically and maintains this singular autobiographical voice throughout. To be sure, Ezekiel's autobiography is received, copied, and even studied by a later scribal community, but the book is presented as the work of an individual, not a community.

Ezekiel thus becomes an exception to the thesis of this book. For me, it is the proverbial exception that proves the rule. Why is Ezekiel unique?

In part because it reflects the circumstance of the Babylonian destruction and exile itself. The campaigns against Jerusalem and Judah systematically destroyed the institutions that provided a foundation for scribal communities. In the case of Ezekiel, he was a priest without a temple to serve. He was removed from his community in Jerusalem. It is reasonable to assume that he had apprentices in Babylon and that he was teaching Hebrew to a small community as a side gig. He claims to be called by God "to go to the house of Israel and speak *my very words* to them" (Ezek 3:4). In this case, God's very words must have been Hebrew. There is a later literary tradition in the Book of Jubilees that makes this explicit (Jub 12:26), but this could easily be inferred from the quotations of God in biblical literature—"God spoke" and "thus says the LORD" is always followed by a Hebrew quote. After all, what other language would He speak? So, we can assume that Ezekiel tried to preserve and teach his own cultural language and tradition, but his location in his book was Babylon. His students or apprentices would have been entrusted with copying and transmitting his teachings that eventually make their way back to Jerusalem, preserved in the library of the rebuilt Temple in Jerusalem.

Ezekiel knew priestly scribal traditions. He probably apprenticed in the Jerusalem Temple learning priestly traditions but then became detached and dislocated from the Jerusalem priestly scribal community. This perhaps explains why Ezekiel casually revises priestly laws. Let's take one example related to marriage, purity, and priestly genealogies—a central concern after the Babylonian exile. In Leviticus 21:13–15, we read,

> A priest shall marry only a woman who is a virgin. A widow, or a divorced woman, or a woman who has been defiled, a prostitute, these he shall not marry. He shall marry a virgin of his own kin, so that he may not profane his offspring among his kin. For I am the LORD, I sanctify him.

Ezekiel 44:22 echoes this law with a minor modification:

> Priests shall not marry a widow, or a divorced woman, but only a virgin of the stock of the house of Israel, *or a widow who is the widow of a priest.*

Ezekiel rewrites the Levitical law that prohibited a priest from marrying a widow! To be sure, there were likely quite a few widows in the aftermath of the Babylonian invasions, so Ezekiel may be revising this law to cope with his times. That Ezekiel makes the point that a priest can marry a priestly widow suggests that he knows the Levitical rule. Such laws, among the priests, would also have been common knowledge. Ezekiel did not need to consult a scroll. Priests probably copied or memorized such laws during their scribal education. Ezekiel probably did not carry a "pocket Leviticus" with him into exile. And Ezekiel also did not treat these rules as permanent. They apparently were not considered "canonical"—that is, fixed and unchanging. They were subject to revision, updating, or clarification.[27]

To conclude, it is important to stress that Ezekiel was a priest, not a prophet—at least in his own book. The Book of Ezekiel never gives him the title "the Prophet." In the later canonical process, Ezekiel is included among "The Former Prophets" and in the Jewish TaNaK with the Nebi'im ("Prophets"). Although he is considered one of the three "major" prophets (along with Isaiah and Jeremiah), Ezekiel was a priest. He came from a priestly family in Jerusalem. He represents the final legacy of the First Temple priestly tradition that would die in the exile. Still, priests would return to Jerusalem, and the priestly community would be reborn with the rebuilding of the Jerusalem Temple at the end of the sixth century BCE. Judging from the genealogical lists in the Book of Ezra-Nehemiah, priests and priestly lineage were a central concern in the post-exilic period. But that's a story for a later chapter in the history of priestly scribal communities (see chapter 12).

11

Working with the Samaritans

One of my old friends in biblical studies was Gary Knoppers. He was a great scholar but, even more than that, a great person. One of my fondest memories was the day I spent showing him around Jerusalem when we were both fellows at the Albright Institute of Archaeological Research. I intended to end the day by walking through Hezekiah's Tunnel with him. The cool waters that run from the Gihon Spring through the tunnel to the Siloam Pool are a great end to a hot summer's day in Jerusalem. Gary was all for it until we got into the cave of the Gihon, and he saw the narrow and low entrance to the tunnel. Gary was a big guy, probably six-foot-six. We got our feet wet, but we did not go through the tunnel that day. Too low, too narrow. I'm reminded of this day because Gary passed away prematurely a few years ago. A great loss. One of Gary's final scholarly contributions was a book, *Jews and Samaritans: The Origins and History of Their Early Relations*, that elevated my understanding of an understudied topic—the early history of the Samaritans.[1] Many people know the Samaritans from the parable of the "Good Samaritan" or through the lens of the New Testament, but their story goes much further back.

What makes the Samaritans so interesting for this book is that they had their own Hebrew scribal community that must have had its origins during the late Iron Age (seventh century BCE). How do we know this? The Samaritans would use and develop the Old Hebrew letters and would preserve their own version of the Pentateuch. To begin with, it is not likely that the Samaritans adopted the Old Hebrew script during the Persian or Hellenistic period because it had already gone out of regular use. No, their script developed organically from an Iron Age script, so it follows that the Samaritan use of this script likely dates back to at least the seventh century BCE. Even though we know the Samaritan script mostly in its later developed versions that were used by the Samaritan community in the Hellenistic, Roman, and later periods, its origins were earlier. The use of the older Hebrew script (as opposed to the later Aramaic script of the Persian period), along with their preservation of their own version of the Pentateuch, suggests that the Samaritan priests were working with Judean priests already in the late Iron Age. In this chapter, I will suggest that they were working with the Jerusalem priests during the seventh, sixth, and fifth centuries BCE in creating the Pentateuch, but eventually they parted ways after they built their own temple.

Scholars have long thought that there was always mutual animosity between Jerusalem and Samaria. This view comes partly from reading the story through the lens of the New Testament. But it is not just the New Testament. The Jewish historian Josephus, who lived in the first century CE, details how a Hasmonean king, John Hyrcanus (r. 134–104 BCE) had destroyed the Samaritan temple on Mount Gerizim. By the second century BCE, the animosity between Jews and Samaritans was well entrenched. Even before this, the books of Ezra-Nehemiah describe the tensions between Sanballat, the Samaritan leader, and his Jerusalem counterparts. And the Book of Chronicles, written during the Persian period, rewrites the history of Israel by editing out the narrative of Samaria and the northern kingdom completely (in contrast with the Book of Kings). So there is lots of history to this fraught relationship.

But the relationship was not always so fraught. The story, as always, is more complex. After all, the patriarchal narratives tell the stories of all twelve tribes, not just the southern tribe of Judah and the priestly heirs of Levi. And while it is true that the Book of Chronicles eliminates the narrative of the kingdom of the northern tribes (1 Chr 10–2 Chr 36), it still prefaces its historical work with the genealogies of all twelve tribes (1 Chr 1–9).[2] In other words, it acknowledges a shared genealogy. But that is as far as it goes in Chronicles. Gary Knoppers highlighted the shared genealogy in Chronicles to suggest that the book was not completely anti-Samaritan, but the shared genealogies are limited. The genealogies in Chronicles focus on the patriarchal period, the levitical and priestly lineages, the Judahite genealogies, and the sons of David. There is a genealogy of Saul, for example, but it serves as a lead-in to the narrative of David's rise—the true king in Chronicles—and that is where the genealogies of the northern tribes end. Just as the narratives of Chronicles do not include the northern kingdom, the genealogies for the northern tribes do not extend chronologically into the days of the divided kingdom. The Chronicler acknowledges northern tribes but not the northern kingdom. So, for example, we read that "the Reubenites, the Gadites, and the half-tribe of Manasseh had valiant warriors, who carried shield and sword, and drew the bow, expert in war, forty-four thousand seven hundred sixty, ready for service. They made war on the Hagrites, Jetur, Naphish, and Nodab" (1 Chr 5:18–19). This is all part of the prehistory of the kingdoms, but the Chronicles cuts short any discussion of the northern tribes and their kingdom by writing only that "they lived in their territory until the exile" (v. 22). There is no shared *history* of Israel but rather a shared *prehistory*. In this respect, the Chronicles genealogies reflect the story in 1 Chronicles 21, where King David took a census of all the tribes of Israel. These were the days of the "united" kingdom. By including King David's census, Chronicles makes a statement about the illegitimacy of the northern kingdom itself. The northern tribes are only legitimate under the auspices of David and Jerusalem, where they are counted among the United Monarchy. Ultimately, the purpose seems to marginalize the Samaritans.

For Chronicles, the kingdom of Judah is Israel, and all true Israelites come to Jerusalem. To promote this, Chronicles tells unique stories like Hezekiah's Passover where the northern tribes are invited to come to Jerusalem: "Hezekiah wrote letters to Ephraim and Manasseh, that they should come to the house of the LORD at Jerusalem, to keep the Passover to the LORD the God of Israel" (2 Chr 30:1). As I have pointed out, Hezekiah seems to be a hero to the early post-exilic scribal community because he accommodates the northern tribes, but this story still has everyone coming to Jerusalem. It does not acknowledge a legitimate alternative place to worship, and it does not show any indication that the history of Samaria was part of the legitimate history of Israel. This reflects the attitude in Jerusalem by the fourth century BCE, even though there had been some cooperation in earlier times.

The Samaritan Temple and Its Scribal Community

The history of the Samaritan community begins where Samaria and the northern kingdom ends, namely, with the Assyrian invasion, the destruction of Samaria, and the exile of many northerners in the late eighth century BCE. Supposedly, Samaria was then resettled by the Assyrians with people from other parts of the empire: "The king of Assyria brought people from Babylon, Cuthah, Avva, Hamath, and Sepharvaim, and placed them in the cities of Samaria in place of the people of Israel" (2 Kgs 17:24). Many people fled south toward Jerusalem as well as to Egypt. According to biblical tradition, the Assyrians later brought back an exiled Israelian priest to his homeland to teach the resettled peoples the local customs and religion (see v. 27), so that the mixed ethnic population created a hybrid religious tradition with Yahwism and local Babylonian cults (v. 33). Such an account works well as a critique of Samaritan religion by later scribes in Jerusalem, but it also acknowledges apparent religious connections between the north and south. To be sure, the Jerusalemite scribes are implying that true orthodoxy was only in Jerusalem.

The account of the fall of Samaria points to an awareness of a unique Samaritan religious tradition that developed in the wake of the Assyrian conquest. It also acknowledges Yahwistic elements to that religion, which was led by a priest of Yahweh. The biblical account places the early location for this tradition at Bethel: "one of the priests whom they had carried away from Samaria came and lived in Bethel, and he was teaching them how they should worship Yahweh" (2 Kgs 17:28). Bethel had an old religious tradition, but archaeological excavations at Bethel demonstrate that the site was largely unoccupied in the later Babylonian and Persian periods (see chapter 4).[3] It did not become a center for Samaritan religion. That honor would belong to Mount Gerizim.

From Sacred Precinct to Samaritan Temple on Mount Gerizim

For two decades, archaeologist Yitzhak Magen excavated a sacred precinct on Mount Gerizim (see Figure 11.1). Magen dated the building of the Samaritan temple to 450 BCE—the middle of the Persian period— but Magen also recognized some early features of the sacred precinct. Another archaeologist, Eran Arie, furthered Magen's observations and argued that the sacred precinct was founded before the Temple in the late Iron Age, perhaps already in the seventh century BCE.[4] The excavations had discovered a sacred precinct, bounded by a wall with a six-chambered gate leading in from the north and probably also on the southern side. The six-chambered gates that served as an entryway into the sacred precinct are known throughout the southern Levant from the Iron Age, but there is not a single example known to have been built during the Persian period.

The sacred precinct was modified in the Persian period with the foundation of the Mount Gerizim temple, built about 450 BCE based on coins, pottery, and carbon-14 (see Figure 11.2).[5] The walls of the sacred precinct were remodeled at this time so that they had eight chambers, which made them conform to the biblical descriptions of the temple gates in Ezekiel as well as those detailed in the later Temple Scroll.[6] The new Samaritan temple was built facing directly east. But this made the walls of the temple askew to the old walls of the Iron Age sacred precinct. Why did they build the temple wall askew to the sacred precinct walls? The orientation of the Samaritan temple was undoubtedly meant to parallel the Jerusalem Temple, which also had an eastern orientation. In that respect, they had no choice. The Samaritan temple copied the orientation of the Jerusalem Temple even though it meant that the walls of the temple and the outer sacred precinct were not aligned. Ideology trumped architectural symmetry! Here it is important to remember that the Judean returnees rebuilt the Jerusalem Temple around 515 BCE. The founding of a Samaritan temple in the fifth century accords with the account of Nehemiah, who mentions that one of the grandsons of the high priest Eliashib was the son-in-law of Sanballat the Horonite, and Nehemiah suggests that he so defiled the priesthood (Neh 13:28–29).[7]

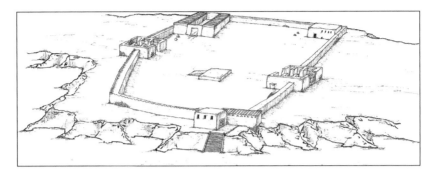

FIGURE 11.1. Iron Age sacred precinct on Mount Gerizim. Drawing by Andrew Herbek.

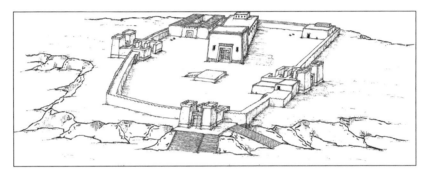

FIGURE 11.2. Persian period Samaritan temple. Drawing by Andrew Herbek.

The outer sacred precinct walls must be older than the temple itself because if they had been built together, they would have been aligned. This observation is underscored by the later remodeled Hellenistic Samaritan temple precinct in the third century BCE, which rectified the misalignment by adding a new partition wall around the Samaritan temple (see Figure 11.3). With this remodeling, the temple was perfectly aligned with retaining walls, and the walls of the old sacred precinct to the south were removed. With this, the architectural tension between the temple and the sacred precinct begins to disappear. The Hellenistic reconstruction of the sacred precinct also further enhanced the eastern orientation and recalls the description of Ezekiel's visionary temple, where God enters both the visionary temple and the city from

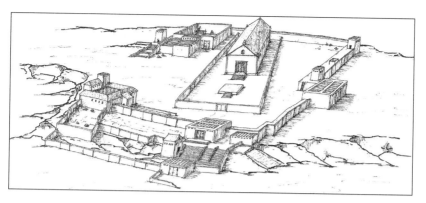

FIGURE 11.3. Hellenistic temple with new partition wall. Drawing by Andrew Herbek.

the east (Ezek 43:1–5). The old traces of the Iron Age sacred precinct were gradually replaced in the successive remodeling of the temple precinct. The misaligned walls tell the story of the sacred precinct and the Samaritan sacred space on Mount Gerizim.

Another archaeological find that points to the late Iron Age for the foundation of the sacred district are proto-Ionian capitals (Figure 11.4). There are two mostly intact capitals and one fragmentary capital. These capitals were excavated in the sacred precinct on Mount Gerizim, and they use a style that is known almost exclusively in the Iron Age. Similar examples have been excavated in Jerusalem, Ramat Raḥel, Arnona, Megiddo, and throughout the southern Levant dating to the Iron Age. In this respect, they further indicate that the sacred precinct on Mount Gerizim must have already been established by the seventh century BCE. Almost fifty comparable examples of proto-Ionian capitals are known from the southern Levant dating to the late Iron Age. Unfortunately, the Gerizim capitals were found in secondary use in the later Byzantine Church. The emperor Zenon demolished the Samaritan sacred precinct and built a church dedicated to Mary Theotokos in 484 CE. At that time, the capitals were trimmed on the sides and used as building blocks, but the old Iron Age artistic elements are still easily visible. These capitals are carved only on one side, so they must have originally served in an ornate doorway in the sacred precinct on Mount Gerizim.

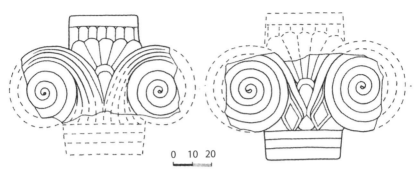

FIGURE 11.4. Proto-Ionian capitals from Mount Gerizim sacred precinct.
Courtesy of Eran Arie.

The excavators also found a large number of inscriptions—395 in
total—in the excavations on Mount Gerizim. The inscriptions are
mostly in Aramaic, but there are also Hebrew inscriptions. The Hebrew
inscriptions use both the old Iron Age Hebrew script as well as the later
Samaritan Hebrew script. There are nine fragmentary examples of inscriptions that use the old Iron Age Hebrew script. These inscriptions
unfortunately suffered the same fate as the proto-Ionic capitals; that is,
they were dismantled from their original contexts and reused in the
building of the Byzantine Church, but they are still instructive. One
example will suffice to illustrate (see Figure 11.5).

Inscription no. 384 preserves three fragmentary lines in Hebrew that
can be translated as follows:

1) [p]ynḥs   [Ph]inehas,
2) [ ] ᵓšr   [ ]who was
3) [hkhn] hgdl   the high [priest].

It is short and fragmentary, but the language and the script still bear striking
similarities to old Hebrew from the Iron Age.[8] This is a monumental inscription, which must have been a dedication inscription for the sacred precinct.
Perhaps Phinehas was the first high priest of the Samaritan sacred priesthood during the Iron Age. The Hebrew name pynḥs is usually translated as
Phinehas in English Bibles (influenced by the Greek spelling), and the

family name is quite well known in priestly genealogies. For example, a certain Phinehas was the grandson of Aaron, the brother of Moses, in the biblical tradition (Num 6:25). And this priest Phinehas is praised for his zeal for Yahweh in wiping out foreign cults (see Num 25:7–15; Ps 106:30). This could be a reference to the biblical figure of Phinehas, but it seems more likely to refer to an early Samaritan high priest. The inscription might be dated by its script to the fifth or fourth century BCE, and it provides early evidence for

FIGURE 11.5. Old Hebrew inscription (no. 384) from Mount Gerizim. Drawing by the author.

a priestly scribal community around Mount Gerizim. It could have been installed with the original Samaritan temple, or perhaps during the Hellenistic remodeling of the Temple precinct. The Samaritan priestly community obviously ascribed to themselves an elite priestly and biblical lineage. The naming of this particular priest suggests they knew the biblical priestly stories.

So what does all this mean? This would have been after 721 BCE, when the Assyrians conquered Israel, razed Samaria, and exiled many Israelites. It is hard to pinpoint a precise beginning of the Mount Gerizim sacred precinct, but the seventh century fits with architectural features like the proto-Ionic capitals, the six-chambered gates, and the old Hebrew inscriptions. Later in the fifth century, a temple oriented to the east was added inside the sacred precinct on Mount Gerizim. The intentional and awkward eastern orientation of the Samaritan temple indicates that it was fashioning itself after the Jerusalem Temple and in doing so setting itself up as a rival temple. The building of a temple emulating the Jerusalem Temple naturally created some competition, especially considering the requirement in Deuteronomy 12 for a single sacred place.

The Samaritan Scribal Community

The administration of Judah during the Babylonian period shows continuing Samaritan influence. The early Yehud Stamp Seals, for example, use Israelian names. One seal that was used frequently reads "Yehud | ʾUriyaw," and a second one reads "Yehud | Malkiyaw." These are distinctly Israelian names as indicated by the *-yaw* theophoric ending. So, some of the early governors of Judah during the sixth century (either during the Babylonian period or in the very early Persian period) identified themselves as Samaritan or Israelian. This suggests even more opportunity for cooperation between the Samaritan and Jerusalem priestly communities in the sixth and early fifth centuries BCE—cooperation that gave rise to the later Samaritan Pentateuch.

Some of our misunderstanding of Samaritan history can be traced to the Jewish historian Josephus. Writing in the first century CE, Josephus (mis)dated the construction of the Samaritan temple to the time of Alexander the Great (*Ant* 11.302–47; 13.254–56). We may suspect that Josephus surely wanted the Samaritan temple to be as late (and therefore inauthentic) as possible. In Josephus' defense, his literary sources (mostly Ezra and Nehemiah) were difficult to decipher, and scholars to this day debate the chronology and dating for the figures of Ezra and Nehemiah. But archaeology has come to the rescue here. We now have a firm date for the construction of the Samaritan temple, and this date shows that Josephus dated the beginnings of Samaritan temple more than a century later than the archaeological evidence. More than this, the sacred precinct and its priestly tradition on Mount Gerizim likely dated from another couple centuries earlier than the founding of the temple. This forces a major reevaluation of the history of the Samaritan tradition.

The Samaritan priestly community, of course, wanted their temple to be as early as possible. To accomplish this, the scribal community revised stories related to their community in the Samaritan Pentateuch. How do we know that the Samaritan revisions are later? The story of the Ten Commandments, which is foundational for Samaritan religion, points to later revisions. The Samaritan Pentateuch inserts a Mount Gerizim tradition into the story of the giving of the Ten Commandments. The Samaritan Pentateuch concludes its account of the giving of the Ten Commandments in Exodus as follows:

> And when the LORD your God brings you into the land of the Canaanites . . . you shall erect these stones which I am commanding you today on Mount Gerizim, and you shall build there an altar to the LORD your God. (Exod 20:17b SP)

The Samaritan Pentateuch borrows directly from Deuteronomy 28 here, attaching verses from there to the conclusion of the Ten Commandments in Exodus 20. This also explicitly connects the "stone tablets" that God gave to Moses on Mount Sinai (see Exod 24:12 and 31:18) with the Ten Commandments, which is another idea borrowed from Deuteronomy. This connection is not made in the Masoretic version of the giving of the Ten Commandments in Exodus 20 where they are only presented orally: "God spoke all these words" (v. 1). We are not told they are written down. Later in the Exodus narrative, chapter 24 mentions "stone tablets," but there is no mention of the Ten Commandments in this context. However, when the Book of Deuteronomy retells the story, it identifies the two stone tablets with the Ten Commandments (or, "Ten Words") (4:12–13; 5:22). It is easy to see a progression of interpretation in these accounts, and the Samaritan Pentateuch reflects an evolving interpretation of the theophany on Mount Sinai. The Samaritan Pentateuch borrows from other accounts to insert this interpretation directly into a story of the placement of the tablets of the Ten Commandments on Mount Gerizim. This revision also expresses the prominent role that the Ten Commandments themselves had in Samaritan religious tradition. In this way, Mount

Gerizim becomes a sacred place that supersedes the Jerusalem Temple itself!

Archaeological excavations can now be used to reset our framework. The origins of the Mount Gerizim sacred precinct date back to the late Iron Age. The sacred precinct seems to have originally had an altar but not a temple. The Samaritan temple, which imitated the Jerusalem Temple, was built in the mid-fifth century BCE. This gives the Samaritan religious history an entirely different view. For example, the Samaritan Pentateuch cannot originate in the Hellenistic period, by which time there was already an inseparable rift between the Jerusalem and Mount Gerizim temple communities. The Samaritan Pentateuch should be dated to the period of cooperation, not the period of competition between Jerusalem and Mount Gerizim.

The Samaritan and Jerusalem priestly scribal communities must have shared the Pentateuch until the communities parted ways. When did this happen? Probably already by the end of the fifth century BCE. A temple in Jerusalem and on Mount Gerizim simply could not coexist with the shared Pentateuchal tradition in Deuteronomy 12. Both communities claimed Deuteronomy as a sacred textual tradition. But Deuteronomy 12 stipulates a central sacred place to put his name: "Take care that you do not offer your burnt offerings at any place you happen to see. But only at the place that the LORD will choose in one of your tribes—there you shall offer your burnt offerings and there you shall do everything I command you" (vv. 13–14). This text is ambiguous enough to accommodate the movement of the sacred space that God would choose—for example, from Shiloh to Jerusalem. It might have also accommodated multiple sacred spaces in different parts of the land or even in the Diaspora. But the interpretative tradition moved toward understanding this to refer to a single sacred space. This could be Jerusalem, or it could be Mount Gerizim. It could not be both. This incompatibility is nicely encapsulated by the later confrontation between the Jewish rabbi Jesus with a Samaritan woman near Mount Gerizim. She says, "Our ancestors worshiped on this mountain, but you say that the place where people must worship is in Jerusalem" (John 4:20). Once Deuteronomy 12 became textualized and studied, it became a prooftext requiring only one sacred place.

The Samaritan priestly scribes addressed the tension between Jerusalem and Mount Gerizim in their copying and transmission of the Samaritan Pentateuch. But how and when did the Samaritans come to have their own Pentateuch? If we follow the Jewish historian Josephus, we might be misled into beginning the history of the Samaritan Pentateuch in the Hellenistic period. The Samaritan Pentateuch has its own long history,[9] but the Jerusalem and Gerizim priestly communities were working together on the formation of the Pentateuch long before the Hellenistic period. The archaeology of Mount Gerizim dates a priestly scribal community back into the late Iron Age. The dedication inscription of a certain Phinehas, the high priest, on Mount Gerizim suggests deeply entrenched connections with the Pentateuchal traditions (see Figure 11.4). We can imagine an ebb and flow to Jerusalem-Samaritan priestly relations. Perhaps they could have worked well together in the early seventh century under the Judean kings Hezekiah and Manasseh. Under the Judean king Josiah, on the other hand, there may have been more tension with a northern cult center. After the destruction of Jerusalem and its temple, one might again imagine a more cooperative relationship between the remnant of Judean priestly scribes and Samaritan scribes. At least two early governors of Yehud seem to have been of Samaritan heritage. However, when the Jerusalem Temple was rebuilt in the late sixth century and then a rival Samaritan temple was built in the mid-fifth century, it must have become increasingly difficult for these two communities to cooperate. As a result, two separate Pentateuchal textual traditions diverged, following two different priestly scribal communities.

The Samaritan scribal community instantiates significant differences that highlight the importance of Mount Gerizim. It is best to begin with the conclusion to Moses' speech to Israel giving them the law. The change between the traditional Masoretic and Samaritan text is small but significant:

	Masoretic Pentateuch	Samaritan Pentateuch
Deut 27:4	So when you have crossed over the Jordan, you shall set up these stones, about which I am commanding you today, on *Mount Ebal*, and you shall cover them with plaster.	So when you have crossed over the Jordan, you shall set up these stones, about which I am commanding you today, on *Mount Gerizim*, and you shall cover them with plaster.

The two sites of Mount Ebal and Gerizim lie above to the north and south of the ancient city and temple at Shechem in the valley below. Shechem itself was an ancient holy site with a monumental temple dating back to the second millennium as well as being the first capital of the northern kingdom (1 Kgs 12:25). According to biblical tradition, it was near Shechem that God first appeared to Abraham and first promised him, "I will give to you and your offspring this land," after which Abraham built an altar there (Gen 12:7). In this respect, the area has an important old tradition as sacred space that the Samaritans could appeal to when they built their temple on Mount Gerizim.

The Gerizim-specific additions and changes date to after the parting of the ways between Jerusalem and the Samaritan communities, but they shared a Pentateuch that was largely the same. There had to be a period when the Jerusalem and Samaritan priestly communities worked together sharing and codifying Pentateuchal traditions. After all, both inherited the Pentateuch, and the two Pentateuchs are strikingly similar in spite of the special Samaritan additions. The Dead Sea Scrolls even attest to an early textual tradition of Samaritan Pentateuch, likely dating to the before the Samaritan-Jerusalem rift.[10] The differences between the Masoretic Pentateuch and the presectarian Samaritan Pentateuch are mostly minor linguistic or spelling differences. Most prominently, the presectarian Samaritan tradition did not include the additions emphasizing the special import of Mount Gerizim. The existence of a presectarian Samaritan tradition shows that the Samaritan and Jerusalemite priestly scribes had a shared heritage in the formation of the Pentateuch. But this shared history had to before the Samaritan-Jerusalem rift, likely even before the building of two competing temples in Jerusalem and

Mount Gerizim. Once the rival temple on Mount Gerizim was built, the two priestly scribal communities had to go their separate ways. Two physical centers were vying for claims to primacy—Jerusalem and Mount Gerizim—and they developed two different priestly scribal communities.

The shared heritage between the Samaritan and Jerusalem priests is illustrated in a story of intermarriage in the family of the high priests told by the later Jewish historian Josephus:

> Now Jaddua succeeded in the high priesthood, and he had a brother whose name was Manasseh. Now there was one Sanballat who was sent by Darius, the last king of Persia, into Samaria. . . . He willingly gave his daughter, whose name was Nicaso, in marriage to Manasseh, as thinking this alliance by marriage would be a pledge and security that the nation of the Jews should continue their good will to him. . . . *Sanballat told Manasseh, the brother of the high priest Jaddua, that he would build him a temple like that in Jerusalem on Mount Gerizim.* Sanballat also promised to give him the honor and dignity of a high priest and make him governor if he would keep his daughter as his wife. Manasseh was elevated with these promises and many priests and Levites in Jerusalem were involved in such matches. (Ant 11.302–313)

Josephus, of course, disapproves. But this is not the point. The story attests to a close relationship between Jerusalemites and Samaritans *before the building of the Samaritan temple.* This suggests that the cooperation between Jerusalem and Gerizim priestly scribes lasted through the fifth century. The choice of the name *Manasseh*, with its connections to one of the northern tribes of Israel, also suggests more friendly relations between Jerusalem and Samaria.

A friendly relationship between the Jerusalem and Samaritan communities is also attested by an Aramaic letter from the Jewish refugees living in Elephantine, Egypt, during the late fifth century. A certain Jedaniah and his fellow priests in Elephantine write a letter to Jerusalem known as "A Request to Build a Temple in Elephantine," which includes mention of another letter sent to the governor of Samaria.[11] The letter specifically appeals to an authorization to rebuild shrines known from the Behistun inscription of the Persian king Darius I. In this respect, Bagohi and Delaiah, the governors in Jerusalem and Samaria, may have felt obligated to give a positive response in their joint reply, dated to 407 BCE, giving permission to rebuild the temple in Elephantine. However, the Elephantine scholar Bezalel Porten notes that the permission to rebuild the temple in Elephantine omits permission to burn offerings at Elephantine, which was specifically requested in the original letter to Jerusalem.[12] In this respect, Deuteronomy 12 is particularly concerned with "the place where people bring *their offerings and sacrifices*" (see vv. 5–6). It is also worth noting that the request letter and the permission memorandum were addressed to and came from the governors in Jerusalem and Samaria rather than the temple priests in Jerusalem and Mount Gerizim. The priests might have felt differently than the governors about the building of more temples and making offerings to Yahweh in more places! Indeed, this is suggested by the fact that Jedaniah and his colleagues complain that the priests in Jerusalem never answered their letter.

The Book of Tobit

One apparent example of a shared literary legacy of Jerusalem and Samaritan priests is the Book of Tobit. This work was known mainly through later Greek copies until five Aramaic and one Hebrew fragmentary copies turned up among the Dead Sea Scrolls.[13] Before the publication of the Tobit Scrolls, there was a lot of confusion about the origin of the Book of Tobit. But now, as Israeli Dead Sea Scrolls scholar Devorah Dimant observes, scholars generally recognize that "Tobit belongs with the Aramaic literature created in the land of Israel during the Second Temple period."[14] The book tells the story of Tobit, an Israelite exile from the tribe of Naphali during the days of the Assyrian empire. It shares some literary tropes of the more widely known Aramaic text of the time known as *Ahiqar*, which was used as school curricula in training Aramean scribes throughout the Persian Empire.[15] The Book of Tobit borrows *Ahiqar*'s trope of a sage working for the Assyrians and even names Ahiqar as Tobit's nephew who interceded for Tobit and brought him to Nineveh (Tob 1:21–22). It is generally thought that *Ahiqar* was composed in Mesopotamia during the seventh or sixth century, but the first known copy is from Elephantine and dates to the fifth century BCE. The Book of Tobit would have been a local story that borrowed from *Ahiqar* and became literary curricula for Aramaic scribes working in Jerusalem or Samaria.

The great scholarly debates about Tobit revolve around its original language and the time and place of its composition. We have Tobit in both Hebrew and Aramaic among the Dead Sea Scrolls, so both languages are possibilities. The similarities to *Ahiqar*, which was widely used Aramaic pedagogical literature, suggests that Tobit was also probably originally Aramaic. Even if Tobit was originally composed in Aramaic, translating it into Hebrew meant that it could also be used as pedagogical literature for training Hebrew scribes as well. More than this, a translation into Hebrew reminds us that Aramaic was the pathway to learning to read and write Hebrew during the Babylonian and Persian periods when Aramaic was the *lingua franca* for the bureaucracy of empires in the eastern Mediterranean.

The time and place of composition is more difficult. When we look closely at the story of Tobit, it certainly looks like the book could have been Samaritan literature.[16] After all, we tend to write about ourselves. The story of Tobit begins in the days of the Assyrian king Shalmaneser (r. 727–722 BCE). Tobit himself comes from the village of Thisbe in Naphtali, and he contends that he was a pious Jew in spite of living in the northern kingdom. Unfortunately, he is exiled to Nineveh, where he pens his story. But for someone supposedly living in Mesopotamia, many scholars point out that the book does not know Mesopotamian geography very well. For this reason (and others), it makes sense to understand the book as being composed in Samaria. The book has themes that recall other biblical literature like Esther and Daniel. Tobit lives under a foreign king who prohibits Jewish practices (in this case, burials), but God saves the pious Tobit, who continues to follow kosher laws and festivals, to do acts of charity, and to give proper Jewish burials. Much of the book is concerned with proper marriage, which means marriage that stays within the tribe and the family.

A difficulty with Tobit as Samaritan literature is its strongly positive view of Jerusalem. For example, we read, "while I was still a young man, the whole tribe of *my ancestor Naphtali deserted the house of David and Jerusalem.* This city had been chosen from among all the tribes of Israel, where all the tribes of Israel should offer sacrifice and where the temple, the dwelling of God, had been consecrated and established for all generations forever" (Tobit 1:4). This does not sound like a Samaritan, but it does echo the explanation of the Fall of Samaria: "When Israel tore away from the house of David, and they made Jeroboam son of Nebat king, and Jeroboam drove Israel from following the LORD and made them commit great sin" (2 Kgs 17:7). It also follows the view of the northern prophet Hosea, who writes, "The Israelites shall remain many days without king or prince . . . and afterward the Israelites shall return and seek the LORD their God, and David their king." And the Book of Tobit ends with a liturgy that praises Jerusalem: "Let all people speak of God's majesty, and acknowledge Him in Jerusalem" (13:8). The Book of Tobit ends anachronistically, knowing that Jerusalem will eventually be destroyed just like Samaria. It looks forward to its rebuilt temple: "God will again have mercy on them and will bring them back into the land of Israel. They will rebuild the temple of God, *but not like the first one* until the period when the times of fulfillment shall come. After this they all will return from their exile and will rebuild Jerusalem in splendor; and in it the temple of God will be rebuilt" (14:5). All this suggests that the final version of Tobit, that is, the book as we now have it, was edited in Jerusalem. Moreover, it was translated into Hebrew from Aramaic, and it became Hebrew literature. The prominence of Jerusalem in the beginning and at the conclusion—but only in the beginning and conclusion—are classic signs of revision through creating a new introduction as well as conclusion.[17]

We can contrast Tobit's appreciation for Jerusalem with the complete absence of Mount Gerizim. Nothing positive, nothing negative—Tobit makes no allusion to it. Since the temple on Gerizim was probably built by the mid-fifth century BCE, it seems strange that there is no mention of it. This might suggest that Tobit was composed in Aramaic and written before there was a Samaritan temple on Gerizim. The main character of Tobit, an exile from the tribe of Naphtali who has a positive attitude toward Jerusalem, suggests a setting within a scribal community where there were still friendly relations between Jerusalem and Samaria.

The Deterioration of Samaritan-Jerusalem Relations

The relationship between the Judeans and the Samaritans deteriorated and eventually led to an irreparable parting of the ways. The destruction of the Samaritan temple by the Hasmonean ruler John Hyrcanus (ca. 111–110 BCE) is the capstone in these deteriorating relations. The New Testament later reflects the animosity in the parable of the "Good Samaritan" (Luke 10:25–37) as well as the encounter between Jesus and a Samaritan woman at a well near Mount Gerizim (John 4).

When does all this animosity begin? Tensions are already evident in Ezra-Nehemiah, which would point to the late fifth or early fourth century BCE. For example, the Book of Nehemiah recounts that one of the grandsons of the high priest Eliashib was the son-in-law of Sanballat the Horonite. On the one hand, the marriage of a highly placed Aaronite priest into the family of Sanballat gives us a good vector for transfer and creation of a Samaritan Pentateuch. On the other hand, Nehemiah suggests that this intermarriage defiled the priesthood (Neh 13:28–29).[18] This story might predate the origin of the Samaritan temple, but the editorializing about the marriage definitely points to a definitive break between the Jerusalem and Samaritan priestly communities. We mentioned that the later Jewish historian Josephus wrote about an Aaronite priest from Jerusalem named Manasseh marrying into the Sanballat family from Samaria and then taking over as high priest for the temple on Mount Gerizim during the time of Alexander the Great (Ant 11.324). Although Josephus has the chronology wrong by a century, he nevertheless got some issues right. Namely, there was intermarriage between the Samaritan and Jerusalem priestly families. It just happened more than a century earlier than Josephus' account. Perhaps Josephus' confusion is understandable because of the practice of papponymy—naming children after the grandparents. As a result, there are at least two Sanballats who are governors of Samaria, one in the fifth century and a second in the fourth century. And a certain Sanballat, governor of Samaria, plays a central role in the conflict stories between the Judeans and Samaria in the Book of Nehemiah. We also know that a Sanballat was the Samaritan governor in the late fifth century BCE from the Elephantine papyri. Another Sanballat is known from the Samaria papyri dating to the early fourth century BCE.[19]

According to the narrative in Ezra, troubles already begin with the building of the Temple in Jerusalem (e.g., Ezr 4:20–24), which would be as early as the late sixth century. Some scholars suggest that the biblical texts are not reliable about Judean-Samaritan relations. They point to the shared Pentateuch as well as Josephus' description of intermarriage of priestly families during the Hellenistic period and suggest that the positive relationship lasted through the Hellenistic period. However, Josephus leads us astray because he misdated the building of the Samaritan temple to the time of Alexander the Great (ca. 333 BCE). Archaeological excavations suggest that the Gerizim temple was built more a century earlier, and the building of the Samaritan temple in the mid-fifth century BCE must have been a catalyst for tensions between Samaritan and Jerusalem priestly communities. In this respect, by the end of the fifth century BCE, the Jerusalem and Gerizim priestly communities would have found themselves in an irreparable situation based on a shared Pentateuch that included Deuteronomy 12, which allowed for only one place for worship.

The relations between the Judeans and Samaritans were undoubtedly complex and changed over time.[20] It is hard to pinpoint the date of an irreparable break. The events that shaped the relationship began with the destruction of Samaria (721 BCE) and deepened with the destruction of Jerusalem (586 BCE). During the Babylonian period, Samaritan and Judean priestly scribes had a shared experience—namely, the destruction of their sacred spaces and the need to preserve their religious traditions. Even amid Nehemiah's conflicts with Sanballat and the Samaritans, he also admits that many Judeans were allied with the Samaritans and their families had intermarried (e.g., Neh 6:17–19). It is easy to oversimplify the relationship between the Judeans and the Samaritans. Still, the rebuilding of the Jerusalem Temple followed by the building of the Mount Gerizim temple fundamentally changed the shared experience of these priestly scribal communities. The development of the sacred precinct and a temple on Mount Gerizim meant that the Samaritans had an independent locus for their own scribal community. One can imagine that some of these shared experiences, heritage, language, literature, and family intermarriage meant a continuing—if fraught—relationship between the communities. Yet with the building of competing temples, they became communities in fundamental conflict, especially as the import and authority of their shared Pentateuch grew.

12

Ezra and Nehemiah

PERSIAN SCRIBAL COMMUNITIES

As a graduate student I took a seminar from Sara Japhet, one of the world's leading experts on the Book of Chronicles. At the time, I was a doctoral student at Brandeis University, but she invited me to join her seminar at Harvard, where she was a visiting professor, so I trekked across town to sit at the feet of a master. I was in the early stages of writing my dissertation on the Book of Chronicles, and this was one of those opportunities not to be missed. Professor Japhet deepened our understanding of Chronicles in many ways, including its authorship. Previously, there had existed a consensus regarding the Books of Chronicles and Ezra-Nehemiah as deriving from a common author. Professor Japhet wrote a devasting critique of this position, noting the many small but significant distinctions in the ideologies of the two works.[1] Of course, there are also a number of similarities between the books that had created the impression of a common authorship. These similarities were not lost on the later rabbis who also suggested a common authorship. However, these commonalities, beginning with the centrality of the Temple and the high regard for the priests, are better explained as deriving from a common scribal community rather than a common author. These books are the products of a priestly scribal community working in the Temple throughout the Persian and Hellenistic periods.

Chronicles itself is unlikely to have had a single author. Rather, scribal communities across several generations compiled and later revised the book. The indications of compilation begin its extensive genealogies (1 Chronicles 1–9), which were their own composition. These genealogies were incorporated as the preface to the work. A first edition of the book was compiled already in the late sixth century. In this early edition, the Davidic lineage was still relevant to the story of Israel. But the book was revised and updated as is demonstrated by genealogies that extend into the fourth century BCE. By this time, the Jerusalem priests had become the leaders of the Jewish community, and the Davidic kings had become a legacy of the past. In the final edition of Chronicles, the concerns about the temple and the role of the priests take a primary role. So Chronicles has two sides to it that reflect the transition that happens in Jerusalem from the sixth through the fourth centuries. There are old historical, royal, and administrative interests, but in the final composition these are overshadowed by concerns about the priesthood and the Temple. As such, the book provides a nice introduction to the two major figures of this chapter, Nehemiah and Ezra.

Ezra and Nehemiah will illustrate two different aspects of the postexilic Hebrew scribal community. Ezra, who is titled both "Priest" and "scribe," represents the main development of the Hebrew scribal community—namely, its association with the temple and temple service. Nehemiah, who was a Persian administrator and governor, illustrates another part of the story of the Second Temple scribal communities. The Persian administration was conducted in Aramaic, not Hebrew. Hebrew literacy was secondary. Aramaic literacy was practical. Hebrew literacy was related to religious ideology and later used for political purposes.

Returning to Jerusalem

Nehemiah and Ezra represent the exilic community that returned to Jerusalem. They embody the last episode of this story of the biblical scribal communities. It begins with the return of the exiles and the rebuilding of the Temple and then the city of Jerusalem. The decree of the

Persian king, Cyrus the Great, in 539 BCE traditionally marks the beginning of the Persian period, which lasts until Alexander the Great's conquest in 333 BCE. During this period, exiles probably returned in several waves to Jerusalem and Judah (or, as the Persians called it, the province of "Yehud").

The first returnees join those people who had remained in the land, and together they rebuild the Jerusalem Temple sometime around 515 BCE.[2] The walls of Jerusalem were later rebuilt in a second phase of the city's restoration in the mid-fifth century BCE under Nehemiah's leadership. There is some debate about when Nehemiah returned from Babylon; some argue under Artaxerxes I (r. 464–424 BCE) and others under Artaxerxes II (r. 404–358 BCE).[3] I prefer the mid-fifth century date because the early leadership in the post-exilic period was not strictly priestly. So, for example, an Elephantine letter written to Jerusalem in the late fifth century is addressed to a Persian governor, Bagohi, not a temple priest. However, by the fourth century, the priests had taken over direct political leadership in Yehud. We see the tokens of priestly leadership physically manifested in coins minted with priests on the inscriptions.

Ezra and Nehemiah seem to be contemporaries, although they rarely appear together in the stories in Ezra-Nehemiah. For example, Nehemiah pops up in the story of the reading of the Torah in Nehemiah 8, but almost as an afterthought. The story focuses on Ezra and the Levites reading and teaching the Torah. Then Nehemiah makes an appearance as we see in:

> Then Ezra blessed the LORD, the great God, . . . and the Levites helped the people to understand the law. So they read from the book, from the Torah of God, with interpretation. They gave the sense, so that the people understood the reading. . . . And Nehemiah, who was the governor, and Ezra, the priest and scribe, and the Levites, who taught the people, said to all the people, "This day is holy to the LORD your God; do not mourn or weep." (8:6–9)

Nehemiah appears together with Ezra and the Levites almost unexpectedly. Then Nehemiah disappears from the story again. Nehemiah is not included among those reading the Torah or teaching to the people. We could argue that there was no reason for Nehemiah to have a prominent role in this story because he was a governor and administrator, not a teacher of religious texts. Ezra and Nehemiah belonged to different communities within Jerusalem; Nehemiah was an administrator, and Ezra was a priestly scribe. But before we go too far with the figures of Nehemiah and Ezra, let's take a closer look at Jerusalem in the Persian period.

Jerusalem in the Persian Period

Jerusalem was a small town in the Persian period. In that respect, it is surprising that Nehemiah and Ezra are not mentioned as working together more frequently. For example, the so-called "Nehemiah Memoir" (Nehemiah 1–7), which is a first-person account of Nehemiah's journey to Jerusalem and work with the people to restore the city walls, never mentions Ezra. Likewise, the short "Ezra Memoir" (Ezra 7:27–9:15) never mentions Nehemiah. Moreover, Ezra does not figure in the stories about Nehemiah rebuilding the walls of Jerusalem. And Ezra seems secondary in the account of Nehemiah. For example, Nehemiah 12 gives two lists of people working with him. One omits Ezra (vv. 41–43), but it is prefaced by another that highlights the priests including Ezra (vv. 31–37). From this perspective, the two lists seem to have been put together later because of the need to highlight the prominent role of the priests. More generally, the books of Ezra and Nehemiah are put together by a later scribal community that combined their stories in one book, and scholars use a hyphenated title for it: Ezra-Nehemiah. In this merger, they become one story. After all, Jerusalem in the Persian period was just too small for them not to have known each other and worked with each other! That their memoirs do not mention each other suggests that they were put together as a literary construct rather than reflecting the historical circumstances.

Each new archaeological excavation in Jerusalem confirms the picture of Jerusalem as a very small town during the Persian period. Persian Jerusalem was mired in something of a Dark Age. There are two aspects to this Dark Age. First of all, geographically, Jerusalem is isolated. It was "on the road to nowhere," as George Adam Smith so poignantly observed in his classic book *The Historical Geography of the Holy Land*.[4] Located up in the Judean hills, Jerusalem was far away from the main highways and commerce of the empire. Second, the Persian empire made no effort to integrate Jerusalem into the empire. The Persian province of Yehud, where Jerusalem was located, had borders that were restricted to the hill country. The borders of Yehud did not reach the coastal plain. As a result, Jerusalem was unimportant within the empire. Jerusalem had little military, commercial, or political import. Its importance would have been related to its proximity to Egypt, if its borders had extended to the coastal plain and the Mediterranean Sea. But since Jerusalem and Yehud did not control any part of the eastern Mediterranean coastal plain, it played no role in the Persian imperial aspirations for Egypt. As a result, Jerusalem itself remained a rather small and poor town throughout the Persian period.

Events of the late fifth century did focus the Empire's attention toward the eastern Mediterranean. Egypt successfully revolted against the Persians around 404 BCE. The Egyptian revolt resulted in increased focus on the eastern Mediterranean gateway to Egypt, but Jerusalem was still isolated up in the Judean hills. The last few decades of intense archaeological scrutiny have only confirmed this portrait. The Persians developed a string of military fortresses along the coastal plain that were pivotal for imperial aspirations in Egypt. Thousands of Aramaic administrative inscriptions point to the intense economic and political interest in the coastal plain *west of Jerusalem and Yehud.* In this respect, archaeological excavations have not illuminated Jerusalem's Dark Age but rather confirmed it. Jerusalem is not mentioned in the hundreds of economic documents from the coastal plain dating to the late fourth century BCE. Jerusalem had no significant contact with the vibrant coastal trade and military development of the late Persian period in the fourth century.

The size of Jerusalem is also related to a question relevant to our project here: How many scribes lived in Jerusalem? Probably not many. Archaeology has provided some evidence as to the relative size of the city from the Iron Age to the Persian period (see Figure 12.1). It used to be

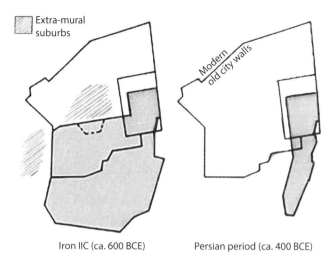

Iron IIC (ca. 600 BCE)   Persian period (ca. 400 BCE)

FIGURE 12.1. Decline and rise of Jerusalem from Iron Age
through the Hasmonean periods. Drawing by the author.

that scholars thought that as many as fifteen thousand people might
have lived in Jerusalem during the Persian period, but the more archaeologists have excavated in Jerusalem, the lower the estimates have gotten.
Archaeologists just do not find much evidence for settlement outside
of the upper part of the eastern hill, or the City of David.

Just how small was Jerusalem? A debate between two old friends of
mine—Israeli archaeologists Israel Finkelstein and Oded Lipschits—is
instructive.[5] I would characterize it as a debate over whether Jerusalem
was really tiny (2.5 hectares, Finkelstein) or just quite small (5 hectares,
Lipschits). Even the "maximalist," Lipschits, still depicts a 90 percent
drop in the size of Jerusalem from the seventh century to the fifth
century BCE.[6] How many people does this translate into? The estimate
will depend on the population density—that is, how many people lived
in the city per acre of land. Finkelstein goes as low as four hundred
people living in Jerusalem, including women and children. That is less
than a hundred adult males living in Jerusalem until the third century
BCE. And, of course, there is no reason to believe they were all scribes!
Lipschits is naturally concerned about the implications for biblical literature and scribal communities. It is hardly possible to posit the kind

of robust editing and composition of literature when you have such a meager population. Even so, Lipschits' more generous approach would envision only about a thousand people living in Jerusalem, and that might be about two hundred adult males. All these certainly were not literate. This does not suggest robust scribal activity in Jerusalem.

The Book of Nehemiah also paints a dismal picture. According to Nehemiah's Memoir, "The city was wide and large, but few people lived in it and no houses had been built" (Neh 7:4). Nehemiah advocates a settlement program for Jerusalem: "Now the leaders of the people lived in Jerusalem, and the rest of the people cast lots to bring one out of ten to live in the holy city of Jerusalem, while nine-tenths remained in the other towns" (Neh 11:1). How many literate people were there in a town that numbered only a thousand people with more than two hundred adult males? Perhaps there were a couple dozen scribes living in Jerusalem who were able to write Hebrew during the Persian period. The problem with envisioning a larger number of scribes is simply that Hebrew had no utility beyond the preservation of religious texts. Nehemiah complains that many could not even speak Hebrew: "In those days I saw Jews . . . that could not speak the language of Judah, but spoke language of various peoples" (Neh 13:23–24). When there was a public reading of the Torah, it had to be translated into Aramaic so that people could understand it (Neh 8:8). All of this is to point out that the book of Ezra-Nehemiah does not imagine widespread Hebrew literacy. It was the job of a small priestly scribal community to read and write and communicate these religious texts to the people.

Writing and scribal communities require affluence, infrastructure, and patronage. Jerusalem was so poor during the Persian period that it could not have been the place of a large scribal community. There are a number of archaeological tools that can be used to measure wealth. For example, archaeologists can quantify and compare things like imported pottery, the characteristics of jewelry, or the number of inscriptions.[7] All these things are indexes of wealth, and the Persian town of Jerusalem has none of them. The number and kind of inscriptions would also tell us something about the infrastructure. Again, we can get a similar picture reading the Book of Nehemiah, which describes a situation where people were complaining about needing "to mortgage our fields, vineyards, and houses in to order to get grain" (Neh 5:3). Some people were even supposedly selling their own children into slavery and prostitution for food (5:5). Nehemiah paints a bleak picture. To be sure, Nehemiah's complaint here addresses the disparity of wealth, but it still paints a dismal economic situation in Persian Jerusalem that accords well with the archaeological evidence. All of this does not bode well for a robust scribal community in Jerusalem.

Let's crunch some numbers about the size of Jerusalem and scribal communities. Begin with the more maximalist view of a population of one thousand, which would be about two hundred adult males. We can also assume that almost all the working Hebrew scribal community were male, since it would have been related to the Temple and biblical literature has no tradition about women working as priests, Levites, or temple administrators. In addition, we should assume that some of the city administrators were literate, but most of them probably would have found Aramaic to be the only useful language for administration in the Achaemenid context. If there were twenty people who had some Hebrew literacy, that would represent 10 percent literacy among the adult male population in the context of a small, isolated town like Jerusalem. That would be quite high, but perhaps religious ideology and temple service created a higher amount of literacy. There also could have also been administrators like Nehemiah that had some Hebrew literacy, although for administration literacy would have focused on Aramaic. Someone like the governor Nehemiah, who makes an ideological point about the knowledge of Hebrew, seems to have added Hebrew scribal literacy to his Aramaic training. Even so, we cannot expect all literate men to acquire advanced Hebrew literacy. Maybe there were a dozen or so scribes actually at work in the Temple copying, updating, and studying traditional Hebrew texts.

Nehemiah's Scribal Community

Nehemiah's scribal community would have been in the Persian administration of Yehud. We may assume this because Nehemiah's primary occupation as governor naturally made him part of the Persian administration, and this would have been an Aramaic scribal community. The broad extent of the Aramaic scribal community is evident in the inscriptional record. Beginning especially in the fourth century BCE (late Persian period), we have thousands of inscriptions from the southern Levant—all in Aramaic.[8] These Aramaic inscriptions include seal impressions, papyri, ostraca, and stone inscriptions and can be found in places like the southern Mediterranean coastal plain (e.g., Mareshah), the Jordan Valley (Jericho), the Judean Negev (Arad), and Samaria (Mt. Gerizim). A few Aramaic inscriptions also come from Jerusalem itself, but the vast majority come from the coastal plain east of Yehud. And they are all administrative. For example, hundreds of Aramaic ostraca dating to the fourth century come from the Judean coast to the west of Jerusalem. The inscriptions are administrative, but they give us some useful information. For example, they give us names and titles of officials (*pḥt* "governor," *khn* "priest," *sgn* "prefect," *dyn* "judge"), and they inform us about the commodities that were being taxed, traded, and recorded.[9] The vast numbers of these ostraca reflect the empire's economic and military development of the southern Levantine coast— the gateway to Egypt.

The large number of Aramaic inscriptions from the Judean coastal plain makes historical sense. The Persian Empire had lost control of Egypt in 404 BCE. As a result, the empire put considerable resources into fortifying the southern Levantine coast that eventually paid dividends in its reconquest of Egypt around 343 BCE. Later in the fourth century, Alexander the Great would also march along the coast on his way to conquer Egypt, but as Jerusalem was also unimportant to Alexander, he bypassed it. The later Jewish historian Josephus tries to raise Jerusalem's stature by narrating the trek of Alexander to meet the high priest (*Ant* 11.302–47),[10] but Jerusalem was not critical to the Achaemenid or Hellenistic administrative, commercial, or military development of the Levantine coast. Nevertheless, Jerusalem was a secondary beneficiary to the increased attention, especially in the third century BCE when Jerusalem began to grow and prosper under Ptolemaic control.

A good measure for the Aramaic scribal infrastructure are seals and seal impressions. We now have a comprehensive study on the topic, *The*

Yehud Stamp Impressions, by a fine scholarly duo—Lipschits, an Israeli archaeologist, and David Vanderhooft, an American expert in inscriptions. Lipschits' excavations at Ramat Raḥel, three miles south of Jerusalem, uncovered an administrative center that inspired him to catalogue and analyze all the Yehud stamp impressions.[11] He argues that Ramat Raḥel served as an administrative center in the sixth and fifth centuries while Jerusalem was still largely in ruins. This argument is bolstered by the excavation of ninety early type Yehud stamps at Ramat Raḥel, while only seventeen were excavated in Jerusalem. The Yehud stamps have a variety of impressions, with most just bearing the Aramaic inscription *yhwd* "Yehud." A few of them bear the names of the governor in the inscription including "Belonging to 'Aḥiab, the Governor" or "Yehud, 'Uriyaw." These inscriptions point to the Persian administration of the Yehud province that required an Aramaic scribal community. But there is not a single Hebrew inscription from Ramat Raḥel that can be dated to the sixth or fifth century BCE. Any scribes working at Ramat Raḥel were part of an Aramaic scribal community. They were trained to write receipts and letters. They oversaw the accounting, taxes, and diplomatic correspondence of the imperial administration.

The seals and seal impressions are a strong confirmation that Aramaic was the language of Achaemenid administration, even in the Persian province of Yehud. Still, Hebrew likely continued to be spoken in some villages. Based on linguistic anthropological analogies, we can expect that the small Judean villages that were not destroyed by the Babylonians continued to speak a local Hebrew vernacular. Yet such places are hardly likely locales for much literacy at all, and the newly established settlements likely spoke Aramaic. Aramaic had become the vernacular.

How did Nehemiah learn Hebrew and how was he trained as a scribe? Aramaic would have been the linguistic foundation for his training. Scribes learned to read and write Aramaic first. Hebrew was a secondary, specialized, and advanced type of scribal training. There was a significant difference between Aramaic and Hebrew scribal communities in the Second Temple Period. Aramaic was the *lingua franca* throughout the near east. This began already with Assyria's use of Aramaic as an administrative language. The use and importance of Aramaic continued under the Babylonians; by the Achaemenid period, the use of Aramaic had reached from India to Egypt. Because Aramaic was an administrative language, the scope of Aramaic literature was rather limited in spite of the thousands of known Aramaic inscriptions and texts. Aramaic scribal education would have generally served as a bridge for Hebrew scribal education. Indeed, biblical figures like Nehemiah as well as Ezra serve as good examples for this. People would learn to read and write in Aramaic, and then some would add Hebrew to their literacy skills. A good analogy for this learning model is the ancient city of Ugarit in the thirteenth century BCE. There, scribes learned to read and write in Akkadian, which was the *lingua franca* of the near east in the second millennium. After acquiring literacy, some scribes added the alphabetic Ugaritic language to their skill set. Since they had already acquired literacy skills and Ugaritic is linguistically related, it was relatively easy to add Ugaritic literacy. This sequence of learning Akkadian and then Ugaritic explains why there are very few Ugaritic school texts compared to Akkadian found at Ugarit, and the number of Ugaritic scribes seems to be far fewer than Akkadian scribes at Ugarit. Ugaritic literacy was a secondary skill. The same was true for Hebrew in Jerusalem during the Persian period. Aramaic was the primary chancellery language, and Hebrew was a secondary language used in the Temple scribal community.

One of the oldest known Aramaic literary texts, *Ahiqar*, was used as a primary curricular text for training in the administrative chancellery. *Ahiqar* would have been part of the curriculum for the Hebrew scribal community since Hebrew scribes would have begun their scribal training by learning Aramaic. So it is not surprising then that *Ahiqar* became a literary template for many other Hebrew works. The vestiges of *Ahiqar* can be seen in a variety of Second Temple texts. Most notably, the Book of Tobit mentions a scribe named Ahiqar in its opening chapter (Tob 1:21–22). Tobit borrows the general theme of the story of *Ahiqar*—a foreigner working in the Imperial court. This theme was localized by Tobit, now a Jew working in a foreign court. Tobit was originally composed in Aramaic, no doubt as a local adaptation for training Levantine scribes, but it was translated into Hebrew as we learn from a copy found among the Dead Sea Scrolls. Its translation into Hebrew would have facilitated the training of Hebrew scribes in the late Second Temple period.

The literary theme of Ahiqar—a foreigner in the Imperial court—appears again and again in Second Temple Hebrew literature. Nehemiah, for example, was a foreigner in the Persian court. The Nehemiah Memoir features a certain Tobiah, which reminds us of the main character of the Book of Tobit. The priest Ezra is also a figure who originally worked in a foreign court. The theme extends to the Book of Daniel, where the book begins with the training of Judeans to serve in Babylonian courts, and later tales in Daniel continue the theme with Judeans serving in the Persian court. The Book of Esther also uses the theme of Jews working in the court of a Persian king. All of these works adapt a literary theme from the most prominent Aramaic curricular text, *Ahiqar*, but they also reflect a reality that began in the Assyrian period and expanded in the Babylonian and Persian periods, namely, the experience of the diverse and multicultural administrators working in the imperial courts. In that respect, *Ahiqar* utilizes a universal experience of Persian scribal communities, and it is hardly surprising that the Hebrew scribal community borrowed and adapted this theme.

According to a later tradition, Nehemiah established a library in Jerusalem. The account of the Jerusalem library is given in 2 Maccabees 2:13–14, a book written in Greek in the second century BCE.

> The same things are reported in the records and in the memoirs of Nehemiah, and also that he founded a library and collected the books about the kings and prophets, and the writings of David, and letters of kings about votive offerings. In the same way Judah (Maccabee) also collected all the books that had been lost on account of the war that had come upon us, and they are in our possession. (NETS)

The purpose of this account seems to be to bolster Judah Maccabee for imitating Nehemiah.[12] In order for this appeal to the past to work, there had to be some tradition of an older library in Jerusalem. Assuredly, a library of classical Hebrew texts was already housed in the Jerusalem Temple. The creation of a library by Nehemiah would have been a secular library, probably inspired (anachronistically) by the Great Library in

Alexandria. A Greek story from the second century BCE, *The Letter of Aristeas*, tells the tale of the translation of the Torah for the Library of Alexandria. According to *Aristeas*, Ptolemy wrote to the high priest in Jerusalem to get official copies of the Torah that were then translated into Greek. The library in the Maccabees' account would also fit nicely with other near eastern royal libraries, but the reference to votive offerings in the Maccabees story suggests this actually refers to the Jerusalem Temple library. We can assume that Maccabees considered the *Torah* as part of a Temple library, in contrast to Nehemiah's library, but it is striking that Nehemiah did not even collect the books of the *Torah*. Maccabees likely thought that the *Torah* was much older than Nehemiah, and therefore there was no need for Nehemiah to collect the books of the *Torah*.

But why is Nehemiah the founder of a Jerusalem library? One really expects Ezra, the priest and scribe, to be elevated by the writer of 2 Maccabees. Why Nehemiah? He is not a priest. He was likely considered to be a literary parallel to Ptolemy, who founded the Library of Alexandria. More than that, there is also a tradition of secular royal libraries in the near east. The most famous example is the library of the Assyrian king Assurbanipal in Ninevah. The Egyptian pharaoh Shabaka also apparently collected a library in Memphis.[13] And these figures are contemporaneous with the Judean king Hezekiah, whose men collected the writings of Solomon (Prov 25:1). We might suggest that Maccabees is merely aware of this tradition of secular leaders collecting libraries. Nehemiah would have collected a more diverse library than the Temple priests, and this makes him an ideal choice for 2 Maccabees.

Nehemiah as a Persian administrator seems to have been instrumental in collecting materials that were used by later scribes. This is indeed suggested by the account of Nehemiah's library in 2 Maccabees, but it is also evident from the writings of Josephus. In contrast to Josephus' account of Ezra, which essentially follows the biblical narrative, Josephus seems to draw on a variety of sources to tell the story of Nehemiah.[14] A review of Josephus' account would suggest that there was more available than what was compiled into the Book of Ezra-Nehemiah. The nature of Ezra-Nehemiah as a compiled work is also suggested by the different ways it is known from antiquity. For example, the Greek *1 Esdras* includes 2

Chronicles 35–36, Ezra 1–10, and Nehemiah 8:1–13. In contrast, the Greek 2 *Esdras* is the combined Book of Ezra-Nehemiah, which was not split up into separate books until the time of Origen and Jerome and perhaps much later than this in Jewish tradition.

Ezra, Priest and Scribe

Ezra serves as the master scribe within the priestly scribal community. He is, in fact, repeatedly given two titles, "Priest" and "Scribe" (e.g., Ezr 7:11; Neh 8:9; 12:16). This emphasis on two different titles is unique in biblical literature. Ezra is not just any priestly scribe. He has a pedigree. According to Ezra 7:1, Ezra's father was Seraiah, which happens to be the same name as King David's scribe (2 Sam 8:17), and it is also the name of the last high priest of the First Temple who was executed by Nebuchadnezzar (2 Kgs 25:18–21). That is quite the potential lineage! Coincidence? I think not. Of course, this could be related to the Hellenistic cuneiform practice that traced scribal lineages to a prestigious ancestor.[15] Hellenistic Greek literature also developed the practice of pseudepigraphy— that is, the ascription of venerable old figures to later literary works. Jewish tradition in the Hellenistic period adopted and adapted this practice. Hellenistic Jewish literature like Enoch, Baruch, and 4 Ezra gets attributed to figures of the past.

Through the editing of the Hebrew Bible, Ezra's ancestor belongs to a scribal family that dates back to the days of King David. According to later Jewish tradition, Ezra wrote his own book as well as the Book of Chronicles (BT, *Bava Batra* 15a), but he is given no role in the composition of the Torah. In spite of this, biblical scholar Richard Elliot Friedman argued in his bestselling book *Who Wrote the Bible?* that it was indeed Ezra that compiled the *Torah*.[16] It is curious, however, that the Bible itself never names Ezra as a compiler, redactor, or editor of the *Torah*. Rather, Ezra is simply a priestly scribe who promotes the authority and prestige of the *Torah* along with his cohort in Nehemiah 8. Interestingly, the Hellenistic book *The Wisdom of Sirach*, composed about 200 BCE, seems to omit Ezra deliberately, perhaps because it considered Moses and Aaron the key figures for the composition of the Pentateuch. The

Books of Ezra-Nehemiah themselves do not present themselves as having a single author, and they look like anthologies of texts collected and edited by the priestly scribal community.

Ezra-Nehemiah is a complex collection of different kinds of writing. They include the personal memoirs of Nehemiah (Neh 1–7, 10–13) as well as narratives about Ezra (Ezr 7–10 continued in Neh 8–10), Hebrew and Aramaic copies of the Decree of Cyrus (Ezr 1:9–11; 6:3–5), Aramaic letters (Ezr 4:8–22; 5:6–17; 6:3–12), inventories of Temple vessels (Ezr 1:9–11), a list of returnees (Ezra 2), and a variety of other lists. Sometimes the lists are reused; thus we find the list in Ezra 2 repeated in Nehemiah 7. Ezra 1–6 is widely regarded as an early composition that deals with the early returnees and the rebuilding of the temple in the late sixth century. Ezra himself does not even appear in the book until the seventh chapter, when the narrative moves to a completely different era. Nehemiah likewise is a complex anthology that begins the so-called "Nehemiah Memoir," which is narrated in the first person. The Memoir concludes with a list of the returnees—supposedly 42,360 (Neh 7:66)—and then the narrative changes to the third person. This overt narrative change points to a variety of different texts gathered together, compiled, and edited by scribes over more than a century.[17] The inflated number of returnees in Nehemiah—much more than archaeology would attest—follows a scribal tradition of using inflated numbers, as is also seen in the books of Chronicles and Exodus. Chronicles retells its history using impossibly large numbers—e.g., a Judean army of 300,000 men (2 Chr 14:8)—that are not present in the Book of Samuel and Kings. The Book of Exodus has one of the most well-known inflated figures in the Bible—the 600,000 *men* (i.e., at least two million *people*) that fled from Egypt (Exod 12:37). All these large numbers seem to be part of a post-exilic priestly scribal tradition that preferred inflated numbers. The use of these inflated numbers points to a unified scribal tradition across diverse works (Exodus, Nehemiah, Chronicles). These books were part of the tradition and even curriculum of the priestly temple scribal community that worked in Jerusalem during and after the Persian period. All of this would have been compiled by priestly scribes in Jerusalem, perhaps in the fourth century BCE.

Inscriptional evidence for a priestly scribal community using Hebrew can be adduced from coins. In the fourth century BCE, coins were minted with a face on one side and the Hebrew inscription of "Johanan, the [high] priest" on the other.[18] The Book of Nehemiah records four high priests that likely date to the early fourth century—Eliashib, Joiada, Johanan, and Jaddua (Neh 12:22).[19] A high priest named Johanan is also mentioned in an Aramaic letter from Elephantine sent to Bogohi, the governor of Yehud. It is hard to precisely equate these figures, however, because the tradition of naming children after ancestors means that the same names keep reappearing. Another silver coin dating to the late fourth century bears a Hebrew inscription reading, "Yeḥezqiyah, the governor"—who can tentatively be identified with a high priest mentioned by Josephus who served as governor toward the end of the fourth century BCE.

Scanty as this evidence might be, it does demonstrate that the Jerusalem priests were in complete control of the government in Jerusalem by the fourth century BCE. More than this, these coins bear inscriptions written in the old Hebrew script, not in the Aramaic script that had become most prevalent throughout the region. There are very few Hebrew inscriptions that can be dated to the Persian period, so the use of Hebrew on coins that bear the names and images of priestly is significant. It seems that the old Hebrew script continued to be a preferred script of the Jerusalem priestly community. Excavations have discovered several more silver coins bearing old Hebrew labels that indicate Jerusalem and the province of Yehud enjoyed a degree of autonomy that allowed the priestly scribal community to mint their own coins using their national language and script.

The Earliest Dead Sea Scrolls of the Pentateuch

When I was a graduate student thirty years ago, we were taught that the earliest biblical manuscripts from Qumran were fragments of the Books of Samuel dating to the third century BCE. However, many of the biblical manuscripts had not been published. I began my own graduate studies in the most troubled days of Qumran scholarship—the 1980s. In those days, only a small group of scholars had access to the Scrolls, and a variety of conspiracy theories rose up to explain why there was not more transparency in the publication of the Scrolls. When I was a graduate student, the Scrolls seemed like a guarded secret, with only a few select Scrolls being published. About the time I finished my PhD, the cartel on the Scrolls was broken and publication proceeded apace. Now all the images of the Dead Sea Scrolls are readily available on the internet to download and study, and critical editions of all twenty-five thousand or so Scroll fragments have been published by a large international team of scholars. I was fortunate to work for the Scrolls editor-in-chief, Professor Emanuel Tov, who can be credited for pushing forward the publication of all the Scrolls, which made them widely accessible. I worked for him twice—once as a graduate student (in 1985) on his Septuagint project before he was the Dead Sea Scrolls editor, and then later (in 1993) just after he became editor when I was a post-doctoral fellow at the Albright Institute in Jerusalem.

The full publication of the Scrolls has changed our understanding of the history of biblical texts. For example, a couple of the Scrolls of the Pentateuch—Genesis (4QpaleoGen^m; see Figure 12.2) and Deuteronomy (4QpaleoDeut^s)—seem to be much older copies. They are written in an archaic paleo-Hebrew script, which was difficult to date until recently. New Samaritan inscriptions from Mount Gerizim along with paleo-Hebrew inscriptions on coins help us reevaluate the dating of these early scrolls. Using this new evidence, French paleographer Professor Michael Langlois dated the early fragments of the Pentateuch as early as the fifth century BCE.[20] Maybe. The fourth century is probably a more conservative estimate, but it is difficult to be precise about dating based on paleography alone. They look later than the Iron Age inscriptions but earlier than Hellenistic paleo-Hebrew coins and inscriptions known from excavations on Mount Gerizim. In other words, they look earlier than the Hellenistic period (333–164 BCE).[21] They represent the earliest biblical scrolls known from Qumran.

What does this mean? It is significant that these examples are Pentateuch Scrolls. The Pentateuch was undoubtedly a focus of the Jerusalem scribal community, as we see in the account of the reading of the *Torah*

Scroll in Nehemiah 8. The use of the old Hebrew script is also significant, probably continuing a tradition of copying Hebrew manuscripts dating back to the First Temple period. It also suggests that the Pentateuch was essentially compiled by the end of the fifth century BCE. The Samaritan scribal community probably would have deposited a copy in their newly built temple in the mid-fifth century BCE. A copy of the Pentateuch would have served as the foundation document for the newly built Gerizim temple. The parallels for a temple "foundation document" can be seen in temples throughout the ancient near east. For the Gerizim temple, the Pentateuch served as foundation documents at the building of the Gerizim temple itself in the fifth century

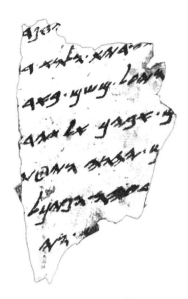

FIGURE 12.2. Fragment from a Genesis scroll in paleo-Hebrew script dating to the fourth century BCE. Drawing by the author.

BCE. After that point, the Samaritan and Jerusalem scribal communities would go their own separate ways and develop their own Pentateuchal textual traditions.

The veneration of religious texts was becoming increasingly important in the Persian period. The story of the reading of the *Torah* in Nehemiah 8 is striking because of the elevated status of the scroll. I have cited this in part above, but it is worth citing here at length:

[1] All the people gathered together into the square before the Water Gate. They told the scribe Ezra to bring the scroll of the *Torah* of Moses, which the LORD had given to Israel. [2] Accordingly, the priest Ezra brought the *Torah* before the assembly, both men and women and all who could hear with understanding. This was on the first day of the seventh month. [3] He read from it facing the square before the Water Gate from early morning until midday, in the presence of the

men and the women and those who could understand; and the ears of all the people were attentive to the scroll of the *Torah*. ⁴ The scribe Ezra stood on a wooden platform that had been made for the purpose; and beside him stood Mattithiah, Shema, Anaiah, Uriah, Hilkiah, and Maaseiah on his right hand; and Pedaiah, Mishael, Malchijah, Hashum, Hash-baddanah, Zechariah, and Meshullam on his left hand. ⁵ And Ezra opened the scroll in the sight of all the people, for he was standing above all the people; and when he opened it, all the people stood up. ⁶ Then Ezra blessed the LORD, the great God, and all the people answered, "Amen, Amen," lifting up their hands. Then they bowed their heads and worshiped the LORD with their faces to the ground. ⁷ Also Jeshua, Bani, Sherebiah, Jamin, Akkub, Shabbethai, Hodiah, Maaseiah, Kelita, Azariah, Jozabad, Hanan, Pelaiah, the Levites, helped the people to understand the *Torah*, while the people remained in their places. ⁸ So they read from the scroll, from the *Torah* of God, with interpretation. They gave the sense, so that the people understood the reading. . . . ¹³ On the second day the heads of ancestral houses of all the people, with the priests and the Levites, came together to the scribe Ezra in order to study the words of the *Torah*. ¹⁴ And they found it written in the *Torah*, which the LORD had commanded by Moses, that the people of Israel should live in booths during the festival of the seventh month, ¹⁵ and that they should publish and proclaim in all their towns and in Jerusalem . . . ¹⁸ And day by day, from the first day to the last day, he read from the scroll of the *Torah* of God. They kept the festival seven days; and on the eighth day there was a solemn assembly, according to the ordinance. (NRSV)

The priestly scribe Ezra is the major figure here, but he is accompanied by another temple group—the Levites. This story recalls the finding of the scroll during the days of King Josiah (as related in 2 Kings 22–23), but this story elevates the text even further as a religious icon. Ezra reads from the scroll with great pomp and circumstance. They make a platform for its recitation. The people listen all day long. The reading even occasions the reinstitution of the Jewish festival of booths (known as *Sukkot*). During the festival, there is a daily reading of the *Torah*.

The reverence for the text in Nehemiah 8 is somewhat muted by the lack of understanding of the text. The people who diligently listen do not understand it. In verse 8, we read that "they read from the book *with interpretation*." The Hebrew word for interpretation (מְפֹרָשׁ) probably refers to the *translation* of the text from Hebrew into the Aramaic vernacular. That is what would have made sense to a large audience in Jerusalem at that time. This suggests that we should curb any enthusiastic suggestion that literacy was widespread outside of the temple and administration. Literacy here is ascribed specifically to Ezra and his Levitical helpers.

A scribal community may get a shout-out in Nehemiah 8. There are a couple of short lists embedded in the narrative. First there is the list of thirteen people who stand beside the priestly scribe Ezra as he reads (v. 4): Mattithiah, Shema, Anaiah, Uriah, Hilkiah, and Maaseiah, Pedaiah, Mishael, Malchijah, Hashum, Hash-baddanah, Zechariah, and Meshullam. These seem to be administrative officials since the narrator does not call them priests or Levites. The second list is more relevant to our search for the scribal community. A list of Levites is named as helping the people to understand the *Torah*—Jeshua, Bani, Sherebiah, Jamin, Akkub, Shabbethai, Hodiah, Maaseiah, Kelita, Azariah, Jozabad, Hanan, Pelaiah (v. 7).[22] It is reasonable to think that this list might include the main people working as temple scribes when this story was written. From their roles in the reading and interpretation, we may surmise that they formed the scribal community at this moment. If the list is complete, then there were about a dozen people that would have been part of the temple scribal community in Jerusalem. This is just a guess, but it makes sense. We might also include the first list as literates, although their role does not involve the reading or interpretation of texts but rather administrative support. Given that Jerusalem was a poor town, twenty-five would be a generous estimate of the larger scribal community working in Jerusalem. Maybe half of those were involved in the copying, editing, and interpreting of traditional Hebrew literature and liturgy. It is not a big group, but it was a big job. They had to preserve the legacy of ancient Israel, which began with the reading and interpretation of a *Torah*.

Lists of Levites appear again in Nehemiah 9–10. First, the people continue to "read from the scroll of the *Torah*" in another event later in the month (9:3). Eight of the Levites from the earlier *Torah* reading are named as standing on the podium and leading the people in reading, prayer, and confession (9:4–5). In chapter 10, the scribal community consisting of "officials, Levites, and priests" draft and sign a covenantal contract:

> [1] Upon the sealed document are the names of Nehemiah the governor, son of Hacaliah, and Zedekiah; [2] Seraiah, Azariah, Jeremiah, [3] Pashhur, Amariah, Malchijah, [4] Hattush, Shebaniah, Malluch, [5] Harim, Meremoth, Obadiah, [6] Daniel, Ginnethon, Baruch, [7] Meshullam, Abijah, Mijamin, [8] Maaziah, Bilgai, Shemaiah; these are the priests. [9] And the Levites: Jeshua son of Azaniah, Binnui of the sons of Henadad, Kadmiel; [10] and their associates, Shebaniah, Hodiah, Kelita, Pelaiah, Hanan, [11] Mica, Rehob, Hashabiah, [12] Zaccur, Sherebiah, Shebaniah, [13] Hodiah, Bani, Beninu. [14] The leaders of the people: Parosh, Pahath-moab, Elam, Zattu, Bani, [15] Bunni, Azgad, Bebai, [16] Adonijah, Bigvai, Adin, [17] Ater, Hezekiah, Azzur, [18] Hodiah, Hashum, Bezai, [19] Hariph, Anathoth, Nebai, [20] Magpiash, Meshullam, Hezir, [21] Meshezabel, Zadok, Jaddua, [22] Pelatiah, Hanan, Anaiah, [23] Hoshea, Hananiah, Hasshub, [24] Hallohesh, Pilha, Shobek, [25] Rehum, Hashabnah, Maaseiah, [26] Ahiah, Hanan, Anan, [27] Malluch, Harim, and Baanah.

The contract claims these three groups as signatories, which explains where the lists in Nehemiah 8–10 come from, but it also may give us a fair sense of the size of the priestly and administrative scribal communities at one particular moment during the late Persian period.

The scope of the Hebrew scribal community was quite narrow. Hebrew, in contrast to Aramaic, had lost any administrative function when Jerusalem was destroyed and Judah was exiled by the Babylonians. When Hebrew script was used during the Second Temple period, it had distinctly ideological overtones. For example, the Hasmoneans use it on their coins (as does the modern state of Israel). The Samaritans use it only for Samaritan religious texts and inscriptions. However, Hebrew no longer served as an administrative language. For example, we do not have a single administrative inscription in Hebrew dating to the Persian period. Of course, we barely have any inscriptional evidence at all for Hebrew. There are a few coins and seal impressions that point to the survival of Hebrew,[23] but such inscriptions point to a political ideology rather than everyday usage. The early Dead Sea Scroll fragments also point to the religious and ideological role of written Hebrew.

Vernacular Hebrew did survive as a language spoken in some villages. This is because vernacular languages continue to be spoken as long as there is a continuity in settlement. I learned this firsthand with Aramaic. When I arrived at UCLA, one of my colleagues—Professor Yona Sabar—was a native speaker of Aramaic. He had grown up in a small village in Iraq where Aramaic had been spoken for more than two thousand years! But his family was forced to move after World War II. Eventually, he ended up as a professor of Aramaic at UCLA, but his children did not learn to speak Aramaic. The displacement of his family from their village had ended the legacy of Aramaic vernacular that had lasted for millennia. This is a generally observable linguistic phenomenon. Vernacular languages are preserved as long as people are not displaced. So Hebrew vernacular would have persisted in the Judean villages that were not destroyed, exiled, or displaced by the Babylonians. Unfortunately, about 80 percent of Judean towns disappeared during the Babylonian period, and so only small pockets of vernacular Hebrew would have continued.

When the exile Nehemiah returns to Jerusalem, he makes Hebrew vernacular a priority. He seems like a precursor to Eliezer Ben-Yehuda, who emigrated to Palestine in the late nineteenth century and revived the everyday speaking of Hebrew. Like Ben-Yehuda, Nehemiah lamented the lack of knowledge of Hebrew. He complains about Jews that had married foreign women and as a result "they could not speak the language of Judah" (Neh 13:23–24). Nehemiah is referring particularly to the knowledge of Hebrew vernacular among the people, and it is couched within the wider issue of marriage to foreign women that pervades the books of Ezra-Nehemiah. But language here is presented as a part of Jewish identity, and the marrying of foreign women casts the inability to speak Hebrew as a religious problem. Of course, the inability to *speak* Hebrew is different from the scribal skill of *reading and writing* Hebrew.

Hebrew survived as a literary language. This is first of all evident in the preservation of the paleo-Hebrew script that we see on some coins and Dead Sea Scroll fragments (e.g., Figure 12.2; Figure 11.5). Hebrew literary texts survived and were collected in the Jerusalem Temple. During the Persian period, they would have been copied and edited by the priestly Temple community. Hebrew was the language of their liturgy and sacred traditions. The earliest Hebrew Dead Sea Scrolls may now be dated to the late Persian period, and these reflect the use of Hebrew as a religious language—as a language of the Temple and its priestly community.

The small Hebrew scribal community in Jerusalem was organized around the Temple. This should not be a controversial observation. Yet many scholars do not want to accept the archaeological data for the Babylonian and Persian periods. Or perhaps they do not seem to understand the import. For example, British scholar Philip Davies argued for a late date for all of biblical literature and as a result he posited "a number of scribal schools with a vigorous scribal activity."[24] Davies understood the implications for dating biblical literature late and hence suggested rewriting—I might say inventing—a new archaeological context for the Persian Yehud. As Davies suggested, "The view of Judah in the Persian period as a cultural backwater and as economically poor perhaps needs to be reconsidered."[25] Davies wanted to rewrite the archaeological data rather than admit that biblical literature must largely date to before the Babylonian exile. Unfortunately for Davies, the archaeological context has only been further substantiated in the two decades since he wrote his book *Scribes and Schools*.

Other scholars do understand the situation. For example, in the introduction to *Chronicles and the Priestly Literature of the Hebrew Bible*, Jaeyoung Jeon and Louis Jonker observe, "Living and working in temporal and spatial proximity to one another, they [scribes] would have been familiar with each other's literary works, which were becoming and/or had already become common religious and intellectual assets of the community."[26] The spatial proximity is more straightforward than the temporal proximity. After all, the Persian period lasted two centuries, and the editing of a few biblical books (e.g., Psalms, Ecclesiastes, Daniel) plausibly continued into the Hellenistic and Hasmonean periods. There was spatial proximity for the Hebrew scribal community—they lived, studied, and worked in and around Jerusalem. But there was not temporal proximity. The community persisted from the Persian period to the destruction of the Temple by the Romans. The books of Chronicles and Ezra-Nehemiah reflect upon a text that was becoming "scripture" and even "canonical" for the priestly scribal community—namely, the *Torah*, which scholars have come to call the "Pentateuch" (literally, "five books").

The Jerusalem priestly temple scribal community would have been a closed and tightly knit group. The scribes would have all known each other. They apprenticed together. They studied together. They worked together. They would have had connections with the Aramaic scribal community. They may have even apprenticed together learning Aramaic, but the larger group would have narrowed when the training advanced to include Hebrew in the curriculum. Hebrew literacy was mainly relevant for the temple, its tradition, its liturgy, and its priestly community. It became a tool of politics and national ideology in especially during the Hasmonean period. At that point, Hebrew literacy could have spread again to different social groups.

Conclusion

This story of scribal communities—that is, who really wrote the Bible—has steered away from the traditional answer to the question. Namely, the search for individual authors. I began with the observation, for me a revelation, that learning to read and write in ancient Israel was done through apprenticeships. This also means that there were no schools as we know them. Education was closer to the model of home schooling with a master scribe and students. This form of education created tight-knit communities of learning that in turn created communities of practice, as anthropologists like to call them. Literature and texts were products of these communities. Of course, individuals could write their own works, but even then their work had to become part of the community in order to be preserved. The emphasis on individual authors especially arose in Hellenistic times and through Greek influence. This is the reason that biblical books usually do not name authors as such. Later tradition, however, would attach traditional authors and authorship to all of biblical literature, but this was not the default for the Bible itself. The Bible was born out of a life of learning together. It was a book collected, copied, and preserved by scribal communities, not authors.

The story of scribal communities has an ebb and flow. It goes from simple to complex and back to simple. In early Israel, writing was relatively uncommon. It was a legacy of the Late Bronze Age in Canaan, a world ruled by the pharaohs of the New Kingdom. They used writing for the colonial administration of the lands of Canaan that they ruled.

We see a variety of languages and scripts used, including Egyptian hieratic, Akkadian cuneiform, and even the early alphabet. When Egypt left, remnants of their administrative system and scribal training remained behind. The early Canaanite polities—that is, Phoenicia, Israel, and Judah—chose the alphabetic writing system and refined it as the local writing system of the newly emerging polities. But early alphabetic writing was quite mundane. It was mostly sponsored by the state for mundane purposes. It would take a couple of centuries before alphabetic writing flourished and new scribal communities emerged.

The rise of the Assyrian empire was a turning point for scribal communities. The empire brought with it urbanization, centralization, and bureaucracy, all of which fostered the use and spread of writing. Scribal skills spread to a variety of new professions, including priests, prophets, and merchants. It also spread outside the major urban centers to the people of the land. Biblical literature reflects this development of new scribal communities and their associated literary works. And women also acquired literacy and worked in various professions. In fact, literacy in ancient Israel was even gendered as feminine by the figure of Lady Wisdom, the master teacher in the Book of Proverbs. In all this, Hebrew literature begins to reflect social and professional diversity.

Diverse scribal communities came to an end with the Babylonian invasions and destruction of Jerusalem. Not all scribes perished, but the social infrastructure that supported their diverse communities collapsed. The scribes were dispersed. Some were exiled to Babylon. Some fled to Egypt. Some were dispersed among the few towns and villages that survived the Babylonian invasions. The Babylonian exile was a period of survival for ancient Israelite literature and Hebrew scribal tradition. And they did survive.

Remnants of various scribal professions and Hebrew literature eventually came back to Jerusalem at the end of the sixth century BCE. At first, this community was probably quite diverse—remnants, fragments, and survivors of a previous generation. For example, there were locals who never experienced exile but worked in the Babylonian administration in places like Ramat Raḥel, south of Jerusalem, or Mizpah, to the north of Jerusalem. There were also returnees from various places in the Diaspora, especially Babylon but also Egypt. The rebuilt temple became the location for the collection of the remnant of classical Hebrew literary traditions. Some texts like the books of the Pentateuch became foundation documents for the new community and its priestly leadership. Yet Jerusalem remained a small, poor town during the Persian period, and its Hebrew scribes would have also been a small, close-knit community that was centered around the temple.

There were two very different scribal communities in and around Jerusalem during the Persian period. The primary one would have been administrators of the Empire. They would have used the Aramaic language, which had been the *lingua franca* in the near east ever since the neo-Assyrian period. During the Persian period it completely eclipsed Akkadian as the primary administrative language of the empire. Not surprisingly, almost all the inscriptions that we have from the southern Levant are in Aramaic. The second scribal community would have been a Hebrew community centered around the temple. Because Aramaic was the *lingua franca* of the Persian period, even Hebrew scribal education would have begun by learning to read and write in Aramaic. After an elementary education in Aramaic, it would have been easy for scribes to add Hebrew to their skill set. We see the influence of the quintessential Aramaic school text—*The Wisdom of Ahiqar*—on a number of books composed in the Persian period, including Daniel, Ezra-Nehemiah, and Tobit. However, Hebrew had limited utility outside of the temple and the preservation of the classical literary traditions.

The temple priestly community was the final collector and editor of classical Hebrew literature. The post-exilic priestly community did not write the Pentateuch, but it did collect, preserve, and canonize it into its new *Torah*. It probably even added a few of its own compositions during the editing of the Pentateuch. The priests also composed and edited their own works—books like Chronicles, Ezra-Nehemiah, and Esther are literature of the priestly temple scribal community.

In addition to the priestly scribal community in Jerusalem, there was a Samaritan community that was closely associated with Jerusalem during the Babylonian and early Persian periods. These communities had old ties reaching back into the Iron Age. The Babylonian crisis likely brought them together again. They must have worked together in editing the Pentateuch, which also became a sacred text in the Samaritan tradition. Indeed, the Pentateuch became a founding document for temples in both Jerusalem and Mount Gerizim. Their priestly communities even intermarried, but the rivalry between the two competing temples eventually tore them apart. When we read Ezra-Nehemiah, we see hints of the old cooperative relationship but also a developing ideology forbidding intermarriage that cemented a permanent rift. The Samaritan priestly tradition focused on its Pentateuch and especially the Ten Commandments.[1] But the Jerusalem Temple developed a much broader collection of Hebrew literature, as we see in our biblical canon as well as the even more diverse collection of the Dead Sea Scrolls.

The Jerusalem priestly community must have been quite small during the Persian period. The town was small, isolated, and poor. There may have been a thousand people living in Jerusalem, and it was centered around a rebuilt temple and its priestly leaders. The Hebrew scribal community would have been drawn mostly from the priests and located around the temple. To be sure, there were administrators that worked for the Persian Empire, people like Nehemiah, who could have also learned Hebrew. They were trained in Aramaic, and this was the language of their professional life. Ideology sometimes inspired them to learn Hebrew, as Nehemiah did, but Nehemiah was likely the exception rather than the rule. The Jerusalem priests were a different case. Someone like the priest Ezra became literate first by learning Aramaic, but Hebrew was essential to his professional life, that is, to his service in the Temple. Ezra would have been a member of a small and closed priestly community. This community was extended by a professional class, the Levites, who were involved in the Temple service. But this community did not include women, so it seems unlikely that there were many female Hebrew scribes during the Persian period. This seems to be reflected in some marginalization of women in the final editing of the Bible. For example, the "Song of Miriam" seems to have become the "Song of Moses" (Exod 15:1, 20–21), and the "Song of Deborah" becomes the "song of Deborah *and Barak*" (Judg 5:1). The small male priestly community became the caretakers of the literary heritage of ancient Israel, and they shaped the literature in their own image. They preserved the Hebrew literature that eventually was canonized in our Bible.

I will conclude with a reflection on the next chapter in the story of scribal communities—a topic that is beyond the scope of this book—namely, the Dead Sea Scrolls. This trove of about nine hundred manuscripts dates mostly from the second century BCE to the first century CE, and it is a story in its own right.[2] The Dead Sea Scrolls known from the Qumran caves were the library of a sectarian religious community—the Essenes.[3] They do not only reflect the scribal community at Qumran, but they also reflect the gathering and collecting of texts from different communities and different locales in the late Hasmonean and early Roman periods. Some scrolls were composed or copied at Qumran. Some scrolls reflect the Essene community that was spread out in various towns throughout Palestine who brought with them personal libraries when they came to Qumran. Some scrolls may have come from Jerusalem, and others probably were brought to Qumran (and Masada) by people fleeing during the Great War with Rome (ca. 66 CE).

One interesting small collection of Dead Sea Scrolls was written with a calligraphic hand. These are ornately written texts, usually written on large scrolls. They are carefully prepared parchments with wide, ruled margins and clearly marked lines. They are sometimes called "deluxe scrolls" or alternatively "presentation copies." They are essentially public scrolls, that is, the kind of Bible you keep on a pulpit in a church or in an ark in a synagogue. They're meant for public reading. Drew Longacre observes, "These manuscripts reproduce well-known contents and were professionally produced by scribes for patrons."[4] These presentation scrolls necessitate a new profession—namely, the scribe as professional copyist. These scrolls were made by scribes who did it for a living. Their job is only to create books. They had to professionally prepare the parchment. They set it up with lines and margins. They had to stitch together multiple parchments—as many as eighteen—to make large scrolls. Then they carefully copied the text using a beautiful calligraphic hand. It takes much longer and would be much more expensive to produce these kinds of scrolls. And the calligraphic writing and the physical features of these scrolls reflect production by a professional class. But who were the

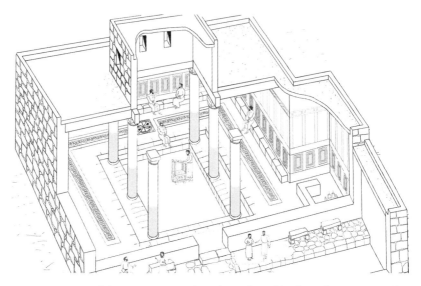

FIGURE 13.1. Magdala synagogue with podium for Sabbath reading. Drawing by Leen Ritmeyer. Used with permission.

"patrons" who purchased such large, ornate, and expensive scrolls? To be sure, there would have been some wealthy elites that purchased books for private libraries, as scholars like Longacre suggest. But that's not enough of a market to create the industry that produced these presentation scrolls. No. I believe these kinds of scrolls arose from the economic demand of a new customer—the synagogue. By the end of the Second Temple period, there were synagogues in every Jewish village and city in Roman Palestine. The synagogue created the demand for professionally produced scrolls and a new profession—the scribal copyist.[5] Synagogues were an important repository for biblical manuscripts.

The reading of biblical texts was part of the early synagogue service. It is not surprising, then, that the synagogue at Masada had a back storage room for scrolls where archaeologists excavated fragments of two calligraphic manuscripts of the Book of Psalms (Mas1e and Mas1f). Every synagogue would have had its own library. In the excavations at Magdala, archaeologists have discovered two synagogues dating to the early Roman period. One of these synagogues even had a large, ornately carved, square limestone block that archaeologists have interpreted as a reading podium in the synagogue (Figure 13.1).

A well-known early example of synagogue reading is from the Gospel of Luke, when Jesus of Nazareth gets up and reads from the Scroll of Isaiah:

> When he came to Nazareth, where he had been brought up, he went to the synagogue on the Sabbath day, as was his custom. He stood up to read, and the scroll of the prophet Isaiah was given to him. He unrolled the scroll and found the place where it was written:
>
> > "The Spirit of the LORD is upon me,
> > because he has anointed me to bring good news to the poor.
> > He has sent me to proclaim release to the captives
> > and recovery of sight to the blind, to set free those who are
> > oppressed,
> > to proclaim the year of the LORD's favor." [Isa 61:1–2a]
>
> And he rolled up the scroll, gave it back to the attendant, and sat down.
>
> (LUKE 4:16–20)

When I was a student learning about ancient synagogues more than thirty years ago, scholars debated the historicity of this story in Luke, with some arguing that there were no synagogues before the destruction of the Jerusalem Temple.[6] How wrong they turned out to be! Archaeological excavations have now uncovered many synagogues dating to the early Roman period, and the earliest known synagogue at Modiʿin, the hometown of the Maccabees, probably dates to the late second century BCE.[7] Archaeologists have also found two early Roman synagogues in the very same ancient village at Magdala. So it now is becoming clear that synagogues were located in every town or village in Palestine with a significant Jewish population.[8]

Even in Jerusalem, there were synagogues in the Second Temple period. The most revealing evidence for this is a first-century inscription that mentions three generations of *Archisynagogoi*—leaders of a Jerusalem synagogue.[9] The Theodotian inscription reads as follows:

> Theodotos, son of Vettenus, priest and ruler of the synagogue [*archisynagōgos*], son of a ruler of the synagogue [*archisynagōgos*],

grandson of a ruler of the synagogue [*archisynagōgos*], built the synagogue [*synagōgē*] for the reading of the law and the teaching of the
commandments, and also the guest chamber and the upper rooms
and the ritual pools of water for accommodating those needing them
from abroad, which his fathers, the elders [*presbyteroi*] and Simo-
nides founded.

The generations of Jerusalem synagogue leaders mentioned push the
date for this particular synagogue back into the first century BCE. That
might make the synagogue contemporary with the enlarging and ag-
grandizing of the Jerusalem Temple by Herod the Great. The reference
to guest chambers suggests that one purpose of Jerusalem synagogues
would have been to accommodate people coming to Jerusalem to celebrate the festivals, which itself requires a pre-destruction dating for the
inscription. It also accords well with the demand for housing created by
Herod the Great's enlargement of the Temple Mount. In addition, the
synagogue was a multipurpose communal space, but the inscription
lists "the reading of the law and teaching" as its first order of business.

Ritual reading and study of classical Jewish literature was a central
function of these synagogues.[10] This would have created a demand for
scroll production in the Second Temple period. One avenue for exploring scroll production at this period is the collection from the Qumran
caves. The Qumran library, however, represented the collection of a particular Jewish group, the Essenes, who had strong objections to the Jerusalem Temple and its priestly leadership. They would not have looked to
the Jerusalem Temple to supply scrolls for their communities. The dis-
tinctives and history of the Essene movement are reflected in the diversity of the Qumran library, which would not have been broadly represen-
tative of Second Temple Jewish synagogue libraries. Yet, the Qumran
scrolls, many of which were brought to the site from outside, still give
hints about book production in the Second Temple period. For example,
the Qumran scrolls give the first evidence for the beginning of the
Masoretic textual tradition, which likely originated among the Jerusalem
Temple scribes. Most synagogues would have looked to the Jerusalem
Temple to supply copies of texts for synagogue libraries. The production

of scrolls for synagogue reading and study would have created the need for a standardized text that would have been copied and distributed, namely, the proto-Masoretic text.

Later Jewish scribes of the Middle Ages (sixth through tenth centuries CE) known as the Masoretes, or "Masters of the Tradition," standardized a system of pronunciation and reading as well as the cantillation of the Hebrew Bible that scholars call "the Masoretic tradition." They represent a very different type of scribal community than we meet in ancient Israel. I would suggest that the very beginning of this much later tradition began already in the late Second Temple period with the Jerusalem Temple scribes producing scrolls for reading in synagogues throughout Palestine. Long before the Masoretes, calligraphic Temple scribes were developing a proto-Masoretic tradition as a textual tradition to be read in synagogues throughout Palestine. The need for a standard text was a direct result of the rise of the synagogue practice of reading biblical texts. Most synagogues would have purchased biblical texts from the Jerusalem Temple, and temple scribes who copied scrolls for synagogues completed the economic circle of supply and demand. Most of the calligraphic scrolls from Qumran, for example, are biblical scrolls. The development of a book industry also meant that other texts beyond just the biblical corpus could have been copied by calligraphic Temple scribes and purchased by wealthy individuals, but the mainstay of this new industry would have been the synagogues that were emerging throughout Roman Palestine. The rise of synagogues was a catalyst for the standardization of a proto-Masoretic scribal tradition, that is, for the text of the Bibles we read today in synagogues and churches.

A model of ritual reading of scripture is provided by the story in Nehemiah 8. It begins by making a podium expressly for the reading of the Torah. Notably, this podium was not erected in the Temple in Jerusalem. It was put in "the square before the Water Gate" (Neh 8:1). There is some debate about where this gate was located, but it may have been near the Gihon Spring on the east side of the City of David (note Neh 3:26). Thus, this instance of the ritual reading of Torah would be taking place well outside of the temple. Since the ritual reading of scripture would become one of the key components of the synagogue service, this story in Nehemiah, which is set in the Persian period, suggests that ritual reading of scripture predates any architecturally known synagogues. Of course, the emergence of synagogues as a social institution may precede the earliest known architecturally identifiable example at Modiʿin from the Hasmonean period.[11] Nehemiah suggests a tradition of ritual reading that precedes the first known synagogues.

Calligraphic scrolls used for ritual reading would have been costly. An entire Torah scroll might have cost as much as six months of wages for one unskilled worker. And, it could have taken one scribe six months to make a single copy of the entire Torah using an ornate calligraphic book hand.[12] Less ornate copies would have been cheaper to produce, but still quite expensive and out of reach for most people. Synagogues, however, could have pooled together community resources to purchase scrolls. Most likely, synagogues would have begun by purchasing smaller, individual scrolls, perhaps a scroll of Deuteronomy and then the Psalms and Isaiah—these are the most common biblical manuscripts among the Dead Sea Scrolls and the most frequently cited books in the New Testament. There is certainly no reason for the Qumran library to own twenty-one copies of Isaiah or thirty-six copies of the Book of Psalms. Many of these copies must have been brought to Qumran, either by initiates joining the community at Qumran or by people fleeing to Qumran during the Great War with Rome. It is probably not a coincidence that Jesus reads from a scroll of Isaiah in the Nazareth synagogue. Most synagogues in smaller Jewish villages probably did not own complete copies of what we know as the Tanakh or Hebrew Bible. They likely prioritized purchasing Psalms, Deuteronomy, Isaiah, and then the rest of the Torah.

The growth of the temple priestly scribal community in the early Hasmonean period also encouraged the fragmentation and dispersal of scribal communities. It was easier for the Jerusalem scribal community to be cohesive when it was small, but as Jerusalem grew, it fractured. There is evidence for a Hebrew scribal community outside of the Temple in Jerusalem by the early second century BCE. The main example is Simon ben-Yeshua ben-Eliezer ben-Sira (or Yeshua ben Sira), who is mentioned in the preface to the *Wisdom of Sirach* as having written a book "for those who love learning." Not surprisingly, the *Wisdom of*

Sirach supported the temple and its priesthood, but he does not seem to be directly affiliated with the temple, and it is unclear whether he himself was a priest, although most scholars believe he was. Manuscripts like the Masada Ben-Sira scroll and the En-Gedi Leviticus scroll reflect this Jerusalem (proto-Masoretic) scribal practice, but other scribal communities emerged, particularly among the Essenes.[13] The Essene community began as an opposition group to the Jerusalem Temple and its priesthood. These renegade priests created their own scribal community of practice that is reflected in the library of texts from the Qumran caves. According to the first-century Jewish philosopher Philo, the Essenes even had their own synagogues, which in turn collected their own sectarian libraries (*Prob.* 81–82).[14] Over more than two centuries this Essene scribal community evolved and developed in various places, including in the scribal center at Qumran.

The rise of the synagogue and the ritual reading of classical Hebrew literature in the synagogue would have made Hebrew literacy possible well beyond the confines of the Jerusalem Temple, its priestly class, and wealthy elites. The story of Jesus in the Nazareth synagogue is a case in point. Whatever the historicity of this particular story, the point is that the story should not be considered remarkable. Namely, it was not remarkable that an adult Jewish male in the late Second Temple period could acquire a measure of Hebrew literacy. Aspects of Jewish life, for example, prayers in Hebrew, required a certain level of fluency in Hebrew even if Aramaic was the vernacular language.[15] To be sure, the ability to read and the ability to write are two different skill sets, and the level and extent of literacy in Roman Palestine is still a debated question. But the synagogue would have spread the availability of Hebrew literature throughout the region, and it would have encouraged a religious ideology requiring some facility in the Hebrew language. After the destruction of the Temple, the synagogue would become the new location for the study of Hebrew as well as for communities of scribes.

NOTES

Preface

1. This saying was attributed to Einstein by Roger Sessions in "How a 'Difficult' Composer Gets That Way," *The New York Times,* January 8, 1950. In Einstein's own writings, we find many statements that fit this general idea, although none of his writings use this formulation. See Alice Calaprice, ed., *The Ultimate Quotable Einstein* (Princeton, NJ: Princeton University Press, 2013).

Introduction

1. This book concerns the Hebrew Bible or Old Testament, although for brevity I will frequently refer to it merely as "the Bible."

2. This point has been made by several recent studies. See especially Karel van der Toorn, *Scribal Culture and the Making of the Hebrew Bible* (Cambridge, MA: Harvard University Press, 2007), as well as my earlier book *How the Bible Became a Book: The Textualization of Ancient Israel* (Cambridge: Cambridge University Press, 2004). On developing concepts of the author, see Hindy Najman, "Reading Beyond Authority," in *Rethinking 'Authority' in Late Antiquity: Authorship, Law, and Transmission in Jewish and Christian Tradition*, ed. A. J. Berkovitz and Mark Letteney (New York: Routledge, 2018), 17–30.

3. This question is the title of an important popular book by Richard Elliot Friedman, *Who Wrote the Bible?* (Englewood Cliffs, NJ: Prentice Hall, 1987). See also Najman, "Reading Beyond Authority."

4. This is nicely expressed in the recent essay by Konrad Schmid, "Die Torah als multiautorielle Diskussionsliteratur Geschichte, Ästhetik und Hermeneutik eines kollaborativen Schreiberprodukts," in *Plurale Autorschaft: Ästhetik der Co-Kreativität in der Vormoderne*, ed. Stefanie Gropper, Anna Pawlak, Anja Wolkenhauer, and Angelika Zirker (Berlin: de Gruyter, 2023), 161–83.

5. Rendtorff's book was translated into English as *The Problem of the Process of Transmission in the Pentateuch* (New York: Bloomsbury, 1990).

6. See, for example, the unsuccessful attempt to "bridge the divide" in Jan Gertz, Bernard Levinson, Dalit Rom-Shiloni, and Konrad Schmid, eds., *The Formation of the Pentateuch: Bridging the Academic Cultures of Europe, Israel, and North America* (Tübingen: Mohr Siebeck, 2016). Note that if the Hebrew Bible was largely a Hellenistic work (as some scholars have suggested), then it would have been a book that focused on its authors.

7. See Konrad Schmid, "The Neo-Documentary Manifesto: A Critical Reading," *JBL* 140 (2021): 473–75.

8. Cited in Schmid, "Neo-Documentary Manifesto," 474, from Hermann Gunkel's *Genesis*, 6th ed. (Göttingen: Vandenhoeck & Ruprecht, 1964), lxxxv.

9. See, for example, James Crenshaw, *Old Testament Wisdom: An Introduction* (Atlanta: John Knox, 1981), 27–29. See also the more nuanced treatment in M. Sneed, "Is the 'Wisdom Tradition' a Tradition?" *CBQ* 73 (2011): 50–71. R. Whybray long ago critiqued this notion of a tradition, arguing that it developed from noninstitutional intellectuals. Whybray is correct in his skepticism, but not in his solution, since it is quite clear in Mesopotamian scribal curriculum that wisdom is simply a genre of educational literature in advanced elementary scribal training, not a special tradition of any distinct scribal community. See Whybray, *The Intellectual Tradition in the Old Testament*, BZAW 135 (Berlin: de Gruyter, 1974).

10. See, for example, J. Blenkinsopp, *Sage, Priest, Prophet: Religious and Intellectual Leadership in Ancient Israel* (Louisville: Westminster John Knox, 1995).

11. Gunkel, "The Literature of Ancient Israel," in *Relating to the Text: Interdisciplinary and Form-Critical Insights on the Bible*, ed. T. Sandoval, C. Mandolfo, and M. Buss, JSOTSS 384 (London and New York: Clark), 69–70.

12. See my own book *The Finger of the Scribe: How Scribes Learned to Write the Bible* (New York: Oxford, 2019), 120–40.

13. There are, for example, no examples of a personal name followed by "the sage" (החכם) as a title in the Hebrew Bible. The concept did develop in later rabbinic tradition as Paul Mandel points out, and then it gets projected back into ancient Israel; see Mandel, "Between סֹפֵר and סָפַר: The Evolution of the Second Temple Period 'Scribe'," in *The Scribe in the Biblical World*, ed. Esther Eshel and Michael Langlois (Berlin: de Gruyter, 2023), 295–320.

14. Dominique Charpin, *Reading and Writing in Babylon* (Cambridge, MA: Harvard University Press, 2010), 17–67.

15. Niv Allon and Hana Navrátilová, *Ancient Egyptian Scribes: A Cultural Exploration* (London: Bloomsbury, 2017).

16. Christopher Rollston, *Writing and Literacy in the World of Ancient Israel: Epigraphic Evidence from the Iron Age* (Atlanta: SBL Press, 2010).

17. James Crenshaw, *Education in Ancient Israel: Across the Deafening Silence* (New York: Doubleday, 1998), 85.

Chapter 1: Scribes and Their Apprentices

1. From the translation by Samuel Noel Kramer, *From the Tablets of Sumer* (Falcon, 1956); see also his critical publication, "Schooldays: A Sumerian Composition Relating to the Education of a Scribe," *JAOS* 69 (1949): 199–215.

2. See Nili Fox, "Royal Officials and Court Families: A New Look at the ילדים (*yelādîm*) in 1 Kings 12," *BA* 59 (1996): 226.

3. See Yoram Cohen, "The Historical and Social Background of the Scribal School at the City of Emar in the Late Bronze Age," in *Theory and Practice of Knowledge Transfer*, ed. W. van Egmond and W. can Soldt (Leiden: Nederlands Instituut, 2012), 120–21. This article summarizes

his book *The Scribes and Scholars of the City of Emar in the Late Bronze Age,* HSS, 59 (Winona Lake, IN: Eisenbrauns, 2009).

4. See Jean Lave and Etienne Wenger, *Situated Learning: Legitimate Peripheral Participation* (Cambridge: Cambridge University Press, 1991), and E. Wenger-Trayner, *Communities of Practice: Learning, Meaning, and Identity* (Cambridge: Cambridge University Press, 1998). This learning model finds a variety of useful applications in the scholarly literature; e.g., J. Kopaczyk and A. Jucker, eds., *Communities of Practice in the History of English* (Amsterdam and Philadephia: John Benjamins Publishing, 2014); E. Wenger-Trayner et al., eds., *Learning in Landscapes of Practice: Boundaries, Identity, and Knowledgeability in Practice-Based Learning* (London: Routledge, 2015).

5. See Nadia Ben-Marzouk, "Forged by Society: An Interregional Investigation into the Social Implications of Metallurgical Knowledge Transfer in the Southern Levant and Egypt," PhD dissertation, UCLA, 2020; and W. Wendrich, ed., *Archaeology and Apprenticeship: Body Knowledge, Identity, and Communities of Practice* (Tucson: University of Arizona Press, 2013).

6. Seth Sanders, *The Invention of Hebrew* (Urbana: University of Illinois Press, 2009), 131–34. See also Sanders, ed., *Margins of Writing, Origins of Culture* (Chicago: University of Chicago Press, 2006).

7. Lave and Wenger, *Situated Learning,* 40.

8. Charpin, *Reading and Writing in Babylon,* 22.

9. Van der Toorn, *Scribal Culture,* 31, 48.

10. This point is made especially by Philip Boyes in his study of writing in ancient Ugarit. See *Script and Society: The Social Context of Writing Practices in Late Bronze Age Ugarit* (New York: Oxbow, 2021).

11. For an application of this observation to ancient Ugarit, see Boyes, *Script and Society.*

12. There are examples from the antiquities market, but these are probably forgeries; e.g., Nahman Avigad, *Corpus of West Semitic Stamp Seals,* revised and edited by Benjamin Sass (Jerusalem: Israel Exploration Society, 1997), nos. 21, 22, 23, 417. See, for example, Yuval Goren and Eran Arie, "The Authenticity of the Bullae of Berekhyahu Son of Neriyahu the Scribe," *BASOR* 372 (2014): 147–58.

13. On the "calligraphic" style, see Drew Longacre, "Paleographic Style and the Forms and Functions of the Dead Sea Psalm Scrolls: A Hand Fitting for the Occasion?" *VT* 72 (2022): 67–92.

14. See Rachel Hachlili, *Ancient Synagogues—Archaeology and Art: New Discoveries and Current Research* (Leiden: Brill, 2013); and Lutz Doering and Andrew Krause, eds., *Synagogues in the Hellistic and Roman Periods: Archaeological Finds, New Methods, New Theories* (Göttingen: Vandenhoeck & Ruprecht, 2020).

15. Texts cited by Allon and Navrátilová, *Ancient Egyptian Scribes,* 74–75.

16. Cited from Irving Finkel, "Assurbanipal's Library: An Overview," in *Libraries before Alexandria,* ed. K. Ryholt and G. Barjamovic (New York: Oxford, 2020), 373; see also Alasdair Livingstone, "Assurbanipal: Literate or Not?" *ZA* 97 (2007): 98–118.

17. Emphasis added. Interestingly, the Qumran Temple Scroll revises this Hebrew text and makes the priests the subject who write the Scroll for the king (see 11Q19 56:20–21).

18. See Allon and Navrátilová, *Ancient Egyptian Scribes,* 41–51.

19. Allon and Navrátilová, *Ancient Egyptian Scribes,* 50–51.

20. *Torah* is a common later synonym for the Pentateuch, but that is not its original meaning. *Torah* is usually translated as "law" in English Bibles because of the influence of its Greek translation as *nomos* "law," but the Hebrew term *torah* originally meant "teaching, instruction" and could refer to any oral instruction and not a particular written text (note, for example, Ps 78:1; Prov 1:8). See my essay, "Diversity and Development of *tôrâ* in the Hebrew Bible," in *Torah: Functions, Meanings, and Diverse Manifestations in Early Judaism and Christianity*, ed. W. Schniedewind, J. Zurawski, and G. Boccaccini (Atlanta: SBL, 2021), 17–36.

21. See, for example, David Davage, *How Isaiah Became an Author: Prophecy, Authority, and Attribution* (Minneapolis: Fortress Press, 2022).

22. Lave and Wenger, *Situated Learning*, 56.

23. On scribal curriculum, see Schniedewind, *Finger of the Scribe*. For a discussion of standardization, see Rollston, *Writing and Literacy in the World of Ancient Israel*, 91–126. Standardization, however, seems to be related to the government bureaucratic "community of practice" and not necessarily forced on other communities. The government bureaucracy likely influenced a standardization, but it is clear that it did not enforce a standard national script.

24. See James Pritchard, *Gibeon, Where the Sun Stood Still; the Discovery of a Biblical City* (Princeton, NJ: Princeton University Press, 1962).

25. Inscription no. 1, from James Pritchard, *Hebrew Inscriptions and Stamps from Gibeon* (Philadephia: University of Pennsylvania Museum, 1959), figure 1.

26. These were first published in a volume edited by Z. Meshel, *Kuntillet ʿAjrud* (Jerusalem: Israel Exploration Society, 2012).

27. See Schniedewind, *Finger of the Scribe*, ch. 2.

28. Charpin, *Reading and Writing in Babylon*, 32.

29. For a list of various administrative titles and discussion, see Y. Avishur and M. Heltzer, *Studies on the Royal Administration in Ancient Israel in the Light of Epigraphic Sources* (Tel Aviv and Jaffa: Archaeological Publication Center, 2000).

30. Lave and Wenger, *Situated Learning*, 56.

31. See J. MacDonald, "The Status and Role of the *Naʿar* in Israelite Society," *JNES* 35 (1976): 147–70; C. Leeb, *Away from the Father's House: The Social Location of the Naʿar and Naʿarah in Ancient Israel* (Sheffield: Sheffield Academic Press, 2000).

32. L. Koehler and W. Baumgartner, eds., *Hebrew and Aramaic Lexicon of the Old Testament* (Leiden: Brill, 2000), ad loc.

33. For the importance of "king" as a divine metaphor, see Marc Brettler, *God Is King: Understanding an Israelite Metaphor* (New York: Bloombury, 1989).

34. Robert Wilson, *Prophecy and Society in Ancient Israel* (Philadelphia: Fortress Press, 1980), 141.

35. Leeb, *Away from the Father's House*, 175.

36. For a comprehensive introduction, see Wilfred Watson and Nicholas Wyatt, *Handbook of Ugaritic Studies* (Leiden: Brill, 1999). Brief overviews can be found in introductory textbooks like William Schniedewind and Joel Hunt, *A Primer on Ugaritic* (Cambridge: Cambridge University Press, 2007), or Dennis Pardee and Pierre Bordreuil, *Manual of Ugaritic* (Winona Lake, IN: Eisenbrauns, 2009).

37. See John Macdonald, "The Unique Ugaritic Personnel Text KTU 4.102," *UF* 10 (1978): 161–73; compare Leeb, *Away from the Father's House*, 176–78.

38. Kevin McGeough, *Ugaritic Economic Tablets: Text, Translation, and Notes* (Leuven: Peeters, 2011), 33–35, 539.

39. David Schloen suggests that *naʿarim* in Ugaritic are subordinate males, part of households, but not necessarily related by blood. Rather, they are part of a fictive kinship group. Schloen, *House of the Father as Fact and Symbol: Patrimonialism in Ugarit and the Ancient Near East* (Cambridge, MA: Harvard Semitic Museum, 2001), 324; see also McGeough, *Ugaritic Economic Tablets*, 27–28.

40. See Avigad, *West Semitic Stamp Seals*, nos. 663; also note seal nos. 24, 25, and 26. It is also found on a seal impression from the recent salvage excavations at Beth-Shemesh.

41. For a more extensive discussion, see Schniedewind, *Finger of the Scribe*, 42–48.

42. For a speculative and expansive view of the Shaphan scribal family, see Preston Kavanagh, *The Shaphan Group* (Eugene, OR: Wipf and Stock, 2011).

43. Avigad, *West Semitic Seal Stamps*, no. 470 (see discussion on p. 40, n. 60). Other possible members of this scribal family seem to be known from seal impressions that come from the antiquities market (see nos. 387, 388, 431). They are probably authentic, but no matter. In this case, archaeologists digging at the City of David have given us striking confirmation for this scribal family.

44. Eilat Mazar, *The Ophel Excavations to the South of the Temple Mount, 2009–2013. Final Reports, Volume II* (Jerusalem: Shoham, 2018), 256–63.

45. E. Mazar and B. Mazar, *Excavations in the South of the Temple Mount, the Ophel of Biblical Jerusalem*, QEDEM, 29 (Jerusalem: Israel Exploration Society, 1989), 42–48.

Chapter 2: The Beginning under Egyptian Dominion

1. See Shlomo Izreel, *Canaano-Akkadian* (Munich: Lincom Europa, 1998).

2. Eminent Assyriologist William Moran uses the term "pidgin" in his introduction to the *Amarna Letters* (Baltimore: Johns Hopkins University Press, 1992). Pidgin is an inexact linguistic description, but I do not have an easy alternative; see Agustinus Gianto, "Amarna Akkadian as a Contact Language," in *Languages and Cultures in Contact: At the Crossroads of Civilizations in the Syro-Mesopotamian Realm*, ed. K. Van Lerberghe and G. Voet (Leuven: Peeters, 1999), 123–32.

3. See Anson F. Rainey, *Canaanite in the Amarna Tablets: A Linguistic Analysis of the Mixed Dialect Used by Scribes from Canaan*, 4 vols. (Boston and Leiden: Brill, 1996), and Rainey, *The Amarna Correspondence*, Volume 1, ed. William Schniedewind (Boston and Leiden: Brill, 2015).

4. EA 289, lines 48–51. For a convenient English translation, see William Moran, *Amarna Letters*.

5. See Allon and Navrátilová, *Ancient Egyptian Scribes*, 2.

6. Allon and Navrátilová, *Ancient Egyptian Scribes*, 128.

7. See *CAD*, "tupšarru," ad loc.

8. See Pearce, "The Scribes and Scholars of Ancient Mesopotamia," in *Civilizations of the Ancient Near East*, volume 4 (1995), columns 2265–78; L. Pearce, "Sepiru and LÚ.A.BA: Scribes of the Late First Millennium B.C.E.," in *Cultures in Contact*, ed. K. van Lerberghe and G. Voet (Leuven: Peeters, 1999), 355–68; Mikko Luuko, "The Administrative Roles of the 'Chief Scribe' and the 'Palace Scribe' in the Neo-Assyrian Period," *State Archives of Assyria Bulletin* 16 (2007): 227–56;

Grant Frame and Caroline Waerzeggers, "The Prebend of Temple Scribe in First Millennium Babylonia," *Zeitschrift für Assyriologie und Vorderasiatische Archäologie* 101 (2011): 127–51.

9. Pearce, Sasson, and Baines, "The Scribes and Scholars of Ancient Mesopotamia," 2265–78. Recently, this Akkadian word, *ṭupšarru*, has also been found in a Hebrew inscription, where it refers to a Babylonian overseer working in Judah in the sixth century BCE (oral communication, Andre Lemaire and Michael Langlois; see *JH* 23, forthcoming).

10. For a convenient English translation along with a brief introduction to the text, see James Allen, "The Craft of the Scribe (Papyrus Anastasi I)," in *Context of Scripture,* vol. 3, ed. William W. Hallo and K. Lawson Younger (Leiden: Brill, 2003), 3.2.

11. From Allen, "The Craft of the Scribe," 28.6–8.

12. See Schniedewind, *Finger of the Scribe,* 130–33.

13. See David Crystal, "The Language of Shakespeare," in *Shakespeare: An Oxford Guide,* ed. Stanley W. Wells and Lena Cowen Orlin (Oxford: Oxford University Press, 2003), 67–78.

14. For a convenient translation, see Miriam Lichtheim, "Instruction of Amenemope," in *Context of Scripture*, vol. 1, no. 47. The critical edition is Vincent Pierre-Michel Laisney, *L'Enseignement d'Amenemope* (Rome: Pontifical Biblical Institute, 2007).

15. Gary Rendsburg, "Literary and Linguistic Matters in the Book of Proverbs," in *Perspectives on Israelite Wisdom: Proceedings of the Oxford Old Testament Seminar* (London: Bloomsbury T & T Clark, 2016), 128–29.

16. I follow Lichtheim's parallels; see "Instruction of Amenemope," in *Context of Scripture*, 1.47. Michael Fox offers some different parallels; see "From Amenemope to Proverbs: Editorial Art in Proverbs 22,17–23,11," *ZAW* 126 (2014): 76–91. The differences in their parallels itself underscores the problem with this as a direct textual borrowing.

17. See Lichtheim, "Instruction of Amenemope," in *Context of Scripture*, 1.47, p. 122.

18. Allon and Navrátilová, *Ancient Egyptian Scribes*, 116; Richard Parkinson and Stephen Quirke, *Papyrus* (Austin: University of Texas Press, 1995), 58–61.

19. See Christopher Eyre, *The Use of Documents in Pharaonic Egypt* (Oxford: Oxford University Press, 2013), 309–15.

20. For ninth-century archives, see the cache of more that 170 bullae published in Ronny Reich, Eli Shukron, and Omri Lernau, "Recent Discoveries in the City of David, Jerusalem," *IEJ* 57 (2007): 156–58.

21. Allon and Navrátilová, *Ancient Egyptian Scribes*, 148.

22. For a convenient introduction and translation, see Miriam Lichtheim, "The Report of Wenamun (P. Moscow 120)," in *Context of Scripture*, 1.41. There is some debate about the dating of the papyrus and its story; see, for example, Arno Egberts, "Hard Times: The Chronology of 'The Report of Wenamun' Revised," *Zeitschrift für Ägyptischen Sprache und Altertumskunde* 125 (1998): 93–108; Bernd Schipper, *Die Erzählund des Wenamun: Ein Literaturwerk im Spannungsfeld von Politik, Geschichte und Religion* (Göttingen: Vandenhoeck & Ruprecht, 2005).

23. See Aaron Burke, "Left Behind: New Kingdom Specialists at the End of Egyptian Empire and the Emergence of Israelite Scribalism," in *Hoffmeier FS* (Winona Lake, IN: Eisenbrauns, 2020), 50–66.

24. William Schniedewind, "The Alphabetic 'Scribe' of the Lachish Jar Inscription and the Hieratic Tradition in the Early Iron Age," *BASOR* 383 (2020): 137–40. It was originally published as "undeciphered" by Benjamin Sass et al., "The Lachish Jar Sherd: An Early Alphabetic Inscrip-

tion Discovered in 2014," *BASOR* 374 (2015): 233–45. Nadav Na'aman (personal communication) suggested reading *spr* "scribe" as a geographical name instead of a title, reasoning that titles were not used in later Hebrew label inscriptions like this; however, titles were routinely used in Egyptian label inscriptions of the New Kingdom.

25. See Schniedewind, *Finger of the Scribe*, 34–35. For an exhaustive treatment, see Stefan Wimmer, *Palästinisches Hieratisch: Die Zahl-und Sonderzeichen in der althebräischen Scrift* (Weisbaden: Harrassowitz, 2008). For Arad, see no. 76 in Yohanan Aharoni, *Arad Inscriptions* (Jerusalem: Israel Exploration Society, 1981), 98–99. I do not agree with some archaeologists who redate Arad stratum XI to the ninth century (e.g., Herzog). I think the archaeology of Arad XI and the paleography of Arad no. 76 also points to the late tenth and early ninth century.

26. William Schniedewind, *A Social History of Hebrew* (New Haven, CT: Yale University Press, 2013), 58–60. For a catalogue and analysis of Egyptian loanwords related to scribes, see Philip Zhakevich, *Scribal Tools in Ancient Israel: A Study of Biblical Hebrew Terms for Writing Materials and Implements* (Winona Lake, IN: Eisenbrauns, 2020).

27. There is some debate about exactly when Ugaritic cuneiform was invented. One could push it all the way back to the fifteenth century; some scholars now place it in the thirteenth century, but I think this is too late to account for the internal developments in Ugaritic cuneiform.

28. For an overview, see Aaron Koller, "The Diffusion of the Alphabet in the Second Millennium BCE: On the Movement of Scribal Idea from Egypt to the Levant, Mesopotamia, and Yemen," *Journal of Ancient Egyptian Interconnections* 20 (2018): 1–14.

29. William Schniedewind, "The Gezer Calendar as an Adaptation of the Mesopotamian Lexical Tradition (Ura 1)," *Semitica* 61 (2019): 15–22.

30. See my discussion in *Finger of the Scribe*, 151–58.

31. This is the subject of some debate among scholars. Compare, for example, David Wright, *Inventing God's Law: How the Covenant Code of the Bible Used and Revised the Laws of Hammurabi* (New York: Oxford University Press, 2009), with Bruce Wells, "The Covenant Code and Near Eastern Legal Traditions: A Response to David P. Wright," *MAARAV* 13 (2006); 85–118, and "The Purpose of the Covenant and Deuteronomic Codes and the Insights of Eckard Otto," *Journal for Ancient Near Eastern and Biblical Law* 25 (2019): 207–10. I prefer the model suggested by Sara Milstein that posits the origin of biblical law in legal-pedagogical texts; see her *Making a Case: The Practical Roots of Biblical Law* (New York: Oxford University Press, 2021).

32. See the overview by David Carr, *The Formation of the Hebrew Bible* (New York: Oxford University Press, *2011*), 404–31.

33. See Antonio Loprieno, *La pensée et l'écriture pour une analyse sémiotique de la culturé égyptienne* (Paris: Cybele, 2001), 124–28.

Chapter 3: In the Service of the State

1. Van der Toorn, *Scribal Culture and the Making of the Hebrew Bible*; see my review in the *Journal of Hebrew Scriptures* 10 (2010), DOI:10.5508/jhs.2010.v10.r29.

2. For the Hebrew expression, see *Hebrew and Aramaic Lexicon of the Old Testament*, ad loc. See also Rendsburg, "Literary and Linguistic Matters in the Book of Proverbs," 112–13.

3. See, for example, Michael Carasik, "Who Were the 'Men of Hezekiah' (Proverbs xxv 1)?" *VT* 44 (1994): 289–300.

4. These include "The Words of the Wise" (Prov 22:17–24:22), "The Words of Agur" (Prov 30:1–14), "Numerical Sayings" (Prov 30:15–33), "The Words of Lemuel" (Prov 31:1–9), and "The Virtuous Woman Poem" (Prov 31:10–31).

5. Anat Mendel, "Epigraphic Lists in Israel and Its Neighbors in the First Temple Period," PhD dissertation, Hebrew University (2015) (in Hebrew).

6. An argument for this text as coming from an archival source can be seen in the classic work by Martin Noth, *The Deuteronomistic History*, translated from the German (Sheffield: JSOT Press, 1981), 90, 93. A good example of a critique of the historical value of such lists can be seen in Paul Ash, "Solomon's? District? List," *JSOT* 67 (1995): 67–86. Donald Redford argued that Solomon organized his tax districts following an Egyptian administrative pattern, "Studies in Relations Between Palestine and Egypt During the First Millennium B.C.: I. The Taxation System of Solomon," in *Studies on the Ancient Palestinian World*, ed. J. W. Wevers and D. B. Redford (Toronto: University of Toronto Press, 1972), 141–56.

7. Halpern, *David's Secret Demons: Messiah, Murderer, Traitor, King* (Grand Rapids, MI: Eerdmans, 2001), 414. See my long discussion in "Solomon from Archival Sources to Collective Memory," in *Congress Volume Aberdeen 2019; Supplements to Vetus Testamentum*, 192 (Leiden: Brill, 2022), 338–57. Also note Donald Redford's argument that Solomon organized his tax districts following an Egyptian administrative pattern, "Studies in Relations Between Palestine and Egypt During the First Millennium B.C.: I. The Taxation System of Solomon," in *Studies on the Ancient Palestinian World*, ed. J. W. Wevers and D. B. Redford (Toronto: University of Toronto Press, 1972), 141–156.

8. For example, *KTU* 4.103, 4.106, 4.77 (RS 11.858, 12.001, 11.744); see McGeough, *Ugaritic Economic Tablets*, 40–49.

9. This is RS 94.2184 + 94.2354 from Pierre Bordreuil, Dennis Pardee, and Robert Hawley, *Une bibliothèque au sud de la ville: Textes 1994–2002 en cunéiforme alphabétique de la Maison d'Ourtenou*, Ras Shamra-Ougarit 18 (Paris: Maison de l'Orient et de la Méditerranée, 2012), 39–42.

10. For ostracon 76, I mostly follow the original readings in Aharoni, *Arad Inscriptions*, 98–99. Nadav Na'aman published some new readings for six Arad inscriptions (including no. 76), supposedly relying on new digital imaging. He shared his digital images with me that I used for my drawing, but I was unable to confirm many of his new readings; see Nadav Na'aman, "New Light on Six Inscriptions from Arad," *TA* 48 (2021): 213–35. His new readings do not substantially alter the interpretation of the text.

11. Nicolas Wyatt, "The Evidence of the Colophons in the Assessment of Ilimilku's Scribal and Authorial Role," *UF* 46 (2015): 399–446.

12. *KTU* 1.6 vi, 54–58.

13. *KTU* 1.4 viii.

14. See Baruch Halpern and David Vanderhooft, "The Editions of Kings in the 7th–6th Centuries B.C.E.," *Hebrew Union College Annual* 62 (1991): 179–244.

15. See, for example, Ronald Wallenfels, "Review: *Shishak and Shoshenq: A Disambiguation*," *JAOS* 139 (2019): 487–500. The tenth-century dating of Shishak's campaign is now supported by a scarab of Sheshonq I excavated in the Wadi Feinan; see Thomas Levy, Stefan Münger, and Mohammad Najjar, "A Newly Discovered Scarab of Sheshonq I," *Antiquity* 88 (2014): 341.

16. Many scholars have envisioned similar transmissions of the traditions. See, for example, Wolfgang Oswald, "Possible Historical Settings of the Saul-David Narrative," in *Saul, Benjamin, and the Emergence of Monarchy in Israel: Biblical and Archaeological Perspectives*, ed. Joachim Krause, Omer Sergi, and Kristin Weingart (Atlanta: SBL, 2020), 93–109.

17. For an overview, see Alice Mandell, "Archaic Biblical Hebrew," in *Encyclopedia of Hebrew Language and Linguistics*, ed. Geoffrey Khan (Leiden: Brill, 2013), http://dx.doi.org/10.1163/2212-4241_ehll_EHLL_COM_00000743. There is some debate about this register, but recent research puts this debate to rest. See Na'ama Pat-El and Aren Wilson-Wright, "Features of Archaic Biblical Hebrew and the Linguistic Dating Debate," *Hebrew Studies* 52 (2013): 387–410; Tania Notarius, "Lexical Isoglosses of Archaic Hebrew: פְּלִילִים (Deut 32:31) and בַּ (Judg 5:15) as Case Studies," *Hebrew Studies* 58 (2017): 81–97.

18. See my discussion in *Finger of the Scribe*, 141–64.

19. The title, "Song of the Bow (קֶשֶׁת)," does not appear in the Old Greek text, so it may be that this is a title given to the lament by later tradition. A second reference to the *Book of Jashar* appears in the Masoretic Text of Joshua 10:12, but it is also missing in the Old Greek, so it seems that the *Book of Jashar* was added to the text there. A third reference to the *Book of Jashar* appears only in the Old Greek (not in the MT) of 2 Kings 8:53a. We can assume that the *Book of Jashar* originally only appeared in 2 Samuel 1:18. See Kristen de Troyer, "'Is This Not Written in the Book of Jashar?' (Josh 10:13c): References to Extra-Biblical Books in the Bible," in *The Land of Israel in Bible, History, and Theology: Studies in Honour of Ed Noort*, ed. J.T.A. G van Ruiten and C. de Vos, VTS 124 (Leiden: Brill, 2009), 45–50; Edward Greenstein, "What Was the Book of Yashar?" *MAARAV* 21 (2014): 25–35.

20. See the overview by Aren Maier and Carl Ehrlich, "Excavating Philistine Gath," *BAR* 27, no. 6 (2001): 22–31.

21. Eleanor Robson, "The Tablet House: A Scribal School in Old Babylonian Nippur," *Revue d'assyriologie et d'archéologie orientale* 93 (2001): 390–66.

22. See Schniedewind, *Finger of the Scribe*, 141–64.

23. Ernst Axel Knauf suggests Saul, Eshbaal (Saul's son), or Jeroboam I (the first king of the divided kingdom in the north) as possible patrons for the poem. See "Deborah's Language: Judges Ch. 5 in Its Hebrew and Semitic Context," in *Studia semitica et semitiohamitica*, ed. Bogdan Burtea, Josef Tropper, and Helen Younansardaroud (Münster: Ugarit-Verlag, 2005), 167–80. Knauf also makes a linguistic argument for a specifically tenth-century Gileadite royal context, but it's difficult to pinpoint the dialect to Gilead (just across the Jordan) as opposed to Tirzah (an early capital of the northern kingdom) or Samaria. There's really not enough evidence to be so precise.

Chapter 4: Refugees from the Samarian Scribal Office

1. See James Kelso and James Swauger, *The Excavation of Bethel (1934–1960)* (Chicago: American Schools of Oriental Research, 1960). See, for example, Anson Rainey, "Looking for Bethel: An Exercise in Historical Geography," in *Confronting the Past: Archaeological and Historical Essays on Ancient Israel in Honor of William G. Dever,* ed. Seymour Gitin, J. Edward Wright, and J. P. Dessel (Winona Lake, IN: Eisenbrauns, 2006), 269–73.

2. See Joseph Blenkinsopp, "Bethel in the Neo-Babylonian Period," in *Judah and the Judeans in the Neo-Babylonian Period,* ed. Oded Lipschits and Joseph Blenkinsopp (Winona Lake, IN: Eisenbrauns, 2003), 93–107; and Ernst Axel Knauf, "Bethel: The Israelite Impact on Judean Language and Literature," in *Judah and Judeans in the Persian Period,* ed. Oded Lipschits and Manfred Oeming (Winona Lake, IN: Eisenbrauns, 2006), 291–349.

3. For example, David Ussishkin, "The Destruction of Lachish by Sennacherib and the Dating of the Royal Judean Storage Jars," *TA* 4 (1977): 28–60.

4. See Israel Finkelstein and Lily Singer-Avitz, "Reevaluating Bethel," *Zeitschrift des Deutschen Palästina-Vereins* 125 (2009): 33–48; see also Oded Lipschits, "Bethel Revisited," in *Rethinking Israel: Studies in the History and Archaeology of Ancient Israel in Honor of Israel Finkelstein,* ed. Oded Lipschits, Yuval Gadot, and Matthew Adams (Winona Lake, IN: Eisenbrauns, 2017), 233–46. Inchol Yang follows Lipschits's interpretation in "The Continuity of the Cult at Bethel after Exile," *Religions* 13, no. 7 (2022), https://doi.org/10.3390/rel13070640.

5. See Daniel Fleming, *The Legacy of Israel in Judah's Bible: History, Politics, and the Reinscribing of Tradition* (Cambridge: Cambridge University Press, 2012); Ginsberg, *The Israelian Heritage of Judaism* (New York: JPS, 1982); and Finkelstein, *The Forgotten Kingdom: The Archaeology and History of Northern Israel* (Atlanta: Society of Biblical Literature, 2013).

6. I am especially indebted to Mahri Leonard-Fleckman for emphasizing the long process of the assimilation of Israel's literature among Judean scribal communities. See Leonard-Fleckman, "When Did Israel's Literature Enter Judah? A Case Study in Biblical Historiography," paper for *Stones, Tablets, and Scrolls* section at the Society of Biblical Literature meeting, Denver, Colorado, November 2022.

7. See Robert Cargill, *Melchizedek, King of Sodom: How Scribes Invented the Biblical Priest-King* (New York: Oxford University Press, 2019).

8. See Karen Radner, "The 'Lost Tribes of Israel' in the Context of the Resettlement Programme of the Assyrian Empire," in *The Last Days of the Kingdom of Israel,* ed. Shuichi Hasegawa, Christoph Levin, and Karen Radner (Berlin: de Gruyter, 2019), 101–24; and Ran Zadok, "Israelite and Judaeans in the Neo-Assyrian Documentation (732–602 B.C.E.): An Overview of the Sources and a Socio-Historical Assessment," *BASOR* 374 (2015): 159–89.

9. On the archaeological context, see Ron Tappy, *The Archaeology of the Ostraca House at Israelite Samaria: Epigraphic Discoveries in Complicated Contexts* (Boston: American Schools of Oriental Research, 2016).

10. See the summary and analysis in Roger Nam, "Power Relations in the Samaria Ostraca," *PEQ* 144 (2012): 156–58; and Lawrence Stager, "The Finest Olive Oil in Samaria," *JSS* 28 (1983): 241–45. For these terms in the Bible, see Isaiah 25:6; 1 Kings 5:25; Exodus 27:20.

11. Nam, "Power Relations," 161.

12. Nam, "Power Relations" cites J. Crowfoot, G. Crowfoot, and Kathleen Kenyon, *Samaria-Sebaste III: The Objects from Samaria* (London: Palestine Exploration Fund, 1957), 155.

13. See Eleanor Beach, "The Samaria Ivories, *Marzeaḥ,* and Biblical Texts," *BA* 55 (1992): 130–39; Tappy, *Archaeology of the Ostraca House,* 5–8.

14. See Tallay Ornan, "Sketches and Final Works of Art: The Drawings and Wall Painting of Kuntillet ʿAjrud Revisited," *Tel Aviv* 43 (2016): 3–26. There has been some debate about the purpose of this fortress, with some scholars believing it was a religious site. But as Ornan points out, all this religious language and imagery was typical of palace art.

15. See the classic article by Magen Broshi, "The Expansion of Jerusalem in the Reigns of Heze-kiah and Manasseh," *IEJ* 24 (1974): 21–26. I drew out some implications of this for biblical literature in my book *Society and the Promise to David: The Reception History of 2 Samuel 7:1–17* (New York: Oxford University Press, 1999), 64–90. In spite of some objections to this analysis, it is the simplest and most elegant explanation of all the evidence; see, recently, Israel Finkelstein, "Migration of Is-raelites into Judah after 720 BCE: An Answer and an Update," *ZAW* 127 (2015): 188–206.

16. For the more conservative estimate of doubling of the population, see Aaron Burke, "An Anthropological Model for the Investigation of the Archaeology of Refugees in Iron Age Judah and Its Environs," in *Interpreting Exile: Interdisciplinary Studies of Displacement and Deportation in Biblical and Modern Contexts*, ed. B. E. Kelle, F. R. Ames, and J. L. Wright, Ancient Israel and Its Literature 10 (Atlanta: Society of Biblical Literature, 2011), 41–56. Ancient communities nor-mally grew at about 0.6 percent per year. Any substantial growth outside of this is due to exoge-nous change. Even a doubling in decades is astronomical growth. Earlier growth estimates for Jerusalem did not sufficiently take into account Jerusalem's growth in the preceding two centuries.

17. See Assaf Kleiman, "A North Israelite Royal Administrative System and Its Impact on Late-Monarchic Judah," *HeBAI* 6 (2017): 354–71.

18. See Oded Lipschits, Omer Sergi, and Ido Koch, "Judahite Stamped and Incised Jar Handles: A Tool for the Study of the History of Late Monarchic Judah," *TA* 38 (2011): 5–41; and Andrew Vaughn, "*lmlk* and Official Seal Impressions," in *Tel Beth-Shemesh, a Border Community in Judah: Renewed Excavations 1990–2000: The Iron Age*, ed. Shlomo Bunimovitz and Zvi Leder-man (Winona Lake, IN: Eisenbrauns, 2016), 480–501. The recent salvage excavations at Arnona must be related to Ramat Rahel; see Neria Sapir et al., "History, Economy, and Administration in Late Iron Age Judah in Light of the Excavations at Mordot Arnona, Jerusalem," *TA* 49 (2022): 32–53.

19. See Crowfoot, Crowfoot, and Kenyon, *Samaria-Sebaste III*, 88, plate XV:29.

20. A. D. Tushingham, "A Royal Israelite Seal (?) and the Royal Jar Handle Stamps (Part One)," *BASOR* 200 (1970): 71–78, and "A Royal Israelite Seal (?) and the Royal Jar Handle Stamps (Part Two)," *BASOR* 201 (1971): 23–35.

21. See, for example, Maria Giulia Amadasi Guzzo, "Tell Afis in the Iron Age: The Aramaic Inscriptions," *Near Eastern Archaeology* 77 (2014): 55–56, esp. figure 3.

22. For my appreciation of naming practices, I am deeply indebted to the research of my former PhD student Moise Isaac. See Isaac, "'You Will Be Named after Your Ancestors': Rep-licating Israelite Tribal Names in Judean Hebrew Inscriptions as Indexes of Refugee Identity Alignment and Community Cohesion," PhD dissertation, UCLA, 2016, and his monograph, *Performing Refugee Identity in Judah: Language Ideologies of Israelite Tribal Names in the Wake of Assyrian Invasions* (Routledge, forthcoming).

23. These prefixes and suffixes are spelled inconsistently in English translations both in the Bible and in scholarly publications. But in Hebrew the prefixes and suffixes are spelled consis-tently and mark Judahite and Israelian identity.

24. See Avraham Faust, *The Neo-Assyrian Empire in the Southwest: Imperial Domination and Its Consequences* (Oxford: Oxford University Press, 2021), 97–99.

25. See Avigad, *West Semitic Stamp Seals*, nos. 676, 677, and 678. See Isaac, "'You Will Be Named After Your Ancestors,'" 306, and *Performing Refugee Identity in Judah*. I discussed these

seal impressions in an article, "Northern Refugees in Jerusalem: The Case of Menaḥem, Son of Yawbana," in *Linguistic and Philological Studies of the Hebrew Bible and Its Manuscripts*, ed. Vincent Beiler and Aaron Rubin (Leiden: Brill, 2023), 262–69.

26. See the discussion in Isaac, "'You Will Be Named After Your Ancestors.'"

27. Fleming, *Legacy of Israel*, 28.

28. See Sara Milstein, *Tracking the Master Scribe: Revision through Introduction in Biblical and Mesopotamian Literature* (New York: Oxford University Press, 2016).

29. See Marc Brettler, "The Book of Judges: Literature as Politics," *JBL* 108 (1989): 395–418; Y. Amit, "Literature in the Service of Politics: Studies in Judges 19–21," in *Politics and Theopolitics in the Bible and Postexilic Literature*, ed. H. G. Revenlow et al. (Sheffield: JSOT Press, 1994), 28–40; Sara Milstein, "Saul the Levite and His Concubine: The 'Allusive' Quality of Judges 19," *VT* 66 (2016): 95–116.

30. See Bernard Levinson, *Deuteronomy and the Hermeneutics of Legal Innovation* (Oxford: Oxford University Press, 1997).

31. See my chapter "Advanced Education" in *Finger of the Scribe*, 141–64.

32. See Gary Rendsburg, "Linguistic Variation and the 'Foreign' Factor in the Hebrew Bible," in *Language and Culture in the Near East, Israel Oriental Studies XV*, ed. Shlomo Izre'el and Rina Drory (Leiden: Brill, 1995), 177–90.

33. See Hugh Williamson's analysis, *Israel in the Book of Chronicles* (Cambridge: Cambridge University Press, 1977).

34. Gary Rendsburg, *Linguistic Evidence for the Northern Origin of Selected Psalms* (Atlanta: Scholars Press, 1990). See also the summary in Gary Rendsburg, "A Comprehensive Guide to Israelian Hebrew: Grammar and Lexicon," *Orient* 38 (2003): 5–35.

Chapter 5: New Scribal Communities

1. See my discussion in *Social History of Hebrew*, 51–74.

2. See the overview by Matthieu Richelle, "Elusive Scrolls: Could Any Hebrew Literature Have Been Written Prior to the Eighth Century BCE?," *VT* 66 (2016): 556–94. Richelle answers "yes" to his question, and he critiques my earlier book, *How the Bible Became a Book*. However, we do not actually disagree. My point is not about whether *any* literature could have been written but about whether literature *flourished* and, for the present book, how diverse scribal communities were.

3. For example, Tel 'Eton was likely destroyed by Sargon II; see H. Katz and A. Faust, "Three Iron Age Ceramic Assemblages from the Tel 'Eton Cemetery," *'Atiqot* 103 (2021): 122.

4. See Gary Rendsburg and William Schniedewind, "The Siloam Tunnel Inscription: Historical and Linguistic Perspectives," *IEJ* 60 (2010): 188–203.

5. See the account of the discovery by his sister, Bertha Spafford, *Our Jerusalem: An American Family in the Holy City, 1881–1949* (New York: Doubleday, 1951), 90–91.

6. This was already suggested by Ivan Kaufman in his dissertation on the Samaria Ostraca and also picked up in F. Briqel-Chatonnet, "Étude comparé de l'évolution des alphabets Judéen, Israélite et Phénicien," *LOAPL* 4 (1993): 1–30. See also Rendsburg and Schniedewind, "Siloam Tunnel Inscription," 188–203.

7. For a convenient translation of Sennacherib's tribute from Jerusalem, see Mordechai Cogan, "Sennacherib's Siege of Jerusalem (2.119b)," in *Context of Scripture*, 2:302–3.

8. See Pritchard's chapter "The Makers of Wine" in *Gibeon: Where the Sun Stood Still*.

9. See the publication in Dobbs-Allsop et al., *Hebrew Inscriptions: Texts from the Biblical Period of the Monarchy with Concordance* (New Haven: Yale University Press, 2005), Gibeon 1.

10. See Avraham Faust, "The Interests of the Assyrian Empire in the West: Olive Oil Production as a Test Case," *JESHO* 54 (2011): 62–86; Aren Maeir, Eric Welch, and Maria Eniukhina, "A Note on Olive Oil Production in Iron Age Philistia: Pressing the Consensus," *Palestine Exploration Quarterly* (2020): 1–16. For "oil" in the Jerusalem inscriptions, see Dobbs-Allsop et al., *Hebrew Inscriptions*, Jerusalem inscriptions nos. 3 and 5

11. Avigad, *West Semitic Stamp Seals*, no. 422.

12. Gabriel Barkay, "A Group of Iron Age Scale Weights," *IEJ* 28 (1978): 209–17, plates 33–34; more generally, see Raz Kletter, *Economic Keystones: The Weight System of the Kingdom of Judah* (Sheffield: JSOT Press, 1998). As Kletter points out, the weight inscriptions have "a tendency for careless writing" (p. 64).

Chapter 6: The Prophetic Scribal Community

1. For the Lachish seal impressions, see Yohanan Aharoni, "Trial Excavations in the 'Solar Shrine' at Lachish. Preliminary Report," *IEJ* 18 (1968): 167, nos. 6–7; and Aharoni, *Lachish V* (Tel Aviv: Gateway, 1975), 19–22, nos. 6–7. Aḥituv discusses this name in light of the unprovenanced seals but also concludes that "*nby* remains unexplained." See Shmuel Aḥituv, "Review: *West Semitic Seals. Eighth–Sixth Centuries B.C.E.*," *IEJ* 53 (2003): 252. These are revisited in Anat Mendel-Geberovich, Eran Arie, and Michael Maggen, "The Lachish Inscriptions from Yohanan Aharoni's Excavations Reread," in *From Shaʿar Hagolan to Shaaraim: Essays in Honor of Prof. Yosef Garfinkel*, ed. Saar Ganor, Igor Kreimerman, Katharina Streit, and Madeleine Mumcuoglu (Jerusalem: Israel Exploration Society, 2016), 111*–133* (Hebrew). I discuss these seal impressions in more detail in my article, "The Isaiah Bulla, Jeremiah the Priest/Prophet, and Reinterpreting the Prophet (*nby/ʾ*) in the Persian Scribal Community," in *Jewish Culture and Creativity: Essays in Honor of Michael Fishbane on the Occasion of His Eightieth Birthday*, ed. Eitan Fishbane and Elisha Fishbane (Academic Studies Press, 2023).

2. For the catalogue, see Avigad, *West Semitic Stamp Seals*, nos. 227, 379, 693; as well as, more recently, Mendel-Geberovich, Arie, and Maggen, "Lachish Inscriptions," 111*–133* (Hebrew). There is an additional antiquities market seal with the reading *nby* published by Robert Deutsch, *Biblical Period Epigraphy: The Josef Chaim Kaufman Collection*, vol. 2 (Jerusalem: Graphit Press, 2011), 17–18 (no. 434).

3. Yohanan Aharoni, "Trial Excavation in the 'Solar Shrine' at Lachish. Preliminary Report," *IEJ* 18 (1968): 167; Aharoni, *Lachish V*, 21–22 (nos. 6–7).

4. See my extended discussion, "The Isaiah Bulla."

5. The ostracon, weights, and seals are published in Aharoni, *Lachish V*. For an updated edition of Lachish ostracon 22 with excellent photos and drawings, see Abigail Zammit, "The Lachish Letters: A Reappraisal of the Ostraca Discovered I 1935 and 1938 at Tell ed-Duweir, Volume 2," PhD dissertation, Oxford University, 2016, 49–50.

6. Avigad, *West Semitic Stamp Seals*, no. 379; see also no. 227.

7. Nahman Avigad, "New Names on Hebrew Seals," *EI* 12 (1975): 71. As A. Vaughn and C. Dobler pointed out, the omission of the word *bn* makes seal no. 227 especially suspect as a forgery; see "A Provenance Study of Hebrew Seals and Seal Impressions: A Statistical Analysis," in *I Will Speak the Riddle of Ancient Times—Archaeological and Historical Studies in Honor of Amihai Mazar on the Occasion of His Sixtieth Birthday*, ed. Aren Maeir and Pierre de Miroschedji (Winona Lake, IL: Eisenbrauns, 2006), 757–71. A close inspection of provenanced Hebrew seals and impressions indicates that *bn* "son of" is usually included (72%) and omitted only when there is no space. Non-provenanced seals omit *bn* with statistically higher frequency, suggesting forgies in the non-provenanced corpus.

8. In the later publication of Avigad, *West Semitic Stamp Seals*, no. 379. Alan Millard tried to explain the name with an etymology related to *nwb* "to fruit." See Millard, "*Corpus of West Semitic Stamp Seals*: A Review Article," *IEJ* 51 (2001): 11. There is apparent example of the name *Nobai* in a genealogical list in Nehemiah 10, but the Hebrew text is garbled (with the *Qere/Ketiv* suggesting both *nwby* and *nyby*). Variants in Hebrew manuscripts suggest that later scribes did not recognize *nwby* as a personal name.

9. Torczyner reconstructed the term "prophet" on Lachish 16, but it is too fragmentary and uncertain to rely on this reading; see Abigail Zammit, "The Lachish Letters: A Reappraisal of the Ostraca Discovered I 1935 and 1938 at Tell ed-Duweir, Volume 1," PhD dissertation, Oxford University, 2016, 272–73. Likewise, Andree Lemaire reconstructed a "prophet" in the Kuntillet ʿAjrud inscriptions, but this also is too fragmentary to be of any use; see Lemaire, "Remarques dur les inscriptions phéniciennes de Kuntillet ʿAjrud," *Semitica* 55 (2013): 86–87.

10. This will contrast with the concept of the prophet that develops in the post-exilic period. The prophet becomes a solitary figure, called by God, and not part of a prophetic community (e.g., Jer 1:1–5).

11. See Terry Fenton, "Deuteronomic Advocacy of the *nābiʾ*: 1 Samuel IX 9 and Questions of Israelite Prophecy," *VT* 47 (1997): 38–39.

12. Cogan and Tadmor correctly understand the Hebrew expression as indicating "a member of a guild," and they suggest that it reflects "loosely organized brotherhoods living together in the towns of northern Israel"; *II Kings* (Garden City: Doubleday, 1988), 31. But Robert Wilson makes the case for "a more rigid structure . . . capable of coordinated social action and a hierarchical structure." See Wilson, *Prophecy and Society in Ancient Israel*, 141.

13. For a full discussion, see Amihai Mazar and Nava Panitz-Cohen, *Tel Reḥov: A Bronze and Iron Age City in the Beth-Shean Valley*, 5 vols. (Jerusalem: Israel Exploration Society, 2020).

14. Nava Panitz-Cohen and Amihai Mazar, "The Exceptional Ninth-Century BCE Northwestern Quarter at Tel Reḥov," *NEA* 85 (2022): 143.

15. See Panitz-Cohen and Mazar, "The Exceptional Ninth-Century BCE Northwestern Quarter at Tel Reḥov," 144.

16. The only other examples of red ink on pottery inscriptions are from Rosh Zayit and Kuntillet ʿAjrud.

17. F. Hatjina, G. Mavrofridis, and R. Jones, eds., *Beekeeping in the Mediterranean—From Antiquity to the Present* (Nea Moudania, 2018), 44.

18. Amihai Mazar, "The Iron Age Apiary at Tel Reḥov, Israel," in F. Hatjina, G. Mavrofridis, R. Jones, eds., *Beekeeping in the Mediterranean*, 44.

19. Mazar and Panitz-Cohen, *Reḥov*, inscription no. 5. It also could be read as the personal name Nemesh, and then the dynasty would be the Nimshides (*nmšy*) spelled with the gentilic.

20. Mazar and Panitz-Cohen, *Reḥov*, inscription no. 6. This could also be translated "belonging to the cupbearer of the Nimshides." See Mazar and Panitz-Cohen for a full exploration of the possibilities.

21. There is more bibliography on Isaiah than can be cited here. For the interested reader, I would suggest H.G.M. Williamson, *The Book Called Isaiah: Deutero-Isaiah's Role in the Composition and Redaction* (Oxford: Oxford University Press, 2005); and Uwe Becker, "The Book of Isaiah: Its Composition History," in *The Oxford Handbook of Isaiah*, ed. Lena-Sofia Tiemeyer (Oxford: Oxford University Press, 2020), 37–56. I find Nathan Mastnjak's description of Isaiah as anthology particularly useful: see "The Book of Isaiah and the Anthological Genre," *Hebrew Studies* 61 (2020): 49–72, as well as Davage, *How Isaiah Became an Author*.

22. The official scholarly publication is Mazar, *The Ophel Excavations to the South of the Temple Mount*, 247–80. A more convenient discussion can be found in Mazar's popular article, "Is This the Prophet Isaiah's Signature?" *Biblical Archaeology Review* 44, nos. 2–3 (2018): 64–73, 92.

23. See Christopher Rollston, "The Yešaʿyah[û] ('Isaiah') Bulla and the Putative Connection with the Biblical Prophet: A Case Study in Proposography and the Necessity of Methodological Caution," in *Biblical and Ancient Near Eastern Studies in Honor of P. Kyle McCarter Jr.*, ed. Christopher Rollston, Susanna Garfein, and Neil Walls (Atlanta: SBL Press, 2022), 409–26.

24. See, for example, texts like Jeremiah 38. See Mazar and Mazar, *Excavations in the South of the Temple Mount, the Ophel of Biblical Jerusalem* and Mazar, *Ophel Excavations*. Rollston has no discussion of the context of the Isaiah seal, but he seems to think that the wet-sifting of archaeological loci means that the bulla wasn't discovered in a controlled excavation. See "The Yešaʿyah[û] ("Isaiah") Bulla," 209. He also doesn't mention the official publication of the bullae.

25. Mazar does not offer a reconstruction for seal impression no. B21 (*Ophel Excavations*), but the royal insignia is clear. Line 2 is the end of a theophoric name. I read it as [*l*-PN]/{winged scarab}/[ʿ*bd* (or, *bn*) *ḥzqy*]*hw*/[*mlk yhd*]*h* "[belonging to PN, servant/son of Hezek]iah, [king of Juda]h." Given the personal name in the first line, I prefer "son of" and then we can only guess which royal prince it might have belonged to. Manasseh is my best guess.

26. Mazar, *Ophel Excavations*, 182.

27. The original excavators thought that it was the area of a royal bakery and suggested reconstructing the inscription as *lśr h ʾw*[*pym*] "belonging to the minister of the bakery." I don't see significant archaeological evidence (like ovens) for a bakery, and they also acknowledge the possibility of reconstructing this as "belonging to minister of the treasury"; see Mazar and Mazar, *Excavations in the South of the Temple Mount*, 20–48.

28. Mazar, *Ophel Excavations*, 266–68 (no. B12).

29. See Mazar, *Ophel Excavations*, 264. The name Isaiah becomes somewhat popular in post-exilic biblical genealogical lists (see Ezr 8:7, 19; Neh 11:7; 1 Chr 3:21; 25:3, 15; 26:25), but this is hardly surprising. It likely reflects the prominence of the historical prophet Isaiah and the Book of Isaiah in later post-exilic tradition. Forgers are also fond of the name Isaiah, which appears at least thirteen times on objects from the antiquities market. Benjamin Mazar also excavated a fragmentary inscription, *lyš ʿ<y>hw*, "belonging to Isa<i>ah," which also would have been contemporary with

the biblical Isaiah, but it is missing a letter, which is hard to explain as a mistake; see Dobbs-Allsop et al., *Hebrew Inscriptions*, 223–24; Yonatan Nadelman, "Hebrew Inscriptions, Seal Impressions, and Markings of the Iron Age II," in Mazar and Mazar, *Excavations in the South of the Temple Mount*, 138.

30. As published in Yair Shoham, "Hebrew Bullae," in *Excavations at the City of David, 1978–1985 Directed by Yigal Shiloh, Volume VI: Inscriptions*, ed. Donald Ariel (Jerusalem: Institute of Archaeology, 2000), 51. More has been published from the City of David by Eilat Mazar, but still no other examples with the name "Isaiah."

31. Rollston, "The Yešaʿyah[û] ("Isaiah") Bulla," 414–17. See my extended critique of Rollston in "The Isaiah Bulla."

32. Mazar, *Ophel Excavations*, 263–64 (no. B9). Mazar translates the name as ʿAdiyahu, which is a possible variant. It is difficult to be certain about the ancient pronunciation, but I choose the variant that makes the etymology of the name and its connections more obvious. See my more extended discussion in "The Isaiah Bulla."

33. Also cognate with another prophetic name, *Oded* (ʿdd; 2 Chr 15). The name *Iddo* also illustrates the variation of spelling with and without a final aleph (see Zech 1:1, 7; 1 Chr 6:6; 2 Chr 12:15; 13:22; 2 Chr 9:29; 1 Kgs 4:14; Ezr 5:1; 6:14; Neh 12:4, 16). The name ʿAdiyahu appears once in the Hebrew Bible (2 Chr 23:1), and the Syriac version there transliterates it as the name Iddo. The name ʿAdiyahu or ʿIddoyahu also appears in Arad 58:1. The LXX spells the name Iddo as Αδδω reflecting both the doubling of the dalet (from the root ʿdd) as well as the interchangeability of the *a* and *i* in the transcription of the name.

34. Stefan Wimmer understands *ḥzyn* and ʿ*ddn* here as parallel terms for "prophets" and points to the use of Egyptian *ḥḏ* (=Hebrew, *ḥzh*) in a Levantine hieratic ostracon from Ashkelon as a local administrative title for "prophet"; see Wimmer, "A New Hieratic Ostracon from Ashkelon," *TA* 35 (2008): 66–68. He also points to the use of the term ʿ*ḏy* in the Tale of Wenamun for an administrative official in the court of Byblos through whom the god speaks (*COS* I, 1.141).

35. Most prominently, Rollston, "The Yešaʿyah[û] ("Isaiah") Bulla."

36. I am indebted to Anat Mendel-Geberovich for discussing this problem with me.

37. For an extended discussion, see my article, "The Isaiah Bulla."

38. See detailed discussion in Schniedewind, "The Isaiah Bulla."

39. I refer to Moussaeiff Ostraca published in Pierre Bordreuil, Felice Israel, and Dennis Pardee, "King's Command and Widow's Plea: Two New Hebrew Ostraca from the Biblical Period," *NEA* 61 (1998), which I cited in *How the Bible Became a Book*. For this reason we cannot use seal impressions like the bulla "Belonging to Isaiah, Servant of the King," from Kaufman's collection of antiquities; see Robert Deutsch, *Biblical Period Bullae: The Josef Chaim Kaufman Collection* (Tel Aviv: Archaeological Center Publications, 2003), 51–53.

40. On the prophetic messenger formula as an adapted scribal rubric, see Schniedewind, *Finger of the Scribe*.

41. See the discussion of the scribal exercises at Kuntillet ʿAjrud in Schniedewind, *Finger of the Scribe*, 23–48.

42. See Schniedewind, "Prophets in the Early Monarchy," in *Enemies and Friends of the State: Ancient Prophecy in Context*, ed. Christopher Rollston (Winona Lake, IN: Eisenbrauns, 2018), 207–17.

43. See, for example, T. Overholt, *Channels of Prophecy: The Social Dynamics of Prophetic Activity* (Eugene, OR: Wipf and Stock, 2003).

44. See Schniedewind, *Finger of the Scribe*, 95–119.

45. See Schniedewind, *Finger of the Scribe*, 95–109.

Chapter 7: Scribes among the People of the Land

1. John Thames summarizes the history of scholarship in his article "A New Discussion of the Meaning of the Phrase *'am hā- 'āreṣ* in the Hebrew Bible," *JBL* 130 (2011): 109–25. Thames dismisses all previous scholarship on this term because of the diversity of views.

2. This development is nicely laid out in *Hebrew and Aramaic Lexicon of the Old Testament*, ad loc., "עַם meaning A: paternal uncle, Latin *patruus*; B: (paternal) relations, clan, kin; C, people; all these meanings concern the same word, the original meaning of which is preserved in A."

3. This is discussed at length in Gabriel Barkay's unpublished Hebrew dissertation; see also Barkay, "The Iron II–III," in *The Archaeology of Ancient Israel*, ed. Amnon Ben-Tor (New Haven: Yale University Press, 1992), 371–72.

4. See, for example, the debate by Israel Finkelstein and Amihai Mazar in *The Quest for the Historical Israel: Archaeology and the History of Early Israel* (Atlanta: SBL Press, 2007).

5. See the classic study by David Schloen, *The House of the Father as Fact and Symbol: Patrimonialism in Ugarit and the Ancient Near East* (Winona Lake, IN: Eisenbrauns, 2001), 135–86; on the changes, see Baruch Halpern, "Jerusalem and the Lineages in the Seventh Century BCE: Kinship and the Rise of Individual Moral Liability," in *Law and Ideology in Monarchic Israel*, ed. Baruch Halpern and Deborah Hobson (Sheffield: JSOT Press, 1991), 11–107.

6. See Faust, *Neo-Assyrian Empire in the Southwest*, 35–59.

7. Translation by Cogan, "Sennacherib's Siege of Jerusalem," in *Context of Scripture*, 2.119B.

8. See Israel Finkelstein and Nadav Na'aman, "The Judahite Shephelah in the Late 8th and Early 7th Centuries BCE," *Tel Aviv* 31 (2004): 60–79; Yehuda Dagan, "Results of the Survey: Settlement Patterns in the Lachish Region," in *The Renewed Archaeological Excavations at Lachish (1973–1994)*, ed. David Ussishkin (Tel Aviv: Sonia and Marco Nadler Institute of Archaeology, 2004), 2672–90.

9. See Yigal Moyal and Avraham Faust, "Jerusalem's Hinterland in the Eighth–Seventh Centuries BCE: Towns, Villages, Farmsteads, and Royal Estates," *PEQ* 147 (2015): 283–98; Faust, *Neo-Assyrian Empire in the Southwest*, 92–100.

10. See N. Ben-Ari, N. Sapir, Ido Koch, and Oded Lipschits, "New 'Private' Stamped Jar Handles from the Mordot Arnona Excavations," *Atiqot*, forthcoming; Ya'akov Billig, Liora Freud, and Efrat Bocher, "A Luxurious Royal Estate from the First Temple Period in Armon ha-Natziv, Jerusalem," *TA* 49 (2022): 8–31; N. Sapir, N. Ben-Ari, L. Freud, and O. Lipschits, "History, Economy and Administration in Late Iron Age Judah in Light of the Excavations at Mordot Arnona, Jerusalem," *TA* 49 (2022): 32–53.

11. On the Holiness Code and Josiah's Reforms, see Lauren Monroe's analysis in *Josiah's Reform and the Dynamics of Defilement: Israelite Rites of Violence and the Making of a Biblical Text* (New York: Oxford University Press, 2011), 130–37.

12. Many scholars limit the original part of the book to chapters 1–3, which is decidedly negative and critical as compared to the rays of hope in the later chapters; for an overview of the scholarship, see James Nogalski, *The Book of the Twelve* (Macon, GA: Smyth and Helwys, 2011), 511–18.

13. Naomi Unwin, *Caria and Crete in Antiquity* (Cambridge: Cambridge University Press, 2017), 34–35.

14. See, for example, Hermann Niemann, "Choosing Brides for the Crown-Prince: Matrimonial Politics in the Davidic Dynasty," *VT* 546 (2006): 225–38.

15. The larger cities of Lachish and Eglon have been identified in studies of historical geography. Most recently, Eglon has been reasonably identified with the site of Tel ʿEton on the basis of excavations; see Avraham Faust and Hayah Katz, "A Canaanite Town, a Judahite Center, and a Persian Period Fort," *NEA* 78, no. 2 (2015): 88–102.

16. Monroe, *Josiah's Reform and the Dynamics of Defilement.*

17. See David Moulis, "Hezekiah's Cultic Reforms According to the Archaeological Evidence," in *The Last Century in the History of Judah: The Seventh Century BCE in Archaeological, Historical, and Biblical Perspectives*, ed. Filip Čapek and Oded Lipschits (Atlanta: SBL, 2019), 167–80.

18. The original publication by Joseph Naveh was followed by a host of scholarly publications. See Naveh, "A Hebrew Letter from the Seventh Century," *IEJ* 10 (1960): 129–39; Naveh, "More Hebrew Inscriptions from Meṣad Ḥashavyahu," *IEJ* 12 (1962): 27–32; Naveh, "Some Notes on the Reading of the Meṣad Ḥashavyahu Letter," *IEJ* 14 (1964): 158–59; F. M. Cross, "Epigraphic Notes on Hebrew Documents of the Eighth–Sixth Centuries B.C. 2. The Murabbaʿât Papyrus and the Letter Found Near Yavneh-Yam," *BASOR* 165 (1962): 34–46; S. Talmon, "The New Hebrew Letter from the Seventh Century B.C. in Historical Perspective," *BASOR* 176 (1964): 29–38; and A. Lemaire, "L'ostracon de Meṣad Ḥashavyahu (Yavneh-Yam) replacé dans son contexte," *Semitica* 21 (1971): 57–79. For a summary of the scholarly literature, see S. Aḥituv, *Echoes from the Past*, 156–63.

19. Naveh, "Hebrew Letter," 136.

20. Usually transliterated as *Hashabiah*. See Gary S. Shogren, "Hashabiah," *Achor Bible Dictionary*, ed. D. Freedman, et. al. (New York: Doubleday, 1992), ad loc.

21. See my article "Commander of the Fortress? Understanding an Ancient Israelite Military Title," *BAR* 45, no. 1 (2019): 39–44, 70.

22. See Naveh, "Hebrew Letter," 137 (n. 8). In addition to Naveh's example, some examples in Avigad, *West Semitic Stamp Seals,* include nos. 700, 1014, and 1161.

23. Some are mentioned in Naveh, "Hebrew Letter," 137 (n. 8). In additional to the idiosyncrasies mentioned by Naveh, the *kaf* is a bit unique in being written with three separate strokes. Naveh's chart illustrates some of the idiosyncrasies of this inscription (p. 138). Comparing the Arad script chart (published well after Naveh's article) further confirms the unique nature of this scribe's hand. See Aharoni, *Arad Inscriptions*, 133–36.

24. See Oded Tammuz, "The Sabbath as the Seventh Day of the Week and a Day of Rest: Since When?" *ZAW* 131 (2019): 287–94.

25. See Jan Joosten, *People and Land in the Holiness Code: An Exegetical Study of the Ideational Framework of the Law in Leviticus 17–26* (Leiden: Brill, 1996).

Chapter 8: Women in the Professions

1. These feminine images are not necessarily completely positive, as some scholars point out. See the overview of scholarship in Alice Ogden Bellis, *Helpmates, Harlots, and Heroes* (Louisville: Westminster John Knox Press, 2007), 172–78.

2. This is nicely developed in David Carr, *Writing on the Tablet of the Heart: Origins of Scripture and Literature* (Oxford: Oxford University Press, 2008).

3. This point is made specifically about female Egyptian literacy in Betsy Bryan, "Evidence for Female Literacy from Theban Tombs of the New Kingdom," *Bulletin of the Egyptological Seminar* 6 (1985): 24n37.

4. Eleanor Robson, "Gendered Literacy and Numeracy in the Sumerian Literary Corpus," in *Analysing Literary Sumerian Corpus-Based Approaches*, ed. Jarle Ebling and Graham Cunningham (London and Oakville: Equinox, 2007), 215–49.

5. Text cited in Robson, "Gendered Literacy," 236.

6. See Claudia Camp, *Wisdom and the Feminine in the Book of Proverbs* (Sheffield: Almond Press, 1985), 283.

7. Meir Bar-Ilan, *Some Jewish Women in Antiquity* (Atlanta: Scholars Press, 1998), 32.

8. J. Greenfield, "Some Babylonian Women," 79, cited in S. Meier, "Women and Communication in the Ancient Near East," *JAOS* 111 (1991): 541.

9. Charles Halton and Saana Svärd, *Women's Writing of Ancient Mesopotamia: An Anthology of the Earliest Female Authors* (Cambridge: Cambridge University Press, 2017), 228.

10. R. Dougherty, "Writing Upon Parchment and Papyrus Among the Babylonians and the Assyrians," *JAOS* 48 (1928): 129.

11. See, for example, Bryan, "Evidence for Female Literacy from Theban Tombs," 17–32.

12. See especially the wide-ranging book by Hennie Marsman, *Women in Ugarit and Israel: Their Social and Religious Position in the Context of the Ancient Near East* (Leiden: Brill, 2003).

13. *KTU* 2.14. Translation by the author.

14. *KTU* 2.11. Translation by the author.

15. See Susan Ackerman, "The Queen Mother and the Cult in Ancient Israel," *JBL* 112 (1993): 385–401; Ktziah Spanier, "The Queen Mother in the Judaean Royal Court: Maacah and Athaliah," in *Proceedings of the Eleventh World Congress of Jewish Studies* (Jerusalem: World Union of Jewish Studies, 1994), 75–82; Elna Solvang, *A Woman's Place in the House: Royal Women of Judah and Their Involvement in the House of David* (Sheffield: Sheffield Academic Press, 2003); Ginny Brewer-Boydston, "Sarah the *gevirah*: A Comparison of Sarah and the Queen Mothers, of Matriarches in the Dynastic Succession of Sons and Nations," *Review and Expositor* 115 (2018): 500–512.

16. See Nahman Avigad, "The Seal of Jezebel," *IEJ* 14 (1964): 274–76, pl. 56. The find did come in an antiquities collection, so we cannot be certain that it is not forged. And it does not use the title "Queen," but the iconography includes royal imagery and the paleography places it appropriately in the days when Jezebel was Queen in Samaria.

17. I avoid most unprovenanced artifacts like the Jerusalem papyrus, which I think is likely a forgery; see Christopher Rollston, "The Putative Authenticity of the New 'Jerusalem' Papyrus Inscription: Methodological Caution as a Desideratum," in O. Lipschits, Y. Gadot, M. Adams, eds., *Rethinking Israel*, 321–30.

18. Bar-Ilan tries to estimate percentages of female literacy, but the statistics are completely conjecture. His point that female literacy tracked overall literacy seems obvious. More to the point is that increases in writing and literacy in the general population likely meant especially marked increases in female literacy; see Bar-Ilan, *Some Jewish Women in Antiquity*, 40–41.

19. See Joseph Naveh, "Hebrew and Aramaic Inscriptions," *QEDEM* 41 (2000): 1–8.

20. Naveh, "Hebrew and Aramaic Inscriptions," 4–5. There is some debate over the interpretation of *ṭet* as an abbreviation for "good wine," but it seems best to read it in relation to the contents of the jar.

21. Also known in Ugaritic accounting texts, see *DULAT*, 377–78.

22. Originally published by Me'ir Ben-Dov, *The Dig at the Temple Mount* (1982), 36 (Hebrew); (1985), 36; see also Nahman Avigad, "A Note on an Impression from a Woman's Seal," *IEJ* 37 (1987): 18–19; Mazar and Mazar, *Excavations in the South of the Temple Mount*, 18, 131, 133; and Andre Lemaire, "Epigraphie palestinenne: Nouveaux documents II—Décennie 1985–1995," *Henoch* 17 (1995): 209–42.

23. See Isaac, "You Shall Be Named After Your Ancestors."

24. Amos Kloner and Irit Yezerski, "A Late Iron Age Rock-Cut Tomb on the Western Slope of Mount Zion, Jerusalem," *'Atiqot* 98 (2020): 17 (figure 13, no. 2); see Avigad, *West Semitic Stamp Seals*, no. 35.

25. See Reich, Shukron, and Lernau, "Recent Discoveries in the City of David, Jerusalem," 153–69.

26. Food security is one of the central issues of refugee populations; see Michael Cernea, "Risks, Safeguards, and Reconstruction: A Model for Population Displacement and Resettlement," in *Risks and Reconstruction: Experience of Resettlers and Refugees*, ed. M. Cernea and C. McDowell (Washington, DC: World Bank, 2000), 11–55; Aaron Burke, "Refugees in the Near East and the Eastern Mediterranean, Archaeology of," in *Encyclopedia of Global Archaeology*, ed. C. Smith (Cham: Springer, 2018), 1–6.

27. Special thanks to James Moore for discussing these texts with me and sharing his forthcoming article "Social and Historical Observations of Women at Elephantine According to the Administrative Papyri and Ostraca," in *Studies on Elephantine*, ed. Verena Lepper (Brill).

28. See the overview in Michael Fox, *Proverbs 10–31*, Anchor Bible Commentary (New York: Doubleday, 2009), 882–88.

29. For a discussion of this collection in Proverbs, see Schniedewind, *Finger of the Scribe*, 126–31.

30. One of the more extensive studies of Huldah is in a popular book, Preston Kavanagh, *Huldah, the Prophet Who Wrote Hebrew Scripture* (Eugene, OR: Pickwick, 2012). Unfortunately, his biography is based on rather fanciful impositions onto texts using methods of Kabbalistic (mystical) interpretation. At least he recognized the importance of Huldah as a figure. Caution is usually the approach by biblical scholars like Pauline Viviano: "Nothing is known of her but she is the wife of Shallum" ("Huldah," in *Anchor Bible Dictionary*, 1992). Similarly, Alice Ogden Bellis gives only one page to Huldah in her comprehensive study *Helpmates, Harlots, and Heroes*, 153–54, and most of this is just a quote of the passage in 2 Kings 22. For an excellent summary of scholarship on Huldah, see Stavrakopoulou, "The Prophet Huldah and the Stuff of State," in Rollston, ed., *Enemies and Friends of the State*, 277–96.

31. See the parallel texts in 2 Chr 34:22 and 2 Kgs 22:14.

32. Stavrakoupoulou, "Prophet Huldah," 290–91.

33. Baruch Halpern calls Huldah the first biblical text critic. See Halpern, "Huldah, the First Biblical Text Critic," *Other Side* 35, no. 2 (1999): 51–53; see also Thomas Römer and Philip Davies, "From Prophet to Scribe: Jeremiah, Huldah, and the Invention of the Book," in *Writing the Bible: Scribes, Scribalism, and Script*, ed. Philip Davies and Thomas Römer (Durham, NC: Acumen, 2013), 96–106.

34. Adrian Bledstein, "Is Judges a Woman's Satire of Men Who Play God?" in *A Feminist Companion to Judges*, ed. A. Brenner (Sheffield: JSOT Press, 1993), 54.

35. See the numerous publications on the excavations by Yuval Gadot and his colleagues, for example, "A Newly Discovered Personal Seal and Bulla from the Excavations of the Givʿati Parking Lot, Jerusalem," *IEJ* 69 (2019): 154–74.

36. See, for example, the popular work by Kavanagh, *Huldah, the Prophet Who Wrote Hebrew Scripture*. Richard Elliot Friedman suggested that Jeremiah was "the Deuteronomist" in his bestseller, *Who Wrote the Bible?*

37. This point is nicely made in Bellis, *Helpmates, Harlots, and Heroes*, 143–48.

38. Whereas we find Hebrew words for the professions of scribe and prophet marked by female suffixes, we find no priestesses in the Hebrew Bible. Perhaps there were some, but the canon of the Hebrew Bible did not record them. See Susan Ackerman, "Why Is Miriam Also Among the Prophets? (And Is Zipporah Among the Priests?)," *JBL* 121 (2002): 71–75. I also thank Professor Ackerman for sharing with me her unpublished ASOR lecture, "Priestesses in the Days of Solomon and Ahab."

Chapter 9: Priestly Scribal Communities

1. On Wellhausen and the dating of priestly material, see Jakob Wöhlre, "The Priestly Writing(s): Scope and Nature," in *The Oxford Handbook of the Pentateuch*, ed. Joel Baden and Jeffrey Stackert (New York: Oxford University Press, 2021), 255–75. In addition, see Avraham Faust's analysis of its archaeological context, "The World of P: the Material Realm of the Priestly Writings," *VT* 69 (2019): 173–218. For the complexities of the priestly writings, see Shara Shectman and Joel Baden, eds., *The Strata of the Priestly Writings: Comtemporary Debate and Future Directions* (Zurich: TVZ, 2009).

2. See the essays in Gertz et al., eds., *The Formation of the Pentateuch*.

3. On bowls, see Gabriel Barkay, "A Bowl with the Hebrew Inscription שדק," *IEJ* 40 (1990): 124–29; Jeremy Smoak, "Holy Bowls: Inscribing Holiness in Ancient Israel and Judah," *MAARAV* 23 (2019): 69–92. For seals and seal impressions, see Avigad, *West Semitic Stamp Seals*. For Arad Temple inscriptions, see Aharoni, *Arad Inscriptions*. For the Ketef Hinnom amulets, see Gabriel Barkay, Andrew Vaughn, Marilyn Lundberg, and Bruce Zuckerman, "The Amulets from Ketef Hinnom: A New Edition and Evaluation," *BASOR* 334 (2004): 41–71; and Jeremy Smoak, *The Priestly Blessing in Inscription and Scripture: The Early History of Numbers 6:24–26* (New York: Oxford University Press, 2015). Another possible priestly inscription is the enigmatic Khirbet Beit Lei inscription, but its priestly connection is uncertain; see Alice Mandell

and Jeremy Smoak, "Reconsidering the Function of Tomb Inscriptions in Iron Age Judah: Khirbet Beit Lei as a Test Case," *JANER* 16 (2016): 192–245.

4. See Gabriel Barkay and Zachi Dvira, "Relics in Rubble: The Temple Mount Sifting Project," *BAR* 42, 6 (2016): 44–55; and most recently, Barkay and Dvira, "Jerusaelm, the Temple Mount Sifting Project—Preliminary Report," *Excavations and Surveys in Israel* 133 (2021).

5. See Z. Dvira and G. Barkay, "Clay Sealings from the Temple Mount and Their Use in the Temple and Royal Treasuries," *Jerusalem Journal of Archaeology* 2 (2021): 41–57.

6. See the survey in Avraham Faust, "Israelite Temples: Where Was Israelite Cult Not Practiced, and Why," *Religions* 10, no. 2 (2019), https://doi.org/10.3390/rel10020106.

7. See Aharoni, *Arad Inscriptions*, nos. 49, 52, 60, 61, 62, 65, 67, 68, 70, 87, 89, 94, 95, 100, 101, 102, 103, and 104. Na'aman also thinks these (and other ostraca from the storeroom area) are evidence of literary activity related to the Arad Temple. Na'aman, "New Light on Six Inscriptions from Arad," 216.

8. The beginnings of the Arad fortress and its temple are the subject of some debate among archaeologists, but it seems clear that the temple went out of use at the end of the eighth century BCE; see Z. Herzog, "The Date of the Temple at Arad: Reassessment of the Stratigraphy and the Implications for the History of Religion in Judah," in *Studies in the Archaeology of the Iron Age in Israel and Jordan*, ed. A. Mazar (Sheffield: Sheffield Academic Press, 2001), 156–78; see also Moulis, "Hezekiah's Cultic Reforms According to the Archaeological Evidence," 167–80.

9. Published by Aharoni, *Arad Inscriptions*, as Arad 49, pp. 80–84. My readings rely on Nadav Na'aman's article and his multispectral images as well as original photos provided to me by West Semitic Research; see Na'aman, "New Light on Six Inscriptions from Arad," 213–35. However, I don't see any compelling reason for Na'aman's reorganization, so I retain Aharoni's general organization of the columns. I have modified Aharoni's original drawing (Figure 9.3) based on Na'aman's multispectral images and images provided by West Semitic Research.

10. I follow Aharoni's organization. Other scholars have offered various "improved" readings, but they do not substantially change the nature of the text. This includes Na'aman, "New Light on Six Inscriptions from Arad," 216–24. It should be noted that Aharoni worked with earlier photos and the freshly excavated ostraca, while Na'aman works from recent multispectral photos in which the ink has considerably faded, which would explain why Aharoni saw things that Na'aman no longer sees. Na'aman gave me his new multispectral images, but I couldn't confirm many of his readings. I relied more on the original publication photos provided to me by West Semitic Research.

11. This connection was pointed out to me by Moise Isaac. See his dissertation, "'You Will Be Named after Your Ancestors,'" 192 (note 130), 251 (note 165).

12. I follow Na'aman's reading here. See "New Light on Six Inscriptions from Arad," 221. Aharoni originally read this name as Aḥa, which also has northern connections (1 Chr 5:15), and it also appears in Transjordanian inscriptions. The name *Aḥa* is also found on two other ostraca from Arad—both are quite early (probably ninth century BCE), found near Arad 49, and near the entrance to the sanctuary.

13. There have been some attempts to down-date the Arad ostraca. For example, Herzog tried to reassign Stratum VIII from the eighth to the seventh century, but he admitted that the pottery of Stratum VIII is like Lachish III (that is, a destruction level in 701 BCE); Herzog now

thinks the temple was dismantled in Stratum IX (eighth century), even though this would mean all the clearly priestly ostraca were written at a time when there was no temple. It makes little sense. The temple did go out of use in the eighth century but in Stratum VIII, which from material culture parallels Lachish III, whose inscriptions still must be eighth century. See Herzog, "The Date of the Temple at Arad," 156–78. As Singer-Avitz points out, Stratum VIII is transitional to the end of the eighth and beginning of the seventh century. L. Singer-Avitz, "Arad: the Iron Age Pottery Assemblages," *Tel Aviv* 29 (2002): 110–214.

14. See the discussion by Smoak, "Holy Bowls," 72 (n. 10).

15. See, for example, Rollston, *Writing and Literacy in the World of Ancient Israel*.

16. Barkay, "Bowl with Hebrew Inscription," 129; Barkay cites Orly Goldwasser, "Hieratic Inscriptions from Tel Seraʿ in Southern Canaan," *TA* 11 (1984): 85.

17. Duncan Mackenzie, "The Excavations at Ain Shems (Beth-Shemesh)," *PEFA* 2 (1912–1913): 86–88, plate 54:13. The interpretation of these letters has been debated, but Barkay offers the most convincing material reading; see Barkay, "'Your Poor Brother': A Note on an Inscribed Bowl from Beth Shemesh," *IEJ* 41 (1991): 239–41.

18. On the execution of chiseled writing, see Yonatan Nadelman, "'Chiseled' Inscriptions and Markings on Pottery Vessels from the Iron II (Discussion and Catalogue)," *IEJ* 40 (1990): 31–41.

19. See Bernard Delavault and André Lemaire, "Les inscriptions phéniciennes de Palestine," *Rivista di studi fenici* 7 (1979): 22.

20. See the overview in Smoak, "Holy Bowls." Frank Moore Cross dismissed the eighth-century archaeological context and argued that these were Phoenician inscriptions from the seventh or sixth century based on his analysis of the paleography; see Cross, "Two Offering Dishes with Phoenician Inscriptions from the Sanctuary of Arad," *BASOR* 235 (1979): 75–78. It's not tenable, however, to dismiss the archaeological context. Rather, it makes more sense to think of retention of Phoenician influence in the peripheral priestly scribal community.

21. There have been attempts to date these amulets to later periods, but the archaeological context detailed in the *editio princeps* make these attempts implausible; see Barkay et al., "The Amulets from Ketef Hinnom," 41–71. See Smoak, *Priestly Blessing*, 13–16.

22. See Gabriel Barkay, "Northern and Western Jerusalem in the End of the Iron Age," PhD dissertation, Hebrew University, 1985 (Hebrew); David Ussishkin, *The Village of Silwan: The Necropolis from the Period of the Judean Kingdom* (Jerusalem: Israel Exploration Society, 1993); Irit Yezerki, "Typology and Chronology of the Iron Age II–III Judahite Rock-Cut Tombs," *IEJ* 63 (2013): 50–77; Gabriel Barkay, "Jerusalem Tombs from the Days of the First Temple," *BAR* 12, no. 2 (1986): 23–39.

23. See, for example, Amihai Mazar, "Iron Age Burial Caves North of the Damascus Gate, Jerusalem," *IEJ* 26 (1976): 1–8; Gabriel Barkay, "Three First Temple Burial Caves North of Damascus Gate and the Date of Jerusalem's Northern Moat," *Cathedra* 83 (1997): 7–26 (Hebrew).

24. This is where the "daughter of Menachem" seal was found (discussed in chapter 8); see Kloner and Yezerski, "A Late Iron Age Rock-Cut Tomb on the Western Slope of Mount Zion," 1–24.

25. Barkay et al., "The Amulets from Ketef Hinnom," 54.

26. The different readings and merits of these readings are reviewed in Smoak, *Priestly Blessing*, 18–42.

27. The association is made in Smoak, *Priestly Blessing*. A later article also further develops Smoak's identification with the Holiness Code; see Mark Awabdy, "The Holiness Composition of the Priestly Blessing," *Biblica* 99 (2018): 29–49.

28. See Faust, "World of P"; Joosten, *People and Land in the Holiness Code*.

29. Most scholars see Exod 34:6–7 as the older formulation upon which Deut 7:9 is drawing. See M. Fishbane, *Biblical Interpretation in Ancient Israel* (Oxford: Oxford University Press, 1985), 335–50; T. Dozeman, "Inner-Biblical Interpretation of Yahweh's Gracious and Compassionate Character," *JBL* 108 (1989): 207–33. Jeffrey Stackert points out the larger influence of the Holiness legislation in the Pentateuch, "The Holiness Legislation and Its Pentateuchal Sources: Revision, Supplementation, and Replacement," in *Strata of the Priestly Writings*, 187–204.

30. For the liturgical background of Psalm 100, see William Schniedewind, "Are We His People? Biblical Interpretation During Crisis," *Biblica* 77 (1995): 540–50; see also John Evans, *You Shall Know That I Am Yahweh: An Inner-Biblical Interpretation of Ezekiel's Recognition Formula* (Winona Lake, IN: Eisenbrauns, 2019).

31. Avigad, *West Semitic Stamp Seals*, no. 28. We do have another seal with the title "Priest" from northern Israel from the antiquities market (*lṣdq bn mk'* and *[lz]kryw khn d'r* WSSS 29). We have to assume it is also a forgery. Another possible title for the temple community would be "servant of YHWH," which is found on the seal of "Miqneyaw, servant of YHWH" (WSSS 27). But it was purchased in Jerusalem and not excavated. There is a strong possibility that it is another forgery.

32. Published as B27 by Shoham, "Hebrew Bullae," 29–57.

33. Lawrence Mykytiuk does an exhaustive study that tries to identify seals and seal impression with biblical figures. This is the one case that he argues can be made with confidence; see *Identifying Biblical Persons in Northwest Semitic Inscriptions of 1200–539 BCE* (Leiden: Brill, 2004), 148–52.

34. Shoham, "Hebrew Bullae," B2.

35. See, for example, Israel Finkelstein and Neil Silberman, "Temple and Dynasty: Hezekiah, the Remaking of Judah and the Rise of the Pan-Israelite Ideology," *JSOT* 30 (2006): 259–85; Saar Ganor and Igor Kreimerman, "An Eighth-Century BCE Gate Shrine at Tel Lachish, Israel," *Bulletin of the American Schools of Oriental Research* 381 (2019): 211–36; Shua Kisilevitz, "The Iron IIA Judahite Temple at Tel Moẓa," *Tel Aviv* 42 (2015): 147–64. In spite of some objections, it makes the most sense of the data to relate it to Hezekiah's Reforms; see the summary by Moulis, "Hezekiah's Cultic Reforms According to the Archaeological Evidence," 167–80.

36. Cult centralization has been a much-debated topic among scholars with no clear consensus. See, for example, Julia Rhyder, *Centralizing the Cult: The Holiness Legislation of Leviticus 17–26* (Tübingen: Mohr Siebeck, 2019), 65–111; and T. Römer, "Cult Centralization in Deuteronomy 12: Between Deuteronomistic History and Pentateuch," in *Das Deuteronomium zwischen Pentateuch und Deuteronomistischen Geschichtswerk*, ed. Eckart Otto and Reinhard Achenbach, FRLANT 20 (Göttingen: Vandenhoeck & Ruprecht, 2004), 168–80.

37. The conceptual framework for this is laid out in Lawrence Stager's classic article, "The Archaeology of the Family in Ancient Israel," *BASOR* 260 (1985): 1–35. The framework is taken up and developed by Mark Leuchter, *The Levites and the Boundaries of Israelite Identity* (New

York: Oxford University Press, 2017). Leuchter conveniently lays it out in a popular essay on *TheTorah.com*, "Who Were the Levites?" (2017), https://thetorah.com/article/who-were-the -levites.

38. Faust, "Israelite Temples," doi.org/10.3390/rel10020106.

39. See, for example, Zeev Herzog, "Perspectives on Southern Israel's Cult Centralization: Arad and Beer-sheba," in *One God—One Cult—One Nation: Archaeological and Biblical Perspectives*, ed. Reinhard Kratz and Hermann Spieckermann (Berlin: de Gruyter, 2010), 169–200.

40. See, for example, my article, "History and Interpretation: The Religion of Ahab and Manasseh in the Book of Kings," *CBQ* 55 (1993): 649–61.

41. See my essay, "Diversity and Development of *tôrâ* in the Hebrew Bible," 1–16.

42. The priestly literature of the Documentary Hypothesis is classically summarized in S. R. Driver, *An Introduction to the Literature of the Old Testament* (1909).

43. See "The Numinous Power of Writing," in Schniedewind, *How the Bible Became a Book*, 24–34.

44. It also parallels near eastern accounts of the divine origin for temples; see Victor Hurowitz, *I Have Built You an Exalted House: Temple Building in the Bible in Light of Mesopotamian and North-West Semitic Writings* (Sheffield: JSOT Press, 1992).

45. See Brian Donnelly-Lewis, "The Tabernacle Manual: Exodus 25:1–31:18 in Light of the Cuneiform Procedural Genre," *JBL* 141 (2022): 617–33.

46. See Alice Mandell, "Writing as a Source of Ritual Authority: The High Priest's Body as a Priestly Text in the Tabernacle-Building Story," *JBL* 141 (2022): 43–64.

47. See Schniedewind, *Finger of the Scribe*, 68–92; Benjamin Scolnic, *Theme and Context in Biblical Lists* (Atlanta: Scholars Press, 1995).

Chapter 10: Exiled Scribal Communities

1. See Avraham Faust, *Judah in the Neo-Babylonian Period: The Archaeology of Desolation* (Atlanta: SBL, 2012), 147, 233. An earlier study by Oded Lipschits calculated a 72 percent decline in the population of Judah; see *The Fall and Rise of Jerusalem in the Neo-Babylonian Period* (Winona Lake, IN: Eisenbrauns, 2005), 270. Yuval Gadot argues that Jerusalem's rural hinterland was not as decimated as suggested in Faust, "In the Valley of the King: Jerusalem's Rural Hinterland in the 8th–4th Centuries BCE," *TA* 42 (2015): 3–26. These are debates about degrees of devastation—the Hebrew scribal infrastructure would have been decimated in any of these models.

2. Oded Lipschits et al., *Ramat Raḥel VI* (Winona Lake, IN: Eisenbrauns, 2021); see also the summary by Lipschits et al., "Palace and Village, Paradise and Oblivion: Unraveling the Riddles of Ramat Raḥel," *NEA* 74, no. 1 (2011): 2–49.

3. In "Bethel Revisited," Lipschits contested Finkelstein and Singer-Avitz's archaeological interpretation, "Reevaluating Bethel." But the eighth-century destruction is not in question. Lipschits wants to find continuity at a nearby shrine. This seems like an attempt to explain away the meager archaeological evidence to support old redactional and source models of biblical literature.

4. See Faust, *Judah in the Neo-Babylonian Period*, 210–11.

5. See Oded Lipschits and David Vanderhooft, *The Yehud Stamp Impressions: A Corpus of Inscribed Impressions from the Persian and Hellenistic Periods in Judah* (Winona Lake, IN: Eisenbrauns, 2011).

6. See Cornelia Wunsch and Laurie Pearce, *Documents of Judean Exiles and West Semites in Babylonia in the Collection of David Sofer* (Bethesda CDL Press, 2014). More generally, see Laurie Pearce, "Cuneiform Sources for Judeans in the Neo-Babylonian and Achaemenid Periods: An Overview," *Religion Compass* 10 (2016): 230–43.

7. Wunsch and Pearce, *Documents of Judean Exiles and West Semites in Babylonia*, 112 (no. 10).

8. From the Staatliche Museen (Berlin, Germany), museum no. 28178. See Ernst F. Weidner, "Jojachin, Koenig von Juda, in babylonischen Keilschrifttexten," *Melanges Syriens offerts a M. Rene Dussaud, Vol. II* (1939), 923–35.

9. These have been edited and published by Bezalel Porten and Ada Yardeni, *Textbook of Aramaic Documents from Ancient Egypt*, 4 vols. (Winona Lake, IN: Eisenbrauns, 1986–99).

10. See the overview by Tawny Holm, "Papyrus Amherst 63 and the Arameans of Egypt: A Landscape of Cultural Nostalgia," in *Elephantine in Context: Studies on the History, Religion and Literature of the Judeans in Persian Period Egypt*, ed. Reinhard Kratz and Bernd Schipper (Tübingen: Mohr Siebeck, 2022), 323–46.

11. For a popular account, see Karel van der Toorn, "Egyptian Papyrus Sheds New Light on Jewish History," *BAR* 44, no. 4 (2018): 32–39. See also Richard Steiner, "Papyrus Amherst 63: A New Source for the Language, Literature, Religion, and History of the Arameans," in *Studia Aramaica: New Sources and New Approaches*, ed. M. Geller, J. Greenfield, and M. Weitzman (Oxford: Oxford University Press, 1995), 199–207; Steiner, "An Aramaic Text in Demotic Script," in *Context of Scripture*, 1.99; and K. van der Toorn, *Papyrus Amherst 63* (Tecklenburg, Germany: Ugarit-Verlag, 2018).

12. The parallel translation borrows from van der Toorn, "Egyptian Papyrus," 37, and Heckl, "Relationship Between Psalm 20 and Papyrus Amherst 63," 365–66. The translation of *ʾḥr* as "Yaho" is problematic and debated. See, for example, Sven Vleeming and Jan Wesselius, *Studies in Papyrus Amherst 63: Essays on the Aramaic Texts in Aramaic/Demotic* (Amsterdam: Juda Palache Instituut, 1985), 42; Zauzich, "Der Gott des Aramaisch-Demotisch Papyrus Amherst 63," *Göttinger Miszellen* 85 (1985): 89–90.

13. See, for example, M. Kister, "Psalm 20 and Papyrus Amherst 63: A Window to the Dynamic Nature of Poetic Texts," *VT* 70 (2020): 426–57; M. Rösel, "Israels Psalmen in Ägypten? Papyrus Amherst 63 und die Psalmen XX und LXXV," *VT* 50 (2000): 81–99.

14. Robert Carroll rightly questioned our ability to discern complex and multiple redactional layers in Jeremiah; see especially his commentary, *Jeremiah*, OTL (Philadelphia: Westminster John Knox, 1986). I prefer to stick with the relatively straightforward short versions of Jeremiah represented by the Septuagint (and DSS) and the Masoretic Text. See also Hindy Najman and Konrad Schmid, eds., *Jeremiah's Scriptures: Production, Reception, Interaction, and Transformations* (Leiden: Brill, 2016).

15. See Emanuel Tov, "The Last Stage of the Literary History of the Book of Jeremiah," in *The Oxford Handbook of the Book of Jeremiah*, ed. E. Silver and L. Stulman (New York: Oxford University Press, 2021), 129–47.

16. See Emanuel Tov, "The Literary History of Jeremiah in the Light of Its Textual History," in *Empirical Models for Biblical Criticism*, ed. Jeffrey Tigay (Philadephia: University of Pennsylvania Press, 1985), 228. My translations for the "long" and "short" versions try to follow the NRSV for the Masoretic Text (long Jeremiah) and the new NETS translation of the Septuagint (short Jeremiah).

17. See especially Reinhard Kratz's introductory essay, "Why Jeremiah? The Invention of a Prophetic Figure," in Najman and Schmid, eds., *Jeremiah's Scriptures*, 197–212, which is followed by three responses.

18. Corrine Patton points out priestly perspectives throughout MT Jeremiah, "Layers of Meaning: Priesthood in Jeremiah MT," in *The Priests in the Prophets: The Portrayal of Priests, Prophets and Other Religious Specialists in the Latter Prophets*, ed. Lester Grabbe and Alice Ogden Bellis (London: T & T Clark, 2004), 149–76.

19. This expanded and harmonizing introduction (vv. 4–10) is framed by repetitions: "The word of the LORD came to me" (vv. 4, 11, 13).

20. The Septuagint itself is complicated; for example, see Emanuel Tov, "The Literary History of Jeremiah in the Light of Its Textual History," in *Empirical Models for Biblical Criticism*, ed. Jeffrey Tigay (Philadephia: University of Pennsylvania Press, 1985), 211–37. We likely have an original translator and then a later revisor who brought the Septuagint more into line with the long (proto-Masoretic) Jeremiah. Tov posits an "Edition I" that was the basis for the MT's "Edition II." The short Jeremiah has its own series of revisions based on "Edition I."

21. Christopher Rollston makes a cogent case for Aramaic as part of Judean scribal curriculum. See Rollston, "Scribal Curriculum During the First Temple Period," in *Contextualizing Israel's Sacred Writing: Ancient Literacy, Orality, and Literary Production*, ed. Brian Schmidt (Atlanta: SBL, 2015), 90–93.

22. See Laurie Pearce, "Ezekiel: A Jewish Priest and a Babylonian Intellectual," *TheTorah.com*, 2017, https://thetorah.com/article/ezekiel-a-jewish-priest-and-a-babylonian-intellectual, n. 10. See also John MacGinnis, "Construction and Operation of Canals in Neo-Assyrian and Neo-Babylonian Sources," in *Water for Assyria*, ed. Hartmut Kühne (Wiesbaden: Harrassowitz, 2018), 41–56.

23. See Laurie Pearce, "Cuneiform Sources for Judeans in Babylonia," 230–43; also Pearce, "Judean Life in Babylonia," *TheTorah.com*, 2018, https://thetorah.com/article/judean-life-in-babylonia.

24. On Ezekiel's knowledge of cuneiform, see Daniel Bodi, "The Mesopotamian Context of Ezekiel," in *The Oxford Handbook of Ezekiel* (Oxford: Oxford Academic, 2020), DOI: 10.1093/oxfordhb/9780190634513.013.1. See also David Vanderhooft, "Ezekiel in and on Babylon," in *Bible et Proche-Orient, Mélanges André Lemaire III*, ed. J. Elayi and J.-M. Durand, *Transeuphratène* 46 (2014): 107–14; Jonathan Stökl, "Ezekiel: Remarks on the Transmission of Learning," *Die Welt des Orients* 45 (2015): 50–61; Abraham Winitzer, "Assyriology and Jewish Studies in Tel Aviv: Ezekiel among the Babylonian *literati*," in *Encounters by the Rivers of Babylon: Scholarly Conversations between Jews, Iranians, and Babylonians in Antiquity*, ed. U. Gabbay and S. Secunda (Tübingen: Mohr Siebeck, 2014), 163–216.

25. For an overview of this question, see Madhavi Nevader, "On Reading Ezekiel by the Rivers of Babylon," *Die Welt des Orients* 45 (2015): 99–110.

26. See, for example, Rainer Albretz, *Israel in Exile: The History and Literature of the Sixth Century B.C.E.* (Atlanta: SBL, 2003), 345–56.

27. See overview by Michael Lyons, "How Have We Changed? Older and Newer Arguments about the Relationship between Ezekiel and the Holiness Code," in *The Formation of the Pentateuch*, ed. Jan Gertz et al., 1055–74; and Christophe Nihan, "The Holiness Code between D and P," in *Das Deuteronomium zwischen Pentateuch und Deuteronomistischen Geschichtswerk*, 81–122.

Chapter 11: Working with the Samaritans

1. Gary Knoppers, *Jews and Samaritans: The Origins and History of Their Early Relations* (New York: Oxford University Press, 2013).

2. Knoppers highlights the shared genealogy in Chronicles to emphasize a pan-Israel perspective. But the genealogies focus on the patriarchal period, and there is no shared history of Israel. For Chronicles, the kingdom of Judah is Israel, and all true Israelites come to Jerusalem.

3. Finkelstein and Singer-Avitz, "Reevaluating Bethel," 33–48; see also Aharon Tavgar, "East of Beitin and the Location of the Ancient Cult Site of Bethel," in *In the Highland's Depth: Ephraim Range and Binyamin Research Studies* 5 (2015): 49–69 (Hebrew).

4. See Yitzhak Magen, *Mount Gerizim Excavations II: A Temple City* (Jerusalem: Israel Antiquities Authority, 2008); Magen, "The Dating of the First Phase of the Samaritan Temple on Mount Gerizim in Light of the Archaeological Evidence," in *Judah and Judeans in the Fourth Century BCE*, ed. O. Lipschits, G. Knoppers, and R. Albertz (Winona Lake, IN: Eisenbrauns, 2007), 157–211; Eran Arie, "Revisiting Mount Gerizim: The Foundation of the Sacred Precinct and the Proto-Ionic Capitals," in *New Studies in the Archaeology of Jerusalem*, vol. 14, ed. Yehiel Zelinger, Orit Peleg-Barkat, Joseph Uziel, and Yuval Gadot (Jerusalem: IAA, 2021), 39*–63*.

5. Magen, "The Dating of the First Phase of the Samaritan Temple," 158–64.

6. See Magen, *Mount Gerizim Excavations II*, 145–48.

7. This is the "high dating" of Nehemiah; some scholars prefer placing the historical figures in the fourth century. See further the two essays on chronology and composition by Sara Japhet and Tamara Eskenazi in *Judah and the Judeans in the Persian Period*, ed. Oded Lipschits and Manfred Oeming (Winona Lake, IN: Eisenbrauns, 2006), 491–530. The related argument of Jan Dušek that the Samaritan inscriptions and script must be post-Temple should be revised—rather, they must be post-sacred precinct; see Dušek, *Aramaic and Hebrew Inscriptions from Mt. Gerizim and Samaria between Antiochus III and Antiochus VI Epiphanes* (Leiden: Brill, 2012), 49–59.

8. See the discussion of this script by Antony Perrot and Matthieu Richelle, "The Dead Sea Scrolls' Paleo-Hebrew Script: Its Roots in the Hebrew Scribal Tradition," in *The Hebrew Bible Manuscripts: A Millennium*, ed. Élodie Attia and Antony Perrot (Leiden: Brill, 2022), 1–74.

9. See Emanuel Tov, *Textual Criticism of the Hebrew Bible*, 2nd ed. (Minneapolis: Augsburg Fortress, 2001), 80–100.

10. See Emanuel Tov, "The Samaritan Pentateuch and the Dead Sea Scrolls: The Proximity of the Pre-Samaritan Qumran Scrolls to the SP," in *Textual Criticism of the Hebrew Bible, Qumran, Septuagint* (Leiden: Brill, 2015), 387–410.

11. See Bezalel Porten and Ada Yardeni, *Textbook of Aramaic Documents from Ancient Egypt* (A4.7, A4.8, and A4.9); and conveniently in Porten, "Request for Letter of Recommendation (First Draft)," *Context of Scripture*, 3.51.

12. Bezalel Porten, "Recommendation for Reconstruction of Temple," *Context of Scripture*, 3.52.

13. For a review of Tobit studies, see Andrew Perrin, "An Almanac of Tobit Studies: 2000–2014," *Currents in Biblical Research* 14 (2014): 107–42.

14. Devorah Dimant, "Tobit and the Qumran Aramaic Texts," in *Is There a Text in This Cave? Studies in the Textuality of the Dead Sea Scrolls in Honour of George J. Brooke*, ed. Ariel Feldman, Maria Cioata, and Charlotte Hempel (Brill: Leiden, 2017), 389.

15. For a brief overview, see James Lindberger, "Ahiqar," in *The Old Testament Pseudepigrapha*, vol. 2 (Garden City, NY: Doubleday, 1985), 497–507. For a more extensive overview, see Herbert Niehr, *Aramäischer Ahiqar* (Gütersloh: Gütersloher Verlagshaus, 2007); and James Moore, *Literary Depictions of the Scribal Profession in the Story of Ahiqar and Jeremiah* 36 (Berlin and Boston: De Gruyter, 2021).

16. For example, Józef Milik thought the author of Tobit was a Samaritan, "La patrie de Tobie," *RB* 73 (1966): 522–30. Frölich observes that the content confirms "familiarity with traditions associated with those historical settings" (2005, p. 59), basically the history of Israel in the late eighth century. This suggests a Palestinian scribal community familiar with the biblical account of the fall of Samaria.

17. The technique of revision by introduction is detailed in Milstein, *Tracking the Master Scribe*. The concept of revision by conclusion is developed in a PhD seminar paper for me by Andrew Bock and in his doctoral dissertation (forthcoming).

18. This is the "high dating" of Nehemiah; some scholars prefer placing the historical figures in the fourth century.

19. See Oded Tammuz, "Will the Real Sanballat Please Stand Up?," in *Samaritans—Past and Present*, ed. Menachem Mor and Friedrich Reiterer (Berlin and New York: de Gruyter, 2008), 51–58.

20. See, for example, Gary Knoppers, "Nehemiah and Sanballat: The Enemy Without or Within?," in *Judah and the Judeans in the Fourth Century B.C.E.*, ed. Oded Lipschits, Gary N. Knoppers, and Rainer Albertz (Winona Lake, IN: Eisenbrauns, 2007), 305–22.

Chapter 12: Ezra and Nehemiah

1. See Sara Japhet, "The Supposed Common Authorship of Chronicles and Ezra-Nehemiah Investigated Anew," *VT* 18 (1968): 330–71; see also Japhet, *The Ideology of the Book of Chronicles and Its Place in Biblical Thought*, reprint ed. (University Park: Pennsylvania State University Press, 2009).

2. Diana Edelman proposed a radical revision of this chronology, in part because she thinks the early Persian period ill suited for any significant temple construction; see Edelman, *The Origins of the "Second" Temple: Persian Imperial Policy and the Rebuilding of Jerusalem* (London: Equinox, 2005). She has a point. As this chapter points out, the archaeological evidence suggests that Jerusalem was quite small in the middle and late Persian periods. But Jerusalem did not

need to be large and prosperous to rebuild its temple, and Ralph Klein has pointed out that Edelman's genealogical analysis does not stand up to scrutiny. See Ralph W. Klein, "Were Joshua, Zerubbabel, and Nehemiah Contemporaries? A Response to Diana Edelman's Proposed Late Date for the Second Temple," *JBL* 127 (2008): 697–701.

3. See the discussion by Sara Japhet, *From the Rivers of Babylon to the Highlands of Judah* (University Park: Pennsylvania State University Press, 2006), 245–67.

4. George Adam Smith, *Historical Geography of the Holy Land*, 25th ed. (London: Hodder and Stoughton, 1931), 215.

5. See Israel Finkelstein, "Jerusalem in the Persian (and Early Hellenistic) Period and the Wall of Nehemiah," *JSOT* 32 (2008): 501–20; Oded Lipschits, "Persian Period Finds from Jerusalem: Facts and Interpretations," *JHS* 9 (2009): Article 20; and Finkelstein, "Persian Period Jerusalem and Yehud: A Rejoinder," *JHS* 9 (2009): Article 24.

6. See Oded Lipschits, "Demographic Changes in Judah," in Lipschits and Blenkinsopp, eds., *Judah and the Judeans in the Neo-Babylonian Period*, 332.

7. This approach was taken up especially in David Jamieson-Drake, *Scribes and Schools in Monarchic Judah: A Socio-Archaeological Approach,* JSOTSS 109 (Sheffield: JSOT Press, 1991). For research that focuses specifically on the economy of the Persian period, see Charles Carter, *The Emergence of Yehud in the Persian Period: A Social and Demographic Study* (Sheffield: JSOT Press, 1999). See also Oded Lipschits's survey of Jerusalem, "Jerusalem Between Two Periods of Greatness: The Size and Status of the City in the Babylonian, Persian and Early Hellenistic Periods," in *Judaism between East and West: The Transition from Persian to Greek Rules (ca. 400–200 BCE),* ed. Lester Grabbe and Oded Lipschits (New York: T & T Clark, 2011), 163–75. The implications are recently taken up in a study by Torleif Elgvin, "Post-Exilic History and Archaeology and the Formation of Biblical Literature," in *Epigraphy, Iconography, and the Bible,* ed. Meir Lubetski and Edith Lubetski (Sheffield: Sheffield Phoenix Press, 2022), 243–79.

8. See André Lemaire, "Administration in Fourth-Century B.C.E. Judah in Light of Epigraphy and Numismatics," in O. Lipschits, G. Knoppers, R. Albertz, eds., *Judah and Judeans in the Fourth Century BCE,* 53–74.

9. See André Lemaire, "Taxes et impôts dans le sud de la Palestine (IVᵉ s. av. J.-C.)," *Transeu* 28 (2004): 133–42.

10. See Shaye Cohen, "Alexander the Great and Jaddus the High Priest According to Josephus," *AJS Review* 7 (1982): 41–68. Even though we must acknowledge the ideological aspects of Josephus' account, there is no reason to think that the priestly officials in Jerusalem would not have sent envoys to meet Alexander.

11. See Oded Lipschits, Yuval Gadot, and Dafna Langgut, "The Riddle of Ramat Raḥel: The Archaeology of a Royal Persian Period Edifice," *Transeuphraten* 41 (2012): 57–79; and the full excavation report, Oded Lipschits, Manfred Oeming, and Yuval Gadot, *Ramat Raḥel IV: The Renewed Excavations by the Tel Aviv–Heidelberg Expedition (2005–2010): Stratigraphy and Architecture* (University Park: Pennsylvania State University Press, 2020).

12. The library of Nehemiah is discussed extensively by scholars, often focusing more on the role of Judas and later canonization than Nehemiah; see, for example, Shayner Leiman, *The Canonization of Hebrew Scripture* (Hamden: Archon, 1976), 51–124; Arie van der Kooij, "The Canonization of Ancient Books Kept in the Library of Jerusalem," in *Canonization and*

Decanonization, ed. A. van der Kooij and K. van der Toorn (Leiden: Brill, 1998), 17–40; Armin Lange, "2 Maccabees 2:13–15: Library or Canon?" in *The Books of Maccabees: History, Theology, Ideology*, ed. G. Xervits and J. Zsengellér (Leiden: Brill, 2007), 155–68.

13. See Miriam Lichtheim, "The Memphite Theology," in *Ancient Egyptian Literature, Volume 1*, ed. Miriam Lichtheim (Berkeley: University of California Press, 1973), 1.52.

14. See Josephus, *Antiquities*, 11.159–83; Theodore Bergen, "Nehemiah in 2 Maccabees 1:10–2:18," *JSJ* 28 (1997): 259–60; Lester Grabbe, "Josephus and the Reconstruction of the Judean Restoration," *JBL* 106 (1986): 232–35.

15. Pearce, "The Scribes and Scholars of Ancient Mesopotamia," 2275.

16. Friedman, *Who Wrote the Bible?*, 232–33.

17. See, for example, Jacob Wright, *Rebuilding Identity: The Nehemiah-Memoir and Its Earliest Readers* (Berlin: de Gruyter, 2004).

18. Dan Barag, "Some Notes on a Silver Coin of Johanan the High Priest," *BA* 48, no. 3 (1985): 166–68; see also John Betlyon, "The Provincial Government of Persian Period Judea and the Yehud Coins," *JBL* 105 (1986): 633–62. More generally, see Lipschits and Vanderhooft, *The Yehud Stamp Impressions*.

19. See, for example, H.G.M. Williamson's commentary, *Ezra-Nehemiah* (Waco, TX: Word, 1985), 358–66.

20. Michael Langlois, "Dead Sea Scrolls Paleography and the Samaritan Pentateuch," in *The Dead Sea Scrolls and the Samaritan Pentateuch*, ed. Michael Langlois, CBET 94 (Leuven: Brill, 2019), 270–71. Drew Longacre, however, has pointed out that these Scrolls seem to employ reed pens and not the earlier (fourth century BCE) rush pens; see his lecture, "Script Interactions and the Development of Formal Hebrew/Aramaic Handwriting," Albright Institute of Archaeological Research, June 2, 2022, on YouTube.

21. A different line of evidence emerged using a forensic methodology, arguing that 4Qpaleo-Deut[s] represents the earliest text form of the Book of Deuteronomy; see Benjamin Ziemer, "A Stemma for Deuteronomy," in M. Langlois, ed., *The Dead Sea Scrolls and the Samaritan Pentateuch*, 127–97. Unfortunately, this is still a relative dating.

22. The Septuagint list is only ten people and may reflect an earlier stage of the list.

23. See the classic work by Yaʿakov Meshorer, *Ancient Jewish Coinage, Volume I: Persian Period Through Hasmoneans* (New York: Amphora, 1982), 13–34.

24. Philip Davies, *Scribes and Schools: The Canonization of the Hebrew Scriptures* (Louisville: Westminster John Knox Press, 1998), 79.

25. Davies, *Scribes and Schools*, 79.

26. Jaeyoung Jeon and Louis Jonker, eds., *Chronicles and the Priestly Literature of the Hebrew Bible*, BZAW 528 (Berlin: de Gruyter, 2021), 2.

Conclusion

1. This is actually something that the Samaritan community shares with the aristocratic Sadducean priestly community, which also focused on the authority of the written Torah; see Eyal Regev, "Were the Priests All the Same? Qumranic Halakhah in Comparison with Sadducean Halakhah," *DSD* 12 (2005): 158–88.

2. There is a mountain of literature on the Dead Sea Scrolls, but two useful books related to this book are John Collins, *Beyond the Qumran Community: The Sectarian Movement of the Dead Sea Scrolls* (Grand Rapids, MI: Eerdmans, 2010); and Sidnie White Crawford, *Scribes and Scrolls at Qumran* (Grand Rapids, MI: Eerdmans, 2019).

3. See especially Crawford, *Scribes and Scrolls at Qumran*.

4. Drew Longacre, "Paleographic Style and the Forms and Functions of the Dead Sea Psalms Scrolls," 82. See also his earlier study, "Disambiguating the Concept of Formality in Palaeographic Description: Stylistic Classification and the Ancient Jewish Hebrew/Aramaic Scripts," *Comparative Oriental Manuscript Studies Bulletin* 5 (2019): 101–28.

5. This distinction is made by Paul Mandel, although he does not connect the new profession of the "scribe-copyist" with the emergence of the synagogue; see "Between סֹפֵר and סֹפֵר: The Evolution of the Second Temple Period 'Scribe,'" 295–320.

6. See the overview by Lee Levine, *The Ancient Synagogue: The First Thousand Years* (New Haven: Yale University Press, 2000).

7. Zeev Weiss et al., eds., *Synagogues in the Hellenistic and Roman Periods: Archaeological Finds, New Mothods, New Theories* (Göttingen: Vanderhoeck & Ruprecht, 2020).

8. Hachlili, *Ancient Synagogues*. For a more recent synagogue, see Machael Osband and Benjamin Arubas, "The Excavation of a Roman-Period Village and Synagogue at Majduliyya," *IEJ* 70 (2020): 189–214.

9. See John Kloppenborg Verbin, "Dating Theodotos (CIJ II 1404)," *JJS* 51 (2000): 243–80.

10. See Levine, *The Ancient Synagogue*, 145–55.

11. See the essays in *Synagogues in the Hellenistic and Roman Periods: Archaeological Finds, New Methods, New Theories*, ed. Lutz Doering and Andrew Krause (Göttingen: Vandenhoeck & Ruprecht, 2020).

12. See, for example, Theo van der Louw and Pieter Hartog, "Physical and Economic Aspects of the Earliest Septuagint Papyri," *JJS* 72 (2021): 1–22.

13. See Emanuel Tov, *Scribal Practices and Approaches Reflected in the Texts Found in the Judean Desert* (Leiden: Brill, 2004); William Schniedewind, "Language and Group Identity in the Dead Sea Scrolls: The Case for an 'Essene Hebrew,'" in *Hebrew Texts and Language of the Second Temple Period: Proceedings of the Eighth International Symposium on the Hebrew of the Dead Sea Scrolls and Ben Sira*, ed. Steven Fassberg (Leiden: Brill, 2021), 280–91.

14. A. Runnesson, D. Binder, B. Olsson, eds., *The Ancient Synagogue from its Origins to 200 CE: A Source Book* (Leiden: Brill, 2010), 70–72.

15. Much has been written the problem of Hebrew literacy in the Second Temple period; see Michael Wise, *Language and Literacy in Roman Judea: A Study of the Bar Kokhba Documents* (New Haven: Yale University Press, 2015); Alan Millard, *Reading and Writing in the Time of Jesus* (New York: New York University Press, 2000); Catherine Hezser, *Jewish Literacy in Roman Palestine* (Tübingen: Mohr Siebeck, 2001).

INDEX OF ANCIENT TEXTS

INDEX OF MODERN SCHOLARS

GENERAL INDEX

A NOTE ON THE TYPE

This book has been composed in Arno, an Old-style serif typeface in the classic Venetian tradition, designed by Robert Slimbach at Adobe.